LITERATURE AND SOCIETY

Studies in nineteenth and twentieth century French literature

presented to

R. J. NORTH

edited by
C. A. BURNS

ISBN 0 7044 0413 3

Published for the University of Birmingham by
John Goodman & Sons (Printers) Limited
Cardigan Street, Birmingham B4 7RS

1980

CONTENTS

FOREWORD

The form and content of a presentation volume such as the present one are determined by the special circumstances which give rise to its publication. A *Festschrift* is, first and foremost, a tribute to a respected senior colleague and the names of the contributors reflect the range and variety of the professional contacts which the person being honoured has maintained over the years. The theme of such a volume is dictated very largely by the nature of the particular area of study to which the retiring colleague has contributed most significantly and the various articles should thus constitute a reasonably coherent pattern of distinct but related elements. The title of the present volume, *Literature and Society*, is a very general one; yet it is hoped that it reflects the wide-ranging and constantly alert attention to literary matters which has characterized Robert North's career. In his writing, as in his teaching, he has been concerned primarily with French literature since 1800, and it is therefore appropriate that the articles which follow should all be devoted to nineteenth and twentieth-century topics. The novel, to which Robert North has committed himself so deeply, is particularly well represented in the following pages; three articles in particular relate to Mauriac with whose work Robert North's major publication (*Le Catholicisme dans l'œuvre de François Mauriac*, 1951) was concerned. But the theatre, too, has commanded much of his attention, and it is fitting in consequence that the drama should also be represented in this volume. Robert North's interest in poetry is, perhaps, less well known, although as a teacher he has always been much concerned to foster in students an understanding and appreciation of poetry; it is appropriate, therefore, that several articles in the book should reflect this interest. A number of articles pay particular attention to stylistic aspects of literature, and they can be seen as a reflection of Robert North's permanent interest in the special relationship between content and expression in creative writing. It is hoped, in other words, that the various essays in the present volume faithfully reflect different aspects of Robert North's many interests in literary matters.

The order in which the articles are printed is not haphazard. While a rigorously chronological order would not have been entirely appropriate, the sequence in which the essays appear does represent a gradual movement forward in time from the Romantic period to the present day. The volume opens with a group of three articles devoted to different aspects of literary and artistic activity in France in the early nineteenth century. There follows a set of six essays devoted to prose fiction written during the nineteenth century and the early twentieth century; some of these articles, appropriately, in a volume presented to an authority on Mauriac, deal with the impact of religious matters on literary figures.

i

FOREWORD

The three essays on poetry which follow are complementary to those which precede them, and it is gratifying to see that music, which means so much to Robert North, figures prominently in this section. The relationship between literature and society is of crucial importance in the essay on First World War novelists, which appears next, as it is, in a different way, in the article on Giraudoux; the shadow of war, which loomed large over the early part of Robert North's career, is clearly visible here. The three contrasting articles on Mauriac which follow reflect, by their very diversity, the richness and subtlety of the work of an author who has long fascinated Robert North. The theme of war reappears in the next article which is concerned with the theatre and its sources of inspiration in the events of the Second World War. There follows a short study of sources in the work of Samuel Beckett. The question of narrative technique, which figured prominently in some of the earlier articles, appears again in the essay on Simone de Beauvoir; the article on Marguerite Duras examines the way in which literary technique and social comment are synthesized in a modern novel; this provides an appropriate conclusion to the volume as a whole.

A *Festschrift* is produced by the contributors with a particular person in mind; this person, in a sense, moulds the volume from a distance, by his character and by the nature of his interests. The contributors earnestly hope that the recipient of this volume of essays will draw satisfaction from the evidence the book contains of the stimulus which his presence, immediate or more remote, has been to them. The editor can testify to the warmth and spontaneity with which colleagues responded to the invitation to contribute; he hopes that *Literature and Society* will not only give pleasure to Robert North himself but will also be seen by readers as a significant contribution to scholarship in its own right.

Thanks are due to all those who, in different ways, have made the publication of this book possible; to the University of Birmingham for sponsoring the publication; to all the contributors for their willing cooperation; to colleagues in the Birmingham French department who have given advice and read manuscripts and proofs; to the departmental secretariat for help in preparing material for the printer; and to John Goodman and Sons and their sales manager for their assistance, courtesy and punctuality.

C. A. BURNS

R. J. NORTH

R. J. NORTH: A BIOGRAPHICAL NOTE

Arnold Bennett wrote of the novelist: 'His mind must be sympathetic, quickly responsive, courageous, honest, humorous, tender, just, merciful. He must be able to conceive the ideal without losing sight of the fact that it is a human world we live in'. The prescription fits Robert North precisely, though he himself, in spite of his gifts and achievements, would scoff at the suggestion that he had ever done anything other than what was necessary.

The major part of his career in university teaching was spent in Keele and Birmingham. Before his arrival in Keele, as a founder member of the then University College of North Staffordshire he had enjoyed a rich variety of experience, both of situations and of people. He had begun grammar school teaching in 1936 after school in London, a University of London First in French at King's College and a Diploma in Education. From 1940 to 1945 he had worked as a Company Officer in the National Fire Service, to which his conscientious objection had led him. His return to grammar school teaching was brief, for in 1947, the year in which he was awarded the Master of Arts with distinction for his thesis on Mauriac, he was appointed an assistant lecturer under the late Professor Clapton in the University of Sheffield.

It was in 1950 that Robert North went to Keele and began the task of setting up, with the Germanist Walker Chambers, the Department of Modern Languages in an institution which represented, in one sense, a whole series of brave innovations and in another, an adherence to traditional humanist values. For a year Robert taught French on his own, before being joined by John Broome in 1951 and Dorothy Page a year later. He was promoted successively Senior Lecturer in 1952, Reader in 1956 and Professor in 1962, the year in which the University College became the University of Keele.

During his eighteen years in Keele he was much involved in administration, notably as Chairman of the Board of Humanities and as Deputy Vice-Chancellor. His outside activities at that time included membership of the National Executive Committee of the A.U.T. When, in 1968, he accepted a newly-established chair of French at the University of Birmingham, in a larger department and a university of a quite different style from that which he had known at Keele, he was quickly drawn into a very wide range of activities. His experience, his administrative skill, his willingness to be of service to his colleagues and, perhaps, also a certain impatience to see things done, brought him into major roles in university government, as Dean of the Faculty of Arts (1970-73), Pro-Vice-Chancellor (1973-79) and, from 1974 to 1979, as Vice-Principal. These were years of difficulty in universities, and Robert North was often entrusted with the execution of painful decisions. He recognised and accepted the responsibility, though ruefully and without relish. His services to Birmingham University were officially recognized by the award of the O.B.E. in the Queen's Birthday Honours in June 1980.

Many colleagues throughout the University in Birmingham have respected his integrity and have been grateful for his helpful and compassionate approach to their problems. Those whose connection with him has been through French Studies have been no less appreciative. Quite early in his university career he became actively involved in the annual conference of university teachers of French, the predecessor of the Society for French Studies. Later, he was pressed into service as a member of the Committee of the Association of University Professors of French and became its chairman in 1978-79.

This university and inter-university work might have absorbed his energies entirely. In the event he has insisted on the interdependence of the different spheres of French Studies and has been much concerned with the encouragement of French in schools. At Keele he produced the annual French play and inaugurated a Schools' Film Society, then launched himself into the vigorously active membership of the Modern Languages Association which he has maintained ever since. He served on the Council of the Association from 1967-77, the National Executive Committee (1969-76) and the Journal Committee from 1972 and held office as National Chairman in 1969-70 and as President in 1978. The Association recognised his distinguished service by nominating him the Twentyman Lecturer in 1976. He represented the M.L.A. on the Joint Council of Language Associations and on the Executive Committee of the Fédération Internationale de Professeurs de Langues Vivantes and he was also a member of the Executive Committee of the Alliance Française in Great Britain.

These preoccupations reflected and came to deepen his awareness of the problems of modern language teaching. As Robert North's nature does not allow him to believe that problems will evaporate spontaneously, he set about looking for reasons and solutions. As Chairman of the 'A' level examiners in French of the J.M.B., for example, he sought to meet criticisms of traditional approaches while at the same time preserving standards and he played a major role in investigating teachers' attitudes and in seeking to adapt the thrust of the curriculum to the needs of successive generations in the light of changing educational circumstances.

In his teaching and scholarship also, Robert North has responded to the needs of students and colleagues; hence his work on Sartre, Ionesco and Malraux after his earlier work on Mauriac, and the accessible editions of texts by these authors which stand to his name, the contributions on nineteenth-century French literature he made to *The Year's Work in Modern Language Studies* from 1949 to 1951 and 1957 to 1959, and the important translations of Maurice Duverger he undertook first with his wife Barbara and later with Ruth Murphy.

His teaching continued with unabated enthusiasm and no diminution of range during the years of heavy administrative responsibility. Robert North himself would no doubt regard this, if his attention were drawn to it (it would not occur to him to think of the matter himself), as no more than a mark of the professional university teacher.

He has regarded it as one of his tasks as Head of Department to encourage his colleagues to be similarly professional, to be wholehearted craftsmen as scholars and teachers. It has always been his aim, as a teacher and as a guide to teachers, to promote a spirit of positive self-criticism, to stimulate the investigation, development and application of new methods where appropriate and their rejection when they serve no purpose.

This encouragement has not always been free of asperity, but the 'respectful hostility' which for Virginia Woolf was 'the only healthy relation between old and young' has always been tempered by humour and compassion. His method is often Socratic. More often still, he guided by his example of dedication, grasp of detail, wisdom of judgement and clarity of exposition.

Robert North has remained diffident, even self-deprecating about his contribution to French Studies. We hope that this volume will convince him that his name is not writ in water, but stands in the minds and memories of his colleagues and friends.

E. J. HATHAWAY
R. E. HALLMARK

BIRMINGHAM

F. W. J. HEMMINGS

A FOCAL FIGURE IN THE ROMANTIC
FRATERNITÉ DES ARTS: SARDANAPALUS

'The poet said to the painter: "You can paint, but you don't know how to use words; I will make you a present of my jargon." To which the painter replied: "You can write, but you don't know how to use a brush; I will make you a present of my beard." And, from that day, painters have been able to write, and men of letters have worn beards'.[1]

This sarcastic comment, voiced shortly after the July Revolution, refers to a process which had started quite early in the Restoration period, when artists and men of letters discovered a new community of interests founded in the first place on the growing popularity among the former of themes and images drawn from contemporary literary masterpieces — *Faust, Atala,* etc. — or from those major poets of the past, Shakespeare in particular, whom Romantic writers also looked on as important inspirational sources. Their meeting-places were artists' studios and literary salons; it was only later in the century that particular cafés came to be favoured as places of rendez-vous. We hear of Géricault, on his return from Italy in 1817, frequenting the studio of his friend Horace Vernet, where he spent hours in familiar talk with poets and playwrights like Béranger and Antoine-Vincent Arnault, though it is likely that this talk ran more on political issues (all these men were ardent Bonapartists) than on aesthetic questions. A more congenial forum, and one more closely involving future luminaries of the Romantic movement, was established only a few weeks after Géricault's death, when on April 14th, 1824 Charles Nodier inaugurated his celebrated Sunday evening receptions in the Bibliothèque de l'Arsenal. Nodier was on friendly terms with most of the regular contributors to the short-lived Romantic periodical *La Muse Française*: Emile Deschamps, the two Toulousain poets Alexandre Soumet and Alexandre Guiraud, and of course Victor Hugo, all of whom were made welcome at the Arsenal. Vigny was another regular visitor, and Lamartine would put in an occasional appearance when he happened to be in Paris. But there were as many artists as writers among the *habitués*, justifying Sainte-Beuve's nostalgic effusion:

> Fraternité des arts! union fortunée!
> Soirs, dont le souvenir, même après mainte année,
> Charmera le vieillard![2]

The sculptor David d'Angers was among the liveliest and most talkative of the guests; others included Louis Boulanger, the painter whom Hugo befriended more particularly, and Achille Devéria. According to Mme Hugo's reminiscences, it was not at the Arsenal that she and her husband first met Devéria, but in a theatre queue.[3] The friendship, inaugurated in this unconventional fashion, ripened rapidly. Hugo took to visiting Devéria in his studio, and it was there that he was first introduced, it would seem, to Delacroix.

At the *salon de peinture* that year it was Delacroix's *Massacres de Scio* that caused perhaps the greatest sensation. 'M. Delacroix,' observed Stendhal drily, 'a toujours cette immense supériorité sur tous les auteurs de grands tableaux, qui tapissent les grands salons, qu'au moins le public s'est beaucoup occupé de son ouvrage'.[4] The reactions of other critics to this picture were varied. Etienne Delécluze, as was to be expected from that staunch classicist, was downright contemptuous; Hippolyte Thiers was cautious, Auguste Jal dithyrambic. At least one journalist used the *Massacres de Scio* as the occasion for a fierce attack on the barbarous new fashion of Romanticism in art. 'Le romantique . . . a je ne sais quoi de forcé, de hors nature qui choque au premier coup et rebute à l'examen. Inutilement, l'auteur en délire combine des scènes atroces, verse le sang, déchire les entrailles, peint le désespoir, l'agonie. La postérité ne recevra point de tels ouvrages'.[5]

Romantic or not in concept and style, the *Massacres de Scio* cannot qualify as an illustration of a scene from a Romantic work of literature. The picture was intended — as had been Géricault's *Radeau de la Méduse* — to recall an event in very recent history; the same, in fact, as was to inspire Hugo with one of the most moving of his propaganda poems in *Les Orientales*, 'L'Enfant': in the autumn of 1822 the Turks, in revenge for a naval defeat inflicted by the insurgent Greeks, had landed on the island of Chios and had put to the sword or deported as slaves the greater part of its population, even though the islanders had taken no part in the revolt against Ottoman rule. But, of course, in 1824 it was hardly possible to allude to the Greek War of Independence without summoning to people's minds the figure of Byron, whose death at Missolonghi had occurred that very year (on January 5th). It was not long before Delacroix's admiration for Byron began to be reflected more directly in his art.

` This admiration was one he shared with many of his fellow countrymen, particularly among the younger generation of writers. The Parisian bookseller Galignani had issued a complete set of Byron's works in English as early as 1818, encouraged no doubt by the presence of so many British tourists in France at this time. But among the French themselves there were a sufficient number conversant with English to provide a nucleus of initiates. Their enthusiasm for Byron communicated itself to others, and young men like Jean-Jacques Ampère, the son of the celebrated physicist who gave his name to the unit of electric current, Pierre Lebrun, who was to win fame with his highly successful adaptation of Schiller's

2

Maria Stuart, and Prosper Mérimée, the future author of the *Théâtre de Clara Gazul* — these three among others taught themselves English for the primary purpose of being able to read Byron in the original.[6] Delacroix, however, had no need to submit himself to this preliminary linguistic grind, having acquired a fair reading knowledge of English at an early stage. One of his closest friends at school, Raymond Soulier, had spent his childhood in England, and was consequently in a position to give him basic tuition in the language. Then, at the age of nineteen, Delacroix had his first love-affair with an English lady's maid in the service of his aunt; one may suppose that his courtship of the girl served among other things to improve his colloquial command of her native tongue. It was with this same aunt, a little later, that he read *Childe Harold* on visits to her home in the valley of Montmorency. With the 6,000 francs the government paid him for *Les Massacres de Scio* he was able to fulfil a long-cherished dream and take a trip to London, there to witness — unforgettable experience — enactments of the major plays of Shakespeare performed in more or less their original versions. He used the time too to pay his respects to a few of the British artists whom he knew by reputation: Sir Thomas Lawrence and William Etty in particular. He may also have spent a few happy hours in the establishments of the more fashionable London tailors and boot-makers, if his efforts referred to in Baudelaire's *L'Œuvre et la vie de Delacroix*, to 'introduire parmi la jeunesse élégante le goût des coupes anglaises dans la chaussure et dans le vêtement'[7] are to be dated, as seems likely, to this period in Delacroix's life.

Given this intense interest in things English, it is hardly surprising that the works of Byron, read and re-read since his earliest youth, should have suggested to Delacroix subjects for pictorial treatment. In the years immediately following the 1824 Salon he executed not only the striking picture, inspired by Byron's play of 1820, of the beheading of Marino Faliero, but also, in 1826-7, two separate compositions based on *The Giaour*, an oil-painting and a lithograph.[8] But the picture which today is probably remembered as the finest of those drawn from Byron's works is that usually referred to as *La Mort de Sardanapale*.

★　★　★

Byron started composing *Sardanapalus*, a five-act tragedy in blank verse, in January 1821; it was published in December of the same year together with *The Two Foscari*. Far from being a Romantic play, in a purely technical sense it could be regarded as anti-Romantic; for Byron made a point of keeping strictly to the classical unities, even though this meant doing violence to the historical tradition. Sardanapalus is plunged

3

from the enjoyment of empire to defeat and death in the course of a single day and night: the action takes places entirely in one hall in his palace. It is, as Byron himself remarked, 'very *unlike* Shakespeare'; but, he added, 'so much the better in one sense, for I look upon him to be the worst of models, though the most extraordinary of writers'.[9]

Of Sardanapalus, the last of the line of Assyrian kings founded by Belus, little was known in Byron's time beyond the semi-legendary stories found in the Greek historians, Diodorus the Sicilian in particular. Their accounts had made his name a byword for extravagant luxury and debauchery. Byron presents him as a reckless voluptuary but a man of peace, intelligent, sceptical, holding Voltairian views about the priesthood. A kind of eighteenth-century 'benevolent despot', he is more inclined to exercise clemency than to exact harsh penalties for treason; and when, in act II, the leaders of a conspiracy to overthrow him are surprised and apprehended, Sardanapalus, against his brother-in-law's advice, pronounces a simple sentence of exile. Once beyond the reach of his guards, they raise the standard of revolt and return to besiege the king in his palace. In act III Sardanapalus shows himself a confident commander and a brave fighter, though still rash even in battle. A fresh act of treachery undoes him, and he dies, in the last act, on a funeral pyre raised and fired in accordance with his own orders.

Delacroix is unlikely to have taken the idea of painting a 'Death of Sardanapalus' from any other source than this tragedy; but that is perhaps as far as one can safely go. His picture is in no sense an illustration of any one incident in Byron's dramatic poem; what seems to have happened is that, after brooding over the story, he emerged with an image quite different from anything that could be discovered in the text from which it originated. Thus, in the final scene of Byron's tragedy, when all is lost, Sardanapalus, having already sent his wife and sons to safety, gives his trusted lieutenant the key to the royal treasure-chamber and orders him to escape from the palace taking with him all the valuables he can carry. He also orders him to free his domestic slaves. The fuel for his funeral pyre consists of logs sprinkled with spices, and it is Myrrha, his favourite concubine, who lights the pile with a torch and then leaps into his arms, committing a kind of suttee, but of her own free will. Thus, in Byron's play, there is no question of the king's possessions being destroyed along with him, nor of his concubines being sacrificed in a wild blood-bath; all this, which we can see in Delacroix's canvas, seems to have come from the artist's own gloomy imagination. Byron's Sardanapalus wishes merely, as he says in his last speech, to light a beacon which will flare for all time, 'to lesson ages, rebel nations, and Voluptuous princes'; his intentions and frame of mind are entirely different from those of Delacroix's Sardanapalus, who glowers from the back of the picture, a sullen, resentful potentate, 'attentive as a spider in his web',[10] easing his own irritation at defeat by enjoying, in godlike indifference, the spectacle of the destruction of all that used to give him pleasure and which the holocaust will deny to his victorious enemies. What Delacroix did, in fact, was to take Byron's philosophical drama, with its overtones of the eighteenth-century enlightenment, and turn it into a romantic nightmare.

The Salon of 1827, at which the picture was first exhibited, counts as a turning-point in the history of French art. The older generation were well represented, Gros sending in a portrait of Charles X on horseback, Gérard a ceremonial view of the Coronation, Guérin an *Expulsion of Adam and Eve*; while the persistence of the classical ideal was emphatically asserted in Ingre's *Apotheosis of Homer*. But also, for the first time, the young Romantics were present in force. Devéria's gaudy historical picture, *The Birth of Henry IV*, attracted most notice, but in addition he had sent in a *Mary Stuart* and a 'modern Greek' picture, *Mario Bozzaris*. The current philhellenism was also responsible for Ary Scheffer's *Souliote Women*, while Victor Hugo's young friend Louis Boulanger was exhibiting his first *salon* picture, inspired by Byron's celebrated poem *Mazeppa* which was to provide Hugo in his turn with the idea for another stirring poem in *Les Orientales*.

The most important of Delacroix's pictures to be seen on the opening day — *Le Christ au Jardin des Oliviers* and *Le Doge Marino Faliero* — were stylistically and compositionally quite acceptable by the standards of the time; unlikely, at all events, to raise any academician's blood-pressure. The second of these two is the more familiar to English art-lovers today, housed as it is in the Wallace collection in London. It strikes the same note of frozen activity as *Les Massacres de Scio*, but the effort to maintain control, which in Delacroix was always at odds with the temptation to let his instincts run wild, is more clearly discernible in the *Marino Faliero* and it is arguable that the control is more successfully imposed. Delacroix has as it were boxed himself in, building up his composition by a rigid system of right-angled lines. The horizontals are represented first by the heads of the patricians, running straight across the top of the canvas; next, below, on the right-hand side, we notice the level stone balustrade and, lower still, the numerous parallel lines of the wide marble steps of the great staircase, quite empty; then, lowest of all, the prone body of the decapitated doge. All these horizontals are crossed by as many verticals; on the left-hand side, a rising tier of heads, on the right, the proud, slim figure of the bearded executioner; finally, at the back, tall pillars, the jambs of a great door, hanging banners, and the sword of justice symbolically raised aloft by a member of the Council of Ten.

This picture, the first drawn directly by Delacroix from one of Byron's works,[11] had been shown the year before, along with two hundred others by Géricault, Devéria, Ary Scheffer and the major surviving artists of the First Empire, at an exhibition opened in the Galerie Lebrun to raise money for the Greek insurgents. In February 1828 Delacroix withdrew it from the Salon and had it shipped to London, replacing it with his new canvas, *La Mort de Sardanapale*.

The sensation was enormous. Conservatives were, predictably, scandalized. 'Le *Sardanapale* de M. Delacroix n'a trouvé grâce ni devant le public, ni devant les artistes,' thundered Delécluze. It was a picture, he went on, in which 'les premières règles de l'art semblent avoir été violées de parti pris. Le *Sardanapale* est une erreur du peintre'.[12] Other critics were more hesitant. The work was certainly a novelty, boldly executed, but difficult to appraise, with the heaped-up confusion of miscellaneous objects, and the straining, writhing bodies everywhere. *Le Moniteur universel* reported that although there were a few who thought it a masterpiece, the great majority judged it to be ridiculous, and in *Le Globe* Ludovic Vitet, who in general was sympathetic to the Romantic movement, expressed the view that if a soldier starts firing on his comrades as well as the enemy, it is time to send him off the battlefield; the new school of painters would be well advised to disown this dangerous ally. Delacroix, quoting these remarks to Soulier, added bitterly: 'Tant il y a que ceux qui me volent et vivent de ma substance crieraient haro plus fort que les autres'.[13]

There was at least one exception to this widespread desertion by his former supporters. For a year or two now it had been fashionable among critics to couple Delacroix's name with Victor Hugo's. Paul Dubois, commenting in *Le Globe* on the announcement of a new volume of Hugo's *Odes et Ballades*, had observed that 'M. Victor Hugo est en poésie ce que M. Delacroix est en peinture: il y a toujours une grande idée, un sentiment profond, sous ces traits incorrects et heurtés; et je l'avoue, pour moi j'aime cette vigueur jeune et âpre'.[14] We have seen how Hugo and Delacroix first made contact in Devéria's studio. Meeting again in the foyer of the Odéon, during the sensational 'Shakespeare season' of 1827-8, the two men struck up a firm friendship, which did not, however, last: Delacroix felt ill at ease in the hot-house atmosphere of Hugo's *cénacle*, while Hugo judged Delacroix to be timid and reactionary except when he had a brush in his hand.[15] But this did not prevent him admiring *La Mort de Sardanapale* and defending it against its detractors, the 'feuilletonnistes stupides'. The picture was, he told Victor Pavie, 'une chose magnifique, et si gigantesque qu'elle échappe aux petites vues. Du reste, ce bel ouvrage, comme beaucoup d'autres ouvrages grands et forts, n'a point eu de succès près des bourgeois de Paris: *sifflets des sots sont fanfares de gloire*. Je ne regrette qu'une chose, c'est qu'il n'ait pas mis le feu à ce bûcher; cette belle scène serait bien plus belle encore si elle avait pour base une corbeille de flammes'.[16]

This curious suggestion can be construed as marking the fundamental difference between Hugo's robust and essentially sane concept of Romanticism and Delacroix's pain-ridden, tormented version, so much nearer Baudelaire's. Hugo would have liked an all-consuming, purifying fire: his Romanticism was molochism. Delacroix's was sadism, the slitting of throats and the severing of arteries, glowing, living flesh agonizing and turned to stillness. No crackling flames but the darkness pressing down from above and welling up from below, the even deeper spiritual darkness in the King's swarthy face and black beard — this darkness is what we see on the point of engulfing the pink and gold glory that streams diagonally across the centre of the canvas. Carnality under the knife, orgiastic passion flaring up briefly before extinction overwhelms it: this was also Romanticism, but an aspect of Romanticism which remained to all intents and purposes concealed until 1828.

It seems certain that it arose from the very depths of the artist's being. He gave it public expression on this one occasion and then, mortified perhaps at the cries of outrage that greeted it, Delacroix took the painting back and hid it away. It was not shown in any subsequent retrospective exhibition of his art and remained in private hands, glimpsed only occasionally in sale rooms, for the rest of the century, in fact down to 1921 when its last purchaser bequeathed it to the Louvre. In none of his paintings after the *Sardanapalus* is this unique conjugation of life and death, voluptuousness and cruelty so apparent.

✶ ✶ ✶

The idiosyncrasy of the creation is highlighted by the fruitless attempts of scholars to discover its genealogy. We have seen already how vastly dissimilar Delacroix's picturing of the death of Sardanapalus was from Byron's. Byron must have derived the story ultimately from Diodorus, who does state that the Assyrian monarch caused his concubines to die with him; but they were not put to the sword beforehand; they were shut up with the eunuchs in a room specially constructed in the very heart of the enormous funeral pyre on which the tyrant then mounted, before giving the signal for it to be fired.[17] Thus neither the Greek historian, whom

Delacroix may or may not have read, nor Byron, whom he certainly did read, could conceivably have provided him with the central idea of his own *Mort de Sardanapale*. At the time the picture was first put on public view in the Louvre, Jean Guiffrey reviewed the evidence as to sources which at that time had come to light and judged it to be quite inconclusive. 'La légende et le poète faisaient périr Sardanapale, ses femmes, ses serviteurs et ses trésors sur un bûcher allumé sur l'ordre du tyran. Delacroix *invente* le massacre préalable'.[18] Art-historians coming after him have not been content to leave it there, but it cannot be said that their efforts to discover the true source, whether literary or iconographical, have been conspicuously successful. One of them, pondering the elaborate description of his picture that Delacroix provided for the Salon catalogue, postulates that he must have seen some other play or opera, in Paris or London, which gave him the idea of the 'massacre préalable'; but she has not been able to find any trace of any dramatic production in the years before 1828 on the subject of Sardanapalus.[19] Another researcher asks us to believe that Delacroix was inspired by a single plate in an album of engravings representing a scene of slaughter copied from an antique sarcophagus in the Palazzo Pitti which has since disappeared.[20] As far as one can judge, this etching represents the irruption of a warrior bearing sword and shield into some domestic interior in which can be seen a couch and a few vessels scattered on the floor. But the nude figures in this scene are all male; the only female one is fully clothed; it seems gratuitous to suppose that this drawing, assuming he saw it, could possibly have given Delacroix the idea of a slaughter of naked girls which is, after all, the salient, certainly the most memorable, feature of his picture.

Unless and until more convincing evidence comes to light, we must continue to assume that *La Mort de Sardanapale* was a purely personal invention of the artist's, though it remains possible that he would never have allowed his imagination to dwell on the mysterious fate of the Assyrian despot, had he not happened to read Byron's tragedy on the subject. What all the art-historians appear to have overlooked, in their anxious scanning of the poem for evidence of Delacroix's borrowing in his own portrayal of Sardanapalus, is the possibility that he remembered at any rate one passage from it when he was composing a slightly later work, *La Liberté guidant le peuple* of 1831. In this well-known picture, Liberty is portrayed as a barefoot, bare-breasted girl, her head turned sideways so that her face is seen in profile, with its straight, 'Grecian' nose very clearly apparent against the billowing smoke in the background. She is striding over a barricade, holding the tricolour flag high in the air with her right hand, while in her left she grasps a musket with a business-like bayonet also silhouetted against the clouds.

Although stories were current of women participating in the fighting of 27-29 July 1830, it is clear, from the title Delacroix gave the picture, that the dominant female figure was intended as allegorical rather than realistic,[21] just as had been the young woman in the foreground of his earlier composition, *La Grèce expirant sur les ruines de Missolonghi.* If we turn back to Byron's *Sardanapalus,* we find in act III a passage spoken by Sardanapalus in which he describes how, in the thick of the fight against the rebel satraps, he caught sight of his favourite, the Ionian slave-girl Myrrha.

> I paused
> To look upon her, and her kindled cheek;
> Her large black eyes, that flashed through her long hair
> As it streamed o'er her; her blue veins that rose
> Along her most transparent brow; her nostril
> Dilated from its symmetry; her lips
> Apart . . . . her
> Waved arms, more dazzling with their own born whiteness
> Than the steel her hand held, which she caught up
> From a dead soldier's grasp; — all these things made
> Her seem unto the troops a prophetess
> Of victory, or Victory herself
> Come down to hail us here.

In this graphic description, the only detail changed by Delacroix when he came to paint his *Liberté guidant le peuple* was that of Myrrha's 'long hair' which he hid under a Phrygian cap. Otherwise, Byron's lines constitute a quite remarkable prefiguration of the picture. The 'steel . . . caught up From a dead soldier's grasp' becomes the bayonet she holds, while any good colour reproduction will show the 'kindled cheek', the 'large black eyes', the one dilated nostril, the parted lips and the 'waved arms'. But these details apart — noteworthy only in accumulation — the last four lines, which sum up the general impression, are perhaps the most significant: for it has been observed already, by critics who never thought to establish any connection between Byron's *Sardanapalus* and *La Liberté guidant le peuple,* that Delacroix's personification of Liberty bears a striking resemblance to certain Roman sculptures of the goddess Victory.[22]

✦ ✦ ✦

We have seen how the Sardanapalus legend, after providing a major Romantic poet with the framework for a verse tragedy, subsequently inspired a major Romantic artist to paint a masterpiece of gloom and horror. It remains to be seen how the same story was metamorphosed into a piece of heady Romantic music.

In the days immediately preceding the July Revolution, Hector Berlioz was competing, for the fourth time, for the Prix de Rome. According to practice, the candidates were confined to the building of the Institut while the examination was in progress. Each was assigned a room containing a piano and a writing-desk; the porter unlocked the rooms at 11 a.m. and 6 p.m., to permit them to eat a communal meal, but they were not allowed to go home until they had handed in their entries for the competition. In 1830 the examination started on July 15th; the rules allowed the candidates up to three weeks, if they needed it, to complete their work. Berlioz had still not finished when the Revolution broke out. Impatiently he dashed off the last pages, distracted by the noisy discharge of grapeshot and the thud of stray bullets against the walls of the Institut. When at last he was free to leave, the 'Trois Glorieuses' had come and gone; all he could do was to wander round Paris with an undischarged pistol, listening to exaggerated stories of the exploits performed by his luckier friends.

Before the competition began, it was the custom for one of the professors of music to dictate to the candidates the verses on which they were to compose their cantata. In 1830, the piece of poetry chosen for this purpose was . . . *La Dernière Nuit de Sardanapale*, by the librettist Jean-Baptiste Gail; all that we know of it is what the composer himself tells us in his memoirs, viz. that 'le poème finissait au moment où Sardanapale vaincu appelle ses plus belles esclaves et monte avec elles sur le bûcher'.[23] Berlioz was attracted by the idea of writing a finale in which the fire itself would be melodically represented, together with the crash of falling masonry as the entire palace went up in flames. But he had missed the prize before by being too exuberantly unconventional, so on this occasion he wisely withheld the finale from the score he submitted — and was awarded the prize. Once he was sure of it, he composed his 'conflagration' which was duly played at the rehearsal for the traditional public performance of the prize-winning entry, and was listened to with interest by the academicians who, if they had heard it in a transcription for piano, would most certainly — or so Berlioz believed — have refused him the prize once more.

But it seems to have been Berlioz's fate to be pursued by misfortunes of a more or less ludicrous nature. The public performance of the Sardanapalus cantata was attended by an unusually large number of music-lovers, attracted by Berlioz's budding reputation; they included Spontini and the opera star Marie Malibran. Unfortunately, protocol did not allow Berlioz to conduct the performance in person; for an account of the calamity resulting from the negligence of the official conductor, one cannot do better than quote his own words:

A l'ouverture de la séance, me méfiant un peu de l'habileté de Grasset, l'ex-chef d'orchestre du Théâtre-Italien, qui dirigeait alors, j'allai me placer à côté de lui, mon manuscrit à la main. . . . . La cantate se déroule sans accident. Sardanapale apprend sa défaite, se résout à mourir, appelle ses femmes; l'incendie s'allume, on écoute; les initiés de la répétition disent à leurs voisins: 'Vous allez entendre cet écroulement, c'est étrange, c'est prodigieux!'

Cinq cent mille malédictions sur les musiciens qui ne comptent pas leurs pauses!!! une partie de cor donnait dans ma partition la réplique aux timbales, les timbales la donnaient aux cymbales, celles-ci à la grosse caisse, et le premier coup de la grosse caisse amenait l'explosion finale! Mon damné cor ne fait pas sa note, les timbales ne l'entendant pas n'ont garde de partir, par suite, les cymbales et la grosse caisse se taisent aussi; rien ne part! rien!!! les violons et les basses continuent leur trémolo impuissant; point d'explosion! un incendie qui s'éteint sans avoir éclaté, un effet ridicule au lieu de l'écroulement tant annoncé; *ridiculus mus*!

Shouting with rage and disappointment, the young red-haired composer flung his copy of the score into the orchestra, upsetting two of the music-stands. 'Madame Malibran fit un bond en arrière, comme si une mine venait soudain d'éclater à ses pieds; tout fut en rumeur, et l'orchestre, et les académiciens scandalisés, et les auditeurs mystifiés, et les amis de l'auteur indignés'.[24]

Happily the disaster was not irretrievable. The final 'conflagration' passage of Berlioz's *Mort de Sardanapale* was performed properly later in the year, in a concert at which the *Symphonie fantastique* was heard for the first time. The audience included a gifted young pianist named Liszt who, as Berlioz reported to his father subsequently, 'm'a pour ainsi dire emmené de force dîner chez lui en m'accablant de tout ce que l'enthousiasme a de plus énergique'.[25] It was the start of an enduring friendship between the two composers; but Berlioz took no further interest in the legend of Sardanapalus.

LEICESTER   F. W. J. HEMMINGS

[1] *Le Figaro*, 30 August 1831; see Malcolm Easton, *Artists and Writers in Paris*, London, 1964, p. 58.

[2] 'Le Cénacle', in *Vie, poésies et pensées de Joseph Delorme*.

[3] *Victor Hugo raconté par un témoin de sa vie*, Brussels and Leipzig, 1863, p. 76.

[4] Stendhal, *Œuvres complètes*, vol. 47 (*Mélanges III: Peinture*, ed. Ernest Abravanel), Geneva, Cercle du Bibliophile, 1972, p. 39.

[5] Auguste Chauvin, *Salon de Mil huit cent vingt-quatre*, Paris, 1825; quoted in Raymond Escholier, *Delacroix peintre, graveur, écrivain*, Paris, 1926, vol. I, p. 133.

[6] See Edmond Estève, *Byron et le romantisme français*, Paris, 1929, p. 62.

[7] Baudelaire, *Œuvres complètes*, ed. Claude Pichois, vol. II (Paris, Bibliothèque de la Pléiade, 1976), p. 759.

[8] At successive *salons* after 1830, Delacroix exhibited several other works based on Byron's poems, notably *Gulnare dans la prison de Conrad* (1831), *Le Prisonnier de Chillon* (1835), and *La Barque de Don Juan* (1841).

[9] Letter to John Murray, 14 July 1821; Byron, *Letters and Journals*, ed. R.E. Prothero, vol. V (London, 1901), p. 323.

[10] Jack Spector, *Delacroix: the Death of Sardanapalus*, London, 1974, p. 23.

[11] Casimir Delavigne's tragedy on the same subject was not seen until 1829.

[12] Quoted in Escholier, *op.cit.*, p. 218.

[13] *Correspondance générale d'Eugène Delacroix*, ed. André Joubin, vol. I (Paris, 1935), p. 213.

[14] *Le Globe*, 4 November 1826; quoted in C.A.E. Jensen, *L'Evolution du romantisme. L'année 1826*, Geneva 1959, p. 196. Cf. also Auguste Jal's remark about Delacroix, in his *Esquisses . . . sur le Salon de 1827*: 'Il y a je ne sais quoi de satanique dans ses créations, je ne sais quoi de fascinateur dans son exécution presque sauvage; le poète Hugo est peut-être le seul homme qui puisse être dans le secret du génie de ce peintre.' (Quoted by Jean Gaudon, 'Hugo juge de Delacroix', *Gazette des Beaux-Arts*, vol. 68 (1966), p. 173.)

[15] 'Révolutionnaire dans son atelier, il était conservateur dans les salons, reniait toute solidarité avec les idées nouvelles, désavouait l'insurrection littéraire.' (*Victor Hugo raconté par un témoin de sa vie*, p. 159.)

[16] Hugo, *Correspondance*, vol. I (Paris, Albin Michel, 1947), p. 454.

[17] Diodorus Siculus, II, 27. Athenaeus (*Deipnosophistae*, XII, 529), gives a slightly different version. The wooden chamber was constructed on top of the pyre, and inside Sardanapalus placed 150 gold couches on which he, his queen, and his concubines lay down. 'He then gave orders to light the pyre, and it burned for fifteen days.'

[18] Guiffrey, '*La Mort de Sardanapale* d'Eugène Delacroix', *Gazette des Beaux-Arts*, vol. 63 (1921), p. 196.

[19] Beatrice Farwell, 'Sources for Delacroix's *Death of Sardanapalus*', *The Art Bulletin*, vol. 40 (1958), pp. 67-71.

[20] Lee Johnson, 'The Etruscan Sources of Delacroix's *Death of Sardanapalus*', *The Art Bulletin*, vol. 42 (1960), pp. 296-300.

[21] A fuller discussion of this point is to be found in Werner Hofmann, 'Sur la *Liberté* de Delacroix', *Gazette des Beaux-Arts*, vol. 86 (1975), pp. 61-70.

[22] See especially G.H. Hamilton, 'The Iconographical Origins of Delacroix's *Liberty Leading the People*', pp. 55-66 in *Studies in Art and Literature for Belle da Costa Greene*, ed. Dorothy Miner (Princeton, 1954). Hamilton quotes in this paper two stanzas (LIV and LVI) from the first canto of *Childe Harold*, in which Byron writes of the 'Maid of Saragossa' who fought alongside the troops in the Peninsular War; but it must be said that with the best will in the world one can only detect a vague and shadowy connection between these verses and Delacroix's *Liberté guidant le peuple*.

[23] Berlioz, *Mémoires*, ed. Pierre Citron (Paris, Garnier-Flammarion, 1969), vol. I, p. 184.

[24] Ibid., pp. 184-5. Another account of the same incident, written the day after it occurred, is to be found in one of Berlioz's letter to his father: *Correspondance générale*, ed. Pierre Citron, Paris, 1972, vol. I, pp. 380-1.

[25] *Correspondance générale*, vol. I, p. 385.

C. CROSSLEY

THE TREATMENT OF ARCHITECTURE IN THE WORKS OF EDGAR QUINET PUBLISHED BEFORE 1851

This article aims to provide a general description of the manner in which architecture is presented in those works which Quinet published prior to his departure into exile in December 1851. Our analysis does not claim to be exhaustive. We have for the most part limited our investigation to references to religious as opposed to secular architecture and our broad intention is to situate Quinet's attitude to architecture within the context of his understanding of the history of religions and the philosophy of history.

However, before we turn to a detailed discussion of the meaning which Quinet attributes to architectural creation we must first indicate briefly the main characteristics of his aesthetic theory.[1] Fortunately for the reader Quinet's views on aesthetics are to be found conveniently summarised in his very short doctoral thesis entitled *Considérations philosophiques sur l'art* (1839). An examination of this thesis rapidly reveals that the author's prime concern is neither with the techniques involved in the production of great art, nor with the analysis of the reactions of a spectator contemplating a work of outstanding beauty. His aim is rather to assign to art a metaphysical meaning, in virtue of which he may proceed to both a classification of the different art forms and to a description of their historical development in relation to religion.

From the outset the writer makes abundantly clear his rejection of the doctrine of art for art's sake and his opposition to the theory that art is essentially an imitation of nature. He argues that the artist's goal should not be to produce a copy of the objects of the natural world since the latter are themselves symbols. The real task of the artist is to represent invisible, ideal beauty in sensuous form, to reveal the spiritual meaning of the universe. Quinet, nevertheless, does not deny the existence of natural beauty; nature is the creation of the divine artist and the objects of sense are already expressions of spirit in sensuous form. He is in no doubt, however, that artistic beauty belongs to a higher sphere than natural beauty. Moreover, like Goethe and Schelling, he stresses that the artist is the rival of nature. The artist transforms, recreates, perfects nature so as to reveal the presence of the divine, of the Idea. Natural beauty is incomplete because it is transient; art, which attains a higher level of reality, is capable of resisting the destructive power of the ravages of time.

Having put forward these general considerations Quinet moves on to develop a classification of the arts based upon a threefold division into Oriental, Greek and Christian art which is in some respects strongly reminiscent of the division into Symbolic, Classical and Romantic art proposed by Hegel. It is immediately apparent that Quinet's approach to the arts cannot be dissociated from his writings on the philosophy of history and the history of religions. For although the artist aspires to ideal beauty, this ideal generally takes the form of the idea of God as it is conceived by the collectivity of which the artist is a member. Consequently aesthetic questions cannot be resolved in isolation from the study of religion in its historical development.

Quinet identifies architecture with that first moment in the history of religions which he terms Oriental pantheism. Freedom and individuality barely existed at this early stage in the development of human consciousness. Man, far from seeking to impose his will upon nature, was content to reproduce the harmony of the universe. Nature was worshipped as divine. Architecture, according to Quinet, was well suited to give expression to the symbolic character of the religions of the East. Moreover, architecture has as its means of expression nature in its most material — hence its least free, least spiritual — form. In addition, it should be noted that Quinet shared the belief of so many of his contemporaries that architecture was essentially an anonymous, collective creation.

The next important stage after Oriental pantheism was the civilisation of ancient Greece. Man now became the measure of all things; freedom, individuality and consciousness of self all increased. This was the moment when, in Hegelian terms, the Absolute was conceived as concrete spirit; in Quinet's terms, man replaced nature as the symbol of the divine. The anthropomorphic character of the Greek idea of God resulted in that apotheosis of humanity which received its finest expression in statuary: in sculpture man represented himself as a demi-god, free from all that was contingent and transient. The serenity of classical Greek art was, however, destroyed by the coming of Christianity which signalled the birth of genuine individuality, of true subjectivity. Now painting came to the fore. In accord with the spirit of the Christian religion, it depicted men not as demi-gods, but as suffering individuals living in history.

In the light of the close link which we have seen Quinet make between architecture and Oriental pantheism it comes as something of a surprise to the reader to discover that nowhere does he undertake a detailed examination of the architecture of the East. Whilst attention is paid to the Greek temple, to the mosque and particularly to the Gothic cathedral, we encounter only passing references to 'les temples des Indiens et des Araméens' or to the influence of planetary worship upon the form of the seven-walled city of Ecbatana.[2] Indeed, insofar as the architecture of the 'Orient' is discussed at all it would appear to be largely synonymous with the monuments of ancient Egypt. And yet, when Egyptian religion is looked at in some detail in *Le Génie des religions* (1842) we learn disappointingly little on the subject of architecture. The truth of the matter is that Quinet does not wish to adhere strictly to his historico-religious framework. The spacio-temporal location of a particular art form is in no way absolute; each art possesses its own history. What is more, the arts can also be said to form a hierarchy in virtue of their increasing spiritual content, a hierarchy rising from architecture through sculpture and painting to music and poetry.

Since architecture takes as the matter of its appearance inorganic nature the first question which we must ask is: to what extent do the origins of architectural form lie in an imitation of nature? Quinet's thesis provides an answer:

Presque toujours la géologie a décidé des formes primitives de l'architecture. La forme pyramidale des monuments égyptiens a des relations avec la nature granitique des terrains. Au contraire, les assises parallèles des temples grecs semblent être le prolongement des couches calcaires des montagnes de la Grèce.[3]

It is to be noted that this idea had already been developed in *De la Grèce moderne et de ses rapports avec l'antiquité* (1830) where Quinet informs us that the famous Cyclopean walls blend so well with their natural setting that the spectator is at a loss to decide at which point the walls themselves begin. In a like manner he asserts that the tiers of seats of the ancient amphitheatres follow directly the shape of the curve formed by the mountains. The best illustration of the relationship between architecture and nature is, however, provided by the Greek temple: '[les temples] bâtis sur le plan de la contrée tout entière, faisaient en quelque manière partie de l'édifice de la nature, achevée, couronnée par l'esprit et par la main de l'homme'.[4]

Quinet was, of course, not alone in wishing to associate a certain architectural style with a particular country, climate and scenery. Chateaubriand, drawing inspiration from Bernardin de Saint-Pierre's *Harmonies de la nature* had had similar ambitions.[5] In his *Itinéraire de Paris à Jérusalem* he drew a close parallel between Greek art and its environment:

Les climats influent plus ou moins sur le goût des peuples. En Grèce, par exemple, tout est suave, tout est adouci, tout est plein de calme dans la nature comme dans les écrits des anciens. On conçoit presque comment l'architecture du Parthénon a des proportions si heureuses, comment la sculpture antique est si peu tourmentée, si paisible, si simple, lorsqu'on a vu le ciel pur et les paysages gracieux d'Athènes, de Corinthe et de l'Ionie. Dans cette patrie des Muses la nature ne conseille point les écarts; elle tend au contraire à ramener l'esprit à l'amour des choses uniformes et harmonieuses.[6]

In the case of Quinet, however, we must also bear in mind the wider philosophical context within which his writings on art and aesthetics are set. In an essay which appeared in 1830 he argues that the Absolute which manifests itself as unconscious nature subsequently aspires to self-knowledge in and through the mind of man. The history of religions is envisaged as a westward movement of peoples; different natural environments are unconscious, objective representations of divine thoughts which are then given subjective, conscious expression by certain collectivities. The idea of God produced by each religion is the fullest realisation possible of the divine thought which is present in nature at that point. Man is the 'parole vivante' of nature which speaks through him. This notion underlies much of Quinet's understanding of both art and of religion.[7] For our purposes a convenient example is provided by the following reference to the frieze of a Greek temple:

De toutes parts les lignes, les formes, les harmonies errantes sur le penchant des monts, viennent à se rencontrer au sommet dans cet organe intelligent [la frise], et donner comme une figure éternelle à la pensée, qui végète ou scintille au soleil, ou s'écoule en grondant au fond des vallées.[8]

Art cannot be explained as an imitation of nature in any restricted sense. Art is the revelation of the idea which lies hidden in nature:

[. . .] le temple, le théâtre, l'enceinte, et le mont diaphane, et la colline aux flancs ouverts, et les couches de marbre, mutuellement se mirent dans leurs formes et s'achèvent l'un l'autre. [. . .] Merveilleux types d'art, toute chose autour d'eux, dans l'ombre et la lumière, tend à s'en approcher sans pouvoir les atteindre; et nous touchons aux lieux où l'architecture n'est rien autre que le moule idéal de la nature, reproduit par l'humanité, et sur lequel se sont mystérieusement organisés, dans l'origine, la cosmogonie et le génie d'une contrée.[9]

This method of interpretation is in fact analagous to that used by Quinet elsewhere, in his analysis of myth and religion. The two worlds of nature and history whose ideal identity is realised in myth also combine in architecture. Architecture becomes a silent epic, having its origins in nature but unfolding in history.[10] An important conclusion follows from these remarks. If, despite obvious superficial differences, the architectural monuments of all periods can be interpreted as reflecting in various ways the relationship between nature and history, then the way is open to consider the history of architecture as a continuity: 'des temples de Thèbes jusqu'à la cathédrale gothique il n'y a qu'une modification continuelle d'une forme primitive'.[11] Moreover, this continuity is the continuity of the history of religions. Architecture becomes a tangible expression of the stages through which the religious consciousness has evolved. The pyramids of Egypt, the temples of Greece, the Gothic cathedral are all visible milestones which mark stages along the road of mankind's quest for the Absolute.[12]

It should be emphasised that the notion of continuity does not invalidate the threefold division which we have described above. Quinet never abandons the belief that the distance separating Greece from the Orient is also that which separates sculpture from architecture. Hence the significance which he attributes to the Lion Gate at Mycenae in which he finds evidence of the Greek achievement in the history of religions. The Lion Gate marks the first appearance of 'l'esprit hellénique' still absent from the surrounding architecture. The monument hovers uncertainly between 'le génie du symbole et la beauté de l'art', between architecture and sculpture, between Asia and Europe. No longer 'purement égyptien' the forms depicted in the bas-relief take on 'un commencement de vie'. Here, for the first time, '[la Grèce] cherche à se mouvoir et à se dégager en groupes plastiques sur le seuil du monument sacerdotal de l'Asie'.[13]

The foregoing example reinforces our view that in Quinet's eyes architecture, far from being identified with the East and with Oriental pantheism in an exclusive manner, is in fact taken to be the art form which most adequately renders the symbolic character of periods of intense religious faith irrespective of time and place. And in point of fact the monument to which Quinet devotes most attention is the Gothic cathedral, the embodiment of the spirit of medieval Christianity:

Cette vaste nef, avec ses deux chapelles latérales en forme de croix, et qui figure le corps du Christ dans le sépulcre, ce mystère, ces demi-ténèbres, cette tour principale, qui, image du pouvoir spirituel, monte dans la nue, n'est-ce pas là l'édifice, non de la chair, mais de l'esprit?[14]

In *Ahasvérus* (1833) the voice of the cathedral rings out:

Les nombres me sont sacrés: sur leur harmonie je m'appuie sans peur. Mes deux tours et ma nef font le nombre trois et la Trinité. Mes sept chapelles, liées à mon côté, sont mes sept mystères qui me serrent les flancs. Ah! que leur ombre est noire et muette et profonde! Mes douze colonnes dans le chœur de pierre d'Afrique sont mes douze apôtres, qui m'aident à porter ma croix; et moi je suis un grand chiffre lapidaire que l'Eternité trace, de sa main ridée, sur sa muraille, pour compter son âge.[15]

As the Greek temple was related to its surroundings, so the Gothic cathedral incorporates into its structure elements drawn from nature:

Tout ce qu'il [le christianisme] a trouvé sur sa route, et tout ce qui vit autour de lui, fleurs, eaux, formes, esprits cachés dans les montagnes, dans les forêts, dans les replis des rocs, pics aiguisés des Alpes, ombres des pins, pierres oubliées des druides, il recueille tout cela, comme l'oiseau fait son nid. Il s'en vêtit ainsi que d'un manteau contre les froids d'hiver, et, sentant que c'est le lieu où il doit s'arrêter, il se bâtit de ces objets épars des abris gigantesques, d'obscures cathédrales pour y passer sans remuer les siècles qui lui restent.[16]

As early as the thirteenth century 'une même architecture, la gothique, s'etait formée depuis les confins de l'Andalousie jusqu'aux extrémités de la Suède'.[17] Gothic is not, therefore, the exclusive property of Northern Europe. It took on new aspects under the influence of different climates, environments and national geniuses. In Italy, for example, the religious architecture of the North was substantially modified as a new element of pagan sensuality manifested itself. This phenomenon, Quinet maintains, is clearly discernible in Milan cathedral:

La voûte ténébreuse du Nord s'est changée en un marbre blanc d'un éclat presque païen. Sur cette terre de Saturne, le mysticisme de l'architecture gothique est dépaysé; le soleil ardent du Midi pénètre, avec une curiosité profane, jusqu'au fond de la nef. Le trèfle et la rose chrétienne ont fait place, dans les ornements, au laurier idolâtre. D'ailleurs il n'y a plus de flèche qui monte dans le ciel.[18]

Turning to the subject of Venetian architecture, Quinet not surprisingly likens St. Mark's to St. Sophia. The strong Byzantine influence meant that the grandeur of the cathedrals of the North was absent: '[l'architecture de Venise] ne porte pas dans les nues la pensée religieuse d'une race nouvelle'.[19] Florence, on the other hand, marks the fusion of Christianity with pagan antiquity. The spirit of the Renaissance is embodied in Brunelleschi's cathedral dome. Having travelled to Rome, Quinet offers the following comment upon St. Peter's: 'Plus de symboles de douleur comme dans l'architecture du Nord ou dans la byzantine; ni croix, ni sépulcre: c'est ici l'emblème du Christ régnant, ou plutôt le temple d'un Jupiter chrétien'.[20] He concludes the account of his Italian journey, by remarking that in Italy Gothic architecture extended no further south than Rome. In other words the genius of the Italian people developed between the twin poles of Milan cathedral and the ruins of Paestum which are taken respectively to stand as symbols of the Germanic and the Greek worlds.[21]

Quinet visited Italy in 1831. More than a decade later and by now a Professor at the Collège de France he undertook a journey to Spain and Portugal. Once again his attention was drawn to the Gothic monuments which he encountered. Thus Burgos cathedral provides an excellent illustration of the role played by climate and vegetation in the development of architectural form:

Oserai-je dire que je retrouve l'aridité de la Castille sur la face de la cathédrale de Burgos? Des soleils séculaires ont tari la sève de la rose gothique; les deux clochers aigus armés de pointes rappellent les tiges hérissées de l'aloès. Quelques statues apparaissent de distance en distance, rares habitants de ces hauts murs gris de bruyères.[22]

Having travelled as far as Toledo, Quinet tried to define the particular nature of Spanish Gothic. He remarks that, whereas elsewhere in Europe the cathedral was primarily a symbol of the Holy Sepulchre, in Spain it took on a new significance since it came to symbolise the victory of Christianity over the forces of Islam. A number of factors, however, come together to produce that which is unique in Spanish Gothic architecture:

En France, en Allemagne, en Angleterre, l'Eglise du moyen âge, c'est le deuil éternel. En Italie, le luxe de l'art moderne va jusqu'à effacer l'impression religieuse du passé; d'ailleurs le gothique n'a jamais pu y prendre profondément racine. L'Espagne est le seul pays qui ait concilié des nefs du Nord avec la splendeur païenne du Midi. Sur la face macérée du moyen âge elle a jeté le linceul de pourpre de la Renaissance. Imaginez Notre-Dame de Paris couverte de l'or des Incas et des Caciques, un mélange de religions et de dieux opposés, l'ascétisme de la cathédrale, les treillages et les jalousies de marbre de la mosquée, la magnificence du temple du Soleil, Cologne, Damas, Mexico, subitement rapprochés dans une légende de pierre.[23]

A visit to the mosque of Cordova provided Quinet with an ideal opportunity to compare and contrast the Gothic cathedral directly with the mosque. Christian cathedrals, we are told, are always firmly rooted in the earth:

Dans nos cathédrales chrétiennes, les plus grandes hardiesses reposent toujours sur un fond de raison. On est rassuré aussitôt qu'étonné. Voyez comme les tours du catholicisme sont profondément enracinées, comme elles posent un large pied sur terre; elles ne tendent pas à renverser les lois de la gravité et les mathématiques éternelles.[24]

The mosque, on the other hand, is described as the house of a capricious deity, far removed in character from the God worshipped in the cathedral:

Logique, expérience, principe, raison, nature, tout cela disparaît devant une fantaisie du sultan de l'univers; en sorte que la gloire de sa maison consiste à contrarier, à renverser toutes les habitudes de l'éternelle géométrie.[25]

Even the manner in which the two types of monument were erected is contrasted. The building of the Gothic cathedral extended over a long period; the mosque, on the other hand, is an example of what Quinet terms spontaneous architecture. Its construction was completed, 'comme le Coran, en une seule époque'.[26] Yet despite the fact that Quinet discerns such differences between the two styles he still asserts that each possesses a particular type of beauty deriving from the character of the religion concerned:

Dans nos cathédrales, la végétation divine plus resserrée monte, aspire de cimes en cimes. Le tronc plus vigoureux des piliers porte haut son branchage. Sa beauté est dans la nue, tandis que la sève arabe va s'épuisant dans la foule des rejetons et des colonnes. Mais, ce que cette architecture perd d'un côté, elle le regagne de l'autre; car le sublime de la mosquée, c'est de n'avoir pas de limites à l'horizon. Elle s'étend, en un moment, comme le royaume de l'Islam, sur une surface sans bornes. Dès que vous êtes engagé dans les colonnes, vous perdez de vue l'enceinte. Point de murailles; il reste l'immensité monotone d'Allah, partout semblable à lui-même, beauté, majesté, solitude incommensurable, religion du désert.[27]

As long as faith remained unquestioned the Gothic spires continued to climb towards the heavens. 'Encore! encore! oh! je veux monter plus haut' is the cry of the cathedral in *Ahasvérus*.[28] But as the Middle Ages fell into decline, so the building of the cathedrals ceased:

[l'architecture gothique] était arrivée à son faîte avec la société qu'elle représentait. Elle n'avait pas la force de monter plus haut. [. . .] La plupart des cathédrales allaient rester inachevées; un vent froid avait soufflé sur ces plantes célestes et les avait étiolées à leurs cimes.[29]

The coming of the Reformation and the Renaissance signalled that the religious aspiration of the age of faith had passed: 'le dôme du seizième siècle s'arrondissait déjà sur les ruines de l'architecture gothique et byzantine'.[30] In Quinet's eyes the cathedral at Brou stands as a highly charged symbol of the last phase of the development of Gothic architecture. The edifice is an example of an 'architecture expirante' and it embodies 'la lassitude et l'affaissement' of the end of an epoch.[31] The spirit of asceticism which characterised the great cathedrals is absent from this church which has become a monument to earthly love, to personal feeling and emotion. Unlike the cathedrals, which were the creation of the collectivity over a period of generations, Brou is the expression of 'une pensée individuelle et isolée'; here, continues Quinet, 'l'individualité triomphante des modernes s'est divinisée'.[32]

In conclusion we should note that Quinet considers the present both as a time of crisis marked by doubt and anxiety and as a period which may presage a new religious rebirth.[33] Does this suggest that a corresponding transformation of religious architecture will take place? In 1831 he certainly points to the possibility of such a transformation: the Gothic cathedral may yet grow and develop new forms.[34] It should be emphasised, however, that this is an isolated example. The lectures delivered at the Collège de France in the 1840s represent an unambiguous call to action. In the modern world, so Quinet maintains, Christianity becomes a reality by advancing the causes of freedom, equality, fraternity and solidarity; the Christian message is inextricably linked to the destiny of revolutionary France. Catholicism, in comparison, stands condemned as the embodiment of sterility and reaction. This hostility towards the Church of Rome means that Quinet cannot allow the Gothic cathedral to play an important role in his vision of mankind's future.[35] For what is the cathedral if not a symbol of the past, of the Middle Ages? Henceforth the encounter between the human and the divine will take place within the spirit of the individual.

BIRMINGHAM   C. CROSSLEY

---

[1] For a more detailed discussion of Quinet's aesthetic thought see Crossley, 'Les Idées esthétiques de Quinet', in *Edgar Quinet. Ce Juif errant*, ed. S. Bernard-Griffiths and P. Viallaneix, Clermont-Ferrand, Faculté des lettres, 1978, pp. 239-50. Unless otherwise stated references to Quinet's works in the present article are to his *Œuvres complètes*, Paris, Pagnerre, 1857-8, 10 volumes.

[2] *De la Nature et de l'histoire dans leurs rapports avec les traditions religieuses et épiques*, essay published as an appendix to *De la Grèce moderne et de ses rapports avec l'antiquité*, Paris, Levrault, 1830, p. 422. See also *Ahasvérus*, p. 85. Ecbatana is mentioned in a similar fashion by, among others, Hegel and Creuzer.

[3] *Considérations philosophiques sur l'art*, Strasbourg, Levrault, 1839, p. 8.

[4] *Le Génie des religions*, p. 319.

[5] See A. Poirier, *Les Idées artistiques de Chateaubriand*, Paris, P.U.F., 1930, pp. 47 and 59.

[6] Chateaubriand, *Itinéraire de Paris à Jérusalem*, Paris, Furne, n.d., pp. 7-8. Cf. *De la Grèce moderne*, pp. 329-30.

[7] These ideas are examined in greater detail in our article 'The Young Edgar Quinet and the Philosophy of History', forthcoming in *Stanford French Studies*.

[8] *De la Grèce moderne*, p. 113.

[9] Ibid., p. 261.

[10] *De la Nature et de l'histoire*, p. 422. Cf. *De la Grèce moderne* (p. 265): 'Si, à l'origine, l'histoire des peuples se confond dans celle des cultes, ainsi la ville est en même temps le sanctuaire. La nation vit dans le temple'.

[11] *De la Nature et de l'histoire*, p. 423. In *De la Grèce moderne* (pp. 65-6) Quinet elaborates on this point in an important passage which requires extensive quotation. He begins with a reference to the Byzantine churches which he visited: '[...] il est impossible de les considérer avec quelque attention sans reconnaître qu'elles sont la première forme et l'ébauche irréfléchie des basiliques du Nord; chaos qui vient de se former des débris d'un monde encore croulant, que le génie naissant du moyen âge lui donne la vie et l'intelligence, ces piliers de diverses proportions, sans cesser d'être unis, vont s'élancer en fuseaux, ces chapiteaux usés vont changer leurs acanthes flétries contre les figures symboliques des dragons de l'Apocalypse. L'esprit de l'humanité, en se relevant indépendant et avide d'infini avec des peuples nouveaux, soulèvera dans les airs ces coupoles écrasées; et la forme pyramidale que la nature fait prédominer dans sa création végétale en avançant vers le Nord, sera celle de cet arbre mystique que chaque siècle a nourri de sa sève. Pendant que dans les épopées du moyen âge, les éléments celtiques et germaniques s'entent sur les traditions de la cour de Byzance, les ogives des cathédrales berceront leurs rameaux sur le tronc dépouillé de la colonne d'Ionie. Ainsi, après sa lente formation, l'architecture gothique représente instantanément les phases diverses du genre humain, et n'est elle-même que le type de l'histoire universelle, rendu sensible et immobile par le prodige de l'art'.

[12] Cf. Quinet's remarks on Voss and Heine in *Allemagne et Italie* (1838), pp. 209-10 and 213.

[13] *De la Grèce moderne*, pp. 247-8. Cf. F. Creuzer, *Religions de l'antiquité*, tr. Guigniaut, Paris, Treuttel and Würtz, 1825, vol. 1, pp. 368-77.

[14] *Le Génie des religions*, p. 98.

[15] *Ahasvérus*, p. 261.

[16] 'De l'Avenir des religions', *Revue des deux mondes*, 1831, p. 123. Cf. *Ahasvérus* (p. 261): 'Les montagnes à pic n'ont point de voix pour dire leurs secrets; les rochers n'en ont point dans leurs grottes, ni les forêts de sapin sur leurs cimes qui grisonnent. Moi [la cathédrale], je parle pour eux'. And in *De la Grèce moderne* (p. 182) Quinet remarks: 'Depuis les frontières de la Géorgie jusqu'à la région boréale, la forme pyramidale croit avec les nations germaniques. Pendant que les familles des ombellifères, des crucifères, étendent sous leurs pas des fleurs à vives arêtes, à cônes renversés, le pin, le mélèze s'élancent comme la flèche d'une cathédrale'.

[17] *Allemagne et Italie*, p. 276.

[18] Ibid., p. 295. See H. Tronchon, 'L'Italie dans les carnets d'Edgar Quinet', *Mélanges Henri Hauvette*, Paris, 1934, pp. 713-4.

[19] *Allemagne et Italie*, p. 298.

[20] Ibid., pp. 343-4. See further pp. 275-6.

[21] Between 1848 and 1852 Quinet published in three volumes his long cultural history of the Italian people entitled *Les Révolutions d'Italie*. In this work (p. 77) he interprets the early development of architecture in Italy as follows: 'Dans le dixième et le onzième siècle, toute l'Italie se couvre sans bruit d'églises, de tours, de dômes, de *palais du peuple*. Plus la langue de ces temps est stérile, plus ces chroniques de pierre parlent haut; peuplées de statues et de peintures, elles expriment ce que les lèvres ne pourraient encore dire. L'architecture de l'ogive et l'architecture à plein cintre se disputent le sol, à la suite du parti de l'Empire et du parti du Sacerdoce. Comme un enfant qui ne peut encore parler s'exprime par une foule de gestes, ainsi l'Italie moderne, déjà pleine de pensées et de factions, mais dont la langue n'est pas encore déliée, s'exprime en gestes de pierre par son architecture guelfe et gibeline'.

[22] *Mes Vacances en Espagne* (1846), pp. 14-5. Many of the points made in this work are also discussed in *L'Ultramontanisme ou l'église romaine et la société moderne* (1844) and *Le Christianisme et la révolution française* (1845).

[23] *Mes Vacances en Espagne*, p. 146. Cf. Quinet's description of the Alhambra, the Escurial and the hieronymite monastery of Belem.

[24] Ibid., p. 207.

[25] Ibid., pp. 207-8.

[26] Ibid., p. 208.

[27] Ibid., pp. 208-9.

[28] *Ahasvérus*, p. 259.

[29] *Des Arts de la renaissance, et de l'église de Brou*, p. 352. Cf. *Le Christianisme et la révolution française*, (p. 171): 'Sans doute, il est à regretter que la cathédrale de Cologne n'ait pas continué de grandir; mais il est plus nécessaire encore que l'homme s'achève et s'édifie jusqu'au faîte'.

[30] *Des Arts de la renaissance, et de l'église de Brou*, p. 353.

[31] Ibid., pp. 358 and 357.

[32] Ibid., pp. 356 and 359.

[33] Cf. Quinet's use of the theme of the ruined church as symbol in *Allemagne et Italie* (p. 320) and *Ahasvérus* (p. 103).

[34] This transformation needs to be envisaged in the light of Quinet's belief that a rebirth of religion may take place in America. See Crossley, 'Quelques aspects de l'américanisme romantique', *Nineteenth Century French Studies*, 1977-8, pp. 82-93.

[35] A reading of the works published during Quinet's exile serves to reinforce this point. Cf. J. Pommier, 'Michelet et l'architecture gothique', *Etudes de lettres*, Dec. 1954, pp. 17-35, and J. Le Goff, 'Le Moyen Age de Michelet', in *Pour un autre Moyen Age. Temps, travail et culture en Occident*, Paris, Gallimard, 1977, pp. 19-45.

MARJORIE SHAW

IN SEARCH OF A DRAMATIC IMAGE IN NINETEENTH-CENTURY FRANCE

'Monsieur, combien avez-vous de pièces de théâtre en France?' dit Candide à l'abbé; lequel répondit: 'Cinq ou six mille. — C'est beaucoup, dit Candide; combien y en a-t-il de bonnes? — Quinze ou seize, répliqua l'autre. — C'est beaucoup,' dit Martin.[1]

We have all reacted, as Voltaire meant us to, to this quip. Did Voltaire count many of his own tragedies amongst the fifteen or sixteen, one wonders. A recent French thesis has produced a vast mass of information about *Le Théâtre et le public à Paris de 1715 à 1750* and we know that Professor John Lough had already looked at *Paris Theatre Audiences in the Seventeenth and Eighteenth Centuries*.[2] M. Henri Lagrave's patient researches confirm what we had all suspected, that, in the period studied, the most successful writers (in terms of numbers of performances and numbers of spectators) were Voltaire for tragedy and Marivaux for comedy. He also has some illuminating figures concerning the number of plays which did not survive the horrendous conditions of performance which he describes, and did not receive the approval of the very vocal audiences of the day. More than ten per cent of the new plays presented at the Comédie Française during those thirty-five years (1715-1750) did not see a second performance, including even the *Mariamne* of Voltaire in 1724 and *La Dispute* of Marivaux in 1744. Voltaire of course refused to take 'No' for an answer, rewrote his play and presented it the very next year under the title *Hérode et Mariamne*. In this guise it was more successful and attained the considerable figure of sixty performances before it finally vanished into oblivion in 1763, except for three (freak?) performances in 1817. I don't doubt for a moment but that similar figures would emerge from a scrutiny of the second half of the eighteenth century. Even a quick glance at A. Joannidès, *La Comédie Française de 1680 à 1900* shows us that sixty new plays were performed at the Comédie in the years 1751 to 1760, of which some fifteen or sixteen appear to have sunk without trace after only one performance and we know that the same fate awaited Diderot's *Le Fils naturel* in 1771.[3]

A striking proof of the same phenomenon is to be found in the career of Talma. Talma's career at the Comédie Française was a long one, probably longer than most of his colleagues, certainly longer than those of his most eminent predecessors or successors. Moreover he was fortunate in that he established himself quite quickly as outstanding, and within a comparatively short time authors were writing plays specifically for him, even with his help in the writing, or perhaps more especially with the arrangement for the stage.[4]

Talma's English biographer, H. F. Collins, has drawn up a list of the parts created by Talma during his thirty-eight years at the Comédie, a list of seventy-six parts, fifty-three of them in tragedies, and we can surely assume that the majority of these were in fact written with Talma in mind.[5] Facts concerning these plays are instructive. Of the seventy-six plays, it would seem that seven (nearly ten per cent therefore) did not receive more than one performance and another thirteen had five performances or fewer, and yet a further fifteen had fewer than a dozen performances.[6]

7 plays had	1 performance only
3 ,, ,,	2 performances
3 ,, ,,	3 ,,
3 ,, ,,	4 ,,
4 ,, ,,	5 ,,
1 ,, ,,	6 ,,
7 ,, ,,	7 ,,
3 ,, ,,	8 ,,
2 ,, ,,	10 ,,
1 ,, ,,	11 ,,
1 ,, ,,	12 ,,

Thus thirty-five of these seventy-six plays, very nearly fifty per cent of the total, received fewer than a dozen performances. Others of course had more success. Nevertheless of the nineteen which Collins lists as Talma's most successful (in terms of numbers of performances) only eight are from this list of new plays created specifically for Talma, and for these eight the numbers of performances descend from ninety down to forty and the dates of creation range from 1789 (the very beginning of his career) to four dating from the 1820s (the last decade of his career).

The mainstay of Talma's repertory was of course to be found in the great classical roles of Corneille, Racine and Voltaire, together with the Ducis adaptations of Shakespeare, which for the most part Talma did not 'create'. Only *Jean Sans-Terre* and *Othello* received their first performances during Talma's time at the Comédie.

All of this spells an enormous effort on the part of Talma himself to discover new playwrights of merit, to say nothing of great plays to be added to the repertory of the Comédie, as well as satisfying roles for himself. The fact remains that all this effort was of no avail. Of all these new plays written for one of France's greatest actors, not one has entered the permanent repertory of the Comédie Française, and the vast majority barely survived Talma himself. We know that Talma contemplated playing the name part in Victor Hugo's half-written *Cromwell*. One can only speculate on how much rewriting he would have stipulated before actually putting the play into production. The situation never arose since Talma died when only the first four acts were completed.

Eight years earlier, in June 1818, another eager young poet had consulted the great actor, hoping that Talma would help him to have his play accepted by the reading committee of the Comédie. Lamartine has left conflicting accounts of the interview accorded him by Talma:

Jeune homme, me dit-il, de sa voix la plus grave et la plus émue, j'aurais voulu vous connaître il y a vingt ans, vous auriez été mon poète; . . .

and in a letter to his friend Virieu:

Il m'a répété vingt fois que c'étaient les plus beaux vers qu'on lui eût lus; que j'étais poète et peut-être le seul; que *Moïse*, de M. de Chateaubriand, était beau, que *Saül* [the play submitted by Lamartine] était fort au-dessus; mais que, dans l'un comme dans l'autre, il y avait des innovations qu'il était certain que le Comité ne passerait pas . . .[7]

One Talma role which was enormously successful was the title role in the Ducis version of *Hamlet*, created in 1769, but considerably rewritten by Ducis with help and encouragement from Talma himself as late as 1811.[8] Madame de Staël waxed lyrical about Talma in this role when she witnessed a performance in Lyons in 1809. Yet even this role, while still remaining in the repertory for some twenty years after Talma's death and having quite considerable success during the decade of the thirties (very understandable in the climate of Romantic enthusiasm) faded away after 1849 and was never performed again at the Comédie.

An examination of Rachel's repertory will be seen to lead to the same melancholy conclusion. It is rather more to be expected in her case, no doubt, since her career was very much shorter than Talma's and her repertory consisted even more exclusively of the classical roles from Corneille and Racine. One exception must be mentioned since it forms a link with Talma. Lebrun's *Marie Stuart*, first performed in March 1820 with Talma in the role of Leicester, had sixty-four performances during his lifetime, with a further twenty-two in the period 1827-1835, was revived in 1840 with Rachel playing the title role, having a further fifty-five performances during the years 1840-1857. Two of these must have been played by Rachel's successor, but twenty belong to the early years of her career (1841-1842). The play had no further performances at the Comédie.

One may continue the same exercise with regard to Sarah Bernhardt, but with rather more encouraging results in that more plays associated with Bernhardt are still being revived. I am thinking particularly of the Rostand plays, *Cyrano de Bergerac* and *L'Aiglon*.

What I have been suggesting is the rather obvious point that in spite of outstanding actors and actresses, who stimulated a number of authors, nothing in the way of outstanding plays was written. Let us therefore look at the problem from a slightly different angle.

I began by referring to Lagrave's recent thesis on *Le Théâtre et le public à Paris de 1715 à 1750*. Lagrave expresses himself surprised at the result of his researches in establishing the contemporary success of Marivaux in the realm of comedy. Marivaux has had a very considerable success story in recent years as an 'academic' author. We can therefore concur with the usual verdict passed on the eighteenth century as a whole, that in spite of all the great dramatic activity during that century nothing now remains but the Marivaux canon and the two Beaumarchais comedies, certainly not Voltaire in spite of his overwhelming success in his own day. This success even lasted some years after his death, with a total of thirty-one plays performed at the Comédie Française, and 3660 performances up till 1830. A further 316 only (mostly during the nineteenth century) were added in the next one hundred and thirty-two years, until 1962. I do not know if the bicentenary will have provided the impetus to add another twenty-four performances so as to push the total over the four thousand mark. Voltaire may be very much alive in some aspects of his work, but these do not include his theatre. How much of his initial success and subsequent lack of appeal can be directly and solely attributed to the fact of his having chosen to use the time-honoured formula of five-act tragedies in verse, according to the Racinian model, would be difficult to establish. We know what a mesmeric effect that model had on writers for such a long time, even into the nineteenth century, with Constant and Balzac (to name but two) attempting to follow where so many others had shown the way. In fact, as Daniel Mornet pointed out in his book on Racine in 1943, no one but Corneille and Racine himself had ever really succeeded in that genre, and that it was virtually impossible that any one else should succeed. 'La tragédie classique était une gageure à peu près impossible à gagner', and yet it took playwrights well over a century to accept that fact.

Professor W. D. Howarth in his history of Romantic drama makes the same point when he asserts that the Romantics did at least break the tradition and open up the way for freer dramatic techniques.[10] Each one of the Romantic poets in turn, even Lamartine marginally as we have seen, as well as Alexandre Dumas père, furnished a valiant effort towards a renewal of the dramatic ethos and they were after all writers of considerable stature, unlike many of those who had sought to write plays for Talma. And yet, in spite of all their efforts, the Romantic drama was indeed short-lived and very soon had to give way before a revival of the Classical repertory as played by Rachel, and it is arguable that the dramas of Hugo and Vigny continue to be read and studied today chiefly because of their interest as 'plays of the moment'. 'La bataille d'*Hernani*' is a date in the history of the French theatre. There was of course a Romantic revival towards the end of the century, which brought together the amazing career of Sarah Bernhardt and the undoubted talent of Edmond Rostand, whose *Cyrano de Bergerac* (1898) and *L'Aiglon* (1900), have had several revivals since their creation, and, as we know in this country, *Cyrano* has even crossed frontiers.

Yet of all these plays from *Hernani* to the end of the century, how many would one classify as an essential part of French culture? An adequate representation (or image) of its own period, perhaps? Of the playwrights, only Musset is showing any sign of vitality today. The Garnier-Flammarion collection, which surely aims at a much more popular public than the original Classiques Garnier, included Musset's *Théâtre* amongst its earliest volumes. The monthly periodical *Europe* has recently devoted a double number to Musset, and a substantial part of the volume is comprised of articles referring to the theatre rather than to other aspects of Musset's works.[11] Musset has now moved up to fourth place in the list of authors most frequently performed at the Comédie Française, and the other three, Molière, Racine and Corneille, had a long start on him. Sylvie Chevalley points out, in drawing our attention to this success, that the copywright ran out in 1907 and suggests that this fact may have contributed to the frequency with which his plays have been performed after that date. The copyright on the Vigny plays ran out in 1913 and on the Hugo plays in 1935. One has not noticed that there has been a great deal of enthusiasm for reviving their plays since these dates. In the case of Musset, it seems to me to be much more to the point that several of his *Comédies et Proverbes* are particularly suitable (and successful) as curtain raisers, and it is a fact that eight out of the fifteen plays which Musset included under that umbrella title are at present being performed. One notes with pleasure that even *Lorenzaccio* was given over fifty performances in the years 1971-1976, for until then the Comédie Française had been remarkably shy of tackling that particular play.

Was Voltaire, then, being over-optimistic in his famous reply suggesting that there might be as many as fifteen or sixteen 'good' plays in five or six thousand? There are, it would seem, very few plays written in the nineteenth century which one feels have the lasting qualities of the great plays of the past. French literature would indeed be the poorer without the nineteenth-century contribution in novels and poetry. How many critics would dare to argue very strongly in favour of any playwright, except perhaps Musset, and even in the case of Musset there are many who would rank him as a very lightweight dramatist, with the obvious exception of *Lorenzaccio*. Rostand had an enormous success in his own time, but will his plays last even as well as those of Marivaux and Musset?

The conclusion to be drawn is the very obvious one, which we have all known for a long time, that the great dramatic flowering of the seventeenth century was quite exceptional, and the intense dramatic activity of the succeeding centuries has been quite unable to equal it.

SHEFFIELD   MARJORIE SHAW

[1] Voltaire, *Candide*, chapter XXII.
[2] Henri Lagrave, *Le Théâtre et le public à Paris, de 1715 à 1750*, Paris, Klincksieck, 1972. John Lough, *Paris Theatre Audiences in the Seventeenth and Eighteenth Centuries*, Oxford University Press, 1957.
[3] A. Joannidès, *La Comédie Française de 1680 à 1900*, Geneva, Slatkine Reprints, 1970. (First published in 1901).
[4] Jean Gaudon, 'Talma et ses auteurs', in *Modern Miscellany presented to Eugène Vinaver*, Manchester University Press, 1969.
[5] Herbert F. Collins, *Talma. A biography of an Actor*, London, Faber and Faber, 1964.
[6] A. Joannidès, op. cit.
[7] A. Augustin-Thierry, *Le Tragédien de Napoléon*, Albin Michel, 1942. See p. 235.
[8] J. Gaudon, op. cit.
[9] Daniel Mornet, *Jean Racine*, Aux Armes de France, 1943, p. 95.
[10] W. D. Howarth, *Sublime and Grotesque: a study of French Romantic Drama*, London, Harrap, 1975, p. 405.
[11] *Europe*, 55, nos. 583-84. See Sylvie Chevalley, 'Musset à la Comédie Française', pp. 17-39.

ALISON FAIRLIE

SUGGESTIONS ON THE ART OF THE NOVELIST IN CONSTANT'S *CÉCILE*

Would *Cécile* stand in the canon of novels which rouse constantly renewed enjoyment if *Adolphe*, the *Cahier Rouge*, the *Journaux* and letters of Constant were not already known? That it remained unfinished need be no barrier — one thinks of Marivaux. In the now nearly thirty years since its near-miraculous rediscovery and first publication, many scholars have shown, from widely differing points of view, its vital place in Constant's work as a whole.[1] An initial tendency was to oppose it to the supreme stylisation of *Adolphe*, and therefore to see it as pure and unadorned autobiography. Certain particularly interesting recent articles have investigated other ways of approach. Taking specific sections of the text as examples, Simone Balayé (on how Mme de Malbée differs from Mme de Staël)[2] and Frank P. Bowman[3] (on the 'quietist' episode) have shown how very far the novel's version may be from the facts of Constant's recorded experience. Both are fully aware of the complex problems involved in contrasting a novel with a supposed 'reality'; their conclusions are based on detailed comparisons with Constant's other and multiple forms of self-expression in diaries and letters and on some of the main omissions or distortions of this material in the novel. W. Pabst[4] has drawn attention to ways in which *Cécile* may fit certain conventions of the novels of its day — in the presentation of the hero between two women, and much else. These approaches, in different ways, rightly stress aspects of conscious selection and emphasis. Tricky problems will necessarily remain; how far are modifications of reality undertaken for aesthetic reasons, or out of Constant's desire to present a skilled case in face of particular personal circumstances?

The present brief article will not be primarily concerned with the problem of transformed autobiography, nor with that of the novel's genesis in relation to that of *Adolphe*. Taking up points raised by the studies mentioned above, and by the excellent outline in Paul Delbouille's '*Adolphe* et *Cécile*: esquisse d'une comparaison stylistique',[5] I hope simply to indicate some of the ways of working of Constant's technique in this particular novel, which would deserve fuller investigation than space will allow here.

In *Adolphe*, Constant's care for construction is visible in his choice of ten chapters, first tracing the development of desire, placing the climax in Chapter 4, then following the prolonged disintegration. Was *Cécile* intended similarly to have ten *époques*? One can only surmise, but this might well fit his outline intentions and dates. Certain immediate ways in which the construction and concentration are much less deliberate than in *Adolphe* are obvious. Where *Adolphe*'s narrative is confined to some four years, *Cécile*, even in its unfinished form, covers fifteen. The length of the different *époques* varies wildly, between two pages and nineteen; the stretch of months or years which each includes is in no way proportionate to the length of the episode. Instead of the ultimate concentration into two figures only, Adolphe and Ellénore, we have the narrator's prolonged tergiversations between the contrasting Cécile and Mme de Malbée; but there is also a relative proliferation of episodic characters: the narrator's first wife and her lover, various court figures; Cécile's two husbands and members of her family, the tutor to Mme de Malbée's children, the narrator's father, the Pietist, servants . . . The theme of the woman acquaintance who harmfully intervenes, confined in *Adolphe* to the one friend of Ellénore, is here made recurrent in the two figures of the 'dame d'honneur' at court (174) and of Mme Marcillon (181-2); the witty and bitter older woman whose influence on the narrator was so strong figures in the first chapter of *Adolphe* simply as a recollection, not as a performer in the story, whereas in *Cécile* Mme de Chenevière plays her part in the action. Altogether, the time-scheme and the sporadic sequence of events, however much Constant omits and changes from the multiple sexual, political and financial preoccupations and pressures of his life,[6] are certainly here far from the deliberate concentration of *Adolphe*.

Many of the episodic characters, of course, simply serve a function in the narrative, without being at all developed in their own right. Yet even the most briefly mentioned may serve to suggest at the same time a point of particular susceptibility in the narrator and some social generalisation: the servant (215) whose ribald comment provokes an ulcerated and exaggerated response (Constant in the *Journaux* reproaches himself on various occasions for his apprehension of what servants may think of him) is a 'vieux Français, familier comme ils le sont tous'. One secondary character is given particular development as representative of the personal reactions that stem from a defined social type: Cécile's second husband, Wenceslas de Saint-Elme: the type of the French émigré (a frequent butt for Constant in other works, as for Mme de Staël in her novels). Various incidents and comments (187, 190, 194, 198-202) display his easily wounded vanity and lack of any depth of feeling; he gives rise to the ironical reflection that fear of a given happening may produce precisely the effects it seeks to avoid (190); finally he is virulently summed up (202):

> Son amour-propre se blessait quelquefois de l'idée qu'une femme avait pu préférer un autre homme à lui; mais sa frivolité qui le replongeait sans cesse dans tous les plaisirs du monde, dissipait bientôt ces petits soulèvements de son amour-propre, et ses préjugés religieux, qu'en sa qualité d'émigré français il alliait avec la frivolité, le disposaient quelquefois à désirer lui-même la rupture d'un mariage que sa religion condamnait.

Other briefly outlined characters would deserve further investigation. Just as Simone Balayé has suggested that Mme dc Malbée, a major figure, might be compared not simply with the biographical facts, but with Constant's very many portraits of Mme de Staël in writings of several different kinds, so too it would be interesting to set Mme de Chenevière by the side of the briefer, but again varying, outlines founded on Mme de Charrière, as a means of studying the art of the portrait in Constant's two novels.

On the contrast between the two main female characters, I can here make only one or two remarks. It is obviously Mme de Malbée who comes by far the more persuasively alive. Cécile, the touchingly dignified, ever-patient Griselda, is given no faults;[7] but Mme de Malbée is no merely contrasting Evil Genius. While rejoicing in Simone Balayé's careful and stimulating examination of how much Constant has left aside or under-played in his debts to Mme de Staël in many realms — political, literary, personal — or has passed over in a few dry phrases, one might, I think, stress that, as the novel proceeds, not only the desire to break but the intensity of a whole shared past comes more and more to the fore. A passage of particularly violent criticism (201) is immediately followed by 'Cependant elle avait tant de grâce dans la douleur, et dans la gaîté qui, vu la mobilité de son caractère, se mêlait quelquefois à cette douleur . . .' and leads up to 'une femme qui avait disposé de ma vie pendant treize ans'. His discovery of her infidelity (203) gives rise, after initial fury, to 'Je la connaissais comme moi-même. Je savais que dans sa conduite il y avait de l'inconséquence et de l'égoïsme, mais non de la mauvaise foi . . .' and, as always, he is haunted by 'le spectre de sa douleur'. It is not simply 'la parfaite convenance de nos esprits' which is at stake; 'mon cœur avait besoin de céder' (204-5); and later, with her live interest in his writing, 'la sympathie de nos esprits fit disparaître l'opposition de nos sentiments'. Finally, as he travels the wintry road towards Cécile (214), 'Immobile dans un coin de ma voiture, je voyais s'élever et grandir tous les spectres du passé'. Once again he remembers their thirteen years together:

J'allais renoncer à une femme à qui j'avais donné, dont j'avais reçu, tant de preuves d'affection. Elle avait été le tyran, mais elle avait aussi été le but de ma vie. Mille souvenirs étaient enlacés autour de mon cœur . . .

But most significant of all is his memory of how 'l'homme qui le premier m'avait inspiré des idées religieuses' had in the past pronounced a sombre prophecy. Insisting that all attempts to break 'des nœuds écrits dans le Ciel' are fruitless, and culminating with 'chacun a sa croix sur cette terre, et Mme de Malbée est la croix que vous devez porter', his speech has a resounding rhetorical ring, within which certain phrases pierce more directly to the core of the matter:

Vous fuiriez au bout du monde que son âme crierait au fond de votre âme. Vous épouseriez une autre femme: cette femme se trouverait avoir épousé non pas vous, mais sa rivale (217).

Here, surely, the Pietist counsellor suggests both a parallel to, and a reversal of the figure of the Baron de T. in *Adolphe*, pronouncing in very different tones a part of the narrator's inner thoughts.[8]

★   ★   ★

To come more closely to Constant's treatment of individual scenes: I have discussed elsewhere how the best passages in *Adolphe* function through the concentration into a page or less of a kind of threefold movement: first, the bringing alive of a scene between individuals, compounding succinct but sharply characterised direct speech with equally succinct indirect summary, and often with brief but suggestive physical notations; second, a moment of penetrating insight into the dramatic turning point from which there is no turning back ('nous avions prononcé des mots irréparables . . .'); finally, the stab of a still wider general axiom on human behaviour. Each of these factors exists (in very differing proportions) in *Cécile*; they are much more scattered in their placing. To look at each in turn may provide one or two surprises.

Both Cécile (173, 190) and Mme de Malbée (183-4) are given more detailed physical description than was accorded in Ellénore; if Cécile is given no unfavourable features, the portrait of Mme de Malbée is the more evocative in using initial critical reactions as a deliberate means of stressing the complex fascination she is eventually to exercise. Simone Balayé rightly stresses Constant's technique of providing continual contrasts in the narrator's presentation of her, where a *mais* may undermine an apparently favorable judgment. Yet, in the first physical description at least, the negative sides are placed first, in order to interpose the *mais* and to culminate in the effect of 'séduction irrésistible'. In the evocations of both Cécile and Mme de Malbée there occurs the sensuous effect wrought by 'un son de voix très doux': again this is more fully defined for Mme de Malbée than for Cécile.

Physical background is only rarely apparent in either novel. The touch of everyday detail, of which there is a momentary glimpse in the scene between Adolphe, Ellénore and the Comte de P., has its parallel here in a similar scene between three characters: the narrator's initial visit to Cécile, where her first husband is seen 'en veste et jouant du violon', beside his wife 'assise sur un canapé avec un air d'ennui trés visible'. In the dramatic scene in which Mme de Malbée will rush to seize the narrator back from his refuge with relatives, we see him with his eyes fixed despairingly on the clock; her incursion itself, by comparison with the scene from life on which it draws, (its melodramatic postures so fully described in other writings by Constant and his family) receives only a bare line or two. Fuller physical detail in seen in Cécile's illness of the last pages; an illness, indeed, that remains on the level of the physical and emotional, with no touch of the metaphysical speculations of the final chapter in *Adolphe*.

The use of natural background as objective correlative to personal feeling is clearly less developed than in those two suggestive scenes in *Adolphe* where the narrator wanders and meditates in the sombre countryside at dusk and through the night, or experiences Ellénore's tranquil resignation in the sunlit frosty garden. But the perilous coach journey on the icy mountain roads in the dark, and Cécile's isolation in the snow-storm, however 'factual' their origin, and potentially melo-dramatic their impact, may well fit and echo the desperation of the one and the sorrowful resignation of the other.

Even given the extended time-scale of *Cécile*, so that a larger part of the narrative will have to be briefly summed up, the relative absence of direct quotation from the characters' speech or their letters is startling. Letters are of course specially significant in this novel where characters lose touch over years of separation or travel across many countries; where postal losses or delays may serve either as genuinely ironical obstacles to understanding or as manufactured means to convenient postponement of decision. A list of all mentions of letters would reach an astonishing total. Yet they remain mentions, or brief summaries, sometimes skilfully concentrating a given tone (202) but without the varied technique and suggestive impact of, for example, Adolphe's pleading letters to Ellénore, or those letters where his father's allusive, inhibited, concerned yet ironical style bears out directly the narrator's analysis. In *Cécile*, there is one direct quotation from a letter — both a significant summary of the submissive Cécile, and a deliberate concentration, in carefully balanced style, of aspects of the narrator's self-examination. A firmly articulated phrase, with its intentional or unconscious alliteration, forces home her appeal: 'Je vous conjure de vous consulter et de vous connaître vous-même'. A series of balanced *Si* clauses evokes the alternative reasons that might draw him away from her (weakness, duty to past commitments, inability to break from them); a subsequent series of beseeching imperatives combines assurance of lasting fidelity with the need to be spared from 'l'incertitude, le scandale, les angoisses et la honte'. This very rare example of direct expression in letters is placed, then, at a key point in the novel, and is carefully stylised and concentrated.

Direct speech, too, is almost as rare: it, also, is placed at key moments. In the first *époque* it occurs at the climax of the break with the narrator's wife (176) — again moving to a carefully stylised conclusion: 'ne pas donner mon nom à un enfant qui me force à mépriser sa mère'. In the sixth *époque* there are several examples: Cécile's declaration (197) (again concentrated and stylised) of total obedience and fidelity; then the central 'Si Mme de Malbée ne me suit pas, je résisterai à ses lettres, mais si elle vient ici, toute résistance sera impossible' (205); later (206), the scene where Mme de Malbée's children are made witnesses to the violent rejection of a possible marriage and its still more violent counter-rejection; and finally the extended passage where the Pietist expounds the doctrine to which Adolphe will for long succumb. In the last *époque*, three examples are significant in very different ways. First, there is the succint interchange between the narrator and Cécile as they meet in the snow near Besançon (215), summing up in two phrases his exasperated fear of *inconvenance* and her quiet simplicity of response. Second, there comes the unexpectedly violent reaction to the servant's mocking laughter at a supposed change of allegiance: 'Ah! Ah! Monsieur! et Mme de Malbée!': the insinuations and echoes of this one phrase provoke his writing to Mme de Malbée 'la lettre la plus passionnée qu'elle eût jamais reçue de moi'. The third and most important is the recollection of that earlier prophecy by the Pietist which I discussed above. Here is still another form of stylisation: so long a pronouncement, and from long since, is yet recalled in lofty direct speech. Its placing at this crisis-point of reversal in feeling is all the more significant in that it is a haunting echo from the past and stretches forward into a lifelong future.[9]

Delbouille has suggested that clinching maxims, 'traits de moraliste', are fewer than in *Adolphe*, and that they show an author who is 'moins désenchanté . . . moins enclin aussi à tirer une leçon de son aventure'. Yet there remain many general reflections, whose function in the novel would deserve further discussion. Constant's love of absolute formulae, shown here in the recurrent epigrammatic formulations on women — 'il y a une inimitié secrète entre toutes les femmes' (174-5); 'la haine secrète que les femmes se portent mutuellement' (182) — stand separate from the character at least of Cécile as he has here created her (but, in her reactions after her seduction, he has deliberately differentiated her from women in general (106)). Other generalisations are less slanted, and stand suggestively beside their parallels in *Adolphe*; among them:

Il y a des choses que l'on soupçonne, qu'on veut ignorer, mais dont on ne peut tolérer la preuve (176), or the echo of La Rochefoucauld in the comment on 'l'opinion française':

cette opinion qui pardonne tous les vices, mais qui est inexorable sur les convenances et qui sait gré de l'hypocrisie comme d'une politesse qu'on lui rend (192).

Still other generalisations are more succinctly insinuated: on the one hand the observation in the passage that leads up to the long-postponed physical 'conquest' of Cécile: 'la conversation se dirigea sur les femmes et fut ce qu'elle est d'ordinaire entre hommes' (195); on the other, ringed round by 'j'avais tort sans doute' and 'mais', the briefest of reflections: 'car une promesse l'est toujours' [referring back to 'obligatoire'] (199).

From the first page, the delight in concise and balanced phrases, playing with parallels, contrasts, reversals of terms and ideas, with paradoxes, ironies and barbed allusions, is evident: 'La Baronne avait imaginé d'en faire son beau-frère, pour qu'il ne cessât pas d'être son amant'. The counterbalancing of several terms within the same phrase gives Constant (and his reader) particular enjoyment: 'L'on motive la haine sur l'amitié, et la calomnie sur l'intérêt'; 'ombrageux par caractère et soupçonneux par situation, ils ne considéraient comme leurs alliés que ceux qui se faisaient leurs complices, et Mme de Malbée, malgré ses efforts pour les captiver, et par ces efforts même . . .' as does the epigrammatic expression of ironies: 'Je m'affligeais du départ de Mme de Malbée, précisément parce que je lui savais gré de partir', or 'Je me sentis des devoirs précisément parce qu'elle paraissait ne m'en croire aucun'.

The arts of concision and allusion in the analysis of the self would obviously require a separate article, discussing perhaps the means by which *bonne foi* is asserted and queried, the lack of inner continuity in feeling (213),[10] yet its resurgence under the stimulus of the obstacle; the ability to insinuate yet leave open a mixture of motives by introducing them under the blanket of 'peut-être aussi parce que . . .', of 'soit que . . .' or more directly as 'des considérations moins pures et plus égoïstes' (192). The presentation of the Pietist episode, so ably analysed by F. P. Bowman in its central implications, might be looked at further, both as regards the ways in which it transforms a religious into a psychological issue, and for the ironical insinuations which irrupt from time to time in expressions such as 'sommeil moral'; 'je pris le désir que j'avais de la revoir pour une inspiration du Ciel'; 'je crus sentir que c'était de cette volonté rebelle à ses ordres que Dieu me punissait', or 'cette imprévoyance commode dont je m'étais fait un devoir religieux'; yet here again Constant doubles back to an open question (212) 'Mais aujourd'hui même, je ne sais si cet abandon complet à la Providence n'est pas [. . .] la plus sûre ressource de l'homme' (and one remembers Adolphe's reflections by Ellénore's death-bed).

Finally, if one were to choose isolated scenes in which the art of the novelist is fully in command, two might serve as examples, for very different reasons. The first (175) is predominantly ironical in tone: that early scene where the young narrator feels obliged to lay down the law to his wife, not from any feeling of jealousy, but because of the convention that ridicules the deceived husband. The desperate effort to whip up either the required feelings or the apposite words, contrary to his underlying sense of justice; his own startled surprise when she seems to accept his unaccustomed authority, the irony of her misinterpretation of his intentions, these and other undertones interplay to provide a basic change in their relationship.

Of a quite different kind is one of the most suggestive of the apparently peripheral scenes — the Bal de l'Opéra in the sixth *époque*. Here the masked ball provides a suggestive analysis of a particular experience of momentary delight:

Cette nuit m'a laissé un souvenir de bonheur qui est aussi vif aujourd'hui que si un long temps ne s'était pas écoulé depuis cette époque. Le sentiment d'être seuls au milieu d'une foule immense, inconnus à tout le monde, à l'abri de tous les curieux, environnés de gens auxquels nous avions intérêt de nous cacher, et séparés d'eux par une barrière si faible, et pourtant invincible, cette manière d'exister uniquement l'un pour l'autre, à travers les flots de la multitude, nous semblait une union plus étroite, et remplissait nos cœurs de plaisir et d'amour (200).

One remembers here Stendhal's Lucien and Mme de Chasteller in the gardens of the Chasseur Vert, experiencing later in the century the sense of lovers' mute understanding among a joyous crowd. In Constant, typically, the delight cannot be prolonged or renewed:

Nous retournâmes au même bal la semaine suivante. Mais notre attente fut déçue, probablement parce qu'elle avait été trop vive.[11]

Once again, there comes the clinching general conclusion:

Cette expérience nous apprit qu'il ne fallait pas transformer en arrangements prémédités les plaisirs inattendus.

But the 'charme de notre réunion mystérieuse' has been preserved both in the memory of the narrator and in the expression of the author.

There is still space for further discussion of *Cécile*, whether as a novel in its own right or as an example of Constant's exceptional skill in presenting a case, as exemplified in his personal letters or in his political writings. Its affinities with the eighteenth-century novels avidly read by Constant in his youth might be further investigated. Beside the extraordinary concentration of *Adolphe*, *Cécile* stands on a particular borderline between self-investigation and stylisation.

CAMBRIDGE   ALISON FAIRLIE

---

[1] I refer below only to recent works directly related to the present article. For other important general works, in some of which *Cécile* is discussed, see David K. Lowe: *Benjamin Constant: An annotated bibliography of critical editions and studies 1946-1978*, London, Grant and Cutler, 1979. (Works specifically devoted to *Cécile*, as apart from more general studies, are listed from p. 104). Page references in my text are to Constant's *Œuvres*, edited by Alfred Roulin, Paris, Gallimard, 1957.

[2] 'Madame de Staël et Madame de Malbée, ou *Cécile*, autobiographie et roman', *Europe*, 467 (1968), 107-15.

[3] 'L'Épisode quiétiste dans *Cécile*', *Actes du Congrès Benjamin Constant, 1967*, Geneva, Droz, 1968, 97-108.

[4] '*Cécile* de Benjamin Constant, document autobiographique ou fiction littéraire', in *Actes du Congrès . . .* (see footnote 3) 45-52; and 'Die Stilisierung des literarischen Selbstporträts in Benjamin Constants *Cécile*' in *Formen der Selbstdarstellung, Festgabe für Fritz Neubert*, ed. Reichenkron & Haase, Berlin, Duncker & Humblot, 1956, 313-30.

[5] *Cahiers d'analyse textuelle*, XVII, (1975), 7-22.

[6] Constant's many other projects of marriage find no place in the novel (though at times it is made abundantly clear that Cécile is in part a sheer means of making a break with the obsessive Mme de Malbée), nor do various other involvements, whether serious (as with Anna Lindsay) or purely sexual. Political beliefs and ambitions emerge much more clearly, if only briefly, than in *Adolphe*. Financial considerations arise mainly as signs of personal generosity (narrator to his wife; Cécile's offer to the narrator); they play no part in the relationship with Mme de Malbée, except for the remark (205) that relatives 'sur qui je pouvais fonder quelque espérance de fortune' sought to make him break with her.

[7] In some incidents, the reasons for her refusals or her break in correspondence are left oddly unexplained.

[8] His words echo in the narrator's mind long after they are pronounced, as do the Baron de T.'s for Adolphe during the night-wanderings in Chapter VII (90).

[9] Two moments where inner reflection is expressed in direct quotation might also be noticed: the reflection on the happiness of lovers which the narrator suddenly longs to share (172; cf. Adolphe's embarking on a love-affair after seeing the joy of a friend in love); the prayers expressing total abnegation (209).

[10] 'Ma fausseté ne consistait point à feindre une sensibilité plus grande que celle que j'avais, mais à laisser croire que cette sensibilité aurait des suites qu'elle ne devait pas avoir'.

[11] Cf. *Journaux* 614, 620.

AN ASPECT OF PORTRAITURE
.IN THE NOVELS OF BALZAC:
PSYCHO-PHYSIOLOGICAL BRIDGES

Honoré de Balzac's technique of character presentation and in particular his style of portraiture are arguably amongst the most distinctive and immediately recognizable in the whole of French prose fiction. The hallmarks of this style are, as numerous critics have pointed out,[1] an insistence on carefully selected details of physical appearance and clothing; frequent recourse to the now discredited pseudo-sciences of physiognomy and phrenology (which permits the close association of physiological and psychological peculiarities in the presentation of characters); the establishment of the social status, financial situation and even social antecedents of these same characters largely as a result of an examination of their articles of clothing, physical traits and individual mannerisms; an eagerness on the author's part to place the highly individualized products of his creative imagination in social groups and behavioural categories pertaining to various types of the human species (these are the so-called *individualités typisées*), and finally the modulation of the viewpoint which is achieved through the inclusion of the evaluative judgements of either fictional characters or imagined observers in addition to the judgements of the narrator himself. Underpinning all of this is a firm fabric of psychological and environmental determinism, presented forcefully by a seemingly omniscient author whose basic premiss is that man, in his various manifestations, is completely 'knowable'. Balzac's portraits are, in fact, more than simple descriptions of externals: they synthesize the social, spiritual and psychological progress of the characters to the point in time when they are described and contain an implicit prognosis of development. As Tahsin Yücel has so aptly put it, 'le portrait balzacien [. . .] est le carrefour des illusions perdues, des espoirs naissants, des passions dévorantes, des intentions cachées et des complots qui se préparent, il est, en un mot, un message complexe dont le déchiffrement livrerait tout l'être'.[2]

One aspect of the 'decoding' of this message which has not received adequate critical attention is the nature, frequency and ultimate signifi-cance of a relatively small number of verbs and verbal locutions which act as bridges between the physiological and psychological traits of the characters portrayed.[3] The close inter-relationship between these two ·elements of Balzacian portraiture stems from the novelist's belief in physiognomy and phrenology: the author of *La Comédie humaine* accepts unquestioningly that psychological characteristics, be it an *état d'âme* or a dominant passion, etch themselves on our facial features, are apparent in our postures and gestures or are contained in the configurations of the skull. It is therefore not surprising that within the framework of a single novel a number of his protagonists are accorded as many portraits as there are social or spiritual stages in their lives. An excellent example of this multiplication of portraits is afforded by *Le Curé de village* and in particular by the presentation of one of the two central characters of the work, Véronique Graslin, née Sauviat. Indeed, the description of Véronique at the age of sixteen (when a number of latent characteristics have yet to develop into the familiar and irresistible Balzacian passions) illustrates well a number of the aforementioned hallmarks of the novelist's style of portraiture:

> Quand un sentiment violent éclatait chez Véronique, [. . .] il semblait qu'une lumière intérieure effaçât par ses rayons les marques de la petite vérole. Le pur et radieux visage de son enfance reparaissait dans sa beauté première [. . .] La prunelle de ses yeux, douée d'une grande contractilité, semblait alors s'épanouir, et repoussait le bleu de l'iris, qui ne formait plus qu'un léger cercle. Ainsi cette métamorphose de l'œil, devenu aussi vif que celui de l'aigle, complétait le changement étrange du visage. Etait-ce l'orage des passions contenues, était-ce une force venue des profondeurs de l'âme qui agrandissait la prunelle en plein jour, comme elle s'agrandit ordinairement chez tout le monde dans les ténèbres, en brunissant ainsi l'azur de ces yeux célestes? [. . .] Son menton et le bas de son visage étaient un peu gras, dans l'acception que les peintres donnent à ce mot, et cette forme épaisse *est*, suivant les lois impitoyables de la physiognomonie, *l'indice* d'une violence quasi morbide dans la passion.[4]

This extract illustrates the patently ridiculous excesses of Balzacian portraiture (the obliteration of pock-marks by violent emotion), underscores the changeability and mobility of physical characteristics ('cette métamorphose de l'œil', 'le changement étrange du visage'),[5] offers a modulation of the authorial viewpoint in the evaluation attributed to the genus *peintres* and contains a prognosis of the development of violent passion. Of greater interest to us here, though, is the fact that the passage ends with a sentence containing a psycho-physiological bridge which may be taken as a paradigm for purposes of this study: the lower part of Véronique's face (and in particular the chin) '*est* [. . .] *l'indice* d'une violence quasi morbide dans la passion'. The italicized expression, which links physiological and psychological features, connotes perceptibility and uniformity: the external characteristic is, by implication, a clear, universally perceptible and accurate index of the inner being. The narrator may be adopting the posture of the learned physiognomist, but his language implies that the phenomenon he observes and interprets could be observed and interpreted by others armed with a knowledge of 'les lois impitoyables de la physiognomonie'.

The outward indices of the inner being are not, however, always as immediately perceptible and clear as the one examined above — or so Balzac would have us believe. We are told of Corentin in *Les Chouans*, for example, that he has 'un de ces visages impénétrables accoutumés par les vicissitudes de la Révolution à *cacher* toutes les émotions, même les moindres'.[6] The psycho-physiological bridge *cacher* may be taken as our second paradigm under the heading *impenetrability*: the physiognomist is here forced to accept (for the moment at least) that no clear indication of the character's psychological make-up is apparent in his facial features.

Of a related nature (related because of a similar lack of connexion between the inner and the outer man) are those examples where Balzac indicates a discrepancy between physical appearance and moral nature. This particular phenomenon is well illustrated in the portrayal of the Bridau brothers in *La Rabouilleuse*: Philippe, we are told, 'avait un air tapageur qui *se prenait* facilement *pour* de la vivacité, pour du courage',[7] whilst it is said of Joseph that 'sa figure si tourmentée, et dont l'originalité *peut passer pour* de la laideur aux yeux de ceux qui ne connaissent pas la valeur morale d'une physiognomie, fut pendant sa jeunesse assez rechignée'.[8] Appearances here are obviously deceptive and even the boys' mother, Agathe, is mistaken when she 'concluait de sa ressemblance purement physique avec Philippe à une concordance morale, et croyait fermement retrouver un jour en lui sa délicatesse de sentiments agrandie par la force de l'homme'.[9] We may now therefore take as our third paradigm the verbal locution *se prendre* (facilement) *pour* (grouping it with the phrase *pouvoir passer pour*).

In the case of the last two paradigms examined (*cacher* and *se prendre pour*) Balzac asserts his intuitive powers of observation[10] and introduces evaluative comments which denote impenetrability and discrepancy: he instinctively places Corentin in a particular category and immediately sees beyond the erroneous impressions which other characters or, indeed, the reader, may form of Philippe and Joseph Bridau.

A fourth paradigm found in portraits is the verb *trahir*: it is related to *cacher* and *se prendre pour* in so far as it again denotes discrepancy.[11] But it is also somewhat ambiguous for it leaves doubt as to whether it is the character (in spite of himself) or the narrator who reveals to the reader the trait(s) or attribute(s) in question. For example, Balzac's *Médecin de campagne*, Benassis, was a man of questionable morality before he became a philanthropist moved by a messianic zeal and we are told that his 'physionomie [. . .] *trahissait* une secrète existence *en désaccord avec* ses apparentes vulgarités'.[12] The verb *trahir* conveys a development of character which highlights a discrepancy between the previous and the present self. But such fundamental changes of direction, such pronounced changes of purpose and destiny are rare in *La Comédie humaine* and belong in the main to such overtly didactic works as *Le Médecin de campagne* and *Le Curé de village*. We shall see shortly that other discrepancies revealed under the paradigm *trahir* are not as pronounced as the one examined here but the verb usually brings into relief the disparity between the false self which the inner man attempts to project and the realities of personality displayed by the outer man.

The dialectic on which Balzac's style of portraiture is founded is, then, the result of a clear polarisation: perceptibility and uniformity on the one hand, varying degrees of impenetrability and discrepancy on the other hand. Psycho-physiological bridges seem to hold the key to this dialectic for they convey the very uniformity or discrepancy which the artist perceives when he brings together the physiological and the psychological characteristics of his creations.

Basing my analysis on the categorisation suggested above, I shall now examine the psycho-physiological bridges which are to be found in five of Balzac's novels: *Les Chouans* (first published in 1829), *Le Médecin de campagne* (1833), *Eugénie Grandet* (1833), *Le Curé de village* (1839-41) and *La Rabouilleuse* (1841-42).[13]

Psycho-physiological Bridges[14]

1) *Perceptibility and Uniformity*   Paradigm: *être l'indice de*[15]
This category is by far the largest of those examined. Indeed the examples are so numerous that instead of quoting the relevant extracts in full, I have simply juxtaposed, in the order in which they occur in the text, the three important elements in question: (a) the external feature(s), (b) the psycho-physiological bridge (a single verb or a locution) and (c) the trait(s) of character, individual attribute or state of mind of the person described. For ease of reference, the examples have been numbered from 1) to 132).

Les Chouans

Une centaine de paysans: 1) (a) Leurs regards (b) *annoncer* (c) l'intelligence humaine (p. 906).

Véritables personnages: 2) (a) Quelques têtes soigneusement poudrées, des queues assez bien tressées (b) *annoncer* (c) cette espèce de recherche que nous inspire un commencement de fortune ou d'éducation (p. 907).

Les autres individus de la troupe: 3) (b) *montrer* (a) sur leurs figures et dans leurs attitudes (c) cette expression uniforme que donne le malheur (p. 908). (c) is here a combination of (a) (cette expression uniforme) and (c) proper (le malheur).

Bourgeois et paysans: 4) (a) tous (b) *garder l'empreinte* (c) mélancolie profonde (p. 908). (a) is not here a precise external feature but refers to the group.

Marche-à-terre: 5) (a) contours de la face (b) *offrir une vague analogie avec* (c) le granit (p. 914).

6) (a) contenance (b) *empreindre (c)* énergie farouche (pp. 915-6).

7) (c) stupide ignorance (b) *graver* (a) traits (p. 916). This is a relatively rare example for the movement is from the internal characteristic (stupide ignorance) to its external manifestation (traits).

Le Gars: 8) (a) contenance (b) *accuser* (c) élégance, force (p. 936).

L'abbé Gudin: 9) (a) teint fleuri (b) *devoir appartenir* (c) ordre ecclésiastique (p. 947).

Francine (seen by Merle): 10) (a) regard de ses yeux bleus (b) *annoncer* (n'annonçait pas [. . .] mais) (c) fermeté mêlée de tendresse (p. 967).

11) (a) attitude (b) *ne pas être dénuée de* (c) dignité (p. 967).[16]

Le Gars (seen by Marie): 12) (a) quelques traits (de la figure) (b) *révéler* (c) âme capable de grandes choses (p. 975).

13) (a) teint bruni, cheveux blonds et bouclés, yeux bleus, nez fin, mouvements pleins d'aisance (b) *déceler* (c) sentiments élevés, l'habitude du commandement (p. 975).

Corentin: 14) (a) œil vert (b) *annoncer* (c) malice, fausseté (p. 976).

Mme du Gua (seen by Corentin): 15) (a) cheveux noirs (b) *faire ressortir* (c) jeunesse d'une tête spirituelle (p. 978).

Marie de Verneuil: 16) (a) réserve (b) *annoncer* (n'annonçait ni [. . .] ni [. . .] mais) (c) indifférence (p. 981). *réserve* could become (c) in another context.

Galope-chopine (seen by Marie): 17) (b) *laisser éclater* (a) figure (c) vices de la civilisation (p. 1122).

Le Médecin de campagne

Genestas: 18) (a) calme de la figure (b) *être un signe certain* (c) les hommes jadis enrégimentés sous les aigles [. . .] du grand Empereur (p. 387).

19) (a) regard, expression (b) *attester* (c) les orages de l'âme (p. 389).

20) (a) front calme (b) *accuser* (c) le pouvoir d'imposer silence aux passions (p 389). In examples 18) and 20) the word *calme*, used adjectivally and nominally, is associated with two different — though not incompatible — aspects of the life and temperament of Genestas.

Benassis: 21) (a) yeux (b) *exprimer* (c) passions amorties (p. 401).

22) (a) cheveux [. . .] gris, rides, sourcils [. . .] blanchis, nez bulbeux et veiné, teint jaune (b) *annoncer* (c) l'âge de cinquante ans et les rudes travaux de sa profession (p. 401).

Jacquotte: 23) (a) geste (b) *annoncer* (c) quelque longue remontrance adressée [. . .] au valet (p. 411).

Taboureau: 24) (a) pommettes (b) *dénoter* (c) vie voyageuse, ruse des maquignons (p. 437).

Gondrin: 25) (a) figure (b) *conserver* (c) vestiges de martialité (p. 458).

26) (a) tout en lui (b) *avoir un caractère* (c) rudesse (p. 458)

27) (a) front (b) *sembler être* (c) quartier de pierre (p. 458).

28) (a) bras, poitrine (b) *annoncer* (c) force extraordinaire (p. 458).

M. et Mme Moreau: 29) (c) histoire de leur vie (b) *graver* (a) leurs physionomies (p. 461). Movement: internal to external characteristic.

30) (a) leurs visages (b) *ne pas manquer de* (c) gaie franchise (p. 461).

Butifer: 31) (a) barbe, moustaches, favoris roux (b) *rehausser* (c) mâle et terrible expression de sa figure (arguably an indirect indication of character) (p. 494).

32) (a) front (b) *respirer* (c) sauvage intelligence (p. 494).

M. Janvier: 33) (a) petite taille, maigreur, attitude (b) *annoncer* (c) faiblesse physique (arguably an indirect indication of character) (p. 499).

34) (a) physionomie (b) *attester* (c) paix intérieure, force qu'engendre la chasteté de l'âme (p. 499).

35) (a) gestes (b) *être ceux de* (c) homme modeste (p. 499).

Eugénie Grandet

Grandet: 36) (a) yeux (b) *avoir l'expression de* (c) basilic (p. 1036).

37) (a) loupe veinée (b) *que le vulgaire disait* (c) pleine de malice (p. 1036).

38) (a) figure (b) *annoncer* (c) finesse dangereuse, probité sans chaleur, égoïsme (p. 1036).

39) (a) attitude, manières, démarche (b) *attester* (c) croyance en soi (p. 1036).

Mme Grandet: 40) (a) elle (b) *offrir* (c) vague ressemblance avec ces fruits cotonneux qui n'ont plus ni saveur ni suc (p. 1046).

Grandet: 41) (c) l'Argent dans toute sa puissance (b) *exprimer* (a) physionomie (p. 1052). Movement: internal to external characteristic.

Eugénie Grandet: 42) (a) symétrie dans sa coiffure (b) *rehausser* (c) timide candeur (de son visage) (p. 1073). (c) is here a combination of (a) and (c) proper.

43) (a) lèvres (b) *être pleines de* (c) amour, bonté (p. 1075).

44) (b) *voir* (le peintre eût vu) (a) sous un front calme (c) monde d'amour (p. 1076).

45) (b) *voir* (le peintre eût vu) (a) dans la coupe des yeux, dans l'habitude des paupières (c) le je ne sais quoi divin (p. 1076).

46) (a) physionomie (b) *communiquer* (c) le charme de la conscience (p. 1076).

Eugénie Grandet (seen by Charles): 47) (a) yeux (b) *scintiller* (c) jeunes pensées d'amour (confirmation of the viewpoint expressed by *le peintre*) (p. 1088).

Eugénie Grandet: 48) (a) régularité de mouvement (Eugénie tirait ses points) (b) *dévoiler* (eût dévoilé à un observateur) (c) les fécondes pensées de sa méditation (p. 1098).

Charles and Eugénie Grandet: 49) (a) leurs yeux (b) *exprimer* (c) un même sentiment (p. 1107).

Charles Grandet: 50) (a) gestes, contenance, regards, son de la voix (b) *avoir* (c) tristesse pleine de grâce (p. 1108).

Grandet: 51) (a) loupe (b) *indiquer* (c) orage intérieur (p. 1116)

Charles Grandet: 52) (a) larmes (b) *accuser* (c) noblesse de cœur (p. 1124).

53) (a) voix, regard, figure (b) *paraître en harmonie avec* (c) les sentiments (pp. 1125-6).

Le Curé de village

Sauviat: 54) (a) front (b) *ne pas manquer de* (c) noblesse (p. 645).

Véronique Graslin, née Sauviat: 55) (a) chevelure (b) *faire ressortir* (c) la pureté de ses traits (p. 648).

M. Graslin: 56) (a) mains maigres (b) *montrer* (c) doigts crochus des gens habitués à compter des écus (p. 661). (c) is here a combination of (a) and (c) proper.

57) (c) l'habitude des décisions rapides (b) *se voir dans* (a) sourcils [. . .] rehaussés vers chaque lobe du front (p. 661). Movement: internal to external characteristic.

58) (a) bouche (b) *annoncer* (c) bonté cachée, âme excellente (p. 661).

L'abbé Dutheil: 59) (a) extérieur (b) *annoncer* (c) une de ces âmes profondes (p. 674).

60) (a) ses lignes (b) *rappeler* (c) celles que le génie des peintres espagnols ont le plus affectionnées pour représenter les grandes méditations monastiques (the basic connexion is between *lignes* and *méditation*) (p. 675).

61) (a) longs plis du visage (b) *avoir* (c) cette grâce que le Moyen Age a mise en relief dans les statues mystiques (Connexion: *visage — grâce mystique*) (p. 675).

Bonnet: 62) (a) dans cette figure (b) *éclater* (c) yeux d'un bleu lumineux de foi (Connexion: *figure/yeux — foi*) (p. 720).

63) (a) yeux (b) *brûler* (c) espérance vive (p. 720).

64) (a) chevelure (b) *annoncer* (c) tempérament pauvre, régime sobre (p. 720).

Jean-François Tascheron: 65) (a) cheveux (b) *annoncer* (c) grande énergie (p. 733).

66) (a) yeux [. . .] trop rapprochés (b) *donner une ressemblance* (c) oiseaux de proie (Connexion: *yeux — nature 'rapace'*) (p. 733).

67) (a) figure (b) *présenter* (c) les caractères de la probité, d'une douce naïveté de mœurs (p. 733).

68) (a) rouge des lèvres (b) *annoncer* (c) férocité contenue (p. 733).

69) (a) maintien (b) *n'accuser aucune* (c) mauvaises habitudes des ouvriers (A difficult example to classify but placed here because the aspect of character in question is 'clearly visible') (p. 733).

Véronique Graslin: 70) (a) menton (b) *révéler* (c) implacable sévérité religieuse (p. 745).

71) (a) le bleu foncé de l'iris (b) *jeter un feu* (c) éclat sauvage (p. 745). cf. no. 62 above. The indicated (*yeux*) become the indicator (*iris*): exactly what blue eyes reveal seems variable.

Farrabesche (seen by Véronique):   72) (a) dents mal rangées (b) *imprimer* (à la bouche) (c) un tour plein d'ironie et de mauvaise audace (p. 765).

73) (a) pommettes (b) *offrir* (c) je ne sais quoi d'animal (p. 765).

74) (a) cet homme (b) *avoir* (c) la taille moyenne, les épaules fortes, le cou rentré, très court, gros, les mains larges et velues des gens violents et capables d'abuser de ces avantages d'une nature bestiale (p. 765). (c) is here a combination of (a) and (c) proper.

Farrabesche's son: 75) (a) regard (b) *deviner* (madame Graslin devina) (c) une de ces affections sans bornes (p. 773).

Farrabesche's son: 75) (a) regard (b) *deviner* (madame Graslin devina) (c) une de ces affections sans bornes (p. 773).

Grégoire Gérard: 76) (a) contenance, attitude, le développement du buste, la maigreur des jambes (b) *annoncer* (c) affaissement corporel produit par les habitudes de la méditation (p. 809).

77) (c) la puissance de cœur et l'ardeur d'intelligence (b) *éclater* (a) sur son front (p. 809). Movement: internal to external characteristic.

78) (a) front (b) *y mettre les signes évidents* (subject: la nature) (c) grandeur, constance, bonté (p. 809).

79) (a) bouche (b) *indiquer* (c) discrétion absolue, le sens de l'économie (p. 809).

Véronique Graslin: 80) (a) front, démarche, les regards (b) *avoir une éloquence qui dit* (c) qu'elle était morte à l'amour (p. 811).

Catherine Curieux
(seen by Véronique):   81) (a) cette fille (b) *avoir* (c) traits d'une excessive douceur (p. 827).

82) (c) douceur (b) *ne pas démentir* (que ne démentait pas) (a) la belle nuance grise de ses yeux (p. 827). Movement: internal to external characteristic.

83) (a) visage, front (b) *offrir* (c) noblesse [. . .] auguste et simple (p. 827).

84) (a) attitude (b) *annoncer* (c) aisance dans les mouvements qui caractérise les filles de campagne (arguably an indirect indication of character) (p. 827).

Véronique Graslin: 85) (a) front (b) *révéler* (c) pensée fixe au milieu de troubles intérieurs (p. 850).

86) (a) figure (b) *offrir* (c) lignes maigres sans sécheresse (indirect indication of inner turmoil) (p. 850).

87) (a) figure (b) *porter les traces* (c) souffrances physiques produites par les douleurs morales (p. 850).

88) (a) yeux (b) *annoncer* (c) empire despotique exercé par une volonté chrétienne (p. 850).

89) (a) visage (b) *expliquer* (c) la vie et les sentiments (p. 863).

La Rabouilleuse

Agathe Bridau: placidité (p. 277).

90) (a) figure (b) *empreindre* (c)

Bridau (painted portrait): (c) fermeté (p. 284).

91) (b) *reconnaître* (a) sur le front

92) (c) sagacité (a) lèvres (b) *témoigner* (p. 284). Movement: internal to external characteristic.

93) (a) physionomie (b) *exprimer* (c) incorruptibilité (pp. 284-5).

la Descoings:

94) (a) visage (b) *offrir* (c) traces d'une dissimulation profonde et d'une arrière-pensée (p. 326).

95) (b) *avoir* [. . .] *quelques indices* (a) dans le mouvement des lèvres (c) gourmandise (p. 326).

Agathe Bridau:

96) (c) souffrances intérieures (a) changement (b) *révéler* (p. 332). The physical change has already been mentioned so the movement is really from the external to the internal characteristic.

Giroudeau:

97) (b) *avoir* (a) physionomie (c) de vieux loup de mer peu rassurante (p. 350).

98) (a) yeux, moustache, chevelure (b) *offrir* (c) je ne sais quoi d'éraillé, de libidineux (p. 350).

99) (a) teint (b) *révéler* (c) vie joyeuse (p. 351).

Philippe Bridau:

100) (a) tête, teint, figure (b) *dire* (c) qu'il sortait du terrible hôpital du Midi (p. 353).

Maxence Gilbet:

101) (a) riche coloris qui nuance les figures berrichonnes (b) *ajouter* (c) à son air de bonne humeur (p. 381).

102) (c) l'intelligence (b) *animer* (a) mouvements (p. 381). Movement: internal to external characteristic.

103) (c) noblesse (b) *éclater* (a) en lui (p. 381). Movement: from the internal characteristic.

Jean-Jacques Rouget:

104) (a) physionomie (b) *respirer* (c) bonheur (p. 399).

Philippe Bridau:

105) (a) visage (b) *illuminer* (fut illuminé par) (c) éclair de joie (pp. 468-9).

Fario:

106) (a) yeux (b) *jaillir* (c) deux douches de feu, de haine et de vengeance (p. 508).

Philippe Bridau:	107) (a) pose (b) *annoncer* (c) duelliste
du premier ordre (p. 508).	
Agathe Bridau:	108) (a) yeux (b) *resplendir* (c)
tendresse (p. 529).	
	109) (a) regards, mouvements d'âme,
gestes (b) *éclater* (c) amour (p. 530).	

In the above examples Balzac predictably concentrates in the main on aspects of the face (particularly the eyes); gestures and postures are also held to be particularly revealing. The usual movement is from the external (a) to the internal (c) characteristic; there are only ten examples out of one hundred and nine where the process is reversed: the order cab occurs twice (although example 96 is perhaps misleading) and cba occurs eight times. The verb is placed between the two other elements in all but eight examples (cab occurs twice as already stated and bac — where syntax rather than stylistic choice usually determines the ante-positioning of the verb — occurs six times). Once the basic pattern of abc has been broken, Balzac sometimes repeats the same variation or introduces another one immediately afterwards: 44, 45 (bac twice); 91, 92 (bac followed by cab); 102, 103 (cba twice). Two possible orders which do not occur at all are acb and bca.

Balzac's favourite psycho-physiological bridge by far is the verb *annoncer* (other recurring verbs include *offrir*, *accuser*, *exprimer*, *empreindre*, *attester* and the less colourful *voir* and *avoir*). The usual tense is the imperfect and in all but eight examples (10, 11, 16, 29, 30, 54, 69, 82) the verbs are used positively. Even where negatives occur they are used for stylistic reasons, understatement being a recurring feature ('Son front ne manquait pas de noblesse' (30)). The only 'absolute' negative is to be found in example 69. When one adds the fact that the subjunctive occurs only three times (the pluperfect subjunctive is used as a literary alternative to the past conditional once in examples 44 and 45 and also in examples 29 and 48) it becomes clear that Balzac's psycho-physiological connexions are placed before the reader in a forceful and unequivocal manner in ten out of every eleven examples. This would seem to underscore the writer's belief in his own 'system'.

The most surprising feature of the extracts examined so far is, perhaps, Balzac's predilection for the juxtaposition of two or even three internal or external characteristics — even when he is establishing traits of character on the basis of a single physical feature — and also the sheer variety of characteristics which he claims to be apparent in the visible features of the human frame.

2) *Impenetrability and Discrepancy*
Examples found under this heading are less numerous; the relevant extracts are therefore quoted in full.

a) *Impenetrability*   *Paradigm: cacher*

Les Chouans

Une centaine de paysans: 110) Ils semblaient courbés sous le joug d'une même pensée, terrible sans doute, mais soigneusement *cachée*, car leurs figures *étaient impénétrables* (p. 908). The order here is (c) (b^1) (a) (b^2).

Corentin: 111) [. . .] un de ces visages *impéné-trables*, accoutumés [. . .] à *cacher* toutes les émotions, même les moindres (p. 966). Order: (a) (b) (c).

Marie de Verneuil: 112) Elle *ne laissa paraître aucune* préméditation de triomphe (p. 981). Order: (a) (b) (c).

Eugénie Grandet

Eugénie Grandet: 113) Quand elle regarda son cousin, elle était bien rouge encore, mais au moins ses regards purent *mentir* et *ne pas peindre* la joie excessive qui lui inondait le cœur (p. 1107). Order: (a) (b^1) (b^2) (c).

114) Eugénie [. . .] *ne laissa percer* sur son visage calme *aucune* des cruelles émotions qui l'agitaient. Elle sut *prendre* une figure riante pour répondre à ceux qui voulurent lui témoigner de l'intérêt par des regards ou des paroles mélancoliques. Elle sut enfin *couvrir* son malheur sous les *voiles* de la politesse (p. 1192). Order: (a) (b) (a) (c) in the opening sentence.

Le Curé de village

Clousier: 115) Sous cette forme quasi grossière, Clousier *cachait* un esprit clairvoyant, livré à de hautes méditations politiques, mais tombé dans une entière insouciance due à sa parfaite connaissance des hommes et de leurs intérêts (p. 812). Order: (a) (b) (c).

La Rabouilleuse

Fario: 116) Mais son teint couleur de pain d'épice et sa douceur *déguisaient* aux ignorants et *annonçaient* à l'observateur le caractère à demi mauritain d'un paysan de Grenade

que rien n'avait encore fait sortir de son flegme et de sa paresse (p. 410).
Order: (a) (b¹) (b²) (c).

Discrepancy

b)   *Paradigm*: *se prendre pour*

Le Médecin de campagne

M. Janvier: 117) Au premier aspect, le visage de
M. Janvier *pouvait paraître* disgracieux, tant les lignes en étaient
sévères et heurtées (arguably an indirect indication of character) (p. 499).
Order: (a) (b) (c).

Le Curé de village

Véronique Graslin: 118) Ce dédain *écrit* sur son front,
sur ses lèvres, et *mal déguisé*, *fut pris pour* l'insolence d'une parvenue
(p. 669). Order: (c¹) (b¹) (a) (b²) (c²).

Bonnet: 119) Ses mains courtes *eussent indiqué*
chez tout autre une pente vers de grossiers plaisirs, et peut-être avait-il,
comme Socrate, vaincu ses mauvais penchants (p. 720). Order: (a) (b) (c).

Clousier: 120) Son teint coloré, son embonpoint
majeur *eussent fait croire*, en dépit de sa sobriété, qu'il cultivait autant
Bacchus que Troplong et Toullier (p. 813). Order: (a) (b) (c).

La Rabouilleuse

la Descoings: 121) Ses yeux, pleins de vie, *semblaient*
animés par une pensée encore jeune et vivace qui *pouvait* d'autant
mieux *passer pour* une pensée de cupidité qu'il y a toujours quelque
chose de cupide chez le joueur (p. 326). Order: (a) (b¹) (c¹) (b²) (c²).

Fario: 122) Des yeux de feu comme percés
avec une vrille et très rapprochés du nez l'*eussent fait passer* à Naples
pour un jeteur de sorts. Ce petit homme *paraissait* doux parce qu'il
était grave, calme, lent dans ses mouvements (p. 410). Order: (a) (b) (c).

c)   *Paradigm*: *trahir*

Les Chouans

Une centaine de paysans: 123) seulement la lenteur de leur
marche pouvait *trahir* de secrets calculs (p. 908). Order: (a) (b) (c).

Corentin: 124) Malgré cette toilette d'empirique, sa tournure *accusait* une certaine élégance de manières à laquelle on reconnaissait un homme bien élevé (p. 966). Order: (a) (b) (c).

Mme du Gua: 125) Les faibles rides du front, *loin d'annoncer* les années, *trahissaient* des passions jeunes (p. 978). Order: (a) (b^1) (b^2) (c).

Galope-chopine: 126) Ce vieux Chouan *ne trahissait certes pas autant* d'idées qu'il y en aurait eu chez un enfant (p. 1122). Order: (a) (b) (c).

Le Médecin de campagne

Genestas: 127) Sa figure brune marquée de petite vérole, mais régulière et *empreinte* d'insouciance apparente, ses manières décidées, la sécurité de son regard, le port de sa tête, tout *aurait trahi* ces habitudes régimentaires qu'il est impossible au soldat de jamais dépouiller (p. 387). Order: (a^1) (b^1) (c^1) (a^2) (b^2) (c^2).

M. Janvier: 128) Ses yeux, où semblait *se refléter* le ciel, *trahissaient* l'inépuisable foyer de charité qui consumait son cœur (p. 499). Order: (a) (b^1) (c^1) (b^2) (c^2).

Le Curé de village

l'abbé Dutheil: 129) Cette grandeur purement physique, d'accord avec la grandeur morale, *donnait* à ce prêtre quelque chose de hautain, de dédaigneux, aussitôt démenti par sa modestie et par sa parole, mais qui ne prévenait pas en sa faveur (p. 675). Order: (a^1) (b^1) (c) (b^2) (a^2)

Véronique Graslin: 130) Les joues étaient creuses et leurs plis *accusaient* de graves pensées (p. 745). Order: (a) (b) (c).

Roubaud: 131) Petit et blond, Roubaud avait une mine assez fade; mais ses yeux gris *trahissaient* la profondeur du physiologiste et la ténacité des gens studieux (pp. 810-81İ). Order: (a) (b) (c).

La Rabouilleuse

Philippe Bridau: 132) Sur un col de velours qui laissait voir son carton, se dressait une tête [. . .] où l'épuisement d'un homme encore vigoureux *se trahit* par un teint cuivré, verdi de place en place [. . .] le front est menaçant par toutes les ruines qu'il *accuse* (p. 472). Order: (a^1) (c^1) (b^1) (a^2) (c^2) (b^2).

The above examples denoting impenetrability and discrepancy are interesting in so far as many of them describe characters who, momentarily or over a long period, feel that they have something to hide (Eugénie Grandet, Véronique Graslin or Corentin for example). Other extracts, however, describe characters who are 'at one' with themselves (M. Janvier, l'abbé Dutheil or Roubaud for instance) and the use of verbs denoting impenetrability or discrepancy in their cases is a trait of style (what could be called the rhetoric of Balzacian portraiture) rather than an accurate index of character.

Another feature of our examples under heading *two* is the recurrence of the basic pattern of abc. A more interesting aspect however is the multiplication of compound sentences containing two 'bridges' and even two examples of (a) or (c). This would have been apparent under heading *one*, had the relevant passages been quoted in full, but to a much lesser degree and this indicates that when he is not simply accentuating a point, Balzac sometimes needs one verb to modify another in order to attenuate the notion of impenetrability and to lessen the idea of a discrepancy. A relatively large number of negatives and past conditionals (or alternatively of pluperfect subjunctives) also lessens the force of some psycho-physiological connexions.

Taking all of our examples into consideration, we may conclude that Balzac's psycho-physiological bridges are relatively few in number: a small quantity of recurring verbs is supplemented by several infrequently used if varied verbal locutions. Verbs from headings *one* and *two* sometimes occur in the same portrait but only rarely do they occur together in the same sentence. By far the most widely found category is the one denoting perceptibility and uniformity (paradigm: *être l'indice de*) and the most frequently used verb is *annoncer*. On the other hand, the ultimately misleading nature of those verbs and verbal locutions which establish or imply impenetrability and discrepancy is revealed in a number of ways. Firstly in the hesitation which we experienced before concluding that *trahir* denotes discrepancy (perhaps *révéler*, *déceler* and *dévoiler*, which we placed under heading *one* should have come under the paradigm *trahir*). Secondly, through the fact that *accuser* connotes both uniformity and discrepancy. Thirdly through the fundamental meaning of the paradigm *se prendre pour* which shows clearly that the author sees beyond any seeming discrepancy. Finally through the very destruction of the illusion of impenetrability: in the final analysis no character is impenetrable, no fictional creation is anything less than the unified sum of his constituent parts. Characters may deceive characters, individuals may mask their true nature from — or present a false self to — other individuals but nothing escapes the all-seeing eye and all-knowing intellect of the narrator.

It is when effecting an overall view of character, when transcending individual psycho-physiological connexions and presenting man in his physical, spiritual and social totality that Balzac shows that the fundamental polarity examined is a false polarity, that the discrepancy between appearance and reality is a false discrepancy. The rhetoric of characterisation gives way to a vision of unity: an imaginative, often intuitive synthesis of all available data reveals the entire man. The illusion of impenetrability and discrepancy fades as the omniscient *docteur ès sciences sociales* re-establishes the total perceptibility and uniformity which lie at the very root of his vision. The world of matter and of spirit are clearly perceived and thoroughly united in what is ultimately a homogeneous picture of mankind.

BIRMINGHAM   IAN PICKUP

---

[1] Tahsin Yücel has devoted a monograph to Balzac's technique of portraiture: *Figures et messages dans la 'Comédie humaine'*, Vienne, Mame, 1972 (Collection: Univers sémiotiques). See also the first chapter of Bernard Vannier's *L'Inscription du corps. Pour une sémiotique du portrait balzacien*, Paris, Klincksieck, 1972. Other works which devote a significant amount of space to Balzac's portraiture include P. Abraham, *Recherches sur la création intellectuelle. Créatures chez Balzac*, Paris, Gallimard, 1931 (see esp. ch. 4 and ch. 5); C. Prendergast, *Balzac, Fiction and Melodrama*, London, Arnold, 1978 (see 6.,*Surface and Depth*); J. Reboul, 'Balzac et la "Vestignomonie"', *Revue d'histoire littéraire de la France*, Paris, Armand Colin, janv.-mars, 1950, pp. 210-233. For a detailed account of the influence of 'les sciences exactes' on Balzac (including references to Lavater, Gall, Saint-Hilaire and so on) see P. Laubriet, *L'Intelligence de l'art chez Balzac*, Paris, Didier, 1961 (2e partie, ch. 1).

[2] Yücel, op. cit., p. 34.

[3] Yücel acknowledges the recurrence of certain verbs (op. cit., p. 17): 'il (le corps de l'homme) "annonce", il "indique", il "dénote", il "trahit", il "dit", il "exprime", il "affirme", il "promet", il raconte, en un mot, l'être profond, l'histoire intime, la destinée de l'homme à qui il appartient.' Yücel, however, does not go on to examine the frequency and significance of such verbs.

[4] Balzac, *Le Curé de village*, vol. IX of *La Comédie humaine*, Bibliothèque de la Pléiade, Gallimard, 1978, pp. 651-2. The italics in this quotation (as in all other quotations from Balzac's works) are mine. All page numbers for the extracts of Balzac's works which I quote refer to the new Pléiade edition. The relevant volume numbers for works cited are as follows: *Les Chouans*, vol. VIII, 1977; *Le Médecin de campagne*, vol. IX, 1978; *Eugénie Grandet*, vol. III, 1976; *La Rabouilleuse*, vol. IV, 1976.

[5] The changeability of human features is given similar prominence in a portrait of Madame Grandet when she is ill and nearing death (see ed. cit., p. 1162).

[6] *Les Chouans*, p. 966.

[7] *La Rabouilleuse*, pp. 287-8.

[8] ibid., p. 289.

[9] ibid, p. 288.

[10] Balzac believed strongly in his own powers of intuition and 'second sight' (See the opening paragraph of *Facino Cane* (on the intuitive dimension of observation) and the preface to *La Peau de chagrin* (on *seconde vue*)).

[11] There is a basic paradox implicit in Balzac's use of *trahir*: although the verb establishes a link between the inner and the outer man (and in this sense it denotes perceptibility and uniformity), it clearly implies a rift or discrepancy: those aspects of personality which the character would like us to see are one thing, what we in fact do see is something else. After hesitating slightly, we are therefore obliged to place the paradigm *trahir* under the general heading *Impenetrability and Discrepancy* whilst acknowledging at the same time that the paradoxical nature of the verb highlights the crudeness yet usefulness of our categorisation.

[12] *Le Médecin de campagne*, p. 401.

[13] The extracts quoted are representative rather than completely exhaustive for I have included only those examples which suggest fairly clearly a trait of character, state of mind or attribute and I have left out of account those 'bridges' which establish a link between character and articles of clothing (see note 14). The novels have been chosen so as to give a broad chronological spread and to embrace a variety of thematic preoccupations; *Le Médecin de campagne* and *Le Curé de village* were chosen because they contain an unusually large number of portraits.

[14] Another related but relatively rare aspect of characterisation which is beyond the scope of this study may be termed psycho-sartorial bridges. In the strictest sense such a term would embrace only those articles of *male* clothing which are held to reveal character. If a neologism may be allowed, *psycho-vestimentary* bridges would convey more fully what is intended; the phenomenon is well illustrated in the following example: *Grégoire Gérard:* La manière dont ses vêtements étaient mis et boutonnés, sa cravate négligée, sa chemise sans fraîcheur *offraient les marques de* ce défaut de soin sur eux-mêmes que l'on reproche aux hommes de science, tous plus ou moins distraits (*Le Curé de village*, p. 809).

For a detailed analysis of the connexion between character and dress, see J. Reboul, op. cit. Reboul, in common with other critics, does not examine the 'bridges'.

[15] The novels examined also contain a number of examples where psycho-physiological connexions are made without the use of verbal bridges; the following is a typical example: *Mme Vigneau:* Quoique son front gardât quelques rides, vestiges de son ancienne misère, elle avait une physionomie heureuse et avenante (*Le Médecin de campagne*, p. 473).

An alternative presentation of the same information could have been, 'ses rides *trahissaient* son ancienne misère'.

[16] This portrait illustrates how Balzac uses one fictional character to describe another fictional character, thereby modulating the purely 'authorial' viewpoint: 'Merle sut *deviner* en elle une de ces fleurs champêtres qui, transportée dans les serres parisiennes [. . .] n'avait rien perdu de ses couleurs pures ni de sa rustique franchise' (*Les Chouans*, p. 967).

The same technique is used in the second portrait of Le Gars for we are told that, 'd'un seul regard, mademoiselle de Verneuil sut distinguer sous ce costume sombre des formes élégantes et *ce je ne sais quoi* (Balzac's italics) qui annoncent une noblesse native' (ibid., p. 975).

MARGARET LYONS

JUDITH GAUTIER AND THE
SŒURS DE NOTRE-DAME DE MISÉRICORDE:
A COMMENT ON *SPIRITE*

Finding the lady has always been one of the more popular pastimes amongst writers on Théophile Gautier. If this article sets out yet again along the same path, it is simply because there is one woman, talented, intelligent and beautiful whose very proximity to the poet has caused her to be neglected, or perhaps the reason for her neglect is that to write of a man's transient liaison with this or that mistress or of his admiration for this or that contemporary beauty is easy but his relationship with his own daughter is of a different order. It is on a more subtle plane which the critic must approach with caution. In discussing the genesis of *Spirite* most writers have managed to avoid almost all mention of the crisis between Gautier and his daughter, Judith, which arose during its composition. Any attempt to redress the balance is in danger of exaggerating her importance so it is as well to state from the outset that this article does not intend to challenge the accepted view of Carlotta Grisi as Gautier's prime source of inspiration for the *conte*.[1] Its aim is solely to remind the reader of the background against which *Spirite* was composed and in the light of that background to examine the contribution which Judith herself claims to have made to its composition.

Towards the end of July, 1865, Gautier left Paris for Carlotta's home, the Villa Grisi at Saint-Jean near Geneva. With Carlotta and members of her family circle he visited the *fête des vignerons* at Vevey and wrote an account of it for the *Moniteur*.[2] He then settled down to the writing of *Spirite*. The project was already mapped out in his mind: the writing may already have begun. Almost immediately the calm of Saint-Jean and Gautier's own tranquillity of mind were broken by letters from Paris. Dalloz, editor of the *Moniteur*, wrote asking for a poem about the charitable works of the Empress Eugénie[3] — a delicate task for Gautier politically — and more alarmingly, Théophile *fils* wrote with disturbing news about Judith's behaviour and the company which she was keeping. Already before leaving Paris, Gautier had rejected a proposal of marriage for Judith from the Persian, Mohsin-Khan. She, herself, had not wished to accept but Mohsin's persistence in his suit had ended by irritating Gautier who, even in Saint-Jean, could not look back on the affair with proper calm.[4] Now Théophile *fils* had revived his anxieties and he quickly wrote to his sisters asking them to go to Neuilly to check up on things.[5] As a result a rather indignant Judith received letters of a high moral tone from her father, warning of the dangers of mixed bathing and urging the need to avoid causing gossip![6] Work on *Spirite* was virtually at a standstill.

The quiet of Saint-Jean and the proximity of Carlotta were certainly not working their accustomed, soothing miracle at this juncture. It was only in September when Judith with her mother and sister had safely arrived at Saint-Jean that *Spirite* began to make progress. As Judith explains:

Mon père était toujours inquiet et tourmenté, quand sa nichée n'etait pas avec lui: il imaginait toutes sortes d'événements, d'accidents, de querelles tragiques, de maladies subites, même quand il nous quittait pour de simples courses: il ne rentrait jamais sans angoisse à Neuilly et était tout heureux, disait-il, de ne pas trouver 'la mère égorgée, les filles violées, le feu à la maison'.

Il travailla plus tranquillement, lorsque nous fûmes tous réunis à Saint-Jean . . .[7]

As usual Judith only tells half the truth. It was not just the effect of writing *Spirite* on his superstitious nature which had disturbed Gautier, as she goes on to suggest, nor was the turbulent arrival of Ernesta particularly calming for him. It was the knowledge that at Saint-Jean the temptations were less and the supervision stricter which allowed him to relax.

At the age of twenty Judith presented her father with a problem. Mohsin-Khan was not the only man attracted by her beauty and intelligence. She had other admirers and Catulle Mendès was already waiting impatiently in the background. Perhaps Gautier would never have willingly consented to her marriage with any man, as has been suggested,[8] but this is a matter only for speculation. One cannot but feel, however, that given this obstinate father and his stubborn daughter, the eventual outcome in 1866 had about it a tragic inevitability. It would have been impossible to frustrate for much longer that independence which her upbringing had always encouraged.

For his part Gautier was a sick man, weary with the continual round of his journalistic activities. At Saint-Jean he found a welcome change from the demands of his life in Paris and, of course, he found the comforting presence of Carlotta. The resemblence between Carlotta and Spirite has been widely commented on, not least by Judith and by Carlotta, herself.[9] This tale of how what might have been is made possible by a return from the dead clearly expresses Gautier's hope that it is not too late for him to revive and transform his relationship with Carlotta. The blond curls and blue eyes of Spirite are Carlotta's. The ethereal Spirite floats along beams of light through swirling vapours just as Giselle floated, seemingly, about the stage. The modesty of Spirite and her 'pudeur offensée' when Malivert's advances are too impetuous remind us of the prudent Carlotta but there is an emphasis on the purity of Spirite who even after death conducts herself with the decorum of a model school girl which makes us wonder if there is not here a different regret and a last attempt to suggest to another young girl a particular mode of conduct. Spirite's eyes express love for Malivert 'mais tel qu'une chaste jeune fille eût pu le laisser voir sur terre dans une liaison permise'. When Malivert is allowed to kiss her hand, she tells him that 'ce que Lavinia peut-être t'eût refusé, Spirite te l'accorde, non comme une volupté, mais comme un signe d'amour pur et d'union éternelle'.[10] This 'chaste roman de pensionnaire'[11] provides a model which any father might wish his daughter to follow.

At Saint-Jean it was Gautier's habit to read aloud to the family the episodes of *Spirite* as they were composed. Judith had always been encouraged to discuss his work with him, just as he kept a proud but watchful eye on hers. Even in the moralising letters of August he had found space to warn her to be more careful in her proof reading.[12] It was inevitable that they should discuss the character of Spirite in the same way that they had discussed Sigognac's behaviour during the composition of *Le Capitaine Fracasse*.[13] When, probably about the beginning of October, Gautier came to the chapter dealing with the time Spirite spent in the convent, it was also natural for them to recall the two years which Judith spent in a convent school as a young girl. In *Le Collier des jours* (1902) Judith recalls the description of the convent and of the ceremony at which Spirite took the veil and claims that she herself in fact provided the detail. There seems no reason to doubt her claim. Clearly, Gautier could recall similar scenes from the Gothic novels which he read so avidly in his youth and from other literary sources. He had even reviewed a theatrical revival of *La Nonne sanglante* as recently as May of the previous year.[14] But three factors lend support to Judith's claim. In the first place Spirite like Sister Sainte-Barbe in Judith's account takes her vows willingly. Admittedly she lacks the vocation of Sister Sainte-Barbe but she enters the convent of her own volition, in contrast to that unfortunate band of Gothic heroines who emulate Diderot's *Religieuse* in their reluctance. The title of Olympe de Gouge's play, *Le Couvent ou les vœux forcés* (1790) aptly sums up the atmosphere in which they live. In the second place Gautier uses virtually the same name for the Order which Spirite enters as that of the Order in whose school Judith was placed. He calls them the *Sœurs de la Miséricorde*. Their full title was *Sœurs de Notre-Dame de Miséricorde*. The most important factor in giving credence to Judith's claim is, however, the link which that particular convent provides between herself and Carlotta.

In 1852 after an early life constrained by a minimum of discipline, first with a wet nurse and then in the home of Gautier's father and two sisters, Judith entered the *pensionnat* of the *Sœurs de Notre-Dame de Miséricorde*. She was seven years old. It is easy to imagine the impact which the sudden transition had on such a young child and how her experiences at the convent remained so vivid in her memory. No-one had prepared her for the move. Disapproving of the venture, the aunts handed her over without explaining anything, for the Gautier family had nothing in common with the Grisis whose nomadic life in the theatre was not to their taste. But Carlotta was Judith's godmother and it was Carlotta who, with the encouragement of her own mother, a redoubtable matron, had decided to take an interest in the life of her niece, and to offer her an education. Carlotta's retirement from ballet to the bourgeois life of Saint-Jean was not far off and she had always questioned Ernesta's home-making talents. If Judith at last left the convent two years later, it was simply because her father finally baulked at a request from Carlotta and Madame Grisi who now wanted to take over all responsibility for Judith's future. Hurt by the suggestion that he was not a fit person to bring up his own daughter, he removed her from the convent and brought her to live at the rue de la Grange-Batelière. When, therefore, Judith writes that it is precisely the same convent to which she was sent at the insistence of Carlotta that Gautier chooses for Spirite to enter, the appropriateness of his choice is apparent. Spirite, the idealised Carlotta, joins the convent which the real Carlotta had picked out for Judith.

From the text of *Spirite* and from *Le Collier des jours* we can build up a picture of the convent of the *Sœurs de Notre-Dame de Miséricorde* and of the ceremony which Spirite and Sœur Sainte-Barbe went through. In addition Judith's account of her two years in the *pensionnat* gives some further details about the community. Where it coincides with her father's account, the originality of her testimony is, of course, open to doubt. She may be merely repeating his earlier version. She was after all writing some thirty-seven years later. Where her version is more interesting and more useful, is where she supplies additional information.

The convent to which Judith was sent was the only house run by the *Sœurs de Notre-Dame de Miséricorde* at the time.[15] The Order was founded in Aix-en-Provence by Father Antoine Yvan in the first half of the seventeenth century. His main aim was to provide a haven for young girls without financial resources who, having no dowry to offer, could neither look for marriage nor expect to be accepted by any other religious order. It was because the Order accepted the need to undertake some form of work to make up for the absence of normal endowments that the Community in Paris was able to survive into the nineteenth century. This Community was established in 1651 in the rue du Vieux Colombier where it remained, although in increasingly impoverished circumstances, until expelled at the Revolution. During the First Empire the Sisters came together again, and as their Rule permitted them to work, they were able to open a *pensionnat* for girls. The need to protect their young charges provided an excuse for their enclosed life and the income from the school kept the Community.

When Judith entered the school, the Order had been living for twenty years in a large house in what was then the rue Neuve-Sainte-Geneviève and is now the rue Tournefort. Judith is mistaken when she describes the convent as being in the rue de la Montagne-Sainte-Geneviève, or at least on the same side of the Place du Panthéon.

Au bout de notre course le Panthéon apparut. Il me sembla colossal, et, pour le voir plus longtemps, je marchais presque à reculons, tandis que la tante me tirait par la main, en contournant la place, afin de gagner la petite rue étroite et grimpante de la Montagne-Sainte-Geneviève.[16]

This description appeared thirty-eight years after the rue Neuve-Sainte-Geneviève had changed its name and she has clearly retained the name Sainte-Geneviève but forgotten the change. She is also confused when she believes that the convent occupied part of the buildings formerly owned by the *Carmel de l'Incarnation* to which Mlle de la Vallière retired. This latter was located further to the west. It is the name of another royal favourite of a different century which is associated with the rue Neuve-Sainte-Geneviève. The Comtesse du Barry was brought up there in a Community of Sister of Sainte-Aure. Traces of their large convent can still be seen on the opposite side of the street and some distance away from the site of the convent of the *Sœurs de Notre-Dame de Miséricorde*.[17]

The convent of the *Sœurs de la Miséricorde* in *Spirite* is described as austere in the extreme. Gautier writes that it 'n'offre pas le moindre recoin obscur pour loger une légende. Rien n'y amuse les yeux; aucun ornement, aucune fantaisie d'art, ni peinture, ni sculpture; ce ne sont que lignes sèches et rigides'.[18] We must remember that Gautier had visited the convent himself but Judith confirms his description in her own way: 'Sauf du côté de la chapelle, dans la partie qui contenait les classes, rien ne paraissait ancien et rien n'avait de caractère'.[19] Both were impressed by the screen dividing the choir of the Sisters from the public part of the church and Judith remembered in addition the heavy grill of blackwood dividing the *parloirs*.

The *Règles et Constitutions pour les religieuses de Notre-Dame de la Miséricorde*[20] confirm these details, as do historians of the Order. An *Iconography* of 1888 lists only a few portraits and engravings in the convent. According to Migne their *clôture* was 'très-exactement gardée'. The *Règles et Constitutions* give precise details for the various grills which all consist of a large mesh metal screen backed by a smaller mesh wooden one. The piano which Judith painfully learned to play was a concession to the Rule allowed for the purpose of giving lessons to pupils; otherwise the only musical instrument permitted was the Chapel organ. Judith's estimate of the size of the school is also accurate. She writes of 'une cinquantaine de pensionnaires'. Darboy in his *Statistique religieuse du Diocèse de Paris* (1856) gives the number as fifty-three.[21] Judith names only nine sisters and novices but writes that there are others, some of whom the children rarely see. Darboy's figures are twenty-four sisters, two novices and four postulants.

If we now turn to the ceremony described by Gautier on the basis of Judith's information, there immediately arises the question of what this ceremony is. Both give to it the name of *prise d'habit* (normally translated into English, in the case of a nun, as taking the veil), thus suggesting a ceremony which takes place when the young girl enters on her Noviciate. After a few weeks of preparation she is questioned in order to make sure that she still wishes to embark on the life of a Religious, and that she is entering the convent of her own free will. This ceremony should not be confused with the ceremony of Profession which takes place at the end of the Noviciate and marks the act by which the nun pronounces the vows which will normally bind her for the rest of her life. However, Gautier writes that during the ceremony Spirite is to 'se vouer pour toujours au Seigneur'[22] and Judith relates that the Novice pronounced 'd'une voix ferme et sonore les paroles qui la liaient à jamais'.[23] It seems that we have here a mixture of the two ceremonies or at least an inaccurate interpretation of the importance and the implications of taking the veil. Judith's misunderstanding is easy to comprehend in view of her extreme youth at the time and of the distress which the ceremony caused her. In the case of Gautier the appearance of the same error confirms the importance of Judith as a source of his *nouvelle*. He had sufficient confidence in the memory of his daughter not to seek confirmation of her account elsewhere. Any work of reference would have shown him the error and in the realm of literature Diderot, for example, had taken care to distinguish between the two ceremonies. The young Suzanne is urged to take the veil in the early pages of *La Religieuse* on the grounds that she will only bind herself to stay in the convent for two years and she accepts this argument but later she categorically refuses to pronounce her vows as she knows this is the major and binding step.[24]

A detail which struck the imagination of Judith, and which Gautier emphasises after her, concerns the moment when the hair of the young postulant is cut. Judith is in love with life: she cannot accept that a young girl 'pleine de vie, de joie et de santé' should shut herself away for ever in this gloomy convent. When she sees that the postulant is even willing to sacrifice her beautiful hair, she is grief-stricken.

. . . ses lourds cheveux noirs roulèrent jusqu'à ses reins et j'aperçus, dans les mains d'une sœur, de grands ciseaux luisants, qui disparurent, en grinçant sous les mèches épaisses. Quand je compris qu'on allait couper ces beaux cheveux, je me mis à crier et à pleurer, et je me jetai sur la sœur pour l'empêcher de continuer . . . Je fus frappée de l'expression extatique de la victime; ses prunelles disparaissaient presque des globes bleuâtres de ses yeux levés, un sourire ravi laissait voir ses dents, entre ses lèvres qui chuchotaient des prières, tandis que, maladroitement, on massacrait sa chevelure . . .[25]

The postulant's ecstasy contrasts with the horror of Judith who cannot understand this sacrifice of beauty accepted with such joy. For her the moment marks the climax of the ceremony and sums up the paradox, which she attempts in vain to resolve, of a young girl who must 'devenir laide, de belle qu'elle était pour plaire à Celui qu'elle disait être son créateur'.[26]

Judith clearly communicated her horror to her father who makes this 'la scène la plus redoutée et la plus lugubre de ce drame religieux'. He compares it to the 'toilette du condamné' and in spite of herself, Spirite feels a shudder of fear.

J'étais atterrée et pénétrée d'une secrète horreur. Le froid du métal, en m'effleurant la nuque, me faisait tressaillir nerveusement comme au contact d'une hache.[27]

Such a *frisson* is a commonplace of Romantic literature but it echoes Gautier's strong dislike for the enclosed life. Ascetic self-denial was a discipline which he found difficult to understand when its rewards were so intangible and the wilful disfigurement of feminine beauty was unacceptable to him. However the importance of the act remains personal to father and daughter for the Church's liturgy sees it as much less important.

Les Cérémonies des Vestures et Professions of the *Sœurs de Notre-Dame de Miséricorde* give no indications as to when the postulant's hair is cut.[28] They attach so little importance to the moment that it is not given any special mention. But the scene brings consternation to Judith and her reaction is taken up and exploited by her father to add depth to the portrayal of his heroine.

Given Gautier's lack of sympathy for the monastic life, it is not surprising that when Spirite enters the convent, the atmosphere of despair surrounding her dying to this world should be expressed in a series of funereal analogies. In Chapter XI of the *nouvelle* death takes possession of the heroine as soon as she passes through the gate of the convent and paradoxically she is restored to life only when her physical death frees her soul and it enters 'l'éternité et l'infini'. The sound of the gate of the convent as it closes behind her is like that of 'le couvercle d'un cercueil'. The silence of the convent is 'aussi profond que celui de la tombe'. When

Spirite's hair was cut, 'une blancheur de mort couvrit [son] visage', 'des sueurs glaciales comme celles de l'agonie baignaient [ses] tempes' and as she fainted she had just time to say unoriginally but appropriately, 'Je me meurs'.[29] In Judith's account, although these images are less numerous, they culminate in a particularly dramatic scene.

... on la reconduisit dans le chœur où elle se prosterna, la face contre terre; on jeta alors sur elle un drap funèbre qui la recouvrit complètement et on chanta l'office des morts, sur celle qui était morte au monde.[30]

This scene perfectly suited the atmosphere which Gautier was trying to evoke but, strangely, he made no use of it. All that is thrown over the head of Spirite is a veil which admittedly is described as 'un linceul symbolique qui ne [la] laissait plus visible qu'à Dieu' and as 'un voile funèbre' but this is still far less dramatic than Judith's pall and funeral office. It is difficult to understand why Gautier should have elected not to use this information if Judith was in a position to provide it when he was writing *Spirite* but it was probably not; in fact, part of her original version and therefore not available to him. It we turn again to the Ceremonial of the *Sœurs de Notre-Dame de Miséricorde*, we find that there exists no scene of this sort. It is possible that the postulant may prostrate herself before the altar without the detail being mentioned in the text but as the pall is not listed with the other articles which the Sister Sacristan has to prepare for the ceremony, and neither it nor the relatively lengthy liturgy involved in the funeral office appears in the text of the ceremony, we may conclude with some degree of certainty that they did not exist. Far from presenting us with a ceremony modelled on obsequies, the text follows the traditional pattern in associating both the taking of the veil and Religious Profession with the parable of the Wise Virgins awaiting the coming of the Bridegroom, and in establishing parallels with the wedding ceremony. It we remember again the long interval between *Spirite* and *Le Collier des jours*, we may conclude that Judith's memory has once more proved uncertain. In writing her autobiography she has added this dramatic touch which harmonises with her interpretation of entry into the monastic life but which she has gleaned elsewhere after her stay in the convent of the *Sœurs de Notre-Dame de Miséricorde* and after the publication of *Spirite*.[31]

A study of the texts, then, confirms the importance of Judith's contribution to this scene in *Spirite* but shows that it was not through the accuracy of her memory that she was most able to help her father, in spite of what she, herself, says. On the contrary she passes on to him her own confusion over the two distinct ceremonies of veil-taking and Religious Profession and the exaggerated importance which she attributes to the moment when the postulant's hair is cut. But the fact that Gautier repeats these inaccuracies demonstrates all the weight which he attaches to the account of his daughter. He could have sought confirmation from other sources. We know from Judith that at other times he was most careful to be accurate in his detail, in *Le Roman de la momie*, for example. However on this occasion he was surely right to prefer the real life experiences of his own daughter to the factually correct but unemotional account of a liturgical dictionary. In the eyes of the young Judith, to take the veil meant already to step irrevocably outside the world of beauty and spontaneity which she loved and the sacrifice of a girl's hair was an inconceivable act of gratuitous disfigurement. Judith did not provide factual information about liturgical practices but displayed the spontaneous reaction of a young girl and this was her direct contribution to *Spirite*.

Judith's deeper contribution to the *nouvelle* remains more difficult to assess. Few critics have even acknowledged the possibility of an impact on Gautier's work of the family crisis of 1865-66, except in terms of an evasion, an escape from the harsh discomfort of home life to the peace of Saint-Jean. But as we have seen, that peace was only complete enough for work on *Spirite* to make real progress when his family was gathered around him.

Maxime Du Camp said of the poems of *Emaux et Camées* that they each 'porte un masque qu'il est facile de soulever'. René Jasinski has echoed Du Camp adding that 'il faudra bien un jour admettre que Gautier fut sensible'.[32] Many examples of this hidden sensitivity have now been revealed. In the case of Judith one of the letters written by Gautier in August, 1865, says it all.

Nous autres, insensibles en apparence, nous sommes sérieux dans les choses sérieuses, et nous les sentons plus vivement que les gens dits expansifs. Tu sais que tu es le dernier espoir de ma pauvre vie, si triste, si fatigante et si tourmentée ... Comprends ta haute valeur; un diamant de ton prix ne doit pas être terni même par un souffle.[33]

In Malivert's love for Spirite there is, of course, a large part of Gautier's love for Carlotta but we would wish to claim also that, in the portrait of this young girl who renounces the world to keep intact her purity, we see the fruit of some of Gautier's last literary discussions with his daughter and his impossible hope of protecting her and keeping her by his side to continue their collaboration.

SHEFFIELD   MARGARET LYONS

[1] Nevertheless there remains the need for a detailed assessment of Carlotta's importance as a source of inspiration for Gautier

[2] *Le Moniteur universel*, 1 August 1865.

[3] 'A l'Impératrice' appeared in *Le Moniteur universel* on 15 August 1865.

[4] J. Gautier, *Le second rang du collier*, s.d. (1903) p. 332 (text hereafter referred to as *Second rang*) & Bibliothèque Spoelberch de Lovenjoul (hereafter Lov.) C.475. fol. 59. My thanks are due to the Bibliothèque and to Monsieur Suffel for his kindness.

[5] Lov. C. 472. fol. 246 - fol. 247.

[6] Lov. C. 472. fol. 244 - fol. 245 & P. Descaves ed., *Les plus belles lettres de Théophile Gautier*, 1962, pp. 105-107.

[7] *Second rang*, p. 323.

[8] M. Dita Camacho, *Judith Gautier, sa vie et son œuvre*, 1939, p. 45.

[9] *Second rang*, pp. 321-322 & Lov. C. 479. fol. 94 - fol. 95.

[10] Th. Gautier, ed. Eigeldinger, *Spirite*, 1970, p. 175. (All quotations from *Spirite* refer to this edition.)

[11] Ibid., p. 180.

[12] P. Descaves, op. cit., p. 106.

[13] *Second rang*, pp. 102-107.

[14] *Le Moniteur universel*, 30 May 1864.

[15] For a detailed history of the Order the best sources are:
   a) J.-P. Migne, *Encyclopédie théologique*, Vol. 21 (R.-P. Hélyot, *Dictionnaire des ordres religieux*, Vol. 2, 1848, Cols. 1020-1033).
   b) Clyseault, *Notice sur le vénérable père Antoine Yvan*, 1888.
Other works on the Order are listed in the *Bibliographie et iconographie de l'ordre des Religieuses de Notre-Dame de Miséricorde* (Petite bibliothèque oratorienne, No. IV), 1888.

[16] J. Gautier, *Le Collier des jours*, s.d. (1902) p. 133 (text hereafter referred to as *Collier*).

[17] F. Bloch & A. Mercklein, *Les Rues de Paris*, 1889-1893, p. 296. The Rue Tournefort is, of course, also the street in which Balzac situated the *maison Vauquer*. In his edition of *Le Père Goriot* (1961) M. P.-G. Castex puts the *Religieuses de la Miséricorde* at no. 25 but Clouseault and other contemporary writers give the no. as 39.

[18] *Spirite*, p. 150.

[19] *Collier*, p. 157.

[20] *Règles et Constitutions pour les religieuses de Notre-Dame de Miséricorde*, 1880.

[21] G. Darboy, *Statistique religieuse du Diocèse de Paris*, 1856, p. 142.

[22] *Spirite*, p. 152.

[23] *Collier*, p. 200.

[24] D. Diderot, *Œuvres complètes*, XI, Hermann, 1975, p. 88.

[25] *Collier*, p. 201.

[26] Ibid., p. 202.

[27] *Spirite*, p. 153.

[28] *Cérémonial de l'office divin pour les Religieuses de Notre-Dame de Miséricorde. Le Martyrologe, Les Cérémonies des Vestures et Professions. Cérémonies des Obsèques*, 1793. My particular thanks are due to the *Bibliothèque de l'Institut Catholique* for allowing me to consult this volume.

[29] *Spirite*, p. 153.

[30] *Collier*, pp. 201-202.

[31] If we were to speculate on this other source, we would suggest Act I of Villiers de l'Isle-Adam's *Axël* as a likely choice. Villiers, in turn, probably gleaned his funereal detail from the Profession ceremony of a Benedictine *monk* during one of his visits to Solesmes. For details see Dom Guéranger, *Cérémonial pour la vêture et la profession des Bénédictins de la Congrégation de France*, Rennes, 1856.

[32] R. Jasinski, *Poésies complètes de Théophile Gautier*, 1970, I, p. LXXXVI.

[33] P. Descaves, op. cit., pp. 105-106.

'UN SACCARD NOUVELLE FORME': THE GENESIS OF THE PROTAGONIST'S ROLE IN ZOLA'S *L'ARGENT*

In his preliminary notes for the *Rougon-Macquart* series Zola distinguishes his undertaking from that of Balzac in *La Comédie humaine*. Whereas his predecessor had offered a wide-ranging portrait of contemporary society, a portrait given depth and unity through reappearing characters, Zola's objective would be more limited and, in his own terms, more scientific: he would chronicle the fortunes of a single family during the Second Empire and explain the destiny of its members according to the supposed interaction of a posited heredity with the pressures of a specific, observed environment. The coherence of his own fictional world would lie not in the device of reappearing characters, but in the simple fact that the scientifically established protagonists were blood relatives.[1]

In turn each member of the *Rougon-Macquart* family would be the focus of attention, but although mentioned elsewhere in the series, would not necessarily play a further role. Gervaise Macquart (*L'Assommoir*) and her son Etienne (*Germinal*) are notable examples. Other members are introduced in one volume before their main appearance in a later work. The eponymous heroine of *Nana* is firmly established in *L'Assommoir*; Claude, the protagonist of *L'Œuvre*, is presented as an Impressionist painter in *Le Ventre de Paris*, and the study of the politician Eugène Rougon (*Son Excellence Eugène Rougon*) is prefigured by his appearance in *La Curée*. Exceptionally, two characters are protagonists for a second time: Jean Macquart in *La Terre* and *La Débâcle*, and Aristide Saccard in *La Curée* and *L'Argent*. Initially portrayed as an unscrupulous property speculator in *La Curée*, Saccard returns in *L'Argent* as the anti-Semitic director of a merchant bank. For this additional role in the series he is necessarily 'un Saccard nouvelle forme'.[2]

His role in *La Curée* had been planned from the outset. In an outline submitted to the publisher Lacroix in 1869, Zola indicates both the subject and his chosen protagonist: 'Un roman qui aura pour cadre les spéculations véreuses et effrénées du Second Empire, et pour héros Aristide Rougon . . .'.[3] His character is intended to represent ruthless ambition:

Un homme emporté par une idée fixe; faire une grande fortune (. . .). Brutal, allant droit au but. Une volonté en somme dans le mal, dans la coquinerie, volonté privée de sens moral et acceptant tout.[4]

The theme of speculation will include share dealings: 'Maintenant toutes les autres spéculations pourront être jetées entre cela. Ainsi jeu de Bourse etc' (fol. 331). Saccard's activities embrace share manipulation, and the future protagonist of *L'Argent* soon becomes a familiar figure at the Bourse.[5] However, in *La Curée* the financial institution remains largely peripheral to the main action. If the presence of the Bourse is registered in later novels, its workings are left unexplored. In *Nana* (1880), for example, Steiner the banker is ruined by speculation; in *La Joie de vivre* (1884) Lazare considers writing a novel about the Bourse;[6] in *Germinal* (1885) the role of shareholders is questioned. It was not until *L'Argent* (1891) that Zola offered a detailed account of the financial institution, with Saccard acting as one of its principal representatives. The decision to include such a study at this point in the series and to focus attention once more on this member of the family requires further examination.

The latter half of the nineteenth century saw a rapid growth in Bourse activity. In the early years of the Second Empire the immense profitability of the railways had encouraged investment: 'De 1853 à 1856, une pléthore de richesse transforma la Bourse en un véritable Eldorado (. . .). Chaque jour se constituaient des sociétés nouvelles'.[7] By the early sixties, despite several sensational crashes, the number of companies quoted rose for the first time above three hundred. It was also during this period that Jewish financiers such as Jules-Isaac Mirès, the Péreire brothers and the Rothschild family dominated the financial market. By the end of the decade the Rothschilds had emerged as the single most powerful force. If the seventies were relatively uneventful in the development of the Bourse, the eighties brought another spate of dramatic collapses:

. . . dès l'année 1881, 19 banques et 13 sociétés industrielles s'écroulaient (. . .). Tout cela prépare le fameux effondrement de 1882: le krach de *l'Union Générale*, 14 autres banques suivent *l'Union*, et le chiffre des faillites des sociétés industrielles s'élève à 20 (. . .). L'effondrement ne fait qu'augmenter en 1883, 20 sociétés font faillite (. . .) avec 50 sociétés industrielles.

Ces chiffres effrayants se maintiennent en 1884.[8]

It seems more than likely that public interest in these crashes, and the success of several novels based on them, were not insignificant factors in Zola's decision to include in his series a novel about the Bourse and the collapse of a merchant bank.[9] *L'Argent*, eighteenth of the completed *Rougon-Macquart* cycle, had not formed part of Zola's original scheme, for neither the preliminary plan of 1869 nor an extended 'liste des romans' of 1872 carries any indication of 'un roman sur la Bourse'. The novel, with Saccard drafted into his second major role, must be considered a late addition inspired by contemporary events.[10]

From the work notes for *La Curée* it is evident that Zola had always envisaged a second appearance for Saccard: 'Les deux hommes [Saccard and Maxime] restent face à face (. . .). Ils auront leur compte dans un autre volume'.[11] There is, however, no specific reference to a novel about the Bourse. Nevertheless, Zola maintains that as early as 1877 he had planned such a novel with Saccard as the protagonist:

... j'ai toujours réservé une case pour ce que j'appelais mon roman sur la Bourse. Je voulais y reprendre Saccard et Rougon, y opposer l'empire libéral à l'empire autoritaire, enfin y étudier la crise politique qui a précédé l'effondrement du règne. Vous voyez que la conception du roman est chez moi très ancienne. Je la place après la publication de *Son Excellence Eugène Rougon*, vers 1877.[12]

Yet it is not until 1883, in the manuscript notes for *La Terre*, that Zola committed himself to his Bourse novel. There, in a revised list of novel subjects, he writes 'La Bourse et les journaux. Saccard, Maxime, Sidonie Oct. [ave] Mouret'.[13]

Now although this is the first mention of the Bourse novel, the proposed newspaper study dates from the second plan of 1872. Here we find: 'Roman sur la débâcle. Faire revenir Aristide, Eugène et les autres. (L'étude sur les journaux à la fin de l'Empire)'.[14] In his 1883 list Zola has given prominence to the Bourse, now incorporating the newspaper into a study of the financial world, with the collapse of France reserved for *La Débâcle*. The name of Aristide (Saccard) remains logically identified with the projected novel about the Bourse.

Zola's first concern in gathering material for the novel was to find a financial enterprise whose activities would permit discussion of the press. Initially the most promising model appeared to be *La Caisse Générale des Chemins de fer* belonging to Jules-Isaac Mirès, who had successfully promoted the company through newspapers in his ownership. In an interview, Zola states: 'Mon action se passe sous l'Empire. L'affaire Mirès me semble indiquée. Je veux donc l'étudier consciencieusement dès aujourd'hui'.[15] However, on investigation, the company's history lacked dramatic interest: 'L'affaire Mirès m'avait séduit; elle est vaste, considérable, étendue, mais elle n'est pas intéressante. Je me déciderai pour l'affaire Bontoux, *l'Union Générale*, ou même pour l'affaire des Métaux'.[16] As others had before him, Zola finally opted for the *Union Générale* affaire.[17] This decision would have several implications for Saccard's second leading role.

Under the energetic direction of Eugène Bontoux, a former èmployee of the Rothschilds, the *Union Générale* had become one of the leading companies in the early eighties. The company drew its support from small investors, mainly Catholic and Conservative, who were inspired by its declared aim of furthering Catholic interests in the world. Bontoux, resenting his dismissal by Rothschild, used the company to challenge the Jewish financier's domination of the Bourse. After a spectacular rise, the *Union Générale* found that its shares were less in demand, and in an attempt to resist downward pressures, exhausted its capital reserves by illegally buying in its own shares. Settlement day brought the inevitable crash, and thousands of small investors were ruined. Bontoux claimed that the company had been destroyed by the concerted efforts of Jewish financiers and masonic elements in the government.[18]

Now, according to Zola's account of his working methods, the creation of a new *Rougon-Macquart* novel would begin with reflections on the temperament of the chosen protagonist.[19] Though this description may reflect his practice in the early novels, later in the series, and especially for those novels in which an established character is used again, Zola's prime concern is no longer with his protagonist but with themes and substance.[20] This change of emphasis is apparent in the *ébauche*[21] for *L'Argent* where after first determining the scope of the novel, Zola remarks, 'Je n'ai guère que Saccard pour héros central' (fol. 383). He now chooses the most appropriate member of his fictional family to fulfil the role required of the protagonist, rather than shaping the role to demonstrate some truth about the individual and his given circumstances. The subsequent depiction of Saccard, his involvement with the press, his attitudes towards speculation, Jewish dominance of the Bourse and social problems, is determined by expressed creative intentions and evidence gathered during documentary investigations.

From the author's opening statements in the *ébauche*, it is clear that Saccard's activities will be governed in this way. The novel's tone is to be positive: 'Je voudrais dans ce roman ne pas conclure au dégoût de la vie (pessimisme)' (fol. 378). It will present an impartial view of money: 'Sur l'argent sans l'attaquer, sans le défendre' (fol. 381); examine the social implications of wealth and poverty, 'la question sociale' (fol. 379); the influence of Jewish financiers, 'la question juive' (fol. 380); the role of the press in company promotion, 'le journal' (fol. 382). A number of character-types are to be included: an aristocratic family, '. . . comme je n'ai pas de noble dans ma série j'aimerais assez mettre le désastre dans une famille de très ancienne noblesse' (fol. 380); a certain Madame Conin, 'Ne pas oublier la petite madame Conin que je veux employer depuis longtemps' (fol. 384); a dishonest office boy, 'J'ai aussi mon garçon de recette, paysan venu de la Franche-Comté et perdu par l'exemple' (fol. 416). These commitments, which owe nothing to detailed documentation of the Bourse and the *Union Générale* affair, inform Zola's conception of a narrative structure given coherence by the role of Saccard.

The purpose of the *ébauche* is to explore potential themes and characters, to clarify relationships, and to link given elements in order to establish a coherent narrative. The protagonist's role is instrumental in achieving this goal and is developed accordingly. Since press involvement in company promotion is to be illustrated, Saccard will become a newspaper owner: 'Il faudrait donc à un moment que mon personnage central achetât un journal' (fol. 382). Members of the aristocratic family will be integrated through some contact with the protagonist: '. . . je ne vois pas trop quels liens nouer entre Saccard et eux. Saccard s'intéressera à eux, pourquoi?' (fol. 392). Similarly, it is through Saccard that the dishonest office boy will be included: 'Je le mettrai chez Saccard, simplement' (fol. 418).

Zola's attitude towards money will be demonstrated through Saccard's ventures: 'C'est lui qui me permet de montrer le bon et le mauvais de l'argent' (fol. 402). Likewise his main character will be an essential element in the depiction of social deprivation, for Saccard will be given a bastard son living in appalling conditions: 'Pour le côté pauvre je lui donnerai un fils d'une ouvrière' (fol. 383). Through the illegitimate Victor another character, Drugeon, can be linked to Saccard: 'Je le [Drugeon] mêle au récit par Saccard dont il retrouve le fils naturel' (fol. 414). Finally, an involvement with the institution where Victor is placed will illustrate the more laudable aspects of Saccard's activities: 'Sur Saccard béni, il faudrait qu'il s'occupât d'une façon directe de l'asile' (fol. 472).

In developing his narrative, Zola realizes that a novel dealing predominently with financial matters might be lacking in general appeal: 'Cela me donne simplement un drame à la Bourse. Mais cela ne suffit pas, car je voudrais un coin de drame passionnel' (fol. 388). Accordingly, several female characters are considered to provide a sentimental interest for Saccard:

Il faut reprendre ça et voir si je ne dois pas mettre une femme au centre conduisant tout. Pourtant je ne crois pas. L'idée de l'argent doit dominer, l'argent donnant les femmes. Il me faudra simplement une femme très chère, très belle que Saccard se paiera (. . .). Si Saccard se paie une déesse, je puis le montrer échouant avec tout son argent auprès d'une jeune fille qu'il désire. (foll. 396-397)

The role of this 'jeune fille' is attributed to the Madame Conin figure. At one point she is to sleep with Saccard 'A la fin une dernière fois avec Saccard en consolatrice' (fol. 422), but he is later denied this pleasure because of the particular moral value Madame Conin has come to represent: 'Et quand elle a dit non, c'est bien non, jamais (le cas de Saccard). N'accepte pas d'argent dans ce monde où l'argent est roi' (foll. 452-453).

Zola's attempts to create a sentimental intrigue are hampered by his earlier presentation of Saccard in *La Curée*, for to make the main female character his wife would involve his already twice married protagonist in perhaps a marriage too many: 'Je pourrais ne pas le faire remarier, peut-être pourrait-il être simplement conseillé par la jolie femme que je mettrai au centre' (fol. 403). Similarly, it would be unreasonable to cast this female character as Maxime's wife, for any subsequent liaison with Saccard would be a repetition of *La Curée*:

Si j'en fais la femme de Maxime, je ne puis plus la faire acheter par Saccard. Ce serait honteux, et cela leur ferait encore partager une femme, ce qui répéterait trop la situation. (fol. 403)

The problem of the sentimental intrigue is finally resolved through an additional character, Madame Caroline. Saccard is not worthy of her: 'Je ne puis guère lui faire épouser Saccard; il n'est pas digne d'elle, il la salirait' (fol. 408). However, through their relationship Zola can show that Saccard does have attractive qualities to merit her devotion:

. . . cela me donnerait même cette originalité: ce gueux de Saccard aimé par une nature foncièrement honnête, et aimé pour des raisons d'activité, de bravoure, de continuel espoir. (fol. 410)

Since Eugène Bontoux had claimed political interference in his company's affairs, Saccard's relationship with the government must be clarified. In *La Curée* he had been portrayed as a fervent supporter of Napoleon III and consequently had enjoyed the protection of his politically ambitious brother, Eugène Rougon. In *L'Argent* he cannot accept the Emperor's more liberal domestic policies and is appalled at the government's failure to defend papal interests in Italy. At the same time, with its crusade in the Holy Land enjoying solid Catholic support, the *Banque Universelle* becomes an embarrassment to the government. In this situation Saccard will inevitably forfeit his brother Rougon's protection:

. . . Bontoux prétend à être tombé sous les coups des Juifs et des Maçons (au gouvernement républicain). Donc sur quoi pourrait bien s'établir Saccard? Ne pas oublier que j'en ai fait un bonapartiste militant (. . .). Admettons un moment que j'en fasse un autoritaire absolu contre l'empire libéral (. . .) il a contre lui les hommes nouveaux qu'on fait entrer dans le gouvernement. Il a même contre lui son frère Rougon le ministre, qui lui portera le dernier coup. (foll. 385-386)

The sequence of events leading to Saccard's fall is set in motion by a treacherous female companion, 'une joueuse, se donnant pour avoir un tuyau' (fol. 455). Initially her role was limited to passing vital information to Saccard's Jewish rival, Gundermann. However, drawing on information about Jules-Isaac Mirès' affair with Edwige Sapia, Zola extends her role to satisfy Bontoux's contention that hostile political forces had assisted Jewish financiers in the destruction of the *Union Générale*. Maxime Du Camp had revealed how a future minister, Chaix d'Est-Ange, surprised his mistress practising fellatio with Mirès, whom he threatened with revenge. These details are now incorporated into the mechanism of Saccard's fall:

> Je pourrais en outre garder l'histoire de Du Camp. Une rivalité entre Saccard et un magistrat, un procureur impérial. Celui-ci aurait surpris Saccard chez une maîtresse qu'il entretenait, nu, et l'explication terrible (. . .). Plus tard, le procureur devient ministre, juste au moment du désastre de l'*Universelle*, et c'est lui qui fait coffrer Saccard. Est-ce que je ne pourrais pas mêler les deux choses? Ma joueuse serait la maîtresse du procureur (. . .) son coup avec Saccard pour le tuyau et l'argent, et elle se fait surprendre. Donc devenu ministre, le procureur se venge. Et c'est ainsi que la passion tue Saccard après l'avoir élevé. Rougon laisserait faire pour se débarrasser de Saccard. Cette fois tout cela va bien. (foll. 455-456)

As Richard Grant[22] has argued, this episode is not altogether consistent with Saccard's portrayal as a man with little interest in sex. Indeed the incident confirms Zola's overriding concern with narrative structure even to the detriment of character consistency. The protagonist's sexual activities are simply a convenient means either to demonstrate social deprivation, as in the case of his bastard Victor, or, through an elaboration of his liaison with 'la joueuse', to create a more unified plot.

Saccard's motivation is not of major concern to Zola. Since his plot requires a man of energy, a man whose ambitious schemes must fail, these requirements are readily fulfilled by the former protagonist of *La Curée*. In a brief section of the *ébauche* headed 'La psychologie de mon Saccard' (foll. 423-429), he establishes the main determinants. For Saccard, money represents power and pleasure:

> Vouloir gagner de l'argent, pourquoi? Pas comme Grandet, pour l'enfouir. (. . .) il veut avoir de l'argent pour l'assouvissement des besoins, pour les jouissances du luxe et de la femme, surtout pour être le maître de Paris . . . (fol. 423)

He has the gambler's instincts:

> Mais il y a aussi la joie pure de se battre, la conquête pour la conquête, la joie en elle-même des joueurs, soit qu'il gagne, soit qu'il perde. Il est là dans son élément, il y vit davantage. (fol. 424)

If this aspect is founded in general observation of speculators, Saccard's desire for revenge is directly attributable to the choice of Bontoux as a model:

> Enfin, cette joie de l'action se double de ce qu'il a des vengeances à exercer. Un prince de la finance, un juif, l'a coulé, et il ne rêve que de l'attaquer. (fol. 424)

Character weakness explains the protagonist's inevitable failure: 'Saccard succombe parce que *passionné*, parce que *jouisseur*, un emballé enfin' (fol. 426), and here Zola recalls Eugène Rougon's judgement of his brother in *La Curée*: '"Tu veux te mettre trop vite à table"'. (foll. 426-427).

The development of Saccard's role in the *ébauche* is governed by several considerations: the demonstration of given themes and values, the inclusion of established character-types, the achievement of a coherent narrative structure. That the role is constantly modified to satisfy changing intentions is evident, but perhaps nowhere is this more apparent than from the opening section of the *ébauche*, where, before the *Union Générale* documentation has been undertaken, Saccard is seen to be triumphant. At this stage he is an affirmation of Zola's optimism: '. . . je voudrais mon homme fort arrivant et nettoyant le juif' (fol. 380).

The role fashioned for Saccard necessitates changes in his previous *curriculum vitae*. Since the action of *L'Argent* requires him to be a free man in 1864, his second wife Renée must be deemed to have died sooner than the year 1867 as indicated by *La Curée*. In the *Personnages* notes,[23] Zola admits that he has little choice other than to ignore this position: '. . . il faudra la faire mourir en 1863, s'il y a moyen' (fol. 267). Similarly, Saccard's unacknowledged bastard must be explained, and here Zola explores dates to correspond to the action of the new novel: 'L'enfant bâtard serait donc de 53 ou 54. J'aime mieux 53, il aurait alors 15 ou 16 en 69' (fol. 273). This position is further refined in the notes for Victor:

L'enfant serait né vers 1852. A ce moment Saccard vivait avec Angèle, rue Saint-Jacques (. . .). J'admets donc des rapports avec la fille d'une ouvrière d'en haut (. . .) lui a 37 ans, la fille en a 18. (fol. 295)

If in *La Curée* Saccard's presentation as a property speculator was achieved without detailed financial discussion, his daring and skilful manipulation of the Bourse in *L'Argent* would require specialized knowledge. Zola recognized that his layman's understanding was insufficient, and, despite extensive documentation, found composition of *L'Argent* unusually difficult.[24] For details of his protagonist's professional role he was prepared to rely heavily on expert opinion. Accordingly, Saccard will reflect the documented characteristics of the successful financier and articulate the accepted attitudes and values of the financial fraternity. In the Feydeau notes,[25] Zola states his intention: 'Donner à mon Saccard les qualités d'homme d'affaires' (fol. 153).

When Saccard defends the capitalist system,[26] his argument is based in two documentary sources: Mirecourt[27] and Feydeau. In the former notes a clear association is made with the protagonist: 'Mais le bien: voies ferrées, machines immenses (les projets de Saccard) amenant du bien-être. Prodiges de l'industrie' (fol. 6). However, it is in Feydeau that the main substance of his defence is found:

L'agiotage ou mieux la spéculation. Défense: améliorer la condition par la science, arts et industrie (. . .) la spéculation vivifie: ce qu'il y a de plus funeste pour une valeur industrielle, c'est la stagnation. Avec ses exagérations, ses baisses, ses hausses, la spéculation donne de l'élan, de la vie, passionne. (foll. 110-111)

The most informed critic of capitalism is Sigismund Busch, and in two contrived meetings, Saccard is required to act as a foil to his exposition of socialist theory.[28] The Schaeffle documentation[29] reveals that this will be a functional aspect of the protagonist's role: 'Saccard au socialiste: "Hein? Vous voulez tout bouleverser?" "Non, vous travaillez pour nous"' (fol. 25). Originally, Schaeffle's misgivings about socialist economic theory were intended to become Saccard's objections: '"Les choses se sont faites ainsi, c'est qu'elles ont suivi la logique humaine", dit Saccard. Et l'autre rêveur' (fol. 29). However, in the novel a change of emphasis occurs, for it is Sigismund himself who acknowledges this argument.[30] This change has implications for both characters: Sigismund appears more self-critical than at first conceived, while Saccard's more passive role diminishes his claim to a theoretical understanding of economics.

Saccard's anti-Semitic comments have not passed unnoticed.[31] It is important to consider these statements in the context of Zola's intentions and the documentary process. The *ébauche* reads:

. . . ne pas oublier que la question juive va se trouver au fond de mon sujet; car je ne puis pas toucher à l'argent sans évoquer tout le rôle des juifs autrefois et aujourd'hui. (fol. 380)

With this aim, details about Jews are simply noted in the course of documentation, as for example in the Feydeau notes: 'Bonne page sur les juifs' (fol. 123). The influence of Jewish financiers had been apparent from the earliest investigations into potential models for *L'Argent*. The majority of cases all involved Jews, as with the career of Jules-Isaac Mirès or the struggle between the Péreire brothers and the Rothschild family. Significantly, in his account of the *Union Générale* crash, Eugène Bontoux cites the hostility of Jewish financiers.[32] Zola's notes read:

Les juifs ont triomphé sur le champ de bataille de la Bourse (. . .). La banque juive, millards depuis 50 ans, monopole sur les 9 dixièmes des affaires financières de l'Europe. Guerre de conquête surtout depuis un quart de siècle. La mort de l'*Union*, épisode de cette grande guerre. (foll. 550-551)

Saccard explains the collapse of the *Banque Universelle* in similar terms.[33]

This anti-Semitic attitude is common to more general works about the Bourse. From Mirecourt, Zola notes: 'Tous les capitaux entre les mains de la juiverie financière' (fol. 11). In the novel this view is duly articulated by Saccard.[34] Again, according to Zola's protagonist, Jews have innate abilities in financial matters.[35] This argument is advanced by Feydeau and noted as follows:

Ne rien perdre, axiome de la race juive. (fol. 121)
Les juifs à la Bourse (. . .). Intelligents, bon calcul d'instinct. Chrétiens pas de force pour lutter, moins tenaces, moins économes, pas d'esprit de corps (. . .) les juifs arrivent jeunes commis chez un juif, carnet de dix sous et tout de suite abattent des affaires. (fol. 123)

There is, however, a certain irony in Saccard's anti-Semitic stance, for his characterization is partly developed through information about Jewish financiers. When noting Feydeau, Zola observes: 'Très bon pour l'intérieur de mon Saccard, à prendre' (fol. 122), and here the details concern the Péreire brothers. Elsewhere, information about Rothschild is used. Feydeau recalls a broker who successfully imitated his Jewish client: 'Tel autre qui hante la maison Rothschild fait exactement en petit toutes les opérations que le célèbre banquier fait en grand'.[36] This becomes for Zola: 'un qui fera en petit ce que Saccard fera en grand' (fol. 131). Similarly, Rothschild's dictum, 'traire la vache, mais pas jusqu'à la faire crier' (fol. 220), is attributed not to his fictional counterpart, Gundermann, but to Saccard.[37] Finally, as we have already shown, Saccard's affair with Baroness Sandorff stems from an episode in Mirès' life.

These elements in Saccard's presentation are doubly instructive: they testify to Zola's flexible response to information, and at the same time illuminate the expression of anti-Semitic views. From the evidence of the documentation, Saccard's attitude is intended to be representative and cannot be defined as the author's. Zola does seem to reflect, uncritically, received opinions, but through Madame Caroline an unanswered counter to Saccard's views is offered.[38] Significantly, it is of his female character, not Saccard, that Zola writes in the ébauche: 'me mettre tout entier là-dedans' (fol. 406).

Documentation of the Union Générale affair brings further precision to Saccard's role. His position in the Banque Universelle mirrors that of Jules Feder as director of the Union. Details were gathered from the official account of the trial:[39]

Ses attributions (art. 41 des statuts); gérer les affaires courantes, assurer l'exécution des délibérations du conseil d'administration; il représentait la société vis-à-vis des tiers, signant tout acte ayant pour objet la réalisation des affaires autorisées par les conseils; il dirigeait le travail des bureaux, effectuant les recettes et les dépenses. En somme, il était la puissance exécutive de la société. (fol. 484)

Saccard's duties are identical.[40] Similarly, the structure of his working day[41] follows closely an outline suggested by Gautherin.[42] Zola's notes read:

Une journée de Saccard, directeur. Il ne loge pas au siège social. Il y arrive vers neuf heures. Il dépouille le courrier et reçoit le galop des agents de change et des courtiers venant demander des ordres de bourse. A onze heures, il va déjeuner. Puis à une heure il va à la Bourse. Il rentre entre 3 et 4 heures, signe la correspondance, donne les avis d'opérer (selon les notes qu'il a rapportées de la Bourse) reçoit des visites, cause des affaires de la Société jusque vers 6 h. (foll. 60-61)

For his presentation of Saccard's professional duties, Zola is clearly prepared to draw extensively on his researched information, and occasionally to transpose specific details with minimal disguise. Undeniable accuracy and authenticity in portrayal is his justification.

However, neither is an inspired reworking of documented detail foreign to Zola's presentation of his protagonist. If, according to Feydeau, a ready wit is essential at the Bourse: 'on égaie les affaires, bonnes ou mauvaises' (fol. 153), Saccard will demonstrate this gift when under pressure. A first draft of the climactic Bourse scene is found in the Lévy notes.[43] Here Saccard covers his distress with the remark, 'Je suis ennuyé, je viens d'apprendre que des voleurs ont dévalisé ma maison de campagne, hier' (fol. 169). In a second draft this comment becomes, 'Est-ce ennuyeux, j'avais un cheval que j'ai dû abattre',[44] finally to appear in the novel as: 'Vous me voyez consterné. Par ces grands froids, on a oublié un camélia dans ma cour, et il est perdu' (p. 325). The basic notion, the exteriorized fear of dispossession, remains, but the form of its expression is subject to repeated revision.

The genesis of Saccard's role in *L'Argent* is instructive for the student of Zola's creative methods. This character's unscheduled reappearance as the protagonist clearly originates in the late circumstantial inclusion of the Bourse novel in the series. To exploit an established character in this way invites difficulties, if only because his previous presentation may limit potential development in character and situation. However, in *L'Argent* Zola is barely concerned with his protagonist as an individual. Here Saccard is deemed valuable, not primarily as an exemplification of the interaction between an inherited temperament and a given set of circumstances, but much more as a generalized representation of values and attitudes in the financial community. Both the *ébauche* and the documentation reveal how the development of his role responds to the author's stated attitudes, general thematic considerations, and the demands of a plot based on the *Union Générale* affair. In the more technical areas of the subject matter, the influence of the documentation is manifest. For the uninitiated reader, Saccard acts as an informed guide through the financial labyrinth, now operating as an inspired speculator, now articulating fashionable anti-Semitic views, now listening to an exposition of socialist economic theory. 'La nouvelle forme' indicated for Saccard is not discovered in an extensively reworked character portrayal: rather the newness lies in the development of his role. Zola unashamedly exploits his established character's second appearance both to unify disparate fictional areas and to introduce a human dimension to a subject which, by its very nature, would be the most technical and, in some respects, the least engaging of the *Rougon-Macquart* series.

BIRMINGHAM   R. COUSINS

[1] See 'Différences entre Balzac et moi' in *Les Rougon-Macquart*, Bibliothèque de la Pléiade, 5 vols (Paris, 1963-1967), V, 1736-1737. All references to the *Rougon-Macquart* novels are from this edition.

[2] The *ébauche* of *L'Argent*, MS 10268, fol. 383. Zola's manuscripts for the *Rougon-Macquart* series are preserved in the Bibliothèque Nationale, Paris (B.N. MS *Nouvelles aquisitions françaises* 10268-345). Hereafter references will be indicated by manuscript number and folio.

[3] 'Premier plan remis à Lacroix' in *Les Rougon-Macquart*, V, 1172. Aristide is renamed Saccard in *La Curée*, II, 364.

[4] MS 10282, fol. 322.

[5] See *La Curée*, II, 465.

[6] See *La Joie de vivre*, III, 1045. The point is made by R. J. Niess in his 'Autobiographical elements in Zola's *La Joie de vivre*', *PMLA*, lvi (1941), p. 1139.

[7] P. Duchâteau, *Guide de la Bourse illustrée*, (Paris, 1901), p. 87.

[8] 'Krachs financiers et industriels' (article signed 'Montguyon'), *Le Figaro*, 20 November, 1892.

[9] See Halina Suwala, 'Le Krach de l'*Union Générale* dans le roman français avant *L'Argent* de Zola', *Les Cahiers Naturalistes*, 27, (1964) pp. 80-90.

[10] For J. C. Lapp one origin of *L'Argent* may be found in Zola's *Les Mystères de Marseille* (1867). See his *Zola before the Rougon-Macquart*, (Toronto, 1964), p. 77.

[11] MS 10282, fol. 303.

[12] Letter to J. Van Santen Kolff dated 12 September, 1890. See R. J. Niess, *Emile Zola's Letters to J. Van Santen Kolff*, (St. Louis, 1940), p. 37.

[13] MS 10329, fol. 299.

[14] MS 10345, fol. 129.

[15] 'Les Trois Derniers Romans des *Rougon-Macquart*' (article signed Henri Bryois), *Le Figaro*, 2 April, 1890.

[16] 'Le Prochain Roman de Zola: *L'Argent*' (article signed Mario Fenouil), *Le Gil Blas*, 8 April, 1890.

[17] See Suwala, op. cit. (above, note 9).

[18] See J. Bouvier, *Le Krach de l'Union Générale (1878-1885)*, (Paris, 1960).

[19] See Edmondo de Amicis, *Souvenirs de Paris et de Londres*, (Paris, 1880), p. 192.

[20] See F. W. J. Hemmings, 'The Elaboration of character in the *ébauches* of Zola's *Rougon-Macquart* novels', *PMLA*, lxxxi (1966), pp. 286-296.

[21] MS 10268, foll. 376-477.

[22] See 'The Problem of Zola's character creation in *L'Argent*', *Kentucky Foreign Language Quarterly*, viii (1961), p. 61.

[23] MS 10268, fol. 260-374.

[24] See above note 16.

[25] E. Feydeau, *Mémoires d'un coulissier*, Paris, 1873. Zola's notes are found in MS 10269, foll. 109-34.

[26] See *L'Argent*, V, 114-115.

[27] Eugène de Mirecourt, *La Bourse, ses abus et ses mystères*, (Paris, 1858). Zola's notes are found in MS 10269, foll. 1-15.

[28] See *L'Argent*, V, 42-47 and 282-286.

[29] Albert Schaeffle, *La Quintessence du socialisme*, (Brussels, 1886). Zola's notes are found in MS 10269, foll. 17-33.

[30] See *L'Argent*, V, 46.

[31] See R. B. Grant 'The Jewish question in Zola's *L'Argent*', *PMLA*, lxx (1955), pp. 284-289.

[32] *L'Union Générale. Sa vie. Sa mort. Son programme*, (Paris, 1888). Zola's notes are found in MS 10268, foll. 539-560.

[33] See *L'Argent*, V, 384-385.

[34] See *L'Argent*, V, 182.

[35] See *L'Argent*, V, 91-92.

[36] E. Feydeau, op. cit., p. 254.

[37] See *L'Argent*, V, 107.

[38] See *L'Argent*, V, 385.

[39] 'Affaire de l'Union Générale', *Le Droit*, 6, 7, 8, 14, 15, 21 December, 1882. Zola's notes are found in MS 10268, foll. 481-538.

[40] See *L'Argent*, V, 134.

[41] See *L'Argent*, V, 139-140.

[42] Zola's notes from a conversation with this financial expert are found in MS 10269, foll. 59-90.

[43] Zola's notes from a conversation with Georges Lévy, a financial expert, are found in MS 10269, foll. 155-171.

[44] MS 10268, fol. 185.

C. A. BURNS

NATURALISM AND RELIGION:
A NOTE ON THE CASE OF HENRY CÉARD

The role of Henry Céard in the development of the Naturalist movement in French literature is now generally recognized to have been important. During the 1870s and early 1880s his name was often linked with that of J.-K. Huysmans.[1] The two men met in 1873 and their literary education was in many ways parallel. Both were fervent admirers of Flaubert and the Goncourts and their enthusiastic discovery of Zola was the starting point for the formation of the so-called Médan group of writers. Although their characters were different — the early Huysmans was essentially an artist in words whereas Céard was primarily a psychologist — their ideas on art and literature, at least up to 1884 when Huysmans published *A Rebours*, were not dissimilar. Thereafter Huysmans broke with Naturalism and was ultimately converted to Catholicism; Céard remained loyal to Zola until 1893 and was not converted. However, since Céard shared so much with Huysmans in the early part of his literary career, it is at least worth asking whether there are not some signs in his writing, either in the Naturalist period properly speaking or in the later years of his life, of some concern at least for religious matters, even if such concern does not amount to an actual conversion. The purpose of this article is to examine briefly some of the relevant evidence and to assess provisionally the nature and importance of Céard's attitude to religion at different stages of his career.

The Naturalist period should, strictly speaking, be limited to the years between 1876 and 1884, that is to say, to the period which separates the publication of *L'Assommoir* from that of *A Rebours*. During these years there is no evidence in Céard's writing, either published or unpublished, of a concern for or an understanding of religious matters. In 1877 he made the following uncompromising declaration:

. . . L'art contemporain est essentiellement désintéressé: il est essentiellement athée, essentiellement anarchique, essentiellement immoral. Athée parce qu'il représente son époque, et qu'aujourd'hui la science a montré que le ciel était vide et qu'il n'y a pas de dieux; anarchique, parce que les républiques lui demanderaient une utilité qu'il ne peut pas leur donner, et que les monarchies exigeraient des soumissions qu'il leur refuse; immoral, parce qu'il ne prend parti pour rien, qu'à ses yeux vice ou vertu, crime ou haut fait, tout a la même valeur.[2]

No doubt such comments should be seen in the context of the frequently violent polemics which surrounded the publication of *L'Assommoir*, and should not be taken as a definitive statement of principles valid for all time. As far as science is concerned, for example, it is clear from Céard's correspondence that, quite early on, he had grave doubts about the validity of the pseudo-scientific theories of literature which Zola proclaimed in his battle to establish his own form of Naturalism.[3] But such doubts were not expressed in public, and it is at least possible that Céard's private view of religion was not as totally negative as the foregoing quotation would imply.

The fiction which Céard published during these early years reveals no interest in matters religious. Broadly speaking his writing at this time can be divided into the 'militant' fiction inspired by the Franco-Prussian war (*Une Attaque de Nuit, Mal-Eclos* and *La Saignée*) and the 'poetic' fiction (*Une Belle Journée, A la Mer*) in which a more mature philosopher replaces the angry young man whose presence dominates the first group of stories. In the works inspired by the events of 1870-71 Céard satirizes vehemently, if rather clumsily, what he saw as the moral bankruptcy of the leaders of the nation at the time of the collapse of the Second Empire. Although there is no specific mention of the church in these works, it may be assumed that it is included in Céard's general condemnation of the 'establishment' of 1870. The bitterness and frustration which this writing reveals leave no place for the serious study of spiritual matters.

Une Belle Journée (1881) is, however, in a different category altogether. Here events as such are unimportant, and the frustrations of life are seen in a much more philosophical perspective. Throughout the book the emphasis is on the inner life of the central character, Madame Duhamain, whose fleeting thoughts and imprecise emotions are analysed in minute detail. The conclusion of the book is deeply poignant, perhaps even tragic, as we observe Madame Duhamain's efforts to achieve a kind of emotional nirvana in which suffering would be neutralized by a total renunciation of all ambition.

... Elle comprit que la misère des cœurs résulte non pas de la douleur continue qui les poigne, mais de l'effort qu'ils font pour échapper à leur condition. L'idéal qu'ils réclament ainsi qu'une délivrance se montrait plus meurtrier encore que les vulgarités auxquelles ils tentaient de se soustraire . . . Et puis l'ennui dont elle croyait souffrir n'était sans doute point si considérable et rien ne le différenciait du bonheur qu'une plus longue accoutumance. L'imagination, toujours, aggravait les tristesses naturelles et puisque les réalités s'imposaient, sans cesse moindres que le rêve, le mieux consistait à s'étendre dans une platitude définitive.[4]

The significance of *Une Belle Journée* from our particular standpoint in this article, lies in the fact that at no point does Madame Duhamain seek, or think of seeking, refuge or consolation in religion. Her suffering is of a moral order rather than of a purely emotional kind, and is not in any true sense spiritual. A comparison with Des Esseintes in *A Rebours* will make the point clear: the moral suffering to which Céard's heroine stoically submits is quite different from the essentially spiritual anguish from which Des Esseintes seeks relief at the end of Huysmans' novel.

The plays which Céard wrote during the 1880s reflect the same preoccupations as those noted in the novels and short stories. A distinction can be drawn, for example, between the plays of violence, such as *La Pêche*, and the philosophical type of drama to be found in *Les Résignés*. Although the plot of *La Pêche* owes nothing specifically to the 1870 war, its mood of brutal passion and blunt realism links it to the 'militant' type of fiction mentioned above. *Les Résignés*, on the other hand, is an expression in dramatic terms of the static melancholy and stoic acceptance of disillusionment that characterize *Une Belle Journée*. In the play the main characters appear even to relish the hopelessness of their dilemma and to make no serious attempt to transcend misfortune either by assertive personal action or by seeking consolation on a higher spiritual plane. They are trapped in a kind of moral paralysis and, as in the novels and short stories, the strictly spiritual dimension of human unhappiness is conspicuous by its absence.

A very different picture emerges, however, when one comes to consider Céard's writing after 1898. The presentation of religious matters in the mammoth novel *Terrains à vendre au bord de la mer*, which appeared in 1906, is extremely complex. It will be remembered that the action of this novel takes place in 'Kerahuel', the fictional name which Céard used for Quiberon, where he spent some ten years in self-imposed exile after his retirement in 1898 from his position as librarian at the Bibliothèque Historique de la Ville de Paris. The novel has many facets. On one level it is an account of the love affair between Malbar, a journalist, and Madame Trénissan, a distinguished singer. On another level it is a description of the latter's attempt to create the role of the heroine in Wagner's *Tristan and Isolda* and an analysis of the fatal mistake the singer makes in trying to bring to life in the starkly beautiful scenery of Brittany the legendary world evoked by Wagner in his opera. On yet another level the novel is simply a long prose poem inspired by the land, the sea and the sky. On another level again it is an exposition of the views held by Malbar and his scientist friend Laguépie on a wide variety of issues ranging from science to literature, including in particular politics. Finally it can be seen as a *roman de mœurs* which satirizes the attitudes of the inhabitants of 'Kerahuel'.

At a first reading the book seems to be fiercely anti-clerical. The satire of the attitudes and religious practices of the Bretons is biting. They are portrayed as ignorant, arrogant, narrow-minded, suspicious of all ideas that do not fit in with their own prejudices, and, above all, shamelessly hypocritical in their rigid observance of religious ritual while indulging in all manner of immoral and dishonest behaviour in their private or public lives. The curé of 'Kerahuel', for example, is ruthless in exploiting Madame Trénissan's generosity, but remains totally insensitive to her need for spiritual guidance, just as l'Abbé Bournisien had been deaf to the appeals of Madame Bovary. Laguépie, the man of science whose lofty humanitarian principles set him apart from the other characters in the book,[5] is frustrated at every turn by the ignorance, envy and hatred of one Astérie, a religious fanatic whose quack remedies for illnesses cause more suffering than they alleviate, but who is held in awe by the local inhabitants because of the aura of power which her religious fervour seems to confer on her. Religion as it is practised in 'Kerahuel' is presented by Céard as a shameful charade.

However, there is much more to the matter than this. It is clear, for example, that the scholar in Céard was fascinated by the phenomenon of religion, and more particularly by the legends he heard related and by the religious rituals he observed during his sojourn in Brittany. These legends and ceremonies are described in the novel at great length and with a kind of awe which contrasts strikingly with the satire of the moral turpitude of individual characters in religious matters. In chapter IX, for example, the ritual surrounding the blessing of the life-boat is described with muted admiration and is skilfully used as a background to a particularly intense emotional scene between two characters, in a kind of literary counterpoint which recalls the scene of the *Comices agricoles* in *Madame Bovary*. In the same chapter, the story of Saint Coulm is related in great detail; the miraculous elements in it are not dismissed disdainfully by Céard, as might have been expected; on the contrary they exert a powerful fascination over him and he is clearly moved by them.

Most of the significant themes in *Terrains à vendre* — the disillusion-ment of the artist, the love of Malbar and Madame Trénissan, the satire of the inhabitants of 'Kerahuel' and the inadequacy of the church — are brought together in the brilliant *ensemble* scene in chapter XXII which depicts the midnight Christmas mass. Madame Trénissan sings Elisabeth's prayer from *Tannhäuser*, but the music falls on the deaf and uncomprehending ears of the resentful townspeople. Unmindful of the solemnity of the occasion, they vent their spite on the 'étrangère', Madame Trénissan, and whisper obscene insults that sully the very essence of the faith they profess to believe in. Malbar, a silent spectator, is torn between his admiration for the music and his disgust at the behaviour of the faithful. He leaves the church in despair, determined never to return. Madame Trénissan, too, crushed and humiliated, vows never again to make the mistake of seeking to link art with religion. Céard appears to be saying quite clearly in this scene that, if true religious feeling exists, it is not to be found in the church.

This impression is confirmed by a small scene in the book, the importance of which it is easy to overlook on a first reading. Quite early in the novel, in chapter VII, at a point, that is, before the satire of religion as practised in 'Kerahuel' becomes particularly intense, Malbar and Madame Trénissan, returning home from an evening walk, happen to overhear a woman in a fisherman's cottage telling her son to say prayers for the peace of the soul of his father, who, like so many others, had been lost at sea. The stark simplicity of this scene, on which Malbar and his companion have unintentionally intruded, is moving both for the characters and for the reader. There is no satirical intention whatsoever. The mood is reminiscent of certain scenes in Flaubert's *Un Cœur simple*, where Félicité's ignorance and naivety bring her very close to the spirit of true religion. Indeed, it may be that, to judge by the evidence of *Terrains à vendre*, we should compare Céard's view of religion with that of Flaubert rather than with that of Huysmans, as was suggested at the beginning of this article. For if Céard was unable to accept the existence of God and if he was repelled by what he saw as the insincerity of the practices of organized religion, he was, like Flaubert, fascinated by the historical phenomenon of religion and touched by the simple faith of uneducated and inarticulate individuals. If this is a fair assessment of his views in 1906, his position is clearly very different from that which is implicit in his work published twenty-five years earlier during the Naturalist period properly speaking.

So far, we have considered only the evidence of Céard's prose writing. To complete the picture some attention would have to be paid to the very considerable amount of verse that has come to light in recent years, and particularly to the many occasional poems written in Brittany during the years 1898-1908.[6] To a certain extent these poems, the great majority of which are still unpublished, reflect the same interest in Breton legends and customs as that which we noted in *Terrains à vendre*. One such poem is that entitled 'L'Eglise qui chante' which was composed in July 1899. According to legend, the church which once stood on the rocks near Quiberon, was swept into the sea by a gale:

> . . . Malgré le temps et l'accident
> L'Eglise existe cependant.
> Elle vit au siècle où nous sommes,
> Et la mer de sa profondeur
> Fait monter le bruit et l'odeur
> Des encensoirs mêlés aux psaumes.
>
> Dans les flots sous les goémons
> Le chantre encor, à pleins poumons,

Debout devant l'antiphonaire,
Chante des motets en latin,
Et la vague n'a pas éteint
Un seul cierge du luminaire.

L'orgue n'a pas perdu l'accord;
Maintenant on l'entend encor
Qui soutient la voix des fidèles,
Et les cloches avec leurs sons
Aujourd'hui font peur aux poissons
Comme autrefois aux hirondelles.

Et voilà pourquoi le marin
Parfois quand le temps est serein,
Et que la mer n'est point méchante,
Dans un passage qu'il connaît,
Se signe en ôtant son bonnet;
Il entend l'église qui chante.[7]

One notes here the disarming naivety of the style and the author's apparent readiness to take seriously the clearly implausible legend.

More revealing still from our point of view here is the piece entitled 'Sur la porte' which also dates from July 1899. Here Céard describes how he intends to conform with local custom by having a statue of the Virgin placed above the door of his house. His thoughts then extend to matters of more general interest:

. . . Bah, faisons comme nos aïeux,
Gardons la foi vaille que vaille,
Puisque l'homme en vain se travaille
Pour ne rien inventer de mieux.

Gardons la foi des pauvres hères,
Oui, à quoi bon chercher si loin
La science qui ne sert point
Sauf à nous montrer nos misères.

Gardons, gardons la foi d'antan,
Celle des saints et des apôtres;
On en a essayé bien d'autres,
Aucune ne valait autant.

Gardons une foi point austère,
La foi facile qui jadis
Ouvrait tout grand le paradis
Aux humbles de cœur, sur la terre,

La foi modeste en son effet
Et dont la pacifique flamme,

En place d'incendier l'âme,
Tout doucement la réchauffait.

Elle suffisait à nos mères,
Que souvent elle consola.
Contentons-nous de celle-là,
Puisque les autres sont chimères . . .[8]

The reasons which impelled Céard to yearn for a simple, traditional and unquestioning faith are no doubt numerous and complex. A full examination of these motives would require more space than we have available here. What is clear, however, is that, in 1898, Céard felt the need to escape from the frustrations and turmoil of life in Paris and to find a new way of life quite different from that of the sophisticated 'boulevardier' which he had led before his retreat to Brittany. In psychological terms he clearly sought a return to the simplicity and certainty that he had known in childhood but which he had lost in adult life. Such a development is not surprising, perhaps, in a man of his age and temperament who had spent many years in the pursuit of elusive intellectual and literary ideals. His new attitude may appear simplistic; it is difficult, however, to deny the sincerity of the feelings expressed in the verse written in Brittany between 1898 and 1908.

A significant number of the Breton poems reveal a fascination with miracles and particularly with the Nativity. The stanzas entitled 'Noël breton', for example, are an account of the birth of Christ which had, ostensibly, been given to Céard by an eccentric Breton character called Perrine la Taupe. The poem describes how Joseph left the stable just before the birth of the child in order to seek help. The only person he can find to assist him is an old woman who is deformed, blind and a deaf-mute; they return to the stable:

. . . La femme entre avec lui. Jésus venait de naître.
Et la Vierge enfantant, les ayant aperçus,
Dit à la femme: 'Femme, en tes bras prends Jésus.'
Et la femme restait béante sur la porte.
La Vierge répéta: 'Prends Jésus et le porte,
Afin qu'il se réchauffe à côté de l'ânon.'

Prendre Jésus! La vieille, hélas! n'a qu'un moignon
A chaque bras. Depuis le jour de sa naissance
Les deux mains lui manquaient; et pleurant d'impuissance,
L'infirme remuait ses inutiles bras.

'Prends Jésus, dit Marie, et Dieu fera le reste.'
Quand de prendre l'enfant, la femme eut fait le geste,
Aux deux extrémités des moignons, il lui vint
Des mains pour soutenir le nouveau-né divin

Qui commençait sa vie avec une merveille,
Et la Vierge Marie alors dit à la vieille:
'Regarde, c'est mon fils.'
                    La femme ayant des yeux
Fermés depuis l'enfance au spectacle des cieux,
De ses nouvelles mains montrait ses deux orbites
Vides de tout regard; quand des clartés subites
Font resplendir ses yeux comme un double soleil;
Et son obscur esprit, aux ténèbres pareil,
S'illuminant quand s'illuminent ses prunelles,
Dans le rayonnement des gloires éternelles,
Elle aperçut l'Enfant Jésus, lui souriant.

Et comme, en ce moment, les Rois de l'Orient,
Dans des vases d'argent, de jaspe et de porphyre,
Apportaient au sauveur l'or, l'encens et la myrrhe,
Retrouvant la parole et poussant un grand cri,
La femme à l'univers annonça Jésus-Christ.[9]

It is surely not unreasonable to conclude from these lines that Céard's interest goes beyond the mere recording of a story related by a colourful local character and extends almost certainly to an acceptance of the miracle and, by extension, to an acceptance of the Christian faith itself.

If such a conclusion is justified, it would seem that, during his years in Brittany, Céard reached a position not entirely different from that of Huysmans, although the route which he had followed to reach that position clearly was very different. It is important to remember that, unlike Huysmans, Céard did not reveal to the world at large in fictional form the evolution of his thinking on religious matters. To some extent we can deduce this evolution from *Terrains à vendre* and from some of the Breton poems just quoted. Such questions were for Céard essentially private matters which would have been discussed, if at all, with only one or two particularly close friends. Nearly all the Breton poetry remained unpublished during his lifetime and has only recently begun to attract the attention of specialists. The closest Céard ever came in his later years to a public statement of his position on religious matters was when he published in 1923, only a few months before his death, an article entitled 'Étoiles de Noël'. Here he returns to the theme of the Nativity and draws a parallel between the recurrence of the religious festival and the continuing search by men of his generation for faith and certainty in different fields of endeavour:

. . . 'Noël, Noël, voici le Rédempteur', chantaient les vieux cantiques de notre enfance. Vieillissants et désabusés, nous voudrions quand même répéter encore ce cri de délivrance et de joie. Pourtant, depuis que nous avons l'âge d'homme, combien n'en avons-nous pas rencontrés de ces rédempteurs qui, sous toutes les formes, art, philosophie, littérature ou politique, ont détruit nos illusions et ajouté à nos mélancolies . . .

Quelles déplorables étoiles n'avons-nous pas suivies ! De combien de suspects rédempteurs n'avons-nous pas été et les mages, et les dupes ? Nous sommes venus vers eux de l'Orient de notre jeunesse et de notre candeur. Nous leur apportions nos aspirations, notre confiance, comme les rois apportaient à l'Enfant-Dieu l'or, l'encens et la myrrhe.

En échange de ces grands cadeaux, désillusionnant même la désillusion, déconcertant même l'ironie, ils ne nous ont donné que du néant. Cependant, irrités contre eux, point satisfaits de nous-mêmes, nous ne pouvons nous résoudre à vivre dans l'indifférence totale et à nous désintéresser complètement du ciel et de la terre. Voilà pourquoi la fête de Noël se célèbre encore, et d'âge en âge se célébrera sans cesse . . .[10]

To judge by the tone of this article, it would seem that, in public, Céard did not wish to go beyond presenting himself as the 'mécréant respectueux' which he claimed to be in a letter he wrote to Huysmans in 1903 after the publication of *L'Oblat*.[11] In private, in his later years, he was almost certainly closer than is generally realized to an acceptance, or re-acceptance, of the faith he had learnt in childhood. This was certainly the view of one of his closest friends, Pol Neveux, who believed that Céard 'est mort réconcilié avec Dieu'.[12]

The presentation of religion in the writings of the Naturalist authors is a large and complex subject. If and when a comprehensive study of the question comes to be written, the foregoing comments on the case of Henry Céard will not, we hope, be entirely without interest.

BIRMINGHAM   C. A. BURNS

[1] See R. Baldick, *The Life of J.-K. Huysmans*, Oxford, Clarendon Press, 1955. It will be recalled that one of Zola's most penetrating articles in *Une Campagne* was devoted to a study of 'Céard et Huysmans' (*Le Figaro*, 11 April 1881); see Emile Zola, *Œuvres complètes*, Paris, Cercle du Livre précieux, 1966-9, XIV, 580-585.

[2] From an article entitled 'Lettre de la fin' which appeared in the Brussels review *L'Artiste* on 25 November 1877.

[3] See the well-known rebuttal of the theories of *Le Roman expérimental* contained in Céard's letter to Zola of 28 October 1879; Henry Céard, *Lettres inédites à Emile Zola*, ed. C. A. Burns, Paris, Nizet, 1958, pp. 107-8.

[4] Henry Céard, *Une Belle Journée*, ed. C. A. Burns, Geneva, Slatkine Reprints, 1970, pp. 338-9.

[5] On one occasion, for example, Laguépie speaks of 'l'église où je ne vais pas, non par dédain, mais parce que ma croyance est plus haute'; *Terrains à vendre au bord de la mer*, Paris, Charpentier-Fasquelle, 1918, p. 138.

[6] There are two main collections of verse by Céard, one in the hands of the author of this article, the other in the Bibliothèque de l'Arsenal in Paris. On the former, see C. A. Burns, 'Nouvelles perspectives sur le Naturalisme', *Studi francesi*, 25, 1965, 41-61; on the latter, see J. B. Sanders, 'Henry Céard's unpublished Breton poetry', *The French Review*, Special issue no. 2, Winter 1971, 38-44.

[7] 'L'Eglise qui chante', an unpublished poem of twenty-four six-line stanzas, is one of the poems in the Arsenal collection of Céard's verse mentioned in note 6, MS. 13431, ff. 12-18.

[8] 'Sur la porte', which comprises twenty-seven quatrains, is also unpublished; Bibliothèque de l'Arsenal, MS. 13431, ff. 6-9.

[9] 'Noël breton' was written in 1900 and was published in the *Revue théâtrale* in December 1904. A prose version of the story appears in chapter XXII of *Terrains à vendre*, pp. 571-3 of the 1918 edition.

[10] 'Étoiles de Noël', *Le Petit Marseillais*, 30 December 1923.

[11] Letter to Huysmans dated 17 March 1903, printed in the *Bulletin de la Société J.-K. Huysmans*, 13, December 1935.

[12] Letter of Pol Neveux to Edouard Gauthier, undated, Bibliothèque de l'Arsenal, MS. 13039 (100). Neveux believed, to judge by this letter, that 'sans qu'il s'en doutât peut-être, notre ami (Céard) gardait au secret de son âme sa fidélité à des croyances familiales et traditionnelles.' This telling comment from one who had been close to Céard since the early 1880s gives strong support to the thesis put forward in this article.

CATHOLICISM AND ISLAM IN PSICHARI
AND HIS CONTEMPORARIES

It is sometimes forgotten that Psichari was a novelist. Critical work upon him has tended to see his novels as the intimate description of personal experience. 'L'histoire de sa conversion au catholicisme est racontée dans *Le Voyage du Centurion*',[1] wrote Jacques Maritain, his close friend. A.-M. Goïchon, his biographer, went further: 'Ce voyage, il l'a vécu', she wrote.

> Avec une sincérité magnifique d'où lui vient cette profondeur de psychologie, cette délicatesse incomparable dans l'analyse, il l'a redit, confirmant par ce récit, de nouveau pensé après une année de vie chrétienne, les impressions et les idées premières que le catholicisme avait éveillées en lui. L'intense personnalité du style est peut-être obtenue moins par le travail proprement littéraire — qui est pourtant considérable — que par l'entière fidélité dans l'expression des nuances d'une âme aussi complexe que droite, et simple à force de clairvoyance.[2]

This statement not only raises the old hare about sincerity in some mysterious way creating literary excellence; it also stresses the personal and anecdotic nature of *Le Voyage* in a way that Psichari himself had denied, in a letter which Mlle Goïchon herself quotes, in part, in her book:

> C'est l'histoire d'une conversion opérée dans le silence des déserts d'Afrique, mais je m'empresse d'ajouter que cette conversion n'est pas *ma* conversion. Dieu me garde de verser dans les détestables excès de la psychologie, dans cet abus de l'observation intérieure, dans cette véritable complaisance de soi-même qui caractérise les écrivains modernes.
> Si l'on considère la littérature actuelle, on y voit partout ce petit esprit qui, au lieu d'aller à la grande et sereine vérité, s'attarde aux imperfections de l'âme humaine, s'y complaît presque, et qui, à la fin, ne se résout à aborder notre sainte religion que par les caractères les plus extérieurs.[3]

In this letter to a priest Psichari is, as a Christian, criticising the tradition of the Catholic novel in his own day, and in particular the personal confession in the manner of Huysmans's *En Route*, the great example of the 'histoire d'une conversion' in the pre-1914 period. For Psichari Huysmans was a 'médiocre' who had been unable to provide 'ces belles analyses dont notre temps a besoin, de l'âme chrétienne, de la sainteté, de la communion des saints'.[4]

This is not, of course, to deny that Psichari was converted to the Catholic faith in the years before the First World War, and that his experiences in the army and in North Africa played some part in that conversion. What is clear is that Psichari's fictional works *cannot* be taken to reflect exact truths about the details of his own experience, as has too often been deduced by those who have studied him.[5] Mlle Goïchon explains Psichari's letter by suggesting that Psichari changed his own experiences slightly, between the originally unpublished *Les Voix qui crient dans le désert* and *Le Voyage du Centurion*, because of a kind of humility which had made him feel that they were too personal to be communicated directly.[6] This interpretation ignores a number of important points. Firstly, *Les Voix* was originally intended for publication, as we shall see, and is in no sense a straightforward diary. Secondly, it was not humility or embarrassment which made him reject personal experience as subject-matter, but a conviction as to the most valid way to express religious truth. Thirdly, the novel was a *roman à thèse*, written in an 'esprit d'apostolat' in which every phrase was weighed according to its 'utilité spirituelle';[7] the experiences of one man were unlikely to contain all the 'spiritual usefulness' which such a work required.

Psichari's works, then, from *L'Appel des Armes* onwards, were based on what he believed to be general truths about human experience, rather than on purely personal memories. A certain amount of personal experience naturally enters them, as it does the work of most novelists; our knowledge of human experience has to come either from personal events, or from the recounted experiences of others, or from our reading. But it would be futile to attempt to interpret Flaubert's novels on the basis of the elements of personal experience which they contain. These elements are transmuted in accordance with the novelist's major interests, and are intermingled with other elements from other sources. The same is true of Psichari. He tells us general truths about religious experience, in the religious idiom of his own day; for this purpose he draws on many sources, and perhaps the most interesting parts of the story are those that are least personal, for they help us to understand that idiom more clearly.

In many ways the approach to the Catholic faith which is found in the works of Psichari is typical of certain trends in Catholic thought in the first two decades of the twentieth century. Traditionalism, the search for an order (whether monastic or military), the rejection of the modern world, the rejection of intellectualism, the belief in the temporal mission of France, 'fille aînée de l'Église', all these views were part of the religious atmosphere of the time. It is fascinating to trace all the philosophical links between Psichari and his contemporaries, whether they be the older generation of Péguy, Barrès and Maurras, or his close friends Maritain and Massis. There is one area in particular, however, which illustrates *à merveille* the way in which Psichari reflects the tendencies of his age, and that is the depiction of Islam in his works. In this article I propose to concentrate on this one area, both for the insight it gives us into Psichari's methods as a novelist, and for the picture it gives us of French reactions to the religious life of the Muslim populations of French North Africa.

★ ★ ★

There had always been sympathy for the Islamic faith in France's North African army. The military had shown themselves, on the whole, to be 'soucieux de ne pas irriter la susceptibilité des musulmans'[8] under the Second Empire, and often to defend the indigenous peoples against the encroachment of the 'colons' (for which they were repaid with an anti-militarism which finds expression in, for example, Alphonse Daudet's *Tartarin de Tarascon*). It was under the Third Republic, however, that a whole series of military men went much further than sympathy, finding in the Islamic faith a message for themselves, and an example which was to plant a firm Christian faith within them.

Count Henry de Castries was the first, and most striking, example of this tendency. He himself, though of a Catholic family, and though he had not, like so many of his contemporaries, lost his faith in face of the apparent triumph of the materialist philosophies of the nineteenth century, was at this stage far from being a devoutly practising Christian. The description he was later to give of the first impact of Islam upon him is of importance not only in itself, but because of the impact it was to have on later writers, and on their view of Islam.

He described how, when he was on a march with thirty Muslim horsemen, in the early 1870's, the hour for prayer had arrived, 'la prière de l'*asser*, la prière commune, plus agréable à Dieu chez les musulmans comme chez les chrétiens'. He stood aside, but nevertheless observed with emotion:

Je m'éloignai; j'aurais voulu rentrer sous terre! Je voyais les amples burnous s'incliner à la fois dans un geste superbe aux prostrations rituelles; j'entendais, revenant sur un ton plus élevé, l'invocation: Allah akber! Dieu est le plus grand! et cet attribut de la divinité prenait dans mon esprit un sens que toutes les démonstrations métaphysiques des théodicées n'avaient jamais réussi à lui donner. J'étais en proie à un malaise indicible, fait de honte et de colère. Je sentais que, dans ce moment de la prière, ces cavaliers arabes, si serviles tout à l'heure, avaient conscience qu'ils reprenaient sur moi leur supériorité. J'aurais voulu leur crier que, moi aussi, je croyais, que je savais prier, que je savais adorer . . . Moi seul, dans cette immensité saharienne, j'étais disparate avec mon costume militaire étriqué, ridicule moulage de la forme humaine, vêtement presque indécent. Mais, dans ce Sahara si favorable à la pensée religieuse, je tranchais surtout par cette attitude mécréante qui me donnait l'apparence d'une brute, *d'un chien*, vis-à-vis de ces gens renouvelant à leur Dieu l'aveu d'une foi sincère et profonde . . . Quand, de retour dans mon bordj, j'essayais de fixer mes impressions, je me sentais attiré de plus en plus par les beautés de l'Islam. Il me semblait que, pour la première fois, dans cette vie nomade du désert, j'avais réellement vu des hommes rendre hommage à la divinité. Ma pensée se reportait à ces temples chrétiens où le plus souvent les femmes seules sont en prière, et l'indignation me venait contre cette irréligion des hommes d'Occident.[9]

This description, coming as it did right at the beginning of Castries's influential book *L'Islam*, was to influence many people far more than their actual experiences did. One finds, in writings about this period, recurrent references to similar scenes. In this context, Psichari's description of the experiences of the military hero of *L'Appel des Armes* is only to be expected:

C'était l'heure de la prière . . . Maurice, les yeux fixés sur son horizon inhabité, éprouvait un mal étrange. Cette ferveur qu'il ne pouvait comprendre, et qui seule mettait une pensée dans ce désert, elle lui faisait une crispation de cœur intolérable. A ce moment-là, il sentait l'âme de ses hommes plus haute que la sienne. Il souffrait de sa race devenue incapable d'adoration.[10]

A similar description, in the same novel, borrows further details from Castries's description:

Il aurait voulu leur crier, à ces Maures: 'Moi aussi, chers enfants, j'ai mes prières et j'ai mon Dieu!' C'était en vain. Aux heures de prières, leur âme était plus haute que la sienne . . . Jamais Maurice n'a vu prier comme ces gens prient . . . Maurice, qui ne pouvait les suivre dans leur voyage, n'osait plus les regarder. Il avait honte d'être resté sur la terre.[11]

What many of the enthusiasts for Castries's description of his experience failed to note was the criticism which he himself added to it, in the succeeding paragraphs of his book. It had been a purely youthful reaction, he wrote:

J'étais à l'âge des solutions simplistes, des généralisations superficielles, où l'enthousiasme tient lieu de critique, où l'on croit à l'absolu en ce monde, âge en un mot où l'on ne devrait jamais écrire. La beauté d'une religion me semblait être la meilleure preuve de sa vérité et, à mon insu, j'écrivais d'abondance *Le Génie de l'Islamisme*. Une pareille œuvre eût été déplorable et aurait certainement mérité le reproche 'd'incroyable légèreté' que s'attirent justement de la part des orientalistes certaines productions algériennes un peu hâtives.[12]

Two kinds of people, said Castries, wrote usefully about Islam in his day: erudite orientalists and 'les arabisants d'Algérie', who, 'vivant en contact journalier avec des musulmans, pénètrent leur pensée, leur vie, leur religion, mieux qu'il n'est possible de le faire en aucun autre pays'. He saw himself as being somewhere between the two, though more related to the latter.

Castries's book was an attempt to bring the French to understand the religion of their Muslim subjects. By the time he wrote the book, he was himself a fervent Catholic; but the book does not contrast the two religions, so much as show the relationship between them.

How many of his readers misunderstood him, however! Even Charles de Foucauld saw the main message of the book as being the centrality of 'adoration' in religion: 'Comme vous comprenez *l'adoration*, mon bien cher ami, et avec quel sentiment irrésistible vous voyez que l'adoration — qui est la plus complète expression du parfait amour — est l'acte par excellence de l'homme!'[13] Amid the many comments he wrote to his cousin Castries on this subject, we find no mention of the central themes of the book — the examination of various crucial aspects of Muslim theology, the assessment of the present temporal status of Islam, the depiction of the spiritual relationship between Islam and Christianity, the attitude to be taken towards Islam by the French in North Africa.

For Castries the relationship between the two religions was so close that the divisions between them could be taken as 'au sein de la même famille'. Christianity, he said, 'ne saurait accuser d'idolâtrie une religion qui présente avec lui assez de points de contact pour que saint Jean Damascène la regardât comme une hérésie chrétienne'. Though the Muslims did not admit the divinity of Jesus, they honoured him as the greatest of the Prophets. The creators of Judaïsm, Christianity and Islam were, in the words of Abd-el-Kader, 'trois hommes dont le père est unique et qui ont plusieurs mères'.[14] Though one must be aware of the relationship, however, Castries did not believe in a merging of the two religions.

With regard to French colonial policy, Castries was, like most French military men, convinced of France's mission. He nevertheless felt that many mistakes had been made in North Africa; the urbanisation of the nomads having, above all, lowered the 'principes de la morale' of the 'régime patriarcal'. This had been further exacerbated by educating them in the French manner. Assimilation was impossible: evangelisation was even more out of the question: 'Irréductibilité de la foi musulmane par l'apostolat, impossibilité de la vaincre par la violence, telles sont les deux raisons qui s'opposent à l'évangélisation de l'Algérie'.[15]

Charles de Foucauld's views were far simpler. There is no need, here, to go into the details of his early life, and his conversion.[16] Suffice it to say that the soldier, and future Saint of the desert himself claimed to have been converted by the impact of Islam.

L'Islam a produit en moi un profond bouleversement . . . la vue de cette foi, de ces âmes vivant dans la continuelle présence de Dieu, m'a fait entrevoir quelque chose de plus grand et de plus vrai que les occupations mondaines: 'ad majora nati sumus' . . . Je me suis mis à étudier l'Islam, puis la Bible, et la grâce de Dieu agissant, la foi de mon enfance s'est trouvée affermie et renouvelée.[17]

For Foucauld, however, after his conversion, there was only one Truth, and anything else, however close it came, could only be falsehood:

L'islamisme est extrêmement séduisant: il m'a séduit à l'excès. Mais la religion catholique est vraie: c'est facile à prouver. Donc toute autre est fausse . . . Or là où il y a erreur il y a toujours des maux.[18]

As Foucauld wrote to the Abbé Huvelin in 1898:

On ne peut pas vivre au milieu de ces malheureux musulmans, schismatiques, hérétiques sans soupirer après le jour où la lumière se lèvera sur eux.[19]

The reasons for this desire to convert the Muslims were not only spiritual, however. Foucauld believed firmly in the temporal mission of France. In this he was typical of the military men of his day. He would not, I am sure, have been shocked by the statement made, after his death, in the *Bulletin de la Sociéte de Géographie du Maroc*, that General Laperrine and the Père de Foucauld had devoted themselves 'au rude labeur d'ajouter à la plus grande France ces immensités sans bornes'.[20]

Castries and Foucauld, then, though they had certain characteristics in common, differed considerably in their approach to Islam. The examination of their views has been important because it was the writings of the one, and the example of the other, which had the strongest influence on the pre-1914 generation in France's colonial empire. Foucauld, by this stage, was almost a cult figure. Lyautey found in his chapel at Beni Abbès 'une émotion religieuse, un sentiment de grandeur que nous n'avions jamais sentis au même degré'.[21] Louis Massignon, who saw Foucauld, together with Huysmans and Al Hallaj, in a vision at the time of his conversion, was to remain obsessed by the figure of the hermit in the desert. There were many others who studied Islam, or were religiously affected by it. As Psichari himself was to write: 'Sur beaucoup de Français qui n'ont plus la foi, mais qui en ont gardé le regret, l'Islam exerce une puissante attraction'.[22] Let us now see how this atmosphere fits into the literary creations of Ernest Psichari.

★ ★ ★

There are four works by Psichari which contain important references to Islam — the novel *L'Appel des Armes*, first conceived in 1909 and published in 1913, the short verse play *La Nuit d'Afrique*, written in 1912, the novel *Le Voyage du Centurion*, published posthumously in 1915, and *Les Voix qui crient dans le désert*, which was first published in serial form in 1919-20.

La Nuit d'Afrique can be left out of our considerations. A heroic drama with no claim for autobiographical interpretations, it does, it is true, use the well-worn theme of the lapsed Christian, admirer of Islam, who in the face of death finds the faith of his youth, recites the Creed, and dies. But this does not necessarily tell us anything about the author, other than that he was immersed in the North African mystique of his time. It is to the other works that we must look for the possibility of more direct evidence.

Les Voix qui crient dans le désert was not originally intended, as is suggested in the introduction to the posthumous first edition, as 'une confession', a straightforward 'récit complet de la conversion d'Ernest Psichari'.[23] Psichari's own description, in his *Journal de Route*, of his intentions in writing it shows a *literary* concern, a desire to produce travel literature of a new kind, far from the exoticism of writers like Loti:

8/6/12 — Je commence une sorte de récit de voyage relatant mes diverses courses africaines pendant ces trois dernières années. La forme en sera philosophique beaucoup plus qu'anecdotique et se rapproche de l'Essayisme'. La Mauritanie permet d'aborder mille sujets. Nous en avons assez du 'pittoresque', et comme la façon de voyager d'un Loti paraît désuète et vaine ! Je crois que ce que j'entreprends est plus dans mes cordes que le roman. Aux yeux de Taine, le roman était la plus haute forme littéraire. Sans doute, mais je ne puis m'y soumettre. Je suis plus à l'aise dans la forme lâche de 'l'essai'.

Les Voix must clearly be treated on the same level as the two novels; they were all three created as works of art. Indeed, the fact that by 1912, three years after the start of the events he is to describe, Psichari still sees Mauritania as a place affording 'mille sujets' shows the lack of centrality the Christian-Muslim theme had, in real life. *Les Voix* is an interesting work, in that it starts out on the lines sketched above, and gradually becomes the story of a conversion, incorporating at the same time some of the stock-in-trade of the post-Castries tradition. While writing it, Psichari was working towards the idea of *Le Voyage du Centurion*. Once he had decided on writing the latter work, he appears to have left *Les Voix* on one side.

1909 was the year in which the events which are supposed to have been transcribed into the end of *L'Appel des Armes*, and into the other two works, started, with the beginning of the expedition in Mauritania. Let it first be said that there is no hint, in any source personal to Psichari, of the events described in *L'Appel des Armes* relating to the shattering effect of Muslim prayer, and they are clearly based on a literary source, as we have seen. What the use of this source shows is a desire, on the part of the author, to plant his hero right in the centre of a tradition relating to the army, to tradition, to Christianity and to North Africa.

In *L'Appel des Armes*, however, with its major themes of the order and tradition personified by the Army, this particular sequence stands out like a sore thumb. In *Le Voyage du Centurion*, written after the author's conversion, an obvious passage of this kind is avoided; but there is still a lot of space devoted to the influence of Islam upon the convert, even though the author now feels compelled to stress, at various points, the superiority of Christianity, in a manner reminiscent of Foucauld.

Just as, in the first novel, the Islamic experience had been a suitable bit of 'local colour' for the soldier in North Africa, so, in the second, which had the object of being the 'histoire d'une conversion', it was almost necessary to depict what was, after all, a commonplace of North African spirituality.

It is interesting to note the transformations that occurred, both in events from the author's travels, and in extracts from his reading, before they were incorporated in *Le Voyage du Centurion*.

Though Psichari was clearly attracted to Christianity at an early stage, mainly through the influence of his friend Jacques Maritain,[24] we find no trace at this stage, in the mentions of Islam made in his letters from Africa, of any spiritual connexion being made between the two religions. These letters are those of an interested traveller, fascinated by the customs of the regions through which he passes, including the more unusual religious manifestations.[25]

It was in the same spirit that Psichari read many books about the country and its customs, and Islam in general, including Poulet's *Les Maures de l'Afrique Occidentale Française*, Depont and Coppolani's *Les Confréries religieuses musulmanes*, and Gobineau's *Les Religions et les Philosophies dans l'Asie centrale*.

A great part of *Le Voyage du Centurion* is made up of a *contaminatio* of various sources; the changes made in them are significant of the author's intentions. Let us take just one example: the famous passage from pages 38 to 43, in which the hero, Maxence, observes some wild Arab mystics, and draws a lesson from them. This is almost certainly based, originally, on observation. In the early part of *Les Voix* the author describes himself as being in Moudjéria in June 1910, and coming across these people. All the surroundings of the description are, however, different.

Psichari had already stated, four pages earlier in *Les Voix*, that the study of the Moors

m'a fait passer de charmantes heures. Mais elle ne m'a pas mené à grand'chose et je ne crois pas qu'elle ait beaucoup servi à m'améliorer. Ce que j'ai vu de plus beau dans le Tagant, ce sont les traces de notre conquête.[26]

The paragraph immediately preceding the description is, however, even more significant:

Sur beaucoup de Français qui n'ont plus la foi, mais qui en ont gardé le regret, l'Islam exerce une puissante attraction. Il ne faut pas trop s'en plaindre. Ce goût nous a donné une habileté extraordinaire dans la conduite et le maniement des Musulmans. Mais de combien d'inquiétudes, de tristes retours sur nous-mêmes payons-nous ce résultat!

The introduction in *Le Voyage* is quite different:

Mais ceux que Maxence recherchait d'instinct étaient les contemplatifs, les rêveurs des steppes, ceux dont le jeûne a rongé les chairs et amenuisé le cœur.[27]

The description then follows, in both accounts, of the cries and sobs of the ecstatics. From here onwards, however, the tone is completely different. *Les Voix* has the tone of impartial, and bookish, observation, *Le Voyage* the tone of involvement.[28]

The description in *Les Voix* abounds with references to Coppolani's book (often repeating Psichari's own analysis of Coppolani in his *Journal de Route*):

M. Coppolani, dans son ouvrage sur les confréries religieuses de l'Islam, nous renseigne admirablement sur ces sectes quelque peu fermées aux profanes . . . M. Coppolani nous apprend que . . ., Coppolani nous cite . . ., Rien n'est plus intéressant que de suivre dans Coppolani . . ., C'est ici que Coppolani nous ouvre des horizons suprenants . . .

In *Le Voyage* some, but not much, of the interesting information from Coppolani is repeated, but without attribution, as though it is Maxence's contribution. Phrases of praise change the whole tone. 'L'esprit habite donc ici, disait Maxence', is added. 'Et n'est-ce pas grand ce que certains disent' replaces 'Coppolani nous cite'.

Both texts contain a passage of enthusiasm:

Tant de rêves élevés, tant de mysticisme fleurissant en plein XXe siècle sur le sol le plus inhospitalier du monde, $\begin{pmatrix} \text{peuvent très bien nous émouvoir.} & \text{Nous avons} \\ \text{pouvaient très bien émouvoir Maxence.} & \text{Il avait} \end{pmatrix}$ la sensation fortifiante d'aller à des excès, de $\begin{pmatrix} \text{nous élever} \\ \text{s'élever} \end{pmatrix}$ au-dessus de la médiocrité quotidienne.

But whereas the conclusion in *Les Voix* was that some 'débris de notre cœur', which 'vingt siècles de civilisation intense' had 'effrité', were perhaps to be found here, the Maxence of *Le Voyage* provides a truly Foucauldian view:

Maxence recevait de ces misérables, de ces hérétiques, prisonniers dans leur hérésie, une véhémente leçon. Cette petite part de vérité que, sombrés à pic dans l'erreur, ils détenaient encore, Maxence la voyait trembler à son horizon de deuil.

The later sections of *Les Voix*, as has already been pointed out, depart from the tone depicted above. Though the 'essayist' is still in evidence, the aim has changed. It was no doubt because of this incompatibility that the first work was scrapped in favour of *Le Voyage*. So, in the latter part of *Les Voix* we find, alongside admiring references to the capacity for 'adoration' of the Muslims ('ces grands rêveurs qui adorent du moins le vrai Dieu, s'ils ne l'adorent pas en vérité'[29]), and to 'la part de vérité éternelle' to be found in Islam, which comes from the 'grand héritage judaïque',[30] the description of a theological dispute with an Arab, in which the hero unwittingly finds himself taking the Christian side.[31]

Of course, it is easy to read too much into a tradition. Just because it exists, does not necessarily mean that the individual experiences were not repeated. The Moor who, in *L'Appel des Armes*,[32] and then in *Le Voyage du Centurion*[33] gestures towards the horizon, saying 'Dieu est grand', and has such a strong effect on the hero, may remind us of the effect the phrase *Allah akber*, and the expanse of the desert, had upon Castries; but we may be affected by the borrowings we already know that Psichari had made from that author. The Moor may indeed have said it in the way described, to Psichari, and had a strong effect. It does not really matter. True or false, it is part of a tradition which might even, as traditions tend to, create its own reality, in that people expect themselves to be affected in particular ways. Nature is affected by art as often as art is affected by nature.

What is clear is that Psichari made little mention of such matters in his letters, in relation to his own beliefs. He was, it appears, above all attracted to Catholicism because of order, of tradition, of race. In a rare comparison of the two religions, made in a letter to Mme Favre, in 1911, he stated that people said that both religions were equal in beauty. Yes, he went on,

mais l'une est la nôtre, celle de nos pères, de notre race, et adaptée à notre race. L'autre n'a pour nous qu'une beauté intrinsèque, nullement utilisable. C'est ainsi que j'admets les catholiques de tradition, mais moins ceux qui 'croient que c'est arrivé', comme l'on dit vulgairement.[34]

'Not much hint of 'adoration', or the effect of spirituality and belief, here! As he was to put it in a later letter, he was attracted to Catholicism because it was 'une des formes du traditionalisme auquel il faut que nous revenions au plus vite si nous ne voulons pas disparaître'.[35] And, writing to Jacques Maritain, he stressed still further this important point:

Il n'est pas de politique qui se puisse passer du catholicisme ... Tout ce que nous avons de beau et de grand en nos cœurs nous vient du catholicisme ... Et je crois que ce sont là, pour nous, les vraies raisons de croire ...

He continued with an attack on false science, schoolteachers, freemasons, radical-socialists, and all those aspects of the *monde moderne* which most offended the traditional Right, and added:

Avec tout cela, je n'ai pas la foi. Je suis, si je puis dire cette chose absurde, un catholique sans la foi . . . Il me semble pourtant que je déteste les gens que tu détestes et que j'aime ceux que tu aimes et que je ne diffère guère de toi qu'en ce que la Grâce ne m'a pas touché.[36]

So, just before his conversion, Psichari appears affected above all by Christianity's mission as perceived by contemporaries such as Maritain.

Perhaps we should finish with a statement that impressed Psichari so much that he included it in two letters, and in *Le Voyage du Centurion*. It is almost certain that the statement was actually made to Psichari by a Moor (though, again, it is extremely close to statements in Castries); it runs as follows:

Oui, vous autres Français, vous avez le royaume de la terre, mais nous, les Maures, nous avons le royaume du ciel.

In the novel, the statement is the occasion for four pages of suffering and self-doubt in Maxence, and he is shaken to the depths of his being, in that he tries to reply, but is only aware that his words condemn his own unbelief. Psichari's response was considerably different.

A letter about it, to the Bishop of Dakar, dating from May 1912, was, Psichari told Maurras, written 'en véritable enfant de l'Église. Feinte, artifice ou hypocrisie? Nul de ceux qui ont aimé l'Église avant d'y croire ne le dira'.[37] In it, despite the Christian tone, Psichari shows himself to be above all concerned with the *temporal* effects that such beliefs among the Moors could have for France. Religion was *necessary* for France's dominance in this area.

. . . Depuis six ans que j'ai fait connaissance avec les musulmans d'Afrique, je me suis rendu compte de la folie de certains modernes qui veulent séparer la race française de la religion qui l'a faite ce qu'elle est et d'où vient toute sa grandeur. Auprès des gens aussi portés à la méditation métaphysique que les musulmans du Sahara, cette erreur peut avoir de funestes conséquences. J'en ai acquis la conviction, nous ne paraîtrons grands auprès d'eux qu'autant qu'ils connaîtront la grandeur de notre religion. Nous ne nous imposerons à eux qu'autant que la puissance de notre foi s'imposera à leurs regards. Certes, nous n'avons plus les âmes des croisés et ce n'est pas à la pensée d'aller combattre un infidèle qu'un officier désigné pour le Tchad ou l'Adrar va se réjouir. Pourtant, j'ai vu des camarades qui, dans les conversations avex les Maures, souriaient des choses divines et faisaient profession d'athéisme. Ils ne se rendaient pas compte de combien ils faisaient reculer notre cause et combien, en abaissant leur religion, ils abaissaient leur race même. Car, pour le Maure, France et chrétienté ne font qu'un . . .

J'ignore le nombre de musulmans qu'a convertis le vénérable et illustre

R. GRIFFITHS

Père de Foucauld dans le Sahara septentrional. Mais je suis assuré qu'il a plus fait pour asseoir notre domination dans ce pays, que tous nos administrateurs civils et militaires. Ce serait un beau rêve de souhaiter des âmes de missionnaires à tous les officiers Sahariens . . .[38]

Psichari, like Foucauld, believed in the temporal mission of France. But, unlike Foucauld, we have no evidence of a strong influence of Islam upon Psichari's conversion, and a great deal of evidence as to other, strong influences. Psichari's works of art, despite his own strong warnings on the subject, have been taken as presenting his own spiritual itinerary. They were intended to be more than that, and in Le Voyage du Centurion, particularly, we get a wide-ranging picture of a conversion that contains much that was central to the religious experience of the years from 1870 to 1914. The references to Islam, in particular, are complex and interesting; in them Psichari sums up in artistic form the experience of many of his contemporaries.

CARDIFF   R. GRIFFITHS

[1] Jacques Maritain, Preface to Le Voyage du Centurion, re-edition by Conard, 1947, p. iii.
[2] A.-M. Goïchon, Ernest Psichari, Paris, Conard, 1946, p. 285.
[3] Psichari, Letter to R. P. Barnabé Augier, 25 January 1914 (Lettres du Centurion, p. 290-1).
[4] Psichari, Letter to Charles Péguy, 4 January 1912 (Lettres du Centurion, p.,153).
[5] Including the author of the present article, in his book The Reactionary Revolution (Constable, 1966), p. 247-9.
[6] Goïchon, op. cit., p. 283.
[7] Psichari, Letter to R. P. Clérissac, 30 January 1914 (Lettres du Centurion, p. 294).
[8] Martine Astier Loufti, Littérature et Colonialisme, Mouton, 1971, p. 7.
[9] Le Comte Henry de Castries, L'Islam: impressions et études, p. 4-6.
[10] Psichari, L'Appel des Armes, 1913, p. 299-300.
[11] L'Appel des Armes, 1913, p. 289-290.
[12] Castries, L'Islam, p. 7.

[13] Foucauld, Letter to Castries, 15 July 1901.

[14] Castries, *L'Islam*, p. 245. The Abd-el-Kader quotation comes from his *Rappel à l'indifférent*, trad. Dugat, 1858.

[15] Ibid., p. 217.

[16] See, e.g., Michel Carrouges, *Charles de Foucauld, Explorateur mystique*, Cerf, 1954, and Denise & Robert Barrat, *Charles de Foucauld et la Fraternité*, Seuil, s.d.

[17] Foucauld to Castries, 8 July 1901.

[18] Foucauld to Castries, 15 July 1901.

[19] Foucauld to the Abbé Huvelin, 3 March 1898.

[20] op. cit., 1924.

[21] Patrick Heidsieck, *Lyautey*, Gallimard, s.d., p. 239.

[22] *Les Voix qui crient dans le désert*, 1920, p. 21.

[23] Au Lecteur, *Les Voix qui crient dans le désert*.

[24] See, e.g., Letter from Psichari to Maritain, 6 August 1908 (*Lettres du Centurion*, p. 34).

[25] See, e.g., Letters to his mother, 27 December 1909 and 2 April 1910. References to the mystical nature of the Moors, in later letters such as those to Barrès (15 June 1912) and to Péguy, are also made from outside, by an impressed observer. No hint is given of any such influence as that described in Castries or in the novels.

[26] *Les Voix qui crient dans le désert*, p. 19.

[27] *Le Voyage du Centurion*, p. 38.

[28] *Les Voix*, p. 21-28, *Le Voyage*, p. 38-43.

[29] *Les Voix*, p. 106.

[30] Ibid., p. 176.

[31] Ibid., p. 171.

[32] *L'Appel des Armes*, p. 288.

[33] *Voyage du Centurion*, p. 132.

[34] Letter to Mme Favre, 2 July 1911, *Lettres du Centurion*, pp. 145-46.

[35] Letter to Mme Favre, 26 August 1912, ibid., pp. 178-79.

[36] Psichari, Letter to Maritain, 15 June 1912.

[37] Psichari, Letter to Maurras, 1913. (In this letter Psichari mis-dates the earlier letter).

[38] Psichari, Letter to Monseigneur Jalabert, Bishop of Senegambia at Dakar, May 1912. (*Lettres du Centurion*, p. 183-4).

L. J. AUSTIN

HOW AMBIGUOUS IS MALLARMÉ?

Reflections on the Captive Swan

'Vos vers sur le cygne, que m'a communiqués Félix Fénéon, sont charmants, profonds, de pure vision complexe'. These words, from a letter by Francis Poictevin to Mallarmé, dated 15 January 1885, are the first recorded comment on Mallarmé's then still unpublished sonnet on the swan.[1] The 'Prose pour des Esseintes' had just appeared in the January 1885 number of *La Revue Indépendante*. On 19 January Mallarmé asked Fénéon, secretary of the review, to defer publication of his sonnet for a number or two;[2] Fénéon duly inserted it (with 'Quelle soie aux baumes de temps') in the March number. Teodor de Wyzewa gave a brief paraphrase of it in July 1886, in *La Vogue*, and from then onwards commentators from Vittorio Pica in 1891 to B. De Cornulier in 1978 have devoted articles to the poem, and the author of every monograph on Mallarmé, from Albert Mockel in 1899 to Malcolm Bowie in 1978, has scrutinized it with varying degrees of perspicacity and perspicuity.[3] There would be scant sense in adding yet another commentary were it not that some recent critical trends have produced such aberrant and sometimes extravagant results that the reformulation of a deliberately sober and straightforward reading — one open, however, to relevant complexities — may not be altogether inopportune.

Mallarmé is, of course, a 'difficult' author. Malcolm Bowie has admirably analysed the nature, and vindicated the virtues, of the teasing intricacies of his style. Mallarmé himself was never guilty of under-estimating his reader's intelligence. When Wyzewa published his commentary, Mallarmé is alleged to have asked: 'Pourquoi explique-t-il mes vers? Il ferait croire qu'ils sont obscurs'.[4] It was not until 1896, when he had only two years to live, that he publicly defended himself against the charge of obscurity, and launched a vigorous counter-attack upon his critics.[5] Once a writer has been branded as obscure, he remarked, he will not be able to utter a word without the public's saying it cannot understand him — even if the poor fellow has simply said: 'I am blowing my nose'. It is part of Mallarmé's irony that this apparently simple statement is expressed in a passage of quite remarkably contorted syntax, which calls for a little more than a cursory glance. The down-to-earth central proposition is hedged around with multiple qualifications and richly illustrative imagery. The obscure writer is ironically presented as a 'devotee of Darkness' ('suppôt d'Ombre', a facetious variant on the comminatory term 'suppôt de Satan'); the credulous mass of the public is personified as a female figure who rejects with a fan-like twitch of her skirts the idea that the real enigma might lie within her own being; the reassuring journalists are shown as exploiting public credulity for mercenary motives. All this is packed into one brief but complex sentence:

> Sa crédulité vis-à-vis de plusieurs qui la soulagent, en faisant affaire, bondit à l'excès: et le suppôt d'Ombre, d'eux désigné, ne placera un mot, dorénavant, qu'avec un secouement que ç'ait été elle, l'énigme, elle ne tranche, par un coup d'éventail de ses jupes: «Comprends pas!» — l'innocent annonçât-il se moucher.[6]

Mallarmé's final retort to his aggressors is to say that 'des contemporains ne savent pas lire'.[7] This stricture is still valid for some readers today, but for different reasons. Mallarmé conceded that his hostile contemporaries could read the newspapers, which had the advantage of not interrupting their usual preoccupations. But they could not read his writings, because they refused the necessary effort of interpretation. The position to-day is reversed. The present threat to the reading of Mallarmé is over-interpretation. The risk is not that lazy readers will not make a minimal mental effort to unravel the real complexities of Mallarmé's matching of syntax to meaning. It is that over-ingenious, over-subtle, over-sophisticated readers apply inappropriate and anachronistic methods to texts written in accordance with a different conception of the nature and function of literature.

Mallarmé was indeed sensitive to homophonies, and was capable of occasional, judicious paranomasia (but infinitely less than Shakespeare in his scintillating word-play). It is, however, doubtful whether any convincing examples of punning are to be found in his serious verse. Mallarmé was no Derrida, and had been in his grave for nearly seventy years before *L'Écriture et la différence* or *De la grammatologie* appeared. To be sure, the homophony of *Cygne* and *signe* would hardly have escaped Mallarmé; and I believe there is a point to be made here. But it is surely improbable, as a number of critics have asserted, that the poem as a whole is to be interpreted on this basis. Can the second line of the poem be read as

Va-t-il nous déchirer avec un coup des livres,

and is this reading really supported by the recurrence of this phonetic structure in line 6 in the word 'délivre'?[8] This suggestion comes from a recent article claiming to present a linguistic analysis of the poem, which leads to the conclusion that the self-reflection of language and literature is an essential component of the poem.[9] Can one accept the suggestion in another article that 'the swan introduced in the second quatrain must be a poem written previously'?[10] Yet another 'linguistic' reading subjects the sonnet to 'une petite cristallographie', based on the belief that 'les allitérations, homonymies, paranomases et anagrammes corrigent sans cesse l'arbitraire du signe';[11] this leads to extraordinary discoveries, such as the hidden wealth of meaning contained in the two words which open the sonnet:

LE VIERGE amène lever, levier, le vers, le verre (du glacier), l'hiver qu'on retrouve anagrammatisé dans *ivre* et *givre* et qui conduirait au Livre [. . .] Mais on provoquera d'autres rencontres, thématiques cette fois, en interrogeant quatre sèmes également contenus dans VIERGE: *verge* bien sûr, connotant le vœu d'érection, de déchirure, d'ensemencement, *vie* ensuite qui engendrera le deuxième épithète, *vivace*, et *air* qui définit l'aspiration de l'oiseau, *hier* enfin qui réfute sourdement la promesse triomphante du «bel aujourd'hui» et annonce dans cette mesure le dénouement de la pièce: aujourd'hui n'est qu'un autre hier, il n'apportera pas de délivrance.

Well may the commentator triumphantly affirm: 'il n'est donc pas exagéré de voir dans ce mot initial un très puissant générateur du sonnet'.[12] But the real triumph of the method is the revelation of 'la secrète noirceur du cygne', achieved by reshuffling the five letters composing the word 'cygne', to obtain, first 'nygce = 'nixe', and finally 'nux' (which apparently has the sense of the Latin 'nox'). Conclusion: 'La nuit, mais déchirée quelque part avec un coup d'aile ivre, par la Constellation blanc sur noir sur blanc du Si/Cygne'.[13]

None of these verbal acrobats has, to my knowledge, pointed out the elementary fact that the French word *signe* normally bears (as does its Latin etymon *signum*) the meaning of 'constellation', as in 'les signes du Zodiaque'. It seems probable, indeed virtually certain, that the capital given to the last word of the poem, 'Cygne', does carry with it the connotation of the constellation.[14] Problems arise when we seek to identify which of the five candidates at least known to classical mythology is the most relevant eponymous hero of the metamorphosis and apotheosis.[15] One commentator confidently affirms: 'The swan which is entitled to this identification is the swan in the guise of which Zeus appeared to Leda and which, having served its purpose, was metamorphosed into Cygnus. In this context, the word *autrefois* indicates a mythical past'. If doubts dawn in the reader's mind about the relevance of Leda's swan to the poem, will they be dispelled by the next revelatory insight? 'The adjective *magnifique*, which is almost the same as *magnificat*, and the verb *se délivre*, which suggests childbirth, allow [but do not oblige, fortunately] the reader to draw an analogy in contrast between the mythical swan and Mary. Both are god-carriers, both are virginal: the mythical swan is only a disguise. But Mary's delivery brings hope to mankind and she is carried to heaven by presumably feathered angels . . . The lifelike swan can but announce the lifeless, featherless constellation'.[16] Finally, if one should query the pious identification between the Virgin Mary and the swan, another critic obligingly suggests her adversary,

Satan-Lucifer, the Fallen Angel: 'after all, Dante's Satan is imprisoned in ice, but the upper part of his body, his three heads and his featherless, bat-like wings [like those of a swan?] are free to move'. The parallel, one may feel, is astounding.[17]

The question may now fairly be asked: is Mallarmé so difficult, obscure or ambiguous as to justify such widely divergent interpretations? Is a simpler reading not possible, setting the poem in the context of Mallarmé's work as a whole, and in the tradition within which he worked? No manuscript exists (apart from the photolithographic copy of the version in Mallarmé's supremely elegant calligraphy published by Édouard Dujardin in 1887, identical, save two commas removed, with the pre-original of March 1885). But it is thought by some critics to date from at least a decade earlier. I should think it is probably a thoroughly revised version of an early work, if not contemporary with the poems of the first *Parnasse contemporain*, at least with *Hérodiade*: the vocabulary and the imagery, especially that of the swan, the wing, the glacier-like cold of the skies, which are present in both the dialogue scene and the *Ouverture ancienne*, suggest this. Other details relate it to certain passages of *Igitur*.

In the 1887 edition of the *Poésies*, the ninth *Cahier* bore the heading *Derniers sonnets*, and began with the group of four regular sonnets which appeared in the same order and with the heading *Plusieurs sonnets* in the posthumous Deman edition of 1899, which Mallarmé had prepared himself with meticulous care. The four sonnets may not have been conceived as a unified whole, but they can be read as a sequence. Certainly the first two sonnets, 'Quand l'ombre . . .' and 'Le vierge, le vivace . . .' have as their fundamental theme a given mood of the poet. In each case, an old theme is treated in accordance with Mallarmé's mature poetic technique. They are still what he had called his *Parnasse contemporain* poems, namely 'révélations de son tempérament'; but they are no longer 'intuitives', as the early poems were: they are subtle and refined, and transform the text into a pretext, the ultimate goal being the 'rhythmical creation of beauty', as Poe had defined poetry. While they evoke the contrasting moods of a poet, the personality of the individual poet is only discreetly hinted at. Although the first poem begins clearly in the first person, and although the second sonnet uses the word 'nous' in the second line, both poems seem to end with a degree of generality or impersonality, the poet now speaking with the voice of what Valéry was to call 'le Moi pur'.

Without necessarily being a sequel to 'Quand l'ombre . . .', the second sonnet, 'Le vierge, le vivace . . .', is nevertheless related to it in several ways. The first had shown the wing of the Dream as having been folded within the poet, whose genius had then shed forth a great light. In the second, the poet identifies himself, in a quite traditional metaphor, with the swan, at least potentially capable of a 'coup d'aile ivre', and endowed with a 'pur éclat', a pure radiance, the source of his glory and of his suffering. But if the first sonnet expressed a moment of ecstasy, the second evokes a growing feeling of distress. The first proclaimed the possibility of denying space; the second shows the vengeance of space denied by the swan. The movement of the two sonnets is exactly opposite. The first moves from darkness to light, from affliction to triumph. The second begins in a great anticipated upward surge and finally congeals in lucid rigidity. Here is the text of the poem.

> Le vierge, le vivace et le bel aujourd'hui
> Va-t-il nous déchirer avec un coup d'aile ivre
> Ce lac dur oublié que hante sous le givre
> Le transparent glacier des vols qui n'ont pas fui!
>
> Un cygne d'autrefois se souvient que c'est lui
> Magnifique mais qui sans espoir se délivre
> Pour n'avoir pas chanté la région où vivre
> Quand du stérile hiver a resplendi l'ennui.
>
> Tout son col secouera cette blanche agonie
> Par l'espace infligée à l'oiseau qui le nie,
> Mais non l'horreur du sol où le plumage est pris.
>
> Fantôme qu'à ce lieu son pur éclat assigne,
> Il s'immobilise au songe froid de mépris
> Que vêt parmi l'exil inutile le Cygne.

The first quatrain should perhaps be taken as a passage of direct speech without quotation marks. The swan is speaking in the name of all swans: hence the 'nous'. In the second quatrain, the poet intervenes in order to comment on this exultant exordium cut across by anxious questioning and to draw conclusions from it. (This same technique is probably used in the following sonnet, on the sunset).

The movement of the first quatrain is indeed 'magnifique'. The first line powerfully evokes the feelings and sensations noted by Baudelaire in the opening of the *Poème du Haschisch*, where, recalling the 'baromètre spirituel' of Hoffman, he describes 'de belles saisons, d'heureuses journées, de délicieuses minutes' and declares: 'il est des jours où l'homme s'éveille avec un génie jeune et vigoureux'.[18] Mallarmé, by relegating the noun to the end of the line, and by telling as it were the beads of the three exceptionally evocative epithets, once again conveys first the sensation, the effect produced, before naming the object.[19] The piercing absolutism of 'vierge', is followed by the echo and expansion of 'vivace' (the new and the lasting) and the conclusion on a monosyllable of a tellingly general kind 'bel'. The long-drawn-out noun 'aujourd'hui',[20] neither past nor present but *now*, evokes the intense moment. The feeling of the purity of the day still intact and full of potentiality, of its lasting strength, the certainty that the weather is 'set fair': these impressions are magically caught in these words, first by their meaning, but also by the rhythm of the line, which, after the momentary pause on 'vierge' and the dancing alliterations in [v], then unfolds into a cry of joy in 'et le bel aujourd'hui', with the word 'bel' thrown into strong relief by its position. This whole line perfectly illustrates Mallarmé's conception of the line of poetry as 'un mot total, neuf, étranger à la langue et comme incantatoire'.[21] The impetus of the opening continues through the second line and the image of the 'coup d'aile ivre', with an even more subtle music built up around the triple alliteration [v] and the double alliteration in [l] and [d] and [k], and the assonance balancing 'nous' and 'coup' at each end of the line. But the question in 'Va-t-il' begins to slow down the movement, and with the third line we realize that the 'bel aujourd'hui' is illuminating a desolate landscape: a frozen lake covered with hoar-frost, motionless but having within it the potentiality of movement of a glacier.[22] The ice holds captive the strokes of the wing which have not taken place, the flights that have not flown. The lake frozen hard is 'oublié', to be taken quite literally as 'forgotten';[23] the swan is imagined as having sunk into oblivion until the new day recalls him to consciousness and he remembers his plight. The symmetry of 'oublié' and 'se souvient' is striking, but has often been overlooked.

The second quatrain suggests that these are the thoughts of a swan awaking and wondering if this new day will at last free him from his prison of ice. Here Gautier's lines have often been pertinently quoted:

> Un cygne s'est pris en nageant
> Dans le bassin des Tuileries . . .

or one may remember Baudelaire's lines from 'L'Irrémédiable':

> Un navire pris dans le pôle,
> Comme en un piège de cristal . . .

For the swan too is caught in a crystal trap. It is 'un cygne d'autrefois', suggesting that it has awakened from a long sleep, whence the 'lac dur oublié' (with perhaps also a suggestion of the solitude of the swan's struggle, forgotten by others). The return of memories with growing awareness is conveyed with extreme concision, suggesting the more developed beginning of *L'Après-midi d'un Faune*, of Proust's novel, or Valéry's *La Jeune Parque*. In this moment of awakening, he remembers both his own being a swan, and then that the icy grip of winter caught him before he had sung his song of the ideal region in which we should dwell:

the swan was captured before he gave his 'swan song'. So he is now striving to set himself free, in a magnificent but already desperate surge of final energy. The rest of the sonnet will elucidate this despair tempered with disdainful defiance. 'La région où vivre' suggests the ideal realm evoked in 'Toast funèbre', and the land, both existing on no map but certain in the imagination, in 'Prose pour des Esseintes': the land of the funeral oration on Villiers de l'Isle-Adam: 'ce pays prestigieux toujours par lui habité et maintenant surtout, car il n'est pas'.[24]

For Mallarmé as for Baudelaire, the favourable moment for singing of this ideal realm was not the spring or summer, but

L'hiver, saison de l'art serein, l'hiver lucide.

('Renouveau').

The poet of 'Renouveau' waited until his 'ennui' arose. The poetic imagination glories in composing at opposite seasons, as Baudelaire proclaimed in 'Paysage':

Et quand viendra l'hiver aux neiges monotones,
Je fermerai partout portières et volets
Pour bâtir dans la nuit mes féeriques palais . . .
Car je serai plongé dans cette volupté
D'évoquer le Printemps avec ma volonté,
De tirer un soleil de mon cœur, et de faire
De mes pensers brûlants une tiède atmosphère.[25]

Had the swan delayed his migration to the last moment, and been caught by the sudden onset of winter?

The tercets fix the limits of possible escape. The contrast between 'espace' and 'sol' may suggest that the swan can intellectually shake off the metaphysical temptations and the suffering they cause (cf. 'L'Azur'), but he is still caught in the contingent world. Or again, the swan has denied space; but space can hold his body captive; only his head remains free. This movement of partial liberation and inescapable bondage is conveyed exclusively in terms of the imprisoned swan.[26] The long neck is suggested by '*Tout* son col', the mortal frost by 'cette blanche agonie', with its blend of concrete and abstract. The confident certainty of intellectual liberation is expressed by the prediction of the future tense: 'secouera'. The sense of the vindictive, if partial, triumph of the world of space that has been rashly denied is reinforced by certain recurrent patterns of sound, especially [i] and [s] in the line:

Par l'espace infligée à l'oiseau qui le nie.

This triumph is defined in the last line of the first tercet, where again 'l'horreur du sol' juxtaposes abstract and concrete.

The last tercet brings the vast potential movement to a standstill. Realizing the impossibility of complete escape, and realizing too that his pure radiance as the citizen of 'la région où vivre' condemns him to being but a phantom on earth (it is as a phantom that he is assigned to this place where he can be only the shadow of himself), the great bird ceases to struggle, his convulsive gestures cease, and he stops still and motionless, enveloping himself in the icily contemptuous contemplation that is his one remaining means of triumph over the insufficiencies whether of self or of circumstance. The definite article, and the capital letter to the final word, replacing the indefinite article and small letter by which the swan was introduced in 1.5, raise the particular instance to the level of universality and impersonality, and suggest both the cold remoteness of the star and the apotheosis symbolized by the Constellation.

In so far as the sonnet expresses a personal feeling, it may well be related to Mallarmé's struggles, during the winters of 1865 to 1867, with the composition of *Hérodiade*, conceived as the Overture of his *Grand Œuvre*, the 'swan-song' of the universe. The swan's attitude of proud and disdainful withdrawal and self-sufficiency is akin to that of the character Hérodiade, and the image of the swan is prominent in the 'Ouverture ancienne' of the poem; and the sharp dichotomy of body and mind evoked in the sonnet underlies the 'Cantique de saint Jean', where the Saint's mind is set free by his execution:

> Et ma tête surgie
> Solitaire vigie . . .
>
> Plutôt refoule ou tranche
> Les anciens désaccords
> Avec le corps . . .

Here the movement is close to that of the line:

> Tout son col secouera cette blanche agonie . . .

Beyond these more personal applications, the poem undeniably echoes and deepens familiar Romantic themes concerning the isolation of the poet in his ivory tower, and his exile on earth amid his uncomprehending fellow-men, such as are to be found in Lamartine and Vigny and the Baudelaire of 'Bénédiction' and 'L'Albatros'. But Mallarmé, here as elsewhere, sees both sides: he is aware of inner shortcomings as well as of the world's inadequacies. To stress either side to the exclusion of the other is to fall equally short of an adequate interpretation of these lines on the swan, which Poictevin so finely described as 'charmants, profonds, de pure vision complexe.' The originality of the sonnet lies in this two-sidedness, in the sharp intensity with which sensations are expressed, giving concrete richness to the symbols, and in the extraordinarily subtle patterning of the verse. It is immediately apparent, and has often been stressed, that the sonnet is built up essentially on the tense, bright, sharp and clear front vowel [i].[27] Not only are all the rhymes in [i], but this sound recurs with obsessive persistency in every line save three, where a momentary respite makes the return of the dominant sound all the more effective when it is again multiplied in the last two lines. Meanwhile a climax has been reached in the line

> Magnifique mais qui sans espoir se délivre,

with *qui* at the hemistitch, and dislocation of the line at its strongest in this sudden movement from magnificence to struggle without hope. The superb ending to the sonnet plays an air on [i], on the liquid [l], and on the [ə]:

> . . . [ex]il inutile le Cygne.

This is also the sonnet of whiteness: the swan, the glacier, the frost. There is not a single suggestion of any colour. Lastly, it is the sonnet of congealed movement, of a great potential soaring flight which remains forever frustrated. The predominance of the sound of [i] should not, moreover, mask the subtle complexity of the other assonances and alliterations, and of the sound-patterning generally: in the first quatrain [v] predominates; in the second, [s], as also in the tercets. And the rear vowel [ɔ] cuts across the prevalent pattern of [i] in the three closed monosyllables 'vol', 'sol' and 'col', with perhaps a suggestion of the repeated beating of the wing. (The suggestiveness of the shape of the letters can be, and has been, much exaggerated: it is perhaps not too fanciful to see in the repeated letter 'v' a suggestion of a wing).[28]

Critics have brought out how the wintry reverie, the metaphors of ice and snow, have numerous echoes in Mallarmé's correspondence for the years 1864 to 1870, and the associations *miroir-glace-froid*, and *glace-horreur* are frequent. For example:

> Après quelques jours de tension spirituelle dans un appartement, je me congèle et me mire dans le diamant de cette glace, jusqu'à une agonie, puis, quand je veux me revivifier au soleil de la terre, il me fond . . .[29]

And again:

> Le miroir qui m'a réfléchi l'Etre a été le plus souvent l'Horreur et vous devinez si j'expie cruellement ce diamant des Nuits innommées.[30]

One passage of *Igitur* in particular combines the three notions of *horreur*, *fantôme* and *glace*.[31]

But there is a little-quoted passage of the letter to Lefébure quoted above[32] in which Mallarmé plays humorous variations on symbolic birds: these indirectly illuminate the imaginative processes underlying the writing of this sonnet, and especially the transition from the first to the second quatrain:

> Comment allez-vous? Mélancolique cigogne des lacs immobiles, votre âme ne se voit-elle pas apparaître, en leur miroir, avec trop d'ennui — qui troublant de son confus crépuscule le charme magique et pur, *vous rappelle que c'est votre corps* qui, sur une patte, l'autre repliée malade en vos plumes, se tient, abandonné? *Revenu au sentiment de la réalité*, écoutez la voix gutturale et amie d'un autre vieux plumage, héron et corbeau à la fois, qui s'abat près de vous. Pourvu que tout ce tableau ne disparaisse pas, pour vous, dans les frissons et les rides atroces de la souffrance! Avant de nous laisser aller à notre murmure, vraie causerie d'oiseaux pareils aux roseaux, et mêlés à leur vague stupeur *lorsque nous revenons de notre fixité sur l'étang du rêve à la vie* — sur l'étang du rêve où nous ne pêchons jamais que notre propre image, sans songer aux écailles d'argent des poissons! — demandons-nous cependant comment nous y sommes, dans cette vie![33]

What is most striking here, apart from the imaginative identification with the birds, is the return to the sense of existence after a prolonged period of motionless meditation. In the sonnet, of course, this is condensed into a few lines of evocative verse. And the anguished mood of the passages quoted above from *Igitur* and the *Correspondance*, and of similar passages that could also be cited, gives way in the sonnet to the masterful serenity which characterises Mallarmé's maturity. The explicit theme of the sonnet may well be one of anguished frustration. But, by the supreme paradox of art, the tragic note on which the poem ends — 'inutile le Cygne' — is belied by the triumph of expression which the poem, by its existence, proclaims.[34]

CAMBRIDGE   L. J. AUSTIN

[1] *Documents Stéphane Mallarmé*, IV, présentés par Carl Paul Barbier, Paris, Nizet, 1973, p. 361.

[2] Stéphane Mallarmé, *Correspondance*, IV, éd H. Mondor et L. J. Austin, Paris, Gallimard, 1973, p. 482 (fragment; the full text will appear in vol. V). Vol. I (1959) was edited by H. Mondor and J.-P. Richard; it is quoted below as *Corr.* I.

[3] The articles and books referred to in this sentence are as follows. Vittorio Pica, 'Les Modernes Byzantins. — Stéphane Mallarmé', *La Revue indépendante*, t. XVIII, n° 52, février 1891, pp. 173-215; n° 53, mars 1891, pp. 316-360; the sonnet is discussed on p. 323. — B. de Cornulier, *Studi Francesi*, n° 64, gennaio-aprile 1978, pp. 59-75. — Albert Mockel, *Stéphane Mallarmé. Un Héros*. Paris, Mercure de France, 1899, pp. 52-56. — Malcolm Bowie, *Mallarmé and the Art of Being Difficult*, Cambridge University Press, 1978, pp. 9-13, gives a particularly sensitive and intelligent reading of the poem. — Space precludes even

attempting a full list here. Readers are referred, for the fullest bibliography to date, to Jean-Pierre Richard: *L'Univers imaginaire de Mallarmé*, Paris, Seuil, 1961, pp. 623-644; see Richard's own penetrating analysis of the poem, pp. 251-256, 276-279.   Of special value among studies published since 1961 are A. R. Chisholm, in *French Studies*, XVI (1962), pp. 359-363; Bernard Weinberg, in *The Limits of Symbolism*, Chicago University Press, 1966, pp. 170-186; E. Noulet, *Vingt poèmes de Stéphane Mallarmé*, Geneva, Droz, 1967, pp. 130-144, an influential study first published in *L'Œuvre poétique de Stéphane Mallarmé, ib., id.*, 1940, and which replaced the traditional one-sided view of the poem by a new, but, in its turn, one-sided interpretation. (There are three serious misprints in the text of the poem, p. 130, e.g. 1.11, 'honneur' for 'horreur'); Alphonse Bouvet, 'Rhétorique, grammaire et poésie', *Istituto Universitario Orientale. Annali. Sezione Romanza*, XII, 1, 1970, pp. 35-42. See also Charles Chadwick 'Mallarmé et ses critiques', in the proceedings of the *Colloque Mallarmé (Glasgow — Novembre 1973) en l'honneur d'Austin Gill*, texte établi par Carl P. Barbier, Paris, Nizet, 1975, pp. 71-82, and, pp. 83-102, the wide-ranging discussion which followed and in which fifteen speakers participated (see, for example, the remarks by the sixteenth-century specialist, Carol Clark, pp. 86-89, etc.).   The measure of *disagreement* revealed by the discussion is striking.   References to other books and articles discussed are given below.
⁴ H. Mondor, *Vie de Mallarmé*, one-vol. edition, Paris, Gallimard, 1946 (first published 1941), p. 645.
⁵ 'Le Mystère, dans les Lettres', *Revue Blanche*, XI, septembre 1896, pp. 214-218; reproduced in the Pléiade edition, Stéphane Mallarmé, *Œuvres complètes*, ed. H. Mondor et G. Jean Aubry, Paris, Gallimard, rev. ed. 1956, pp. 382-387 (subsequently referred to as *OC*).
⁶ *OC*, p. 385. The pre-original version has three interesting variants: 'à l'infini', for 'à l'excès'; 'selon eux', for 'd'eux'; 'l'arcane', for 'l'énigme'.
⁷ *OC*, p. 387.
⁸ Gerhard Goebel, 'Le signe du Cygne. Zur negativen Poetik Mallarmés', *Lendemains*, II, 6, Januar 1977, p. 111-124.   Goebel suggests 'ent-bucht' as a translation of 'se dé-livre' (p. 116).
⁹ See the summary in French at the end of Goebel's article, p. 124.
¹⁰ Robert Champigny, 'The *Swan* and the Question of Pure Poetry', *L'Esprit Créateur*, Vol. I, No. 3, Fall 1961, special number on *Stéphane Mallarmé*, p. 153.
¹¹ Daniel Bougnoux, 'L'Éclat du signe', *Littérature*, IV, 14 (mai 1974), pp. 83-93 (this ref. p. 83).
¹² Bougnoux, p. 85.
¹³ Bougnoux, p. 93.
¹⁴ See Alan Boase, in *The Poetry of France*, London, Methuen, 1952, p. xliv, followed by J. R. Lawler, p. 80 of his 'reading' of the sonnet in *AUMLA*, N⁰ 8, November 1958, pp. 78-83.   At the Glasgow conference in honour of Austin Gill, the late Carl Barbier rightly drew attention to the difficulty of distinguishing between small 'c' and capital 'C' in Mallarmé's manuscripts (see *Colloque Mallarmé*, p. 83-84). But he seemed unaware of the fact that, in the photolithographic edition of his *Poésies*, published by É. Dujardin in 1887, Mallarmé's calligraphic manuscript shows clearly that he had deliberately transformed a small 'c' into a capital 'C' for the last word of the poem, thereby confirming the reading of the pre-original printed version published in *La Revue indépendante* (and indeed all the printed versions seen through the press by Mallarmé in his lifetime).
¹⁵ See Pierre Grimal, *Dictionnaire de la mythologie grecque et romaine*, 2ᵉ ed., Paris, PUF, 1958, pp. 108-110.   The association of the swan with Apollo, with poets and poetry, and with singing only at the point of death is so traditional that it is idle to seek a single specific source. The *loci classici*, with which Mallarmé would be familiar from his Latin studies at the Lycée de Sens, are the passages in Virgil's *Aeneid* and Ovid's *Metamorphoses* evoking the Ligurian king Cycnus. He was endowed by Apollo with the gift of sweet song. While singing a threnody for his beloved Phaethon when he had been stricken by the thunderbolt of Zeus, Cycnus was transformed into a Swan and flew into the stars; there he became the constellation which immortalizes his name. These are Virgil's lines (*Aeneid*, X, 189-193):

> manque ferunt luctu Cycnum Phaethontis amati,
> populeas inter frondes umbramque sororum
> dum canit et maestum Musa solatur amorem,
> canentem molli pluma dixisse senectem,
> linquantem terras et sidera voce petentem.

(For they say that Cycnus, mourning for his beloved Phaethon, while he sang beneath the shady leaves of the poplar trees that had once been his sisters and sought solace in music for his tragic love, became clad with soft plumage as if by the white hairs of old age, and leaving the world, soared as he sang into the stars). See also Servius's gloss (quoted in W. H. Roscher, *loc. cit.*); Ovid, *Metamorphoses*, II, 367 ff; Hyginus, *Fables*, no. 154.

Among the most famous passages on the Swan in French poetry, certainly familiar to Mallarmé, who loved Ronsard, are these lines from the sonnet in *Les Derniers vers*:

> Il faut laisser maisons et vergers et jardins,
> Vaisselles et vaisseaux que l'artisan burine,
> Et chanter son obsèque en la façon du Cygne,
> Qui chante son trépas sur les bors Maeandrins.
>
> C'est fait, j'ay dévidé le cours de mes destins,
> J'ay vescu, j'ay rendu mon nom nom assez insigne,
> Ma plume vole au Ciel pour estre quelque signe . . .

(Ronsard, *Œuvres complètes*, texte établi et annoté par Gustave Cohen (Bibliothèque de la Pléiade), Paris, Gallimard, 1938, vol. II, p. 637).

[16] R. Champigny, *art. cit.*, p. 150. The swan concerned is not one of the five listed by Grimal. In the oldest form of this legend, it was not Leda, but Nemesis, whom Zeus seduced in the form of a swan when she had changed into a goose. See W. H. Roscher, *Ausführliches Lexicon der griechischen und römischen Mythologie*, Leipzig, Teubner, 1890-1897, t. II, cols. 1698-1699.

[17] Alexander Fischler, 'The Ghost-making Process in Mallarmé's "Le vierge, le vivace", "Toast funèbre", and "Quand l'ombre menaça"', *Symposium*, XX, 3, Fall 1966, pp. 306-320.

[18] Baudelaire, *Œuvres complètes*, I, ed. Claude Pichois, (Bibliothèque de la Pléiade), Paris, Gallimard, 1975, p. 400.

[19] See L. J. Austin, 'The Mystery of a Name', *L'Esprit Créateur*, I, 3, Fall 1961, pp. 130-138.

[20] I regard as completely unacceptable the suggestion by B. de Cornulier (see n. 3 above) that 'aujourd'hui' is an adverb, and that 'vierge', 'vivace' and 'bel' (= 'beau') are adjectival nouns. It is not in accordance with French usage to take 'le vierge' as a noun (the same applies to 'la nue', frequently misinterpreted as a naked woman by commentators). — This is one point I would query in Malcolm Bowie's comments on the poem, when he says: 'we have read seven words of the poem before we are able to know that a male virgin and a male sprite are not among the characters in the drama. But by the time "vierge" and "vivace" have assumed their rightful status as adjectives (and not adjectival nouns), these phantom presences have already appeared on the stage'. (*Op. laud.*, pp. 10-11). Each of Mallarmé's poems, as Alan Boase reminds us, needs to be apprehended as a whole: 'His poems only fully reveal themselves when we know them almost by heart and have, as it were, a whole sonnet present in our mind at once' (*The Poetry of France*, vol. III, 1800-1900, Methuen, 2nd ed., 1967, p. xliv).

[21] *OC*, pp. 368, 858.

[22] See the article by A. R. Chisholm (ref. in n. 3 above), p. 363: 'a glacier, as geologists had discovered, long before the sonnet was written, is a mass of latent movement'.

[23] The etymological meaning of 'livid' would seem to be pleonastic, given the white colouring of 'givre' (see Charles Chassé, *Les Clefs de Mallarmé*, Paris, Aubier, 1954, pp. 121, 151-152, who first suggested this sense of the word).

[24] *OC*, p. 510. — Alphonse Bouvet makes the interesting suggestion (p. 36 of *art. cit.*, n. 3 above), that there may be an allusion here to 'la légende delphique et délienne d'Apollon Hyperboréen: 'Apollon quittait chaque année ses sanctuaires de la Grèce, pour gagner, sur un char attelé de cygnes, la lointaine Hyperborée, «royaume de l'éternelle lumière», où il vivait une partie de l'année «au milieu d'un peuple d'hommes heureux et justes, occupés à chanter ses louanges». Et ce départ était pleuré à l'automne par les hymnes de

l'*apodèmia*, en attendant les hymnes d'appel (*klètikoi*) qui, au printemps, salueraient son retour (*épidèmia*)'. These hymns, however, were sung by priests, not swans, and A. Bouvert is obliged to some jugglery to get over this difficulty. — The *Observer* of Sunday, 13 January 1980, had a photograph of the migratory swan Lancelot who for the last seventeen years has spent the summer in Siberia and the winter in England. Without indulging in absurdly naïve 'realistic' considerations, one may find this piece of zoological lore suggestive.

[25] Baudelaire, *op. cit.*, p. 82.

[26] Cf. Malcolm Bowie, *op. cit.*, p. 13: 'And these awesome generalities are checked, kept in focus and given delicate gradations of sensuous appeal by a single complex image: the image not of a poet with the emblems of his craft, but of the white plumed and muscular neck of an ice-bound swan'. — Cf. also André Rouveyre, 'Mallarmé, Matisse et le Cygne', *Mallarmé*, special number of *Le Point*, XXIX-XXX, Février-Avril 1944, pp. 55-57, where Matisse's admirable illustrations to the poem are discussed (and reproduced pp. 58-61).

[27] See Jacques Duchesne-Guillemin, 'Au sujet du «divin Cygne»', *Mercure de France*, 1er septembre 1948, pp. 62-68, and 'Encore le divin Cygne' (the same article), in *Stéphane Mallarmé*, special number of *Empreintes*, No. 5, novembre-décembre 1948, pp. 44-50; also Cl. Estève, *Études philosophiques sur l'expression littéraire*, Paris, Vrin, 1939, pp. 142-163. A. R. Chisholm gives an admirable analysis of 'vocalic and consonantal effects' (*art. cit.*, p. 362).

[28] A point made by Daniel Bougnoux, *art. cit.*, p. 85. — Robert Greer Cohn, *Toward the poems of Mallarmé*, Berkeley and Los Angeles, University of California Press, 1965, p. 127, detects other suggestions: 'The v's of *vierge* and *vivace*, and of other words, are sharp, cutting, by the outer shape and sound, like saw-teeth or icicles (in this respect they go with the tearing wing thrust). But, oddly [indeed!], they also add a quality of virginal femininity by the inner shape of receptacle (see Letter Table: v and w)'. — The pages in Cohn's book on this sonnet (pp. 124-132) bring together many interesting parallels from Mallarmé's work as a whole; his own comments are sometimes suggestive, sometimes wildly fanciful. He aptly comments (p. 131) on the Matisse illustrations mentioned in n. 26 above.

[29] *Corr.* I, p. 247 (letter to Eugène Lefébure, 17 May 1867).

[30] *Corr.* I, p. 259 (letter to Villiers de L'Isle-Adam, 24 September, 1867).

[31] *OC*, p. 441.

[32] See n. 29 above.

[33] *Corr.* I, p. 244-245 (my italics).

[34] This poem, like so many others by Mallarmé, ends with the shining glory of a constellation or a star. One thinks of the end of Valéry's 'Ode secrète', in which some have seen a veiled hommage to Mallarmé:

> Fin suprême, étincellement
> Qui, par les Monstres et les Dieux,
> Proclame universellement
> Les grands actes qui sont aux Cieux!

MUSIC, MATHEMATICS AND *LA JEUNE PARQUE*[1]

La musique qui est en moi,
La musique qui est dans le silence, en puissance
qu'elle vienne et m'étonne (C II, 1267; 1916-1917).

Valéry believed, like the Pythagoreans, that music and mind are bound together by mathematical links. When we listen to music:

Nous savons aussitôt qu'il existe en nous-mêmes un 'univers' de relations possibles, dans lecquel la Musique nous permet et nous contraint de nous soutenir quelque temps, — comme si la succession de sensations choisies et commensurables nous faisait vivre une vie de qualité supérieure et alimentait d'énergie pure notre durée . . . (II, 1313).

Je pose que: La Science mathématique dégagée de ses applications telles que la géométrie, l'arithmétique écrite etc. et réduite à l'algèbre, c'est-à-dire à l'analyse des transformations d'un être purement différentiel, composé d'éléments homogènes — est le plus fidèle document des propriétés de groupement, de disjonction et de variation de l'esprit (C I, 775, 1894).

Mathematics deals with relations between numbers; these relations are commensurable. Music deals with relations between pitches, tones and rhythms. A pitch is a frequency; a tone is a set of harmonics; rhythm is traditionally 'number', and was analysed as such by Augustine and Boethius. Though rhythm is by no means as readily 'numerable' as pitch and tone, Valéry accepts that it is a matter of relations that *should* be mathematically expressible. So musical relations are 'commensurable'. Valéry then makes a Pythagorean leap into the conviction that mental states, like musical structures, are combinations of commensurable elements; these he calls 'faits mentaux purs'. They are more like images than concepts — units of meaning involving body as much as mind, the sensible as much as the intelligible. The senses affect the nerves, which stimulate the 'psyche' — compounded of physical and mental — to respond with a pattern of 'faits mentaux purs'; this pattern determines the nature of consciousness. Within the psyche is the 'moi pur', the intellectual element, the patterning power itself. Like the 'mind' (nous) of the Greek tradition, it is both passive and active; responsive to the stimulus of the sensible world, projecting meaning into it, tending ideally to the extreme self-consciousness which would be awareness of its own capacity for generating meaning. The 'moi pur' is the seat of 'divinity' as Valéry understands it.

Music, he argues, is the equivalent at once of a state of mind and of a system of relations. Awareness of the relations may help the 'moi pur' to become more clearly conscious of itself. But the sound of music acts upon the central nervous system more directly and more vividly than do the sensations the soul receives from the sensible world; it can make our soul live, in imagination, experiences as powerful and strange as any that real life could ever offer, and can draw out of us awarenesses that, without music, we might never know in real life. The sense of power in music is therefore ambivalent. It can mean awareness of the power of mind to create significant form — a power provided by the composer and intuited by the informed listener; but it can be also the *illusion* of power as the mind *surrenders* to the feeling in the music, and lives more intensely instead of removing itself from the emotions of life through intuition of form. Music moreover can mislead us into supposing that intuition of form corresponds to some transcendent reality; that through it the mind is becoming aware of a 'divinity' other than that of the intuiting intellect itself. Music can create a metaphysical illusion. Worse still, it can be used to promote Christian faith. Like Plotinus and Augustine Valéry is wary of music's power to provide strong life-substitutes; unlike them he mistrusts also what most of the Symbolists prized — its magical suggestion of another world than this.

This ought, on the face of it, to lead Valéry into a preference for 'formal' over 'expressive' music. He often, in the *Cahiers*, thinks in terms of such a distinction. Bach principally, and Mozart largely, belong to the 'formal' group; Wagner mainly, Berlioz to some extent, belong to the 'expressive' group. Aware of the reaction against Wagnerism among the composers of his time, Valéry notes more than once that musicians do not like the second group as much as the first. At one point he even suggests that the historical development of music might have happened in the reverse direction — Bach's music arising out of Wagner's as a simplified, more schematized kind of musical form.

But for all his reservations about the metaphysical misuse of Wagner's music — and the metaphysical misuse of music by Wagner himself in the religious persuasiveness of *Parsifal* — the *Cahiers* show clearly that when Valéry pondered the power of music, Wagner was his model and his spiritual master. He sometimes rebels against this domination, and writes of 'la perfide musique'; or points out that music acts more upon the 'personality', as he calls the part of himself involved in living, than upon the 'moi pur'. There are bursts of what looks like bad temper, like Faust's cry in *Le Solitaire* that he is 'excédé d'être une créature'; for a creature is what Valéry's imagination becomes under Wagner's — and sometimes Beethoven's — spell. But he always comes back to acceptance of the fascination, and to admiration for Wagner's insight into affectivity and his ability to articulate it in the language of music.

For Valéry's notion of form is centred on form as expression. He sometimes uses the word 'composition' for the notion of 'form' in the more usual sense of 'the way the parts of the poem are put together'; but this is still a different notion from the classical 'beginning, middle and end' or the musical 'ABA¹B¹A'. 'Form' is finding symbols for a particular state of mind and finding how to manipulate those symbols to 'modulate' from one state of mind to another, thus miming the 'durée' of consciousness. Sometimes his 'moi pur' seems to be pure mind — consciousness divorced from what it is conscious of. But this is uncharacteristic. Mainly Valéry supposes, like Sartre, that consciousness is conscious of something; and, unlike Sartre, he supposes that the informing power of the 'moi pur' is at its most effective when it brings the organic relationships of the body into consciousness or — putting the same thing another way — when the conscious self can say, like the Parque:

> Je me voyais me voir, sinueuse, et dorais
> De regards en regards, mes profondes forêts (I, 97).

This could come about, Valéry holds, if what are now 'inarticulate' expressions of sensation-affectivity could be articulated; if a perfect language, with an alphabet of symbols exactly corresponding to the 'faits mentaux purs' could be created. And what Valéry most admires in Wagner is that his musical language can articulate the inexpressible; can unite 'physis' and 'psyche' more completely thereby; can extend 'resonance' into such subtle and complex musical figures that consciousness penetrates into the lowest reaches of 'being'. Wagner's listener, ideally, 'lives' in imagination the 'durée' of his own physiology and intuits its organic form, which is analogous to, if not identical with, the informing power of the 'moi pur'.

Admiration perpétuelle

Dans Wagner — je n'admire jamais assez la *suite* incomparable des thèmes, situations — et leurs combinaisons ou déductions de tout le IIIme acte de *Valkyrie*. Il y a 50 ans que je ne puis me lasser de cette extraordinaire magnificence génératrice — Tous les plans de passion et d'action et les passages de l'un à l'autre — à la température du 'Sublime' — Tout travaille.

Et l'on y trouve, chose inouïe, — les changements d'état des 'personnages' comme fonctions du flux d'énergie sonore — qui leur est comme une sève, une raison d'être, se manifeste par eux, s'oppose à lui-même, se fait colère, tendresse, vouloir, tellement que . . . la 'pensée' (supposée) devient une des variables de cette vie du système de l'œuvre! C'est le triomphe de la possession totale des moyens et des forces d'application à un but absolument connu.

Pour que l'opinion des connaisseurs en musique soit bien établie, il faudrait que l'on puisse considérer les *possibilités de W(agner)* comme cas particuliers des *possibilités* de Bach —?

Imagination W(agner) de physico-mathématique.

Imagination B(ach) de math(ématique) pure — formes.

W(agner) a créé un espace, un champ. Ici se poserait le grand problème de l'enchaînement — *vrai de tous les arts* (C II, 980, 1941).

Les timbres, ici, ne sont pas seulement *couleurs* mais modification des *thèmes*. Chef-d'œuvre de synthèse psychophysique (C II, 982, 1943).

Valéry's position is a retreat from the contention that music transports the soul into a state of being outside the sensible world, but he keeps the Pythagorean conviction of an exact correspondence between mathematical structure and expressive effect. Over this, as over the importance of imagination in thinking, he differs from Descartes. Descartes knows all about the mathematics of consonance and of the diatonic scale; but a composer, in his view, is *not* a calculator:

Les calculs ne servent que pour montrer quelles consonances sont les plus simples ou si vous voulez les plus douces et parfaites, mais non pas les plus agréables . . . C'est autre chose de dire qu'une consonance est plus douce qu'une autre, autre chose de dire qu'elle est plus agréable. Car tout le monde sait que le miel est plus doux que les olives, et toutefois force gens aimeront mieux manger des olives que du miel (Letters to Mersenne, January and March 1630).

Over this issue musicians still differ among themselves about the importance of the mathematics of music in its composition and its expressive effect. A musical score tells the musicians to make the air vibrate in a wave-pattern which can be broken down, by Fourier analysis, into these regular frequencies, to be produced by these instruments, each of which has its own overtone-producing characteristics, for these periods of time. Thus, Valéry would hold, the whole experience is reducible to pure number. It becomes a system of intelligible relations: and this system of intelligible relations is the equivalent of a complete psychic experience.

On the other hand one can say that the diatonic scale and the harmonic system based on key-signatures and the various positions of the common chord provide a conventional language which the composer learns to use with no more 'calculation' than is involved in the observance of the conventions. The conventions themselves are more 'numerical' than those of the poet: but the composer is no more number-conscious in his use of them.

Valéry believed firmly that the composer can calculate his effects, as Poe said the poet should do; and bewailed, when he returned to poetry, the poet's lack of a technique based on a commensurable system like the musical scale. A proper psychology would analyse states of sensibility into discrete 'faits mentaux purs' which would be like the x's and y's of the mathematician's expressions. The flow of sensibility which is the experience of music is controlled by discrete sounds; the flow of meaning in the operations of the mathematician is symbolized in the 'transformations' and 'substitutions' which result from a limited number of operations, for instance 'factorize', 'multiply out', 'regroup'. To take a simple example: $(ax + by)^2 + (ay - bx)^2 = a^2(x^2 + y^2) + b^2(x^2 + y^2) = (a^2 + b^2)(x^2 + y^2)$. What does it matter, to the pure mathematician engaged in manipulating his expression, what these variables really stand for? He is interested only in manipulating them, in the laws which govern the shift from one form of the expression to another; in, perhaps, the relative elegance, or aesthetic perfection of one form as compared with another — its symmetry, its balance, its tidiness. *La Jeune Parque* was to try and bring verbal expression into line with music and, as far as possible, with mathematics.

As far as possible. Valéry never managed to analyze out the 'faits mentaux purs' that would prove 'commensurable' like the notes and rhythms of music or the number that gives meaning to the mathematician's symbols.

Si le poète pouvait arriver à construire des œuvres . . . où les relations des significations seraient elles-mêmes perpétuellement pareilles à des rapports harmoniques, *où la transmutation des pensées les unes dans les autres paraîtrait plus importante que toute pensée*, où le jeu des figures contiendrait la réalité du sujet, — alors l'on pourrait parler de *poésie pure* comme d'une chose existante. Il n'en est pas ainsi . . . (I, 1463).

Poetry can never be made of commensurable elements like music; the best that can be done is to transfer to poetry through analogy and through the poet's subjective comparisons of effects what Valéry observes about the effects of music. More important still, perhaps, is it to appropriate, as far as they can be analyzed or intuited, the technical means of previous poets who have written the kind of poetry that Valéry thinks musical — poetry 'qui chante'. Valéry told Valery Larbaud that the poem represents a 'copulation assez monstrueuse de mon "système", de mes "méthodes", de mes exigences musicales et des conventions classiques'.

Valéry's first principle seems to have been that words must be, as far as possible, separated from reference to particular events, beliefs, objects — to particular 'causal' sequences of happenings, logically arranged sequences of ideas, or the arrangement of objects in particular surroundings. In this he is close to Mallarmé — 'narrer, enseigner, décrire' are all proscribed. The effect to be generated must be generalized. Music awakens emotions that might be awakened, in life, by any number of particular sets of circumstances. We may even be prepared to experience, through music, emotions that we would be embarrassed to have brought out into the light of words: Valéry will allow more liberties to Wagner than to Victor Hugo. He tries, in his poetry, to do what Wagner does. The affect is to be in the form, which includes the generalized references of words, their meaning in dictionary terms, but avoids creating, in the reader's imagination, particular life-situations. The reader can fit any life-situations he likes into the affective pattern, into the successive states of mind, just as some listeners tell themselves stories to fit the moods of the music. His poems, Valéry said, had whatever meaning the reader chose to give them; and 'meaning' here means virtually 'story-telling'. Through their form they have another kind of meaning like that Valéry finds in Wagner's music — articulated affect. Valéry's theory of 'le moi pur' implies that the articulation is more important than the affect; but only the quality of the affect guarantees the authenticity of the articulation.

When Valéry said of *La Jeune Parque* that he had written his auto-biography into its form, he surely recognized that the general patterns of his own most familiar states of sensibility were in it. To Gide he admitted more frankly, if still with a certain coy surprise: 'j'ai trouvé après coup dans le poème fini quelque air d' . . . auto-biographie (intellectuelle, s'entend, et mis à part le morceau sur la Primavera qui a été improvisé en grande partie vers la fin)' (*Corr. Gide-Valéry*, p. 448).

The poem does, like Mallarmé's *Hérodiade*, strike at the reader's feelings before any kind of 'content' becomes clear. I have watched generations of students respond to the poem's moods before they could lay claim to any understanding of what the poem is about. But where words are concerned Valéry's theory has a limited application, as he recognized himself; and the history of the poem's exegesis confirms that readers respond more completely to the poem's transformations of sensibility when they can attach them to some kind of life-pattern — more particularly to Valéry's attempt at a 'system' to end all philosophizing and to the intellectual dramas and frustrations that attended it. The more one pores over the *Cahiers*, the more these correspondences between Valéry's mind and the Parque's become particularized and defined — and, I think, add to the poem's legitimate and intended effects. The Parque's consciousness has not only feelings but a content, however difficult this may be to fix and define.

Valéry admitted that although his 'ideas' — meaning the notions which make up his 'system' — should ideally direct the poem from the outside, he allowed them to intrude when it became too difficult not to: 'réservant le fond à ma pensée — et l'exprimant quand je ne pouvais le laisser dans les coulisses du poème — dirigeant sans se montrer' (C I, 292). He could not, any more than Flaubert could, be 'présent partout et visible nulle part' like God, and create a form 'qui se tiendrait de lui-même par la force interne de son style'.

3 juin 17.

Je suis dans l'état si remarquable de l'éfrit dont enfin le pêcheur ouvrit la bouteille. J'ai dégagé ma fumée, et maintenant je veux décapiter le pêcheur.

L'éfrit c'est mon ouvrage. Et le pêcheur, moi (C I, 246).

What Valéry tried to create in *La Jeune Parque* was not unlike what Baudelaire envisaged for the *Petits Poèmes en prose* — a language that would 's'adapter aux mouvements lyriques de l'âme, aux ondulations de la rêverie, aux soubresauts de la conscience'; except that rhyme and rhythm and all the 'classical conventions' were still to play their part in its 'music'. Rhythm, in particular, was always, for Valéry, a prime determinant of mood. In a letter to Louÿs in 1891 he said that through rhythm the poet can 'donner le Mode majeur et mineur', and gave as examples 'Crimen Amoris' and 'L'Après-midi d'un faune'.

Mais mon 'rêve de poète' eût été de composer un discours — une parole de modulations et de relations internes — dans lequel le physique, le psychique et les conventions du langage pussent combiner leurs ressources. Avec telles divisions et changements de ton bien définis (C I, 293).

This was what Valéry meant by 'modulation'. He noted at one point that his idea of modulation in music was vague; yet it was one of the terms he used most often. The mastery of 'modulation' was what he chiefly admired in Wagner. 'L'idée de modulation comme je l'entends me ravit plus que toutes' (C I, 297). Sometimes the emphasis is on the intensity of the affect:

La grande puissance et beauté de ces dernières scènes de la V(a)lk(yrie) est la plénitude, obtenue par entretien de l'état émotif — à haute et pure intensité très riche en éléments (tendresse, tristesse, grandeur) — *action* et émotion bien représentées et se succédant.
La modulation généralisée est le comble de l'art (C II, 956).

Sometimes the emphasis is on the form, the combining power which can seem independent of any identifiable affect, and which is therefore nearer the abstract manipulations of the mathematician:

Miraculeuse Suite en Ré majeur de Bach — Exemple *adorable* — où je n'entends ni melos, ni pathos, ni rien qui ne soit . . . *réel*, qui ne se développe qu'en soi-même, et s'expose sous toutes ses faces *sans me voir*. Intensité de pureté . . .

This is, for Valéry, escape from human nature into nature itself, into a state of mind matching the structure of the sensible world, the organically interrelated movements of the cycle of nature such as the Greek Hermeticists envisaged it: microcosm into macrocosm — what Valéry often referred to as his 'mysticisme du réel'.

Ma sensation pourrait . . . se passer de moi. Le systématique ronflement identique rythmé des violoncelles, comme le sol, la masse, la constance sur quoi l'édifice, la croissance, la φύσιϛ [= physis], la force des cordes hautes s'élève, se meut, s'exalte — — (C II, 955).

121

Whatever the particular music that Valéry thought of, its capacity to take the consciousness of the listener down into the patterns of the physiology of his sensibility or through a kind of 'dance' of the components of his sensibility was what he called 'modulation'.

When he came to write *La Jeune Parque* he chose as his principal model neither Wagner nor Bach, but Gluck, whom he associated with Racine. Lulli, Valéry would have read in Romain Rolland, learned something of the art of his recitatives from La Champmeslé's verse-speaking in Racine's plays:

J'ai pensé à Gluck. J'ai joué avec deux doigts. A l'inverse de Lulli au Th(éâtre) Français j'ai mis des notes sur le S(onge) d'A(thalie) —

j'ai supposé une mélodie, essayé d'attarder, de ritardare, d'enchaîner, de couper, d'*intervenir* — de conclure, de résoudre — et ceci dans le sens comme dans le son (C I, 246).

His immediate stimulus, however, was in the same direction as Lulli's; he read Brisson's article in *Le Temps* in 1913 with Prince Georges de Hohenzollern's notes on Rachel's delivery of Racine's verse, analyzing her breath-groups, accents and intonations. This gave him an insight into Racine's 'musicality'. Close analysis of Esther's prayer and Athalie's dream — the content as well as the form is significant here — took him further into Racine's rhetorical resources and led him to take a fresh look at the 'purest' parts of the French poetic tradition. He noted in 1942 — by which time his 'system' and its aesthetic correlatives had come to seem more fanciful than true:

Sottise
La sottise immédiate a donc sa valeur.
Je pensais à ce qui est attribué à Wagner: combiner Shakespeare à Beethoven. Cela est absurde, mais plein de *force initiale*. J'y songe à propos de la J(*eune*) *Parque* — car il y a eu dans le désir ou dessein de cette fabrication l'intention absurde — (peut-être faut-il de l'absurde dans les projets de certaines œuvres?) de faire chanter une *Idée* de l'être vivant — pensant? — 'Chanter' — c'est-à-dire utiliser tout ce qu'il y eut de chantant dans la poèsie française — entre Racine et Mallarmé . . . (C I, 303).

A marginal note refers to 'Virgile, Racine, Chénier, Baudelaire, Wagner, Euripide, Pétrarque, Mallarmé, Rimbaud, Hugo, Cl. Gluck — Pr(ière) d'Esther' (C I, 246. 'Cl.' seems more likely to refer to Claudel than to Clédat, as a Pléiade note suggests).

Gide spotted the presence of Racine and Mallarmé as soon as he read the poem and was inclined to deplore it. Subsequent critics have supplied a long list of other possible or likely presences. Nadal brought together the Parque's:

> Tout-puissants étrangers, inévitables astres . . .
> Je suis seule avec vous, tremblante, ayant quitté
> Ma couche . . .

and Esther's:

> O mon souverain Roi
> Me voici donc tremblante et seule devant toi.

The link between the two could be the passage Soulairol quoted from Ronsard's 'Hymne des Etoiles';

> De là faut que chacun
> Souffre l'arrest commun
> Des Parques filandières . . .
> . . . Je vous salue, heureuses flammes,
> Estoiles, filles de la Nuit,
> Et ce Destin qui nous conduit,
> Que vous pendistes à nos trames.

Valéry's list of 'singing' models was from Racine to Mallarmé — the most obvious of the 'poètes purs'. Closer to him in time was Paul Fort, 'Prince des Poètes' in 1912 when Valéry was turning back to poetry, prefaced by Valéry when his work was reprinted in 1941. Paul Fort's *Vivre en Dieu* appeared in 1912:

> vivre . . . en homme divin, connaissant, respectant sa nature élevée et pour tout dire enfin, conscient dans ses rêves, étonné doucement de leurs créations, enthousiaste du monde à recréer sans trêve, enfin poète, enfin: dieu de sa religion.

And in 'Le Bonheur', part of the sequence called 'Naissance du printemps à la Ferté-Milon', Valéry would have read:

> Un souffle me réveille. Oh! quel bonheur pourtant! Tout mon corps est poreux au vent frais du printemps . . . Partout je m'infinise et partout suis content . . . je passe mes mains, sans bouger . . . jusqu'au bout du monde, me croyant sans limite, — je suis heureux d'hier, d'aujourd'hui, de demain, me croyant dieu et sans commencement ni fin . . . Or, malgré cette joie d'un corps immatériel, plus léger qu'une houppe, je me dis dans le cœur: Est-ce le bonheur cette vie d'Ariel? cette vie sans déirs? — Non, la joie est au ciel, chez les anges en secret toujours révoltés, toujours plus désireux de plus de voluptés, toujours plus fous de croître en Force et en Beauté. La joie pure n'est pas dans les bonheurs humains. Le grand bonheur n'est pas dans les bonheurs atteints, et ni plus tard dans la contemplation de Dieu, mais bien dans l'éternelle attente d'être un dieu, et pour tout dire enfin, d'être ce dieu suprême, ne fût-ce qu'un moment, qui domine Dieu même et qui commande à tout l'univers — le Destin.

The Parque, 'poreuse à l'éternel qui me semblait m'enclore', is a soul-sister to the speaker in Paul Fort's poems. But she is also, as Daniel

Halévy, Soulairol and Nadal pointed out, close to Racine's Phèdre in the anguish of her divided self:

> . . . Insensée, où suis-je? et qu'ai-je dit?
> Où laissé-je égarer mes vœux et mon esprit?
> Je l'ai perdu: les Dieux m'en ont ravi l'usage . . .
>
> Mon cœur fut-il si près d'un cœur qui va faiblir? . . .
> La pensive couronne échappe à mes esprits . . .
>   Moi si pure, mes genoux
> Pressentent les terreurs de genoux sans défense . . .

Valéry's essay 'Sur Phèdre femme' shows him reacting violently — and as physically as he hoped his own readers would react to *La Jeune Parque* — to Racine's poetry. He feels its power in much the same terms as he feels Wagner's, as articulation of the visceral. Racine's verse was at once classical form and physically-rooted affect.

From Racine as his main poetic model to Gluck as his ideal musician was an easy step. 'L'apogée de l'art "classique", l'extrême point de Racine est peut-être le récitatif de Gluck et consorts' (C II, 938), he notes soon after the composition of *La Jeune Parque*. It has been said that *Phèdre* is put together like an opera; in it, indeed, lyrical probings into the deep affective resonances of a particular situation alternate with dialogues of interaction which move from that situation into another, once more to be sounded in depth. The general 'composition' of *La Jeune Parque* is on the same lines — and differs in this from the uninterrupted 'modulation' that is characteristic of Wagner.

But there is another imaginative link between Valéry and Gluck. The poem was first intended as an 'adieu à la poésie', a kind of 'récitatif pour contralto' of twenty-five lines at most. Valéry had noted in 1910:

Thermométrie.

A un certain âge tendre, j'ai peut-être entendu une voix, un contr'alto profondément émouvant . . .

Ce chant me dut mettre dans un état dont nul objet ne m'avait donné l'idée. Il a imprimé en moi la tension, l'attitude suprême qu'il demandait, sans donner un objet, une idée, une cause, (comme fait la musique). Et je l'ai pris sans le savoir pour mesure des états et j'ai tendu, toute ma vie, à faire, chercher, penser ce qui eût pu directement restituer en moi, nécessiter de moi — l'état correspondant à ce *chant de hasard*; — la chose réelle, introduite, absolue dont le creux était, depuis l'enfance, préparé par ce chant — *oublié*.

Par accident, je suis peut-être gradué. J'ai l'idée d'un maximum d'origine cachée, qui attend toujours en moi.

Une voix qui touche aux larmes, aux entrailles; qui va presser, sans obstacles, les mamelles sacrées / ignobles / de l'émotion / bête /; qui, artificiellement et comme jamais le monde réel n'en a besoin, éveille des extrêmes, insiste, remue, noue, résume trop, épuise les moyens de la sensibilité . . . elle rabaisse les choses observables . . . On l'oublie et il n'en reste que le sentiment d'un degré dont la vie ne peut jamais approcher (C I, 53).

This, perhaps, was the imagined contralto aria he thought of when he planned to write his 'adieu à la poésie'; it was natural enough that with it and Racine in mind he should turn to Gluck, out of the musicians he knew best, as his model. In 1931 he noted: '28 juin — *Iphigénie en Tauride*. Et voilà le "beau" à l'état pur (du moins les 2 premiers actes)' (C II, 960). And, a year later:

La beauté est la qualité de ce qui nous rend sensible, visible — ce que n(ous) aimerions d'*être*, ou de *faire*, ou de *ressentir*, — en même temps que l'*improbabilité* que cela soit, et cela est — La belle chose est incroyable et *est*. Possession de ce qui nous passe, et Ceci nous possédant en retour. En quoi l'infini se montre — L'eau excite la soif et la soif exige l'eau (C II, 962).

The poem conceived as 'une seule phrase longue pour contralto' became in his mind more like a section from an opera by Gluck — a 'melodic' continuity in the theme with 'modulations' in the 'harmony', a constant set of preoccupations with changes of mood. As some early critics suggested, the poem can be divided into a succession of 'arias' linked by transitional passages. The latter, Valéry said, gave him a great deal of trouble. In one transition at least the attempt to translate a true musical modulation into poetic terms seems obvious enough.

In music we can, to take a simple example, hear the note G as the tonic of the chord of G major, then the same note as the mediant of the chord of E minor; a melodic continuity with a dramatic change of mood, of tonality. Valéry produces a comparable effect when the Parque passes from awareness of her mortal, sensual, temporal self to that of her immortal, purely intellectual self: the suspended 'note' is the word 'MOI', picked out in capitals:

Adieu, pensai-je, MOI, mortelle sœur, mensonge . . .

Harmonieuse MOI, différente d'un songe . . .

Valéry's technical experiments began, as Nadal's presentation of the drafts shows clearly, with the attempt to feel poetry primarily in terms of what it has *literally* in common with music. The 'units' he worked with, single words, or the groups of words that presented themselves spontaneously as what he called 'phrases musicales', were spread over the page in clusters related primarily by sounds, secondly by the 'harmonics' or 'vibrations in sensibility' of the meanings — for Valéry still 'felt' words as he described them in his letter to Louÿs of 1891 — as 'élémentaux'; 'elemental spirits' such as Ficino found in music. So the first dance that Valéry's poetry provides is a dance of the organs of speech.

Les analyses de la poésie par la métrique, la prosodie, la phonétique — sont tout à fait insuffisantes. Elles ne peuvent servir à rien car elles omettent ce qui joue le plus grand rôle dans la formation interne-externe des vers.

Elles ne retiennent, en effet, que les caractères de répétition, les accents théoriques, les intensités.

Noter ici que l'enregistrement vibratoire des sons est extrêmement *trompeur* dans cette affaire car il confond des facteurs très différents, tandis que ces différences *jouent le plus grand rôle* dans l'action de formation du produit et dans son effet.

Du reste, dans cette formation, *l'auditif est inséparable du moteur* — c'est l'acte d'*articulation* ou plutôt la structure successive de ces actes — qui fait le *dessin du discours* (et le fait si différent de la mélodie sans paroles), dessin très expressif par lui-même — dont il n'est pas question chez les théoriciens . . . Comment veut-on raisonner sur des 'temps' et des intensités seuls — sur des vides et des pleins?

La question capitale des *consonnes* — et des passages de voyelle à voyelle, et celle des cycles — omises (C II, 1131).

Sound comes before sense. Then words as 'elemental spirits'. When the words have to be worked into a pattern of meaning the most 'resonant' of the 'elemental spirits' are found to be those that call up Valéry's obsessions. He wrote in one of his earliest notebooks:

J'ai été amené à regarder les phénomènes mentaux vigoureusement (sic) comme tels à la suite de grands maux et d'idées douloureuses. Ce qui les rendait si pénibles était leur obsession et leur insupportable retour; plus insupportable était cette forme de leur retour, selon laquelle on prévoit qu'elles reviendront. Je finis par détacher leur répétition de leur signification. Je détachais aussi les images qui les motivaient et les constituaient de la peine que je sentais. Peu à peu je fis subir à ces états toutes les transformations possibles — grâce à cette furieuse reproduction qui me les a redonnés tout neufs pendant longtemps chaque jour à chaque heure (C I, 20).

This is what he found himself doing in *La Jeune Parque*.

LUDGVAN   J. M. COCKING

---

[1] References are to the Pléiade texts; I and II refer to the verse and prose, C I and C II to the *Cahiers*.

L. ALLEN

'D'UNE ASIE L'AUTRE' —
UNE 'SOURCE' D'*ANABASE*

Le rêve oriental, ou l'expérience orientale, a été pour la génération de Chateaubriand un puissant indicateur religieux, pour celle de Flaubert et plus tard celle de Gide une révélation sensuelle. Le cas des poètes est beaucoup plus complexe. Selon Supervielle, un voyage se trouve souvent à l'origine d'une vocation poétique, et le voyage en Orient peut fournir un décor exotique dont l'intérêt reste purement anecdotique — c'est le cas de Nerval. Il peut aussi transformer les données et le sens même d'une vocation — ce sera le cas de Claudel et de Segalen. Lafcadio Hearn, un de leurs contemporains anglais — romancier plutôt que poète — y a puisé la source d'une métamorphose totale de l'être: au terme d'un voyage au Japon, il est devenu sujet de l'Empire du Soleil levant et s'est marié avec une Japonaise, achevant ainsi le transfert d'une personnalité occidentale en celle d'un Japonais de l'ère Meiji, non sans blessures et ennuis, et — parfois — des regards douloureux en arrière.

Si, parmi les écrivains français, Victor Segalen seul a pénétré aussi loin dans une civilisation d'Extrême-Orient que Lafcadio Hearn, son aîné Claudel a eu intuitivement une connaissance que Segalen a approfondie en apprenant à lire le chinois (Hearn ne lisait pas, ou peu, le japonais). Dans les *Cinq Grandes Odes*, dans *Connaissance de l'Est*, un curieux amalgame de littérature globetrotteresque prend forme avec des aperçus très profonds sur la religion et la civilisation chinoises. Segalen, au contraire, à partir des inscriptions funéraires des Stèles — la plus ennuyeuse des littératures — établit un point de départ pour des voyages à l'intérieur de lui-même, rejoignant ainsi la tradition française introspective à travers l'Empire du Milieu, pour atteindre l'autre, le cinquième, centre et Milieu 'Qui est Moi'. Derrière la surface chinoise, une substance rigoureusement personnelle.

Henri Bouillier a déjà montré que l'intérêt porté par Claudel et Segalen à l'idéogramme chinois fait écho à la fois à l'ésotérisme mallarméen et au futurisme d'Apollinaire (*Victor Segalen*, pp. 181-5). Pour Mallarmé, l'hiéroglyphe égyptien, pictogramme plus pur que le caractère chinois, constitue l'image de la barrière parfaite — serrure de missel ancien ou page de musique — qui empêche le profane de mettre les pieds trop facilement dans le champ poétique. Pour Apollinaire, il s'agit plutôt d'entamer une révolution dans les arts de l'écriture: le XXe siècle est l'âge apocalyptique, l'âge où prend fin le caractère d'imprimerie comme véhicule de la pensée. Bientôt le cinéma finira par transformer le roman en lui ôtant la nécessité de tout décrire ou évoquer comme paysage, ainsi que le besoin de raconter des histoires; et la peinture cubiste introduira le mouvement et la vision simultanée dans les beaux-arts. Le Livre serait une forme moribonde, et l'expérience des *Calligrammes* un rite funéraire. Dans ces jeux, Apollinaire s'est proposé de créer l'objet à travers son image et en même temps à travers le langage qui l'exprime: c'est-à-dire, de parfaire la création simultanée qui a été la grande conquête des peintres cubistes. Ce ne sont là, en effet, que des expériences picturales sans grande portée esthétique, dans lesquelles Apollinaire essaie de dépeindre l'objet évoqué par des moyens qui ne sont pas idéogrammatiques autant que typographiques: un cigare qui prend forme à travers la page, une pluie qui tombe verticalement, une mandoline, un morceau de bambou — est-ce autre chose qu'un piètre effort pour atteindre à la simultanéité, pour dépasser le fait que l'acte de lecture est forcément linéaire?

On retrouve des idées semblables dans les théories du poète américain Ezra Pound, dont les premiers essais poétiques sont contemporains d'*Alcools*. Pendant toute sa vie, Pound reste fasciné par l'idéogramme chinois, sans réussir jamais à en comprendre la structure véritable, bien qu'il sème ses poèmes de caractères crûment dessinés. Ses notions sont faussées, dès le début, par leur dépendance des travaux du japonophile américain Ernest Fenollosa, conservateur de musée et historien d'art. Il ne s'agit pas — c'est tout le contraire de Mallarmé — de créer des frontières entre le lecteur et l'objet-à-lire. Le but de l'idéogramme est d'offrir à l'image des contours nets, de soustraire au langage poétique l'élément facilisateur qu'est la parole. L'opuscule de Fenollosa, sur le caractère chinois considéré comme instrument poétique (*The Chinese Character As a Medium For Poetry*) remonte aux premières années du XXe siècle, et semble avoir été écrit à la même époque — à peu près, — que les *Cinq Grandes Odes*. Obsédé par la racine picturale cachée à l'intérieur du caractère moderne formalisé de l'écriture chinoise (ou japonaise, très peu différente), Fenollosa enseigne que le chinois écrit est fondé non sur l'arbitraire d'un symbolique capricieux, mais s'enracine dans un tableau tachygraphique très vivant des opérations de la nature. Dans la parole, l'unité qu'est le mot est une convention, rien de plus. Elle correspond exactement à l'unité mathématique constituée par le symbole algébraïque. La méthode chinoise suit une suggestion naturelle: 'En premier lieu, un homme sur ses deux jambes [人]. Deuxième temps, son œil [見] traverse l'espace — une forme nettement dessinée représentée par des jambes courantes situées sous un oeil [見] — le tableau d'un œil, modifiée, le tableau d'une paire de jambes, modifiées, — mais, une fois aperçues, inoubliables'. Fenollosa évoque ainsi la naissance des caractères 'homme' et 'voir'.

Pas besoin d'être sinologue pour apprécier la naïveté de ces observations d'érudit. L'essai de Fenollosa demeure pourtant une *felix culpa*, une de ces erreurs fructueuses de la littérature. Bien que parfaitement erronées, ses idées ont exercé, à travers l'interprétation d'Ezra Pound, une influence profonde sur la poésie anglaise et américaine. La *felix culpa* est, bien entendu, caractéristique de l'influence de Pound, qui crée, à partir de traductions souvent inexactes ou approximatives, des poésies merveilleuses. (Il faut savoir oublier le texte original et se féliciter de la découverte d'un talent nouveau qui s'exprime à travers les dons d'autrui.) Le Pound de la Belle Epoque, jeune barbare féru de culture méditerranéenne et provençale, s'occupe de poésie chinoise et japonaise *parce qu'il est* américain. Aucun paradoxe: la culture bostonienne est l'une des premières à s'approprier l'art et la littérature d'Extrême-Orient: Percival Lowell poursuit à Boston et au Japon des recherches sur le bouddhisme japonais qui — même cent ans plus tard — conservent beaucoup de leur saveur; et c'est en partie grâce à Ernest Fenollosa que les Japonais eux-mêmes — trop désireux de tout oublier du passé pour entrer plus librement dans l'époque moderne — apprendront à apprécier leurs beautés anciennes. Commentant l'essai de Fenollosa, le critique chinois James Liu a fait observer qu'il est faux de dire que les caractères chinois soient tous des pictogrammes ou des idéogrammes. En refusant d'admettre, ou simplement en ignorant, l'élément purement phonétique de tel caractère chinois, Fenollosa a tout misé sur l'image. Les caractères pour les objets communs — soleil, lune, homme, cheval, arbre — sont des tableaux schématiques, formalisés. Mais ils constituent une minorité dans le vaste trésor lexique du chinois. C'est ce que Paul Claudel, moins habitué à la fréquentation des caractères que Fenollosa, mais qui n'en est pas dupe, ressent intuitivement, lorsqu'il parle de la Religion du Signe:

Que d'autres découvrent dans la rangée des caractères chinois ou une tête de mouton, ou des mains, les jambes d'un homme, le soleil qui se lève derrière un arbre, j'y poursuis pour ma part un lacs plus inextricable.

Claudel distingue un principe horizontal dans le trait essentiel du caractère chinois, par opposition à la ligne verticale de la Lettre romaine. Le signe chinois est le développement du chiffre, tous les deux étant des images abstraites. Le signe, d'ailleurs, est un être sacré, d'où la révérence des Chinois pour l'écriture. Son essence est d'exister, de parler. La Lettre, au contraire, est analytique:

Tout mot qu'elle constitue est une énonciation successive d'affirmations que l'œil et la voix épellent; à l'unité elle ajoute sur une même ligne l'unité, et le vocable précis d'une continuelle variation se fait et se modifie.

La Lettre est donc constitutive du mouvement écritural; le caractère, de l'élément statique ou pictoral. Tous les deux s'unissent — pour Fenollosa sinon pour Claudel — dans la poésie chinoise, combinaison de la vie statique du tableau et du mouvement de la parole. L'esprit saisit l'image et la progression de l'idée dans le temps au même instant. Cette jonction a été réalisée, parfois, dans des moments heureux, par l'école des poètes qui ont tiré leur inspiration de Pound, et donc, à la longue, de Fenollosa: les Imagistes (Richard Aldington, la poétesse H.D., et ainsi de suite). Le Manifeste des Imagistes, — c'est Pound qui en formule les définitions — met l'accent sur le traitement direct de la 'chose', dépouille le poème de tout mot qui ne sert pas la présentation. Cette nudité, qui combine le mouvement avec des traits de pinceau brusques et sonores, on la voit mieux dans tel poème de H.D.:

Whirl up, sea —
Whirl your pointed pines,
Splash your great pines
On our rocks,
Hurl your green over us —
Cover us with your pools of fir.

Le cas de Segalen ne diffère pas tellement de celui de Claudel. Autodidacte en archéologie ainsi qu'en sinologie, Segalen arrive en Chine la même année que Claudel la quitte. Il devient vite expert en calligraphie; mais lorsqu'il essaie de transposer l'expérience de l'idéogramme en français, il aboutit soit au simple pastiche du *Che-king* que sont ses *Odes*, soit au style purement décoratif des *Stèles*, qui en effet rehaussent la valeur des stèles chinoises pour en faire le véhicule d'une poésie courte, péremptoire, et introspective, qui commence par faire écho au genre mémorialiste et finit dans l'exploration de soi, le sens du recueil allant de l'Empire du Milieu à l'Interieur de l'esprit poétique. Segalen, en un mot, dé-chinoise la Stèle pour en faire l'instrument d'une poésie universalisante: 'unique, sans date et sans fin'.

Dans la 'Préface' des *Stèles*, Segalen se livre à des spéculations qui rappellent le Claudel de *Connaissance de l'Est*: ils font cas tous les deux de la dureté et de la clarté de contour offertes par le caractère chinois — encore une fois, indiquant le chemin que devrait choisir l'école imagiste en Angleterre et aux Etats-Unis:

De là cette composition dure, cette densité, cet équilibre interne et ces angles, qualités nécessaires comme les espèces geométriques au cristal . . . Ils ne réclament point la voix ou la musique. Ils méprisent les tons changeants et les syllabes qui les affublent au hasard des provinces. Ils n'expriment pas; ils signifient; ils sont.

Il faut remarquer, pourtant, que la 'matière de Chine' reste accidentelle, si l'on peut dire, pour Victor Segalen. 'Ce n'est pas l'esprit ni la lettre, mais simplement la forme stèle que j'ai empruntée', écrira-t-il à Jules Gaultier. 'Je cherche délibérément en Chine non pas des idées, non pas des sujets, mais des formes, qui sont peu connues, variées et hautaines . . . dans ce moule chinois, j'ai placé simplement ce que j'avais à exprimer'. A Debussy il confesse à peu près la même intention: 'J'y dirais toutes sortes de pensées miennes — vêtues de notions et d'habits archaïques chinois, mais dépouillés de toute chinoiserie'. (H. Bouillier, *Victor Segalen*, p. 189-91).

Cette tentative, esquissée par Segalen, de partir d'une donnée chinoise pour parvenir, à la longue, à quelque chose d'universel dépouillé de toute référence circonstantielle, anticipe en quelque sorte sur le trajet de Saint-John Perse. Comme Claudel, Perse n'a pas appris le chinois; toute théorie sur l'écriture chinoise est donc assez éloignée de ses propos. Ce qu'on trouve chez lui, dans *Amitié du Prince* ou *Anabase*, ce sont des reflets ou des échos, parfois de Claudel ou de Segalen, parfois de la poésie chinoise vue à travers des traductions.

Dans son article, 'La Chine dans la poésie française' (*Cahiers de l'Association Internationale des Etudes françaises*, juin 1961, No. 13, pp. 71-83) Mme Liang Païtchin a relevé comme caractéristiques d'une forme d'expression chinoise: 'semelle blanche des lettrés', 'la femme qui s'étire sur son ongle', 'les clepsydres en marche sur la terre'. 'Si la Chine n'est pas absente de son œuvre, sa plume l'a affleurée seulement comme une libellule rasant l'onde' (Mme Liang, op. cit., p. 81). Elle établit aussi des parallèles plus sérieux. 'Et l'amitié est agréée, comme un présent de feuilles odorantes' (*L'Amitié du Prince*) ferait penser à telle phrase du *Che-king*, 'Si l'amitié est vraie pour agréer, l'offre de l'herbe odorante suffirait'; — 'trop longues, les fleurs s'achèvent en des cris de perruches', (*Pour fêter une Enfance*) au vers du poète des Song, Houang Ting-kien, 'L'arbre printanier s'élève en chants des oiseaux'. Tel verset d'*Eloges*, 'C'est le soir, couleur de paupières, sur les chemins tissés du ciel et de la mer', se rapporterait au vers de Fan Tchong-an, autre poète de la dynastie des Song, 'La montagne se baigne dans le couchant; le ciel touche aux flots'. Enfin, la vision des oies sauvages, en migration, évoquée par Perse, serait un lieu commun de la peinture chinoise.

Ce sont là de bien brèves évocations, aussi suggestives, et aussi exaspérantes dans leur peu de poids, que telle autre phrase — 'Et la lessive part/Comme un prêtre mis en pièces!' qui rappelle 'L'Esprit et l'Eau': 'Soudain le vent de Zeus dans un tourbillon plein de pailles et de poussières avec la lessive de tout le village!' Quel lecteur d'*Anabase*, d'ailleurs, manquerait d'entendre cet écho du vent du temps et de l'histoire qui traverse ces premières pages de l'*Ode* de Claudel? .

> C'est ainsi que dans le vieux vent de la terre, la Cité carrée dresse
> ses retranchements et ses portes,

Etage ses Portes colossales dans le vent jaune, trois fois trois portes comme des éléphants,
Dans le vent de cendre et de poussière, dans le vent gris de la poudre qui fut Sodome, et les empires d'Egypte et des Perses,
et Paris, et Tadmor, et Babylone.

Ce vent va nous mener fort loin. *Anabase*, en effet, suit ses traces de façon inverse: créé, pour l'essentiel, dans un temple taoïste des abords de la capitale chinoise, le poème porte les marques non de la Chine mais de l'Asie centrale, ses rares points de repère — spirituels autant que géographiques — étant ceux d'un itinéraire nomade à travers un désert comme le Gobi pour fonder des villes dans un occident lointain.

Les allusions à la poésie chinoise ne devraient donc pas nous tromper. Claudel, Segalen, Perse ne font pas un trio de poètes français qui auraient vécu en Chine et auraient tiré tout le suc d'une inspiration — de récits, d'images, de formes — d'une source proche et immédiate. Il n'en est rien. Claudel et Segalen ont profité directement de leur contact avec la Chine. Le profit poétique de Saint-John Perse est bien plus difficile à discerner. Il faut le chercher d'une façon tangentielle. Il est curieux que ni Maurice Saillet, suivant une fausse piste aux traces d'Arrien, ni F. J. Carmody, dont on connaît les annotations érudites sur les lectures orientalistes de Perse, n'a songé à évoquer les vestiges parsemés dans le texte d'*Anabase* qui renvoient au livre de Marco Polo. Il y a là des rappels qu'on ne peut guère ignorer: l'importance du *sel* (la montagne de sel au Livre I, ch. XXVIII), les *almanachs* qu'on consulte chez les devins avant d'entreprendre le voyage (Livre II, ch. XXXIII), la *divination* (Livre I, ch. XXXIII), la ville (Camul) dont les citadins donnent leurs épouses aux étrangers de passage (Livre I, ch. XLI), la note sur l'*amiante* (le Salamandre du Livre I, ch. XXII), surtout les noms propres, *Saba* (Livre I, ch. XIII), *Tauris* (Livre I, ch. XI), et enfin le mystérieux *Arbre Sec* (Livre I, ch. XXII) qui pourrait être aussi bien, chez Marco Polo, l'Arbre du Soleil.

Mais il s'agit là de références éparses, qui ne dictent ni le ton de l'œuvre, ni ses lignes directrices. L'Orient est un continent reculé dans le temps et dans l'espace. Le diplomate Alexis Léger peut passer son temps en terre chinoise; l'ombre d'un poète se détache de lui et d'elle, traverse le cœur désertique de l'Asie, suivant *à rebours* les traces de Marco Polo, vers Jabal, l'Arbre Sec et les Mers Mortes pour aborder enfin à un pays autrement lointain, dans un temps transfiguré: nous voici, en plein *Anabase*, à la fois dans la poésie de la transhumance ... et dans l'âge des fondateurs des villes de Mésopotamie ... et de Perse.

Rechercher dans l'œuvre de Saint-John Perse autre chose que de brèves notations scéniques, c'est donc perdre son temps. Ce qu'il a trouvé pendant son séjour en Chine n'est pas l'exotisme psychologique de

Segalen ni l'imagerie philosophico-théologique de Claudel, mais ce seuil qu'offre la Chine dans un réalité géographique et historique, ce seuil entre l'Orient et l'Occident, le désert. Toute l'attraction, tout le mouvement, d'un poème comme *Anabase*, on peut les tracer dans un sens contraire à celui de Segalen, un mouvement qui ne cesse de s'occidentaliser, et qui correspond à l'exploration dont témoignent d'autres parties du poème: cette préoccupation non pas avec la Chine, antique ou moderne, mais avec cet autre Orient antique, le monde de Sumer et de Babylone.

Anabase est suprêmement le poème de la terre, un poème situé, selon l'expression de Claudel, au plus terre de la terre. Tous les poèmes qui l'ont suivi sont des façons de repenser la terre d'en haut, du vertical et non plus de l'horizontal — *Pluies, Neiges, Vents* — géométriquement contraire à l'*Anabase*, pour finir avec *Amers* qui en constitue le contraire idéologique. A propos d'*Anabase*, on a évoqué Arrien, Xénophon et ainsi de suite — mais il existe, je crois, une source plus profonde, non pas d'allusions précises ni de notions individuelles, mais d'esprit, une source qui reflète un Orient beaucoup plus ancien que les stèles chinoises de Segalen, et qui fait penser à la carrière du diplomate-poète — frontières, limites, rivières, ports; et qui, enfin, suggère ce style péremptoire qui est l'équivalent linguistique de cette violence qui 'commandait à nos mœurs', — style de faiseur de lois qui n'admet pas qu'on le contredise.

Cet Orient-là est réglé par un code de lois célèbre: celui du roi Hammurabi. Les thèmes de ses lois peuvent se résumer très brièvement: il s'agit de peines contre les actes de sorcellerie, contre la corruption des témoins, contre la prévarication des juges — autant dire que le roi est obsédé par le besoin d'établir sa justice; de la condition des officiers et des serviteurs du roi; de la culture des terres; de l'organisation de la famille, des dots, des successions; des indemnités pour coups et blessures; des droits et obligations des médecins, des architectes, des bateliers — professions significatives pour le lecteur d'*Anabase*; des salaires; de la discipline des esclaves. Un détail piquant: la traduction française des Lois de Hammurabi paraît dans la version du Père Scheil, dominicain, en 1902, sous le patronage du Ministère de l'Instruction Publique et des Beaux-Arts, et constitue le quatrième tome des *Mémoires* de la 'Délégation en Perse'. L'on sait que le diplomate Alexis Léger a choisi son pseudonyme, comme il le confie à Pierre Mazars, pour pouvoir 'mieux se renier' ou — autre version donnée à l'Argentin Marcos Victoria, — pour être, en littérature, comme ces navires à quai 'qui offrent seulement leur poupe à la curiosité des passants; un nom, un port d'attache, c'est là tout leur état civil. Le reste est aventure et n'appartient qu'a eux'. Mais il est bien d'autres façons de se renier que d'adopter le nom Perse, et ce curieux préfixe anglicisé Saint-John.

Dans une note parue à la *NRF* (no. 304, mai 1978, pp. 126-127), Roger Little, un des plus érudits parmi les jeunes perséens, a proposé une solution intéressante au problème du choix de ce pseudonyme. Il suppose une rencontre qui aurait eu lieu entre le poète et le romancier irlandais James Joyce, chez Adrienne Monnier. Joyce aurait parlé de son livre nouveau, *Finnegan's Wake*. Il a incorporé dans le texte de ce roman expérimental le poème bizarre intitulé 'The Ballad of Perse O'Reilly', et c'est à ce nom, lui-même déformation du nom irlandais bien connu Pierce or Pearse, que Perse aurait songé pour s'affubler du pseudonyme, rendu nécessaire, pensait-il, par son activité diplomatique (recours jugé inutile, pourtant, par un Claudel, un Giraudoux, un Morand).

La suggestion ne manque pas d'ingéniosité. La rencontre elle-même n'aurait pas manqué d'intérêt. Il n'en est pas moins vrai qu'il n'existe pas la moindre preuve qu'elle ait jamais eu lieu. Dans les premières ébauches de son livre, d'ailleurs, rédigées à la date où une rencontre avec Perse aurait été du moins vraisemblable (aux environs de décembre 1924), le titre de la chanson (ou *rann*) ne figure pas, ni le paragraphe qui la précède dans le texte, où le nom apparaît pour la première fois. (La première ébauche complète date de décembre 1923, Livre I, ch. ii, cf. *A First Draft Version of Finnegan's Wake*, ed. David Hayman, London, Faber, 1963). Les dates semblent donc exclure la possibilité de l'emprunt. Je pense qu'il faut préférer la solution banale: un mélange de snobisme anglophile et de 'la voix de celui qui crie dans le désert'; sur ce mélange le poète aurait calqué un souvenir de cet empire de Perse qui régnait autrefois sur toute l'Asie centrale, et dont le nom est peut-être entré dans sa mémoire au hasard d'une lecture de la traduction des Lois de Hammurabi dans le grand in-folio de Scheil.

Mais il y a beaucoup plus qu'un nom, et qu'un écho stylistique, dans les *Mémoires* de cette Délégation en Perse. Dans le détail aussi, les parallèles offrent un certain intérêt. Voyez, par exemple, la façon dont Hammurabi s'établit et se proclame (les chiffres renvoient à la pagination de la traduction Scheil):

Hammurabi,
roi de justice,
à qui Samas la rectitude
a octroyé, moi-même !
Mes volontés sont nobles !
mes œuvres
un rival
n'ont pas !
en haut, en bas
(je suis) un ouragan (qui)
dans les hauteurs hurle ! (p. 123)

— ou la façon dont il décrit ces œuvres:

Droit
et Justice
dans la contrée
j'instituai,
je fis le bonheur des peuples
en ce temps-là (p. 22) . . .

Décrets
d'équité
que Hammurabi
roi vaillant,
a établis;
au pays une police sûre
et un régime heureux
il a procuré (p. 117)

[Sur trois grandes saisons m'établis-
sant avec honneur, j'augure bien du sol
où j'ai fondé ma loi (*Anabase*, I)]

Le Soleil a son rôle à jouer:

Alors —
(moi) Hammurabi,
insigne, noble . . .
justice dans la contrée
pour créer . . .
Comme le Soleil
aux humains
pour apparaître
la contrée
pour éclairer (p. 14)

[Et le soleil n'est point nommé, mais
sa puissance est parmi nous . . .
(*Anabase*, I)]

Sa justice doit demeurer ferme; aucun ennemi ne doit la troubler:

la justice du pays
que j'ai formulée,
les lois de ce pays
que j'ai codifiées,
qu'il ne les change pas!
mes reliefs
qu'il ne dérange pas!

Le style du traducteur du Code utilise parfois un langage dénué d'articles,
caractéristique du style de Perse:

que le dieu Ê-A, le prince grand
entendement
et sagesse
lui retire! (p. 125)

[N'est-ce pas à ce même dieu que fera
ainsi appel plus tard l'auteur de *Vents*?]

Echo aussi du style péremptoire de Perse quand le traducteur emploie le subjonctif de souhait pour exprimer les volontés du roi touchant son ennemi:

Que Zamalmal
le guerrier grand
l'aîné
du temple d'Ekur

qui marche à ma droite
sur le champ de bataille
brise ses armes!
le jour en nuit
qu'il lui convertisse!

son ennemi au-dessous de lui
qu'il place!
que Ištar, la dame
des batailles et combats
qui décoche
mes armes,
mon génie
protecteur
qui aime mon gouvernement
dans son cœur

courroucé
dans sa colère
immense,
maudisse sa royauté
ses faveurs
en maux
qu'elle convertisse!
sur le champ des combats et batailles,
ses armes
qu'elle brise,

trouble,
et révolte,
qu'il lui destine
ses guerriers
qu'il terrasse!
de leur sang
qu'il abreuve la terre! (pp. 128-9)

Le Code trace les rapports entre un prince justicier et son peuple:

l'opprimé
qui un litige
a,
devant mon image
de roi de justice,
qu'il vienne!
et ma stèle
écrite
qu'il lise!
mes ordres
précieux

[Duc d'un peuple d'images . . .
Anabase, V)]

qu'il écoute!
que ma stèle l'affaire
lui éclaircisse!
sa cause qu'il comprenne!
que son cœur
se dilate en disant:
Hammurabi,
c'est un maître qui comme un père
un vrai parent
pour ses sujets
se montre. (pp. 190-1)

[Lois sur la vente des juments.
Lois errantes. (*Anabase*, VIII) . . . Les
mers fautives aux détroits n'ont point
connu de juge plus étroit . . . (*Anabase*, III)]

Un grand principe de violence commandait aux lois de Hammurabi, ainsi qu'aux mœurs d'*Anabase*:

Si un esclave à son maître
'tu n'es pas mon maître'
a dit,
comme son esclave
il le fera comparaître
et son maître lui coupera une oreille (p. 117)

Si un fils son
père a frappé,
ses mains
on coupera (p. 95)

Si cet homme
du grain ou des plants
a volé
et si dans ses mains
cela est trouvé
on lui coupera les mains (p. 109)

Une des formes de violence et de cruauté les plus frappantes dans *Anabase* trouve son écho deux fois répété dans le Code:

Si quelqu'un
a loué un bœuf,

et son œil a crevé,
la moitié de sa valeur en argent
du maître du bœuf
il donnera (p. 107)

Si quelqu'un   [. . . et le poulain poisseux met son
l'œil d'un homme libre   menton barbu dans la main de l'enfant,
a crevé,   qui ne rêve pas encore de lui crever un
son œil   œil . . . (*Anabase*, V)]
on crèvera (p. 95)

Ce corps de femme que le poète fait brûler dans les sables (*Anabase*, IV),
serait-ce le corps d'une prêtresse?

Si une prêtresse
qui dans le cloître
ne reste pas,
la taverne a ouverte
et pour là boisson
dans la taverne
est entrée,
cette hommasse,
on la brûlera (pp. 56-7)

Dans les sacrifices il faut observer la note de pureté si visible dans les
premières pages d'*Anabase*:

qui, à Êa . . .
pour jamais a affecté   [Aux ides pures du matin . . . l'idée
des offrandes pures,   pure comme un sel . . . au pur commerce
prince royal de ville (capitale)   de mon âme . . . (*Anabase*, I)]
qui a rendu denses
les habitations
sur l'Euphrate . . .
qui place des mets purs
devant NIN-A-ZU (p. 20)

Un même homme a-t-il brûlé pour une femme et pour sa fille (*Anabase*, III)?

Si un homme
sa fille
a connu
cet homme
on le chassera de la ville (p. 74).

Ce feu d'épines en plein vent (*Anabase*, I) et cet autre feu de ronces à
l'aurore qui met à nu les grandes pierres vertes et huileuses (*Anabase*, IV),
peut-il être aussi un feu de punition?

puissant parmi les dieux,
lutteur sans pareil,
qui m'a fait obtenir
mon triomphe,
dans sa vigueur

grande,
comme un feu
puissant de roseaux
ses habitants
brûle! (p. 129)

La poésie énumérative des métiers (*Anabase*, I, X) joue un rôle chez Hammurabi aussi:

le salaire d'un briquetier . . . le salaire d'un tailleur d'habits . . . le salaire d'un charpentier . . . le salaire d'un maçon . . . (pp. 114-15)

[Le tailleur pend à un vieil arbre un habit neuf d'un très beau velours — *Anabase* III]

Comme n'importe quel prince, celui d'*Anabase* avertit son peuple contre les rebelles et les dissidents. Le Soleil lui-même est qualifié de 'fauteur de troubles, de discordes'. Hammurabi esquisse quelque chose d'un peu plus précis, et l'évocation ne manque pas de saveur:

Une marchande de vin
quand des rebelles
dans sa maison
se réunissent,
ces rebelles
n'a pas saisi (*sic*)
et au palais
n'a pas conduit (*sic*)
cette marchande de vin
sera tuée (p. 56)

Insister davantage sur ces fragments, ce serait peser d'un poids trop lourd sur quelques échos de lecture, quelques allusions éphémères — et pourtant, qui manquerait de trouver une résonance perséenne, beaucoup plus forte que n'importe quelle citation chinoise, ou tel souvenir de Pékin, dans ces phrases lapidaires d'un autre Orient, vieux de quatre mille ans?

DURHAM   LOUIS ALLEN

J. CRUICKSHANK

CRITICAL APPROACHES TO SOME NOVELS
OF THE GREAT WAR

There is much to be said for the view that the basic function of criticism
is to understand and interpret rather than to classify. If such critical
priorities are accepted, a good deal can be learned from the scrutiny of
writers not generally regarded as outstandingly gifted or successful. It
seems clear that the early Great War novelists come into this latter
category. Novelists who responded immediately to the experience of
mobilization and trench warfare did not, on the whole, produce artistically
memorable writings. The few works of this time that are still read —
Barbusse's *Le Feu* (1916), Duhamel's *Vie des martyrs* (1917) or Dorgelès's
Les Croix de bois (1919) — are admired more as moral outcry than
aesthetic achievement, more as documentation than art. Indeed, most of
the thirty or so novels and collections of short stories published by 1919
have long been out of print. This fact may certainly be attributed in some
measure not only to changes in literary taste but to the limited talents of
these authors. Nevertheless, these writers also faced particular moral and
technical difficulties which need to be stated, however briefly, before the
attempt is made to sketch the broader critical problem of a legitimate
and balanced approach to their work.

The basic difficulty was one of finding appropriate ways of articulating
experiences which, at their worst, were totally horrifying and totally
unfamiliar to the participants. The scale of the casualties, the nature of
the killing and wounding, the increasing assault on human flesh by
industrialized technology and machine-made ingenuity, the loss of
personal identity and dignity in the names of discipline and military
necessity — all these things were experienced and had to be absorbed
not by a small professional army but by civilians suddenly uprooted by
mobilization from normal life in villages and towns. The writers among
them lacked an adequate rhetoric with which to express these unparalleled
experiences. The traditional language of war writing was not only
inadequate but inappropriate. It suggested high chivalry, the heroic trial
of valour, a confidence in resounding moral absolutes. But these are
precisely things which the Great War finally denied and destroyed. The
phenomenon of industrialized and total war was one which required time
and some detachment for its proper understanding and expression.
Significantly, the most successful and admired novels of the war were
almost all written in the 1920s and 1930s.[1]

It can be argued that some of these later novels, because of their literary
skill, lack the immediacy and also the authentic imperfection of less fully
realized works of the 1914-18 period. The immediate pressure of their

subject-matter urged the early war novelists in the direction of documentation and witness. It was a pressure that left only limited room for conscious craftsmanship. Most writers were forced, by the requirements of authentic testimony, into an indeterminate area on the borders of autobiography and fiction. A measure of generic definition was lost, but there were gains in terms of human conviction and a sense of actuality. However, while the experience of fighting on the Western Front provided immediate and dramatic material for some established and many aspiring writers, not all were anxious to appear in print while the holocaust was still taking place. A few even regarded their experiences as inappropriate material for literary treatment and kept silence. Those who did write fall into two main categories. Some, like Dorgelès, were reluctant to 'exploit' their sufferings and those of their comrades.[2] They published their work when the war ended. Dorgelès *Les Croix de bois* and Léon Werth's *Clavel soldat* both appeared in 1919. On the other hand there were writers who, for equally honourable reasons, sought publication as soon as possible in order to tell the truth to those at home and, in some cases, to counteract war propaganda.[3] Barbusse's *Le Feu* was published in 1916 and Duhamel's *Vie des martyrs* in 1917. None of these writers attempted to belittle the nightmare of the battlefield and each succeeded, in considerable measure, in the task of true testimony. The only writers who really emerge as failures are those who, through lack of moral imagination or for propagandist reasons, used a discredited heroic rhetoric to minimize the horror and disguise the folly. It is only right to add that this type of novel, exemplified by René Benjamin's *Gaspard* (1915), was mainly a product of the early months of the fighting. This was a period when, even for many honest witnesses, the true nature and significance of the war were still very unclear.

★   ★   ★

On the face of it the novel seems the most suitable literary form in which to give expression to the facts and conditions of war. As Holger Klein puts it: '. . . prose narrative, taking over in part the tradition of the great epics, is especially suited to the full re-creation of historical events and states of society. Moreover, as prose is the most frequently read genre of the modern era, this is the medium in which the war had its widest impact on the reading public'.[4] Nevertheless, these early war novels differed in emphasis from ordinary fiction in terms of their subject-matter and their aims. The more closely they dealt with the nature of the fighting in Flanders, the more they used what might be called ready-made material. The major facts were witnessed, not invented. They resembled the traditionally heavily autobiographical 'first novel' of other writers and were in fact first novels in a number of cases. Again, their subject was a public and historical experience shared by thousands, and eventually millions, of their compatriots. Therefore, the more the war became central to these works, the more authenticity and actuality became required major aims. In other words there were limits, more strictly marked than in ordinary novels, to the extent to which truth could be modified or changed in the interests of art.

Two consequences affecting the form of these novels follow. One, resulting from the distinctive nature of their subject, is the repetition of certain incidents and scenes from novel to novel. Such set pieces as the baptism of fire, the infantry attack, the artillery barrage, or withdrawal from the front line recur on a number of occasions. These set pieces, in their turn, are given a common background of mud, rain, lice, barbed-wire, exhausted men, flooded trenches and ruined villages. Such repetition, if not aesthetically exciting, is some guarantee of truth. Again, a more significant feature, and one which must affect our critical approach, is the complex mixture of fact and fiction. It has already been pointed out that these books possess characteristics of both the war memoir and the novel (particularly when a first-person narrator is employed). It would therefore be pointless, even irrelevant, to follow the example of some commentators and apply to these works, in a rigidly normative way, those critical expectations which we bring to the analysis of ordinary novels. In fact, it is part of the interest of these narratives that they respond with what may be called generic flexibility to their subject-matter and their authors' purpose. They offer considerable justification of the present-day critical view that works should be appraised as 'texts' and not in terms of strict fidelity to a particular genre. At the level of form, therefore, a strictly genre-based approach is inappropriate. At the same time, this is not a disguised plea for a fully structuralist analysis. The case against a structuralist treatment of these texts is put clearly and firmly by Maurice Rieuneau:

. . . au risque de paraître rétrograde ou attardé, nous affirmons les plus expresses réserves vis-à-vis des théories qui veulent réduire un récit romanesque à une aventure du langage. Ceux qui ont écrit sur la guerre avaient une tout autre aventure à raconter et s'il est artificiel de distinguer une forme et un fond, il n'en est pas moins vrai que l'expérience a précédé l'écriture et l'a déterminée dans sa réalité verbale et idéologique. C'est ce qui en fait, à nos yeux, l'intérêt, en dépit d'évidentes faiblesses.[5]

There is perhaps a danger or an injustice in insisting too heavily on the artistic limitations of the early war novels. It is well to remember that *Le Feu* and *Les Croix de bois*, for instance, were highly praised by many writers and both have continued to be bought and read more than sixty years after their original publication. It may be that one clue to their persistent appeal lies in their successful use of the repetitive element mentioned above. In novel after novel we find a three-part sequence consisting of anticipation of battle, experience of battle, withdrawal from battle. This cycle of anticipation, action, withdrawal — a variation on departure, quest, return — is met many times and we know that it is deeply imprinted in the human spirit. At a formal level, then, a number of war novels contain a mythic structure which has pervaded Western literature in a multitude of versions from the travels of Odysseus and the quest of Orpheus to Dante's *Divine Comedy* and Bunyan's *Pilgrim's Progress*. Making a rather similar point in connection with English writing about the Great War, Paul Fussell uses one of the many valuable insights to be found in Northrop Frye's *Anatomy of Criticism*: 'As Frye reminds us, a standard "quest" has three stages: first, "the stage of the perilous journey and the preliminary minor adventures"; second, "the crucial struggle, usually some kind of battle in which either the hero or his foe, or both, must die"; and third, "the exaltation of the hero, who has clearly proved himself to be a hero even if he does not survive the conflict". It is impossible not to be struck by the similarity between this conventional "romance" pattern and the standard experience re-enacted and formalized in memoirs of the war'.[6] There is much truth in Fussell's comment. But it is important to note that the best of the early war novelists modified this 'romance pattern' in markedly unromantic ways. Barbusse and Léon Werth probably took this tendency furthest. They transformed the crusade pursued by the hero into the chaos experienced by the victim — experienced in the mud and rain of Flanders. But whether the tone is patriotic or pacifist, complaisant or debunking, there exists a structure to which we appear to make an instinctive response.

The presence of mythic patterns in a work should not be taken as necessary evidence of literary sophistication. Indeed, in the case of these particular novels, the basic nature of the material — individual or collective experience of modern warfare — imposed a mythic structure independently of authorial intention. There is little evidence that they consciously exploited the cycle of anticipation, action, withdrawal. We are dealing, in general, with aesthetically innocent narratives. This is a further reason why so many of them have remained out of print. They appear naïve to readers of a more knowing age whose sensibilities are attuned to ironic and oblique modes of writing. Their episodic, anecdotal style seems crude and unformed in comparison with later techniques of cross-cutting, counterpointing and general narrative control.[7] And yet it may be argued, with some justification, that the relatively simple narrative techniques of a Bertrand or a Dorgelès, a Barbusse or a Werth, convey most accurately the pre-ordained existence of the front-line soldier with its regular rhythm of fear, danger and boredom, set against a background of death and destruction.

As regards the subject-matter of these narratives, it is of course obvious that war, in common with love and death, has been a literary theme from the earliest times. Like love and death, too, it often served as a background or narrative framework against which quite other concerns were primarily explored. However, as Stanley Cooperman was one of the first to point out clearly, the early war novel broke with tradition under the pressure of a war which itself destroyed many precedents. With the spectacle of mass mechanized slaughter war ceased to be a narrative device and became a totally invasive narrative subject. Cooperman says: 'No longer one subordinate element among many contributing to a total aesthetic structure, environment — the war itself — became the chief protagonist; when this happened readers were left floundering in a situation where the traditional critical implements simply could not be applied'.[8] This shift of war to a position as central subject, together with its presentation as a form of mass martyrdom, demanded a moral response.

While these novels, then, were aesthetically innocent narratives, most of them also belong firmly to the literature of moral persuasion. The degree of persuasion naturally varies, but whether they are novels of honest witness and high traditionalist ideals, like Bertrand's *L'Appel du sol*, or novels of honest outrage and left-wing values, like Barbusse's *Le Feu*, they call for an ethical response. They work through direct emotional impact, not through subtle artistic effects. This is not to say that they are propagandist works, though no doubt Barbusse's book does come into this category. But it means, given the subject, that the moral stand they take will be judged, to a large extent, in terms of fidelity to the facts. The assumption is easily and naturally made that the moral message will derive its status and its strength from the fundamental truthfulness of the narrative.

Inevitably, then, these novels have given rise to a critical approach which has been broadly ethical. Their subject, particularly while the fighting continued, seemed to demand it; the authors themselves appeared to encourage it. Nevertheless, critical practice has proved neither clear nor simple. It is notoriously difficult to obtain agreement on moral criteria and these war narratives have not proved an exception. The convictions of critics and those of authors have clashed in a variety of ways. In general, the criteria in question have been the truthfulness of what is said and the passion with which it is expressed. Ideally, the truth and the passion should coincide, but in practice they often sort ill together. In the case of

the early war novels — documents about the war and frequently denunciations of it — two forms of response arose. Some critics, concerned above
all with documentary accuracy, admired only those novels which avoided
shrillness, were not unsympathetic to the traditional virtues of the
battlefield, and presented war as a natural, if cruel phenomenon. Other
critics, chiefly sensitive to military mismanagement and the appalling
sacrifice of human life, regarded novels of protest as alone worthy of
attention, judging them according to the intensity of their denunciations.
If the first group appeared to require a moderate account of unexampled
violence, the second seemed to accept passion and unbalance as morally
and artistically self-justifying.

While these contrasting critical approaches existed in some degree
from the early days of the war, they became more clearly defined in the
late 1920s and early 1930s. As the war began slowly to recede, and as
technology and violence became seemingly inevitable features of modern
society, there were those who experienced a measure of reconciliation
with the fact of mechanized killing. Others, in the wake of a victory
obtained at such enormous cost, contributed to a growing mood of
pacifism and war repugnance. Critics seeking balance and restraint
profited from the first of these attitudes. Those seeking an uncompromising
denunciation of war profited from the second. The argument between
these two sets of critics found what is perhaps its fullest and most precise
form in the debate in America between Archibald MacLeish and Malcolm
Cowley. The subject was *The First World War*, edited by Laurence
Stallings, and it appeared in the *New Republic* during September and
October 1933.[9] MacLeish complained of the partiality and lack of balance
in many war novels (he had in mind post-war as well as wartime novels).
Too many, he asserted, concentrated on the futility and slaughter to the
exclusion of the courage, the comradeship, the long periods of inactivity
which also formed an integral part of the war experience. MacLeish's
position implied that the role of literature is to explore and exhibit,
not to preach and persuade. And it is true that the great works of art —
Hamlet or *Middlemarch* or *The Brothers Karamazov* — contain the
woven texture of human contradiction and complexity rather than the
single thread of partisanship.

Cowley, in reply, defended partisanship in terms of the special, even
unprecedented, nature of the Great War. A balanced, exploratory
approach would have betrayed its character and placed it falsely in the
continuing perspective of traditional warfare. Selectiveness and passionate
commitment were necessary to convey the exceptional horror of trench
warfare and mechanized killing. Cowley, and the novelists who felt like
him, saw the war as absurdly pointless slaughter; MacLeish believed that

the truth still demanded a recognition of heroism and generous sacrifice. This aspect of the debate was at least as much about terms as about facts.

While the writing of a novel of protest can be reconciled, at least in theory, with respect for the facts, some critics have been particularly sensitive to the distortions of fact, in the interests of propaganda or of art, which occur in novels of protest — and are by no means totally absent from 'traditionalist' narratives. As recently as 1968 C. E. Carrington wrote of his own lengthy experience of the Great War: '. . . I never came across a glorification of war; I heard no bloodthirsty sermons by militant clergy; I remember no invocations of the joys of battle . . . We were deadly serious about our assignment, without finding a necessity of often saying so, and there seemed no reason why we should not have fun when off duty, since we expected to die tomorrow'.[10] This is some way from the war as Barbusse or Werth describe it. No doubt it is a very anglo-saxon approach, phlegmatic and down-to-earth. But it also reminds us that if a writer were to confine himself to what he had actually experienced and seen with his own eyes, his account of the war might appear very limited and even positively unbalanced. The overall view of the individual was necessarily severely restricted. Referring to the sheer physical dimensions of the front, in terms of trenches and salients, Fussell writes of 'a series of multiple parallel excavations running for 400 miles down through Belgium and France'. He adds: 'From the North Sea coast of Belgium the line wandered southward, bulging out to contain Ypres, then dropping down to protect Béthune, Arras, and Albert. It continued south in front of Montdidier, Compiègne, Soissons, Reims, Verdun, St. Mihiel, and Nancy, and finally attached it southernmost end to the Swiss border at Beurnevisin, in Alsace. The top forty miles — the part north of Ypres — was held by the Belgians; the next ninety miles, down to the river Ancre, were British; the French held the rest, to the south'.[11]

This was a setting of such physical extent that the different types of terrain alone gave rise to a variety of war experiences. Also, it was so extensive that a total picture could not be obtained by a single individual. Rieuneau writes:

Une bataille de Napoléon pouvait être suivie, comprise et décrite dans son ensemble, par un observateur judicieusement placé. Ainsi fit Hugo pour Waterloo, et Stendhal dut fausser les données, restreindre le champ de vision de Fabrice pour créer son fameux épisode de *La Chartreuse de Parme*. En 1914 ou en 1916, point n'était besoin d'artifices de cet ordre, pour donner l'impression de désordre, de décousu, de chaos. Aucun observateur, fût-il le Général en chef, ne pouvait décrire la bataille dans son ensemble. Guerre de millions d'hommes, se jouant sur des centaines de kilomètres, et mettant en œuvre les ressources des nations européennes jusqu'en leurs arrières lointains, elle échappait totalement, par son échelle, au pouvoir de connaissance d'un personnage.[12]

For writers such as Barbusse, and indeed Dorgelès,[13] the attempt to create an overall picture of the war necessarily meant an element of 'invention' and an account of episodes which they themselves had not witnessed. In an apparently paradoxical way — one no doubt peculiar to art — the pursuit of a fuller 'truth' meant the creation of 'fictional' elements. This is something which J. Norton Cru criticized severely in 1930. Displaying a resolutely non-literary approach which demanded documentary realism and rejected the imaginative apprehension which art can provide, he complained of novelists who show their failure to understand war and their betrayal of it 'en la découpant en chapitres de roman feuilleton'. He even hints at an unworthy playing to the gallery when he adds: 'Cette trahison a d'autant plus de succès que le public y retrouve ses épisodes favoris'.[14] Cru's uncompromisingly documentary stand means that the war novel apparently favoured by MacLeish proves guilty of 'l'erreur traditionaliste: l'héroïsme' while that defended by Cowley betrays 'l'erreur pacifiste: la brute sanguinaire'.

This division into traditionalist and pacifist fiction, although too categorical, makes general sense if we turn to specific novels. Also, a brief consideration of two novels in particular helps us to put into clearer focus the question of moral impact raised above. Adrien Bertrand's *L'Appel du sol* and Henri Barbusse's *Le Feu* both appeared in 1916 and were both awarded the Prix Goncourt. *L'Appel du sol*, representing the more traditionalist view of war, is not widely known and copies are hard to come by. *Le Feu*, an uncompromising denunciation of war, was greatly admired by Wilfred Owen and Siegfried Sassoon when they read it in 1917 in the Everyman translation. It sold extremely well and is the most famous novel of the 1914-1918 period.[15]

Although the differences between them remain fundamental, Bertrand and Barbusse share some broad characteristics as war novelists. Both are preoccupied by the horror of trench warfare. Both are natural preachers and proselytisers pursuing a positive emotional effect. Their fictional characters (mostly officers in the case of Bertrand and other ranks in that of Barbusse) are immensely talkative. The conversations which result are a major means of conveying their 'message' to their readers. Their descriptions of human suffering are vivid and harrowing, but the narrative element is fairly fragmentary. Rather than tell a story with a strong and distinctive linear form, they work with a series of scenes and episodes — almost set-pieces — which create something like a mosaic. However, in spite of such similarities, they have very different attitudes to the presentation of war and place their common experience in contrasting moral perspectives. Bertrand wrote from a humane and traditionalist position, showing a sympathetic — but certainly not uncritical — understanding of the classical military virtues of duty, discipline, honour, courage. Barbusse wrote from outside the military tradition as a civilian of strongly left-wing persuasion caught up in the horror of modern war. Bertrand opens a debate on war and the military experience whereas Barbusse insists on a single and exclusive interpretation of these events. Bertrand's novel is two-dimensional and seeks a measure of exploration. Barbusse's novel is one-dimensional and is concerned with demonstration and proof.

Bertrand, although the balance of his attitude is towards a conservative outlook, understands and articulates opposing viewpoints. He argues a case for military discipline and patriotism. His novel ends with the words: 'Mais la France continue! . . .' But several of his characters also express a sceptical attitude towards military ideals. Acceptance and protest are juxtaposed to convey a sense of the moral complexity inherent in the Great War. On the side of acceptance we must place Bertrand's use of the traditional rhetoric of patriotism and war. Within the first six chapters we meet many predictable terms and phrases: *grandeur morale, acceptation résignée, obéissance passive, grand sacrifice, abnégation, mission rédemptrice, mourir pour son pays, ce que la Patrie attend, appel autoritaire du sol de France*, etc. Within the general tone created by this type of vocabulary the main characters (some of them regular soldiers) take a high moral view of both patriotic duty and military discipline. Several passages recall Vigny's *Servitude et grandeur militaires* in both language and moral emphasis.[16] The following is part of a long Vigny-like speech by Nicolaï, a captain in the *chasseurs alpins*:

Vous verrez, dit-il, que l'obéissance passive, la servitude sont les vertus de la campagne. L'enthousiasme s'en va. L'abnégation demeure. Ce qui fait notre force en temps de paix le fera plus encore en temps de guerre. Il ne s'agira pas d'être crâne un jour en courant à l'assaut. Il s'agira d'obéir, d'attendre, d'oser, d'entreprendre, de persévérer . . . Il s'agira de se faire tuer pour des gens inconnus, à l'arrière, là-bas, qui ne se soucient pas de nous, qui s'ingénient à ne point grossir nos rangs, qui édifient des fortunes scandaleuses sur nos cadavres.

Voilà, mon enfant, ce que la Patrie attend de vous. Voilà la nature du grand sacrifice: sacrifice morne, triste, simple et patient.[17]

In passages such as this Bertrand is aware of those evils of exploitation which Barbusse denounces. But he conceives of a duty which overrides them and of an honour which can only be served by stoical acceptance. War is accepted clear-sightedly; it is not glorified. Stoicism is the attitude of other characters such as Vaissette, *ancien normalien* and *agrégé de philosophie*, who speaks of his 'soumission aux lois mystérieuses du destin et de la raison' (p. 259).

At the same time, Bertrand recognizes weaknesses in this position. Patriotism does not prevent him from showing the French army in a state of considerable confusion and disarray due to a lack of intelligent and responsible leadership. Vaissette, although a patriot, is used to counter Nicolaï's ideas when he sees the wounded and dying in a field hospital:

Vaissette n'avait point découvert de beauté morale dans ces souffrances, ni de grandeur dans ces agonies. Il n'avait pas entendu les phrases impérissables qu'il attendait confusément. Il n'avait pas éprouvé, au sein de cet asile de détresses, l'ivresse sacrée du combat. Nulle part il n'avait trouvé l'acceptation du martyre qui endure, avec une foi passionnée, un supplice pour une cause sainte (p. 219).

One of the ordinary soldiers, Rousset, puts the anti-war case succinctly when he exclaims: '. . . c'est pas la guerre, c'est la boucherie' (p. 158). This view is confirmed by the terrible deaths and maimings described. And in the course of the novel the main characters — Nicolaï, Vaissette, Fabre, de Quéré — are all killed, while Angielli loses his reason. The final moral impression is one of extreme confusion and tragedy. There is much that is horrific; there is much that compels admiration.

If Bertrand is ready to encourage discussion and debate, Barbusse is determined to carry conviction. This determination is reflected in his use of first-person narrative which allows direct contact with the reader. Frequent authorial interventions serve a similar purpose and leave the reader in no doubt as to how events must be interpreted. Indeed, there are moments when the final chapter reads like a *Pravda* editorial. Not least, by forsaking the dynamic relationships of linear plot for something approaching the cumulative, static, patterning of a mosaic, Barbusse (and Bertrand to some extent) is able to repeat, and therefore emphasise, the moral points he wishes to make.

The first of these points is the outrageous horror of war as experienced by soldiers the majority of whom are 'des civils déracinés'.[18] The following passage is typical, in its painful realism, of Barbusse's direct assault on the reader's sensibility:

C'est un homme qui n'a pas plus de pieds. Il porte aux jambes des pansements terribles, avec des garrots pour refréner l'hémorragie. Ses moignons ont saigné dans les bandelettes de toile et il semble avoir des culottes rouges. Il a une figure de diable, luisante et sombre, et il délire. On pèse sur ses épaules et ses genoux: cet homme qui a les pieds coupés veut sauter hors du brancard pour s'en aller (pp. 288-9).

Barbusse also preaches, through his fictional characters, an explicit anti-militarism. One of the soldiers (named Bertrand, as it happens) cries:

'Honte à la gloire militaire, honte aux armées, honte au métier de soldat, qui change les hommes tour à tour en stupides victimes et en ignobles bourreaux. Oui, honte: c'est vrai, mais c'est trop vrai, c'est vrai dans l'éternité, pas encore pour nous' (p. 259).

Towards the end of the novel the moral tone takes on an increasingly political character. War is interpreted as a particularly dramatic form of a continuing exploitation of the poor by the rich: '. . . les peuples entiers vont à la boucherie, rangés en troupeaux d'armées, pour qu'une caste galonnée d'or écrive ses noms de princes dans l'histoire, pour que des gens dorés aussi, qui font partie de la même gradaille, brassent plus d'affaires' (p. 342). Finally, Barbusse sees the war as preparing revolution — 'cette guerre, c'est comme la Révolution Française qui continue' (p. 340) — and looks forward to 'l'entente des démocraties, l'entente des immensités, la levée du peuple du monde, la foi brutalement simple' (p. 348).

★　★　★

It seems appropriate to end with a brief analysis of the effects likely to be achieved by these two very different presentations of war. One's first reaction is probably to say that *Le Feu* makes the greater impact because of its anti-war militancy. Barbusse does not run the risk of confusing the reader with antithetical arguments or of undermining his desired effect by presenting a 'human' picture of the slaughter. He works with such concepts as exploitation and class conflict. He interprets modern warfare as an intensification of capitalist evils. Nevertheless, history since 1918 has not confirmed Barbusse's message. It now seems naïve compared with that of Bertrand. Furthermore, the methods Barbusse uses to convey his message to the reader are open to considerable criticism. Kenneth Burke, in the course of his comments on the MacLeish/Cowley debate mentioned earlier, argues that militant pacifism, fed by unrelievedly horrifying details of war, may prove an aesthetic basis for essentially warlike and violent reactions. He maintains that horror, repugnance and hatred can provide 'the firmest basis upon which the "heroism" of a new war could be erected'.[19] If Bertrand's approach is less positive, its subtle balance of opposites does not run the risk of creating a counter-violence. Barbusse's method, by contrast, with its fundamentally conflictual view of society, risks encouraging a counter-violence at variance with its anti-militaristic message. As Burke puts it: 'Sunday-school texts have ever been considered by sophisticated moralists the essential stimulus to "sin" — and I see no reason why the same fact should not apply to a Sunday-school simplification in dealing with the problems of war'.[20] The single thread of partisanship can all too easily prove self-defeating.

Finally, Burke argues that readers would have to respond in the direct and automatic manner of machines for the kind of persuasion used by Barbusse to have its intended effect. Fortunately, the widely canvassed machine model of human beings can be shown to be an illusion. Human stimulus and response, not least in the field of literature, are more complicated, more wayward, less predictable. In fact, *Le Feu* has been frequently admired for its dramatic rendering of war. It has been much more rarely praised as a stimulus to pacifism. If it is true that '*contradictoriness of response* is basic to human psychology',[21] *L'Appel du sol* may turn out, a trifle ironically, to be the more potent pacifist document.

SUSSEX   J. CRUICKSHANK

---

[1] Examples from France would include Montherlant, *Le Songe* (1922), Kessel, *L'Equipage* (1923), Giono, *Le grand troupeau* (1931), Céline, *Voyage au bout de la nuit* (1932), Drieu La Rochelle, *La Comédie de Charleroi* (1934), Romains, *Prélude à Verdun* and *Verdun* (1937).

[2] Dorgelès, in *Souvenirs sur les Croix de bois* (Paris, 1929), p. 36, writes: '. . . j'aurais eu honte de faire des phrases avec leur agonie, d'exploiter leurs souffrances, de trahir leurs secrets'. The consciously literary rhythm and balance of this remark tend to confirm Dorgelès's claim that a commercial and literary presentation of these events could have appeared highly inappropriate, at least while they were still going on. A different though related point is made by one of Barbusse's fictional characters in a succinct phrase: 'Ça étouffe les paroles' (*Le Feu*, p. 331).

[3] Duhamel, in *Vie des martyrs, 1914-1916* (Paris, 1917), writes on the final page: 'Il ne suffit pas de porter le couteau bienfaissant dans la plaie, ou d'en renouveler les linges avec exactitude et adresse. Il faut encore, sans en rien altérer, pouvoir retracer dans sa vérité et sa simplicité votre histoire de victimes émissaires, l'histoire de ces hommes que vous êtes pendant la douleur'.

[4] Holger Klein (ed), *The First World War in Fiction* (London, 1976), p. 4.

[5] Maurice Rieuneau, *Guerre et révolution dans le roman français de 1919 à 1939* (Paris, 1974), pp. 8-9.

[6] Paul Fussell, *The Great War and Modern Memory* (London, 1975), p. 130.

[7] The point is well made by John Flower in Klein, op. cit., p. 59: 'We do not find in this early war literature . . . the kind of careful interweaving of themes and images which Giono achieves in *Le Grand Troupeau* (1931) nor the sustained, highly personalized, even fantasied, reaction to war which Drieu offers us in *La Comédie de Charleroi* (1934)'.

[8] Stanley Cooperman, *World War I and the American Novel* (Baltimore, 1967), p. 194.

[9] See ibid., pp. 198 ff. I am much indebted to Cooperman's full account of this debate. An interesting, and very different, interpretation is to be found in Kenneth Burke's 'War, Response and Contradiction' in his *The Philosophy of Literary Form* (New York, 1957, revised and abridged edition), pp. 201-220.

[10] C. E. Carrington, 'Some Soldiers', in G. A. Panichas, *Promise of Greatness. The War of 1914-1918* (London, 1968), pp. 158-9.

[11] Fussell, op. cit., p. 36.

[12] Rieuneau, op. cit., p. 23. This point is also well made by René Pomeau, 'Guerre et roman dans l'entre-deux-guerres', *Revue des sciences humaines* (janvier-mars, 1963), pp. 77-95.

[13] See Dorgelès, op. cit., p. 33: '. . . ne pas raconter *ma* guerre, mais *la* guerre'.

[14] J. Norton Cru, *Du Témoignage* (Paris, 1930, new edition Paris, 1967), pp. 104-5.

[15] According to A Schinz, *French Literature and the Great War* (New York/London, 1920), p. 30, *Le Feu* sold 230,000 copies in the two years following publication.

[16] The last three words of the epigraph to Vigny's *Servitude et grandeur militaires* — 'Ave, Caesar, morituri te salutant' of Suetonius — are used by Bertrand as the title of his sixth chapter.

[17] André Bertrand, *L'Appel du sol* (Paris, 1916), p. 231. Further page references are given in the text.

[18] Henri Barbusse, *Le Feu* (Paris, 1916), p. 243. Further page references are given in the text.

[19] Burke, loc. cit., p. 205.

[20] Ibid., p. 206.

[21] Ibid., p. 209 (Burke's italics).

G. V. BANKS

GIRAUDOUX'S ULYSSE IN WORD AND DEED

If it is true, as R. Lewis suggests,[1] that over the ages Ulysses has had a bad press, it is equally true that the Ulysse of Giraudoux's *La Guerre de Troie n'aura pas lieu*[2] has had a good one. The description offered by Stanford in *The Ulysses Theme*, quoted approvingly by Lewis,[3] is fairly representative of the weight of critical opinion:

A salty Homeric humour and an unusual candour of phrase make it clear that this is neither the discreet negotiator nor the callous power politician . . . He is both fatalistic and energetic, realistic and compassionate, logical and imaginative, flippant and serious . . . One recognises, despite Giraudoux's twentieth century ethics and idiom, the innate honesty and tolerance of the Homeric hero. As in the *Iliad* and in *Troilus and Cressida*, the Ulysses of *La Guerre de Troie n'aura pas lieu* stands for the civilised mind in a world of unbridled passion. This is his highest function as a politique.[4]

In less fulsome yet equally unequivocal terms critics and commentators such as Mankin,[5] Albérès,[6] Lesage,[7] Lewis,[9] Van der Louw,[9] Frois[10] and Mauron[11] subscribe in general to this favourable and sympathetic view.

Critical opinion of the character and motivation of Ulysse has been based — solely based as far as one can judge — upon analysis and interpretation of the justly famous dialogue between Hector and Ulysse, the *duo avant l'orchestre* as Ulysse himself describes it, Act II, scene 13 of the play. In this most literary of scenes the Greek leader reveals all his own considerable 'literary skills'. He is a master of rhetoric: eloquent, rich in allusion, argument and example, measured and controlled at all times, above all persuasive. So charming are his words, so enchanting the elegance of his expression that it is difficult to resist the force of his argument. And, essentially, his argument is an age old argument: man is powerless to resist or influence the will of 'Destiny'. Hence the Trojan war in unavoidable for Destiny has willed it. However sympathetic he, Ulysse, may be towards Hector's desire for peace, however keen he may be to help him in the pursuit of this desire — and no one, he protests, could be keener — he knows in his wisdom that all attempts to influence the course of events are in vain. For the workings of Destiny are external to the will of man, are independent of and impervious to his actions, desires and aspirations. Ulysse's definition of Destiny is epitomised in his description of Hélène as:

une des rares créatures que le destin met en circulation sur la terre pour son usage personnel.[12]

This description implies neatly and effectively an absence of human free-will and a concomitant absence of human responsibility for that which might befall. Such a view of the role of an all-powerful destiny in human affairs is a morally comforting one, and one perfectly in keeping with the manner in which Ulysse presents himself in Act II. scene 13. For it is impossible to separate Ulysse's presentation of his argument from his projection of himself. The aim of this consummate rhetorician and actor is not just to propound his argument as persuasively as possible but also to present himself in as favourable a light as possible.

Ulysse portrays himself as a man of the world and one who knows its ways. In sadness, in wisdom, with reluctance yet resignation he bows to the way of the world. He is the elder statesman, helping, humouring, soothing the younger, impassioned idealist. He is tolerant and compassionate, demonstrating a good deal of sympathy for Hector's feelings, even indicating as their encounter moves towards its climax, that he is prepared to let his heart rule his head and side with Hector against the ineluctable. It is warming to feel that humanity in general and Ulysse in particular are devoid of all ill-will. In everything the Greek leader says, he displays grace, ease, wit and even-temperedness. Taken on his face value, this attractive and winning personality is hard to fault. He charms us.

He fails to charm Andromaque. Having eavesdropped upon the debate between Ulysse and her husband, Hector, the Trojan woman is in a state of great distress:

HECTOR: Tu étais là, Andromaque?
ANDROMAQUE: Soutiens-moi. Je n'en puis plus!
HECTOR: Tu nous écoutais?
ANDROMAQUE: Oui. Je suis brisée.
HECTOR: Tu vois qu'il ne nous faut pas désespérer.
ANDROMAQUE: De nous peut-être. Du monde oui. Cet homme est effroyable. La misère du monde est sur moi.
HECTOR: Une minute encore et Ulysse est à son bord . . . Il marche vite. D'ici l'on suit son cortège. Le voilà déjà en face des fontaines. Que fais-tu?
ANDROMAQUE: Je n'ai plus la force d'entendre. Je me bouche les oreilles. Je n'enlèverai pas mes mains avant que notre sort soit fixé . . .[13]

This exchange between Hector and Andromaque opens the last scene of the play and follows immediately, of course, the *duo avant l'orchestre*. It is the last exchange which takes place between the Trojan couple and, in fact, Andromaque speaks here her last words in the play. Husband and wife contrast strikingly in their reactions to Ulysse. Hector has come to trust and believe him. Andromaque is appalled by him and is convinced that all is lost. The events of the final scene, unfolding with bewildering and terrifying swiftness and leading to the catastrophe of war, prove her right. But as the final scene opens she cannot know the detail of what is to follow. It is her reaction to and assessment of Ulysse which cause her distress. She sees him as being instrumental in her own downfall and that of Troy. She seems alone in finding him 'effroyable'.

It has been argued that the reaction to Ulysse of the emotionally involved Andromaque is a naïve and subjective one.[14] Certainly everything she holds dear is at stake at this point in the play so she is scarcely in a state of mind conducive to detached objectivity. Moreover we know her to be an affective and impulsive creature. However, it can also be argued that Andromaque is a woman of unerring insight and instinct, one who has much in common with that other beguiling Giralducian character, Le Mendiant, in *Electre*, when he says:

Moi, j'ai une qualité. Je ne comprends pas les paroles des gens. Je n'ai pas d'instruction. Je comprends les gens . . .[15]

Does Andromaque understand Ulysse? An examination of Ulysse's overall contribution to the unfolding of events suggests strongly that she does.

It is easy to gain the impression, when reading critical interpretations of *La Guerre de Troie n'aura pas lieu*, that Ulysse appears only in one scene of the play — namely Act II, scene 13. For, almost invariably, this is the only scene mentioned, let alone discussed, in relation to his role. But Ulysse appears in two scenes. Act II, scene 12 depicts Ulysse's arrival in Troy and his encounter with Hector, Priam, Pâris, Hélène and the citizens of Troy. We witness him in action.

In tone, pace and style, Act II, scene 12 contrasts greatly with the scene which follows it. Whilst the Hector-Ulysse debate is an elegant scene of high comedy, conducted between two civil, polished, articulate and intelligent characters, Act II, scene 12 is, in large measure, a scene of low comedy, of burlesque, a scene in which coarseness and vulgarity have their vital role to play. Perhaps this is why it has been largely ignored. Yet Ulysse's behaviour in this scene is crucial to the whole outcome of the play. Any attempt to interpret his words, motivation and behaviour in Act II, scene 13 without a constant awareness of the nature and significance of his achievement in the preceding scene, fails to avoid one of the major pitfalls in the criticism of dramatic literature: that is to see the scene and not the play, to listen to the character and not the dramatist.

When Ulysse arrives in Troy he finds to his surprise that things seem to be moving towards a peaceful settlement. Oiax, the coarse and inebriated Greek who on his first appearance insults Andromaque and strikes Hector, taunting him with cowardice, is now a reformed character. Impressed by Hector's strength and athletic prowess, and sharing with him a contempt for the war-mongering versifier, Demokos, Oiax promises the Trojan leader that he will work for peace:

Je ne me bats pas contre ceux qui ont avec moi pour ennemis les fils d'Achichaos. Ne parlons plus de guerre. Je ne sais ce qu'Ulysse rumine, mais compte sur moi pour arranger l'histoire.[16]

Furthermore, more surprisingly perhaps and certainly more importantly, Pâris and Hélène seem for the first time ready to accord Hector their positive help and support. Up until this point in the play each of the young people has seemed indifferent to the arguments and pleadings of both Hector[17] and Andromaque.[18] Now, however, Hélène is prepared to return to Greece. Uncharacteristically, Ulysse is caught unawares by this turn of events and is, momentarily, taken aback:

ULYSSE: Qu'Hélène nous soit donc rendue dans l'heure même. Ou c'est la guerre.
OIAX: Il y a les adieux à faire.
HECTOR: Et c'est tout?
ULYSSE: C'est tout.
OIAX: Ce n'est pas long, tu vois, Hector?
HECTOR: Ainsi, si nous vous rendons Hélène, vous nous assurez la paix.
OIAX: Et la tranquillité.
HECTOR: Si elle embarque dans l'heure, l'affaire est close.
OIAX: Et liquidée.
HECTOR: Je crois que nous allons pouvoir nous entendre, n'est-ce pas Hélène?
HÉLÈNE: Oui, je le pense.
ULYSSE: Vous ne voulez pas dire qu'Hélène va nous être rendue?
HECTOR: Cela même. Elle est prête.[19]

Thus to Ulysse's surprise his ultimatum leads not to discord but to agreement. Given goodwill on both sides there seems to be nothing standing in the way of peace. But this does not suit Ulysse. He has been led, perhaps tricked by Hector and Oiax into agreeing to a settlement which he does not want. Recovering quickly from his initial surprise, the wily political negotiator demands a further guarantee, one which he knows full well to be impossible:

ULYSSE: Pardon! Je ne garantis rien. Pour que nous renoncions à toutes représailles, il faudrait qu'il n'y eût pas prétexte à représailles. Il faudrait que Ménélas retrouvât Hélène dans l'état même où elle lui fut ravie.

HECTOR: A quoi reconnaîtra-t-il un changement?
ULYSSE: Un mari est subtil quand un scandale mondial l'a averti. Il faudrait que Pâris eût respecté Hélène. Et ce n'est pas le cas . . .
LA FOULE: Ah non! Ce n'est pas le cas!
UNE VOIX: Pas précisément!
HECTOR: Et si c'était le cas?
ULYSSE: Où voulez-vous en venir Hector?
HECTOR: Pâris n'a pas touché Hélène. Tous deux m'ont fait leur confidences.
ULYSSE: Quelle est cette histoire?
HECTOR: La vraie histoire, n'est-ce pas Hélène?
HÉLÈNE: Qu'a-t-elle d'extraordinaire?
UNE VOIX: C'est épouvantable! Nous sommes déshonorés!
HECTOR: Qu'avez vous à sourire Ulysse? Vous voyez sur Hélène le moindre indice d'une défaillance à son devoir?
ULYSSE: Je ne le cherche pas. L'eau sur le canard marque mieux que la souillure sur la femme.
PÂRIS: Tu parles à une reine.
ULYSSE: Exceptons les reines naturellement . . . Ainsi, Pâris, vous avez enlevé cette reine, vous l'avez enlevée nue; vous-même, je pense, n'étiez pas dans l'eau avec cuissard et armure, et aucun goût d'elle, aucun désir d'elle ne vous a saisi?
PÂRIS: Une reine nue est couverte par sa dignité.
HÉLÈNE: Elle n'a qu'à ne pas s'en dévêtir.[10]

Ironically, he who seeks the truth seeks war, they who lie seek peace. Thus in support of Hector and pursuit of peace, Pâris and Hélène, those two promiscuous, sexually vigorous and hitherto irresponsible young lovers, understandably proud of their physical attractiveness and the prowess which accompanies it, are prepared to deny that they have made love, to claim that they spent three days or more together on the boat from Greece to Troy in perfect innocence. It is not easy for them to do so.

It is impossible to overestimate the importance of the role played by the Trojan crowd in this scene. We have seen in the passage quoted above how ready the citizens of Troy are to participate in and contribute to the proceedings; it is easy to note what their convictions are and where their sympathies lie. In responding as they do to Ulysse's reaction to the 'innocence' of Pâris and Hélène, they give the Greek the hint he needs, the momentary insight enabling him to choose the direction of his attack.

Ulysse takes the floor and turns the situation into a parody of a court-room drama. He himself plays the role of the eloquent, amused, incredulous counsel for the prosecution, cross-examining Pâris and Hélène, the ever less convincing and increasingly ill-at-ease prisoners at the bar. The Trojan crowd warms to playing the part of an unruly, boisterous, coarse and totally partial public gallery. It is a hilarious scene but one which is deadly in its consequences.

The interrogation of Pâris and Hélène by Ulysse is, of course, a game. No one is deceived for a moment. It is a question as to whether or not the characters are prepared to play the game, to pursue the lie in order to further the cause of peace. Ulysse is not. His performance is admirable, his mental agility, his insight, his lightning reactions, his powers of persuasion and manipulation magnificent. He probes, he taunts, he insults. He casts aspersions on the Trojan navy, above all on Pâris's manhood and virility, and by broad implication on all Trojan manhood and virility. He thus reduces the lusty Pâris to a state of acute annoyance and unbearable embarrassment and at the same time whips the Trojan crowd into an ever-increasing rage, a chauvinistic and xenophobic fury. A Greek has insulted their military and sexual prowess. It is too much to bear.

Ulysse pursues his interrogation until he achieves his aim, until he makes certain that the truth — the truth he wants out — will out. Finally, in defiance of Hector's orders, urged on and cheered by the Trojan crowd, Le Gabier and Olpidès launch into a vigorous, earthy and admirably detailed account of Pâris's and Hélène's cavortings in the boat.

Through a masterly exercise in individual and collective psychology, Ulysse has achieved his ends. Having once recovered from his initial surprise he never again loses control of the situation. He knows precisely when to speak, precisely when to keep silent. He speaks, he holds the centre of the stage until the Trojan sailors take up his cause. He then falls silent for his work is done, and remains so until the die is cast. He speaks again briefly when the sailors' account of the voyage is complete, only to make assurance double sure:

ULYSSE: Hélène écoute, charmée.
HÉLÈNE: J'oublais qu'il s'agissait de moi. Ces hommes ont de la conviction.
ULYSSE: Ose dire qu'ils mentent, Pâris.
PÂRIS: Dans les détails, quelque peu.[21]

The two all too recently converted disciples of Hector's cause capitulate finally — with a certain understandable sense of pride and even wonder — to the promptings of Ulysse. Now that the evidence is complete, Ulysse speaks for the last time in this scene. He turns to Hector and says, in what must surely be a tone of quiet satisfaction and triumph: 'Et voilà, Hector'.[11]

Whilst recognising an element of playfulness in Ulysse's nature, a gratuitous pleasure found in the manipulation of other people, in the exploiting of their discomfort and ridiculousness, we cannot ignore a further and more serious motivation guiding his behaviour in this scene. If in the moments following Ulysse's arrival in Troy a peaceful settlement seems a distinct possibility, by the end of Act II, scene 12 the situation has deteriorated greatly. Consciously, deliberately, Ulysse has engineered this deterioration. He can now leave it to 'Destiny' to fill in the details. And 'Destiny' is, of course, the nub of the matter.

The 'Destiny' to which Ulysse refers so blithely during his debate with Hector in Act II, scene 13 — that nebulous, abstract, inhuman force, so beloved of pseudo-fatalists, — is different indeed from the destiny which he intuits, senses to be at work, seizes upon and exploits throughout Act II, scene 12.

This latter force of destiny is constantly at work in the play. Hector combats it ceaselessly and unavailingly, Ulysse exploits it fruitfully. It is the collective will of the people of Troy, the collective will of a society in a state of moral decay, a society in which bellicosity is wedded to licentiousness.

Throughout his *comédie-tragédie*,[23] Giraudoux portrays his ideal couple, Hector and Andromaque, as the embodiment of the ideal of peace, individual and collective. Defeated they may be, because for them the times are out of joint, mistaken they may be, for they do not have the power to control either their own destiny or that of Troy, but this monogamous, loyal and pacific couple never lose honour or dignity. The Giralducian moral ideal, embodied in *La Guerre de Troie n'aura pas lieu* in the characters of Hector and Andromaque, is as subjective as any other. But it constitutes the mainspring of the drama and lends the play its tragic dimension.

Until the arrival of Ulysse upon the scene, and her own belated conversion to Hector's cause, Hélène is the mirror-image of that force of destiny, that collective will with which Hector grapples in vain. Herein lies her power, here is to be found the nature of this *femme fatale*. Young, sensual and promiscuous, irresponsible, carefree and amoral, the exotic Hélène flatters the dreams of Trojan youth, Pâris and Troilus, the fond, sentimental memories of the elder statesman, Priam, the lusty appetites of the Trojan crowd, the perverted blatherings of the war-mongering poetaster, Demokos, and the fantasies of the lascivious old men of Troy. The image of all they envy and desire, she is the image of their moral values — or lack of them — and therefore of their destiny. Thus, rightly or wrongly, but unmistakably, Giraudoux draws a close parallel between a nation's moral decay and the advent of its downfall.

Ulysse replaces Hélène as the principal adversary of Hector and of peace. Whatever his protestations to the contrary in the subsequent debate with Hector, the Greek leader, by his behaviour in Act II, scene 12, contributes wilfully and vitally to the unleashing of the forces of destruction. Ulysse is not, of course, solely responsible for the outbreak of the Trojan war. He is not responsible for the moral state of the majority of the citizens of Troy, nor for their aggressive chauvinism. He is, however, responsible in part — and importantly so — for the outbreak of hostilities for he goads the Trojans into fury and thus renders the outbreak of war more certain and precipitates it. He moves with the tide, having helped to move it. It is this part-responsibility which Ulysse seeks above all to deny in Act II, scene 13. But not even his rhetorical powers succeed in concealing the fact that, despite an apparently remarkable change in behaviour and attitude, Giraudoux's Ulysse is all of a piece.

After the initial verbal fencing which opens the *combat de paroles*,[24] a verbal fencing which takes the form of a *pesée*[25] in which both Greek and Trojan present themselves and what they stand for, Ulysse embarks upon a speech which is to set the tone for all which is to follow in scene 13. It is worthy of our close attention:

Vous êtes jeune, Hector! . . . A la veille de toute guerre, il est courant que deux chefs des peuples en conflit se rencontrent seuls dans quelque innocent village, sur la terrasse au bord d'un lac, dans l'angle d'un jardin. Et ils conviennent que la guerre est le pire fléau du monde, et tous deux, à suivre du regard ces reflets et ces rides sur les eaux, à recevoir sur l'épaule ces pétales de magnolias, ils sont pacifiques, modestes, loyaux. Et ils s'étudient. Ils se regardent. Et, tiédis par le soleil, attendris par un vin clairet, ils ne trouvent dans le visage d'en face aucun trait qui justifie la haine, aucun trait qui n'appelle l'amour humain, et rien d'incompatible non plus dans leur langages, dans leur façon de se gratter le nez ou de boire. Et ils sont vraiment combles de paix, de désirs de paix. Et ils se quittent en se serrant les mains, en se sentant des frères. Et ils se retournent de leur calèche pour se sourire . . .Et le lendemain pourtant éclate la guerre . . . Ainsi nous sommes tous deux maintenant . . . Nos peuples autour de l'entretien se taisent et s'écartent mais ce n'est pas qu'ils attendent de nous une victoire sur l'inéluctable. C'est seulement qu'ils nous ont donné pleins pouvoirs, qu'ils nous ont isolés, pour que nous goûtions mieux, au-dessus de la catastrophe, notre fraternité d'ennemis. Goûtons-la. C'est un plat de riches. Savourons-la . . . Mais c'est tout. Le privilège des grands, c'est de voir les catastrophes d'une terrasse.[26]

The speech has all the neatness and elegance of a mathematical equation — *quod erat demonstrandum* — but none of its proof in logic. But then Ulysse is not in the business of proving by logic or reason (although, very cleverly, he gives the impression here, at least at first sight, that he is), but in that of persuading through rhetoric.

The principal rhetorical device he employs is the accumulation of a series of detailed observations, concrete, vivid, immediate, instantly recognisable and acceptable, all of them convincing in themselves, used as a means of demonstrating a generalised, absolute truth. Each detail has the irresistable ring of truth: the lakeside village with its garden, its terrace, its magnolias, its warming sun and welcoming wine; the heads of state drinking and conversing together, exuding friendship and goodwill, protesting their hatred of war, their love of peace; the final handshake, the friendly and official wave from the coach of state.[27] The setting, the pattern of events, the responses and behaviour of the participants are all too familiar. The whole affair is presented as a play, a ritualised game, the necessary preliminary to an inevitable subsequent event ('Et le lendemain pourtant éclate la guerre'), an event upon which the heads of state have apparently no influence and over which they have no control. Here is the main burden of Ulysse's argument in this speech and indeed throughout the scene. For his later references to economic greed,[28] national pride,[29] human folly and brutality,[30] — and he is as convincing in detail on these matters as he is in the detail of the speech quoted above, for all he refers to is, alas, quite obviously and constantly present in human affairs — are used in the service of one overriding 'truth'. The 'truth' is that if Destiny wills two people to go to war, there is nothing that statesmen can do about it; they can in no way be held responsible.

Like all masters of rhetoric, Ulysse pays as much attention to the structure of his speech as he does to the detail of its content. Having set the role of statesmen in the period immediately preceding the outbreak of war in a general framework, having absolved them from all responsibility, having accepted the inevitability of war, Ulysse moves from the general to the particular:

Et le lendemain pourtant éclate la guerre . . . Ainsi nous sommes tous deux maintenant . . . Nos peuples autour de l'entretien se taisent et s'écartent mais ce n'est pas qu'ils attendent de nous une victoire sur l'inéluctable.

Thus, Ulysse, having described an identifiably recurrent pattern of events in the history of human conflict, and having elevated that pattern to the level of an absolute truth, now invites Hector to accept that they too are part of this pattern of events, and to bow to the inevitability of a Trojan war which they have no power to prevent and for which they are not responsible.

Ulysse goes further than this. The closing lines of his speech are surely nothing short of an exercise in aristocratic cynicism, an invitation to Hector to join forces with him, exploit his privileged position, profit from the situation and enjoy the war. Taken in this way — and it is difficult to see how they may be taken in any other — these closing lines, betraying as they do the cynicism, self-interest and callousness of Ulysse, may be seen as reason enough for Andromaque's later outburst.[31]

It seem likely, however, that there is further reason for Andromaque's troubled reaction to Ulysse. The Greek leader refers twice to Andromaque in his conversation with Hector. Both references occur towards the end of the scene. On the first occasion he is assuring Hector of his sincere desire to side with him against Destiny:

Je ruse en ce moment contre le destin, non contre vous. C'est mon premier essai et j'y ai plus de mérite. Je suis sincère, Hector. Si je voulais la guerre, je ne vous demanderais pas Hélène, mais une rançon qui vous est plus chère . . . Je pars . . . mais je ne peux me défendre de l'impression qu'il est bien long, le chemin qui va de cette place à mon navire.[32]

On the second occasion Ulysse brings the scene to an end as he explains to Hector what it is that has persuaded him to leave:

ULYSSE: Vous savez ce qui me décide à partir, Hector . . .
HECTOR: Je le sais. La noblesse.
ULYSSE: Pas précisément. Andromaque a le même battement de cils que
           Pénélope.[33]

Now both these references to Andromaque are decidedly ambivalent. Undoubtedly, Ulysse's conscious intentions are to avow his desire to help Hector and to explain his reasons for having decided to do so. But also, unwittingly, Ulysse reveals perhaps something of the workings of his own imagination. Whether or not he would ever consider seriously demanding Andromaque's favours as the price of peace is not the point; the point is that such a possibility springs to his mind, and, eventually, to his lips. This terrifies Andromaque. So too does his highly evocative and disturbing reference to his wife, Penelope. Whilst Ulysse shares none of the coarseness or vulgarity of the Trojan mob which he has, at an earlier stage, understood so instinctively and provoked so effectively, there is present the innuendo that he shares, at least imaginatively, some of their sexual proclivities. Taking his ambivalent references to Andromaque in conjunction with the insights and attitudes he reveals in Act II, scene 12, it is fair to say that a certain moral decadence is more than hinted at.

Towards the end of Act II, scene 13, Giraudoux shows us an Ulysse willing to help Hector secure the peace. In doing so he shows us this character at his most complex. Ulysse is sincere in his impulse to help Hector at this point. However, the nature of his sincerity and the quality of the feelings which inform it are open to question.[34] For Ulysse's feelings and their sincerity are surely closely akin to those of the statesmen he himself describes so ironically earlier in the scene. We recall:

Et ils sont vraiment combles de paix, de désirs de paix. Et ils se quittent en se serrant les mains, en se sentant des frères. Et ils se retournent de leur calèche pour se sourire . . . Et le lendemain pourtant éclate la guerre . . .[35]

Here, with a keen sense of dramatic irony, Giraudoux portrays Ulysse hoisting himself on his own petard. He becomes one of the statesmen he describes. We have seen earlier how he identifies consciously with them in disclaiming all responsibility for the outbreak of war. But now, unconsciously, he identifies with their gestures and feelings. His sincerity is of the moment, and of the moment only. It is shallow, instantaneous, ephemeral. It has no roots in past behaviour or experience — emotional or moral —, no bearing whatsoever on future events. It is born of sentimentality. Like Homer's Ulysses, like many a warrior far from home, Giraudoux's Ulysse has a strong sentimental streak in his make-up.

Because of their sentimental nature, Ulysse's feelings at this moment in the play are short-lived and inefficacious; they have no influence upon the course of events. As we have seen, other, deeper layers of his character have been at work in the shaping of things to come.

In his portraits of Hector and Ulysse, and in their confrontation, Giraudoux shows the conflict of two contrasting characters, each of them the embodiment of a partial truth, neither of them possessing the whole truth.

Hector believes that he is arbiter of his own and of his people's destiny, that he has the power and the responsibility to dictate absolutely the future course of events. He believes in the unlimited power of the individual human will. In this Giraudoux shows him to be mistaken. Ulysse claims that destiny operates entirely independently of human will, that man is powerless to influence its workings and therefore free from all responsibility for what befalls humanity. In this Giraudoux shows him to be mistaken.

The overall burden of the argument presented by Giraudoux in *La Guerre de Troie n'aura pas lieu* is that destiny is made up of an immense complex of interacting phenomena, constantly at work within human society; we do not have absolute control over these phenomena, but our own individual behaviour is an essential, contributory part of the pattern, and for this, and its consequences, we are responsible (The Giraudoux who writes *La Guerre de Troie n'aura pas lieu* has much in common with Sartre).

Thus each of the characters, convinced that he possesses the whole truth, possesses only a partial vision of the whole truth proposed through his play by the dramatist.

But there is an essential difference between the two men in the way in which they are portrayed; it is a difference in moral quality. Hector, blind to an important part of the truth of his condition though he may be, acts in good faith; committed, responsible and embattled, he is a man of moral integrity. He is the hero of the play, a flawed but noble creation.

Ulysse, *rusé*, deceitful, at times self-deceiving, is devoid of moral conscience. He is devious and self-interested, a man portrayed by Giraudoux as a man of *mauvaise foi*, whose actions belie his words. He

163

is also portrayed as witty, intelligent and charming, a character with whom it is difficult to disagree, whom it is perhaps impossible to dislike. But that is because Giraudoux, a dramatist with an intuitive knowledge of the theatre and its ways, knows that in *La Guerre de Troie n'aura pas lieu*, this entertainment with a serious moral purpose, he must give the enemy he creates the freedom to oppose him.

BIRMINGHAM   G. V. BANKS

[1] R. Lewis, *Giraudoux: La Guerre de Troie n'aura pas lieu*, Studies in French Literature, 19 (London, Arnold, 1971), p. 49.

[2] All references to the play (hereinafter referred to as *Guerre de Troie*) are drawn from Jean Giraudoux, *Théâtre*, Volume II (Paris, Grasset, 1959), pp. 245-329.

[3] Lewis, op. cit., p. 50.

[4] W. Stanford, *The Ulysses Theme* (Oxford, Blackwell, 1954), pp. 173-74.

[5] Mankin, *Precious Irony; the Theatre of Jean Giraudoux*, (The Hague, Mouton, 1971). See in particular pp. 114 *et seq.*

[6] R. M. Albérès, *Esthétique et Morale chez Jean Giraudoux* (Paris, Nizet, 1957). See in particular pp. 396 *et seq.*

[7] L. Lesage, *Jean Giraudoux: His Life and Works* (Pennsylvania State University Press, 1959). See in particular pp. 139 *et seq.*

[8] Lewis, op. cit., pp. 48-57.

[9] G. van der Louw, *La Tragédie grecque dans le théâtre de Giraudoux* (Université de Nancy, Publications du Centre Européen Universitaire, Collection des Mémoires, no. 24, 1967). See in particular pp. 22 *et seq.*

[10] E. Frois, *Giraudoux: La Guerre de Troie n'aura pas lieu* (Paris, Hatier, 1971). See in particular pp. 38 *et seq.*

[11] Charles Mauron, *Le Théâtre de Giraudoux; Etude psychocritique* (Paris, Corti, 1971). See in particular pp. 106 *et seq.* Mauron's judgement on Ulysse is in part favourable, in part unfavourable. He does recognise, to some extent, the actively sinister role played by the Greek in Act II, scene 12. He does also, however, aver his belief in Ulysse's sincerity, good faith and goodwill, in Act II, scene 13. Overall, it is a study of the character which suggests that Mauron has some difficulty in making up his mind.

[12] *Guerre de Troie*, Act II, scene 13, p. 325.

[13] ibid., Act II, scene 14, p. 327.

[14] Lewis, op. cit., p. 59. In contrast, in her book, *Le Théâtre de Giraudoux et la Condition Humaine* (Paris, Domat, 1954), M. Mercier-Campiche asserts firmly — and in our view rightly — 'Andromaque ne se trompe pas quand elle appelle le chef grec un homme effroyable' (p. 67). See pp. 55-73 for this critic's (in our opinion) convincing interpretation of Ulysse's role in the play.

[15] Giraudoux, *Electre* in *Théâtre*, Volume III (Paris, Grasset, 1959), Act I, scene 3, p. 26.

[16] *Guerre de Troie*, Act II, scene 11, p. 311.

[17] ibid. See in particular Act I, scene 4, pp. 257-62, and Act I, scenes 8 and 9, pp. 274-81.

[18] ibid., See in particular Act II, scene 8, pp. 302-07.

[19] ibid., Act II, scene 12, p. 312.

[20] ibid., Act II, scene 12, pp. 313-14.

[21] ibid., Act II, scene 12, p. 318.

[22] ibid., Act II, scene 12, p. 318.

[23] Giraudoux's own definition of his play in *L'Echo de Paris* (6 November 1935) p. 4, 'Interviews rapides avec Jean Giraudoux'. Interviewer: Maurice Dabadie.

[24] *Guerre de Troie*; Hector's words in Act II, scene 13, p. 320.

[25] ibid. Ulysse's words in Act II, scene 13, p. 320.

[26] ibid., Act II, scene 13, pp. 321-22.

[27] A description which surely brought to the minds of the 1935 audience and readers both the Peace agreement signed between the representatives of France, Belgium, Britain, Germany and Italy at Locarno in 1925, and the conference held in Stresa in 1935 between France, Britain and Italy after the re-establishing of obligatory military service in Germany in that same year.

[28] *Guerre de Troie*, Act II, scene 13, p. 324.

[29] ibid., Act II, scene 13, p. 323.

[30] ibid., Act II, scene 13, p. 323.

[31] ibid., Act II, scene 14, p. 327.

[32] ibid., Act II, scene 13, p. 326.

[33] ibid., Act II, scene 13, p. 327.

[34] ibid., Act II, scene 13, pp. 326-27.

[35] ibid., Act II, scene 13, p. 322.

J. FLOWER

TOWARDS A PSYCHOBIOGRAPHICAL STUDY OF MAURIAC — THE CASE OF *GENITRIX*

Quelque chose ne meurt pas, Vincent, c'est notre passé, mon passé dont je suis obsédé. *L'Enfant chargé de chaînes.*

L'enfance est le tout d'une vie, puisqu'elle nous en donne la clef.
Mémoires Intérieurs.

In his notes on the genesis of *Le Fleuve de Feu* in the first volume of the Pléiade edition of Mauriac's work Jacques Petit, commenting on Daniel Trassis' search for a lost purity and innocence through his affair with Gisèle de Plailly, remarks that the novel 'demanderait un commentaire psychanalytique autant que religieux'.[1] The proposition is an interesting one and could surely be extended to the whole of Mauriac's work. The role which Gisèle is required to fill in this novel ('on disait que les garçons cherchent en nous leur pureté perdue')[2] is one shared by Colombe in *Le Mal* (finally published in book form in 1935 though begun much earlier),[3] and in different ways and at later stages by characters like Marinette in *Le Nœud de vipères* (1932), Mathilde in *Les Anges noirs* (1936) or Jeannette Séris in *Un Adolescent d'autrefois* (1969), for example. Furthermore it could be argued that this particular aspect of Mauriac's work is not the only one to which such an approach might be profitably applied. Indeed given the frequency with which critics have drawn attention to the abnormality of many of the relationships between characters in his novels, and given too the manner in which his generally pessimistic view of life also dominates much of his non-fictional and more personal writing, it is surprising that some form of psychoanalytical study on an extensive scale has not been undertaken. There are some exceptions; Emile Glenisson, a psychologist by training, in his *L'amour dans les romans de François Mauriac* (1970)[4] does examine some of the heterosexual relationships depicted in Mauriac's work, and in the same year J. P. McNab published an interesting article 'The Mother in François Mauriac's *Genitrix*'[5] in which he restricts himself to a consideration of the novel as a self-sufficient subject for critical analysis in its own right, making few attempts to link it with any literary material or information concerning the author. Since these publications the influence of psychoanalysis on literary criticism has grown apace, with the psychocriticism pioneered by Charles Mauron and the rather more orthodox psychobiographical work of critics like Marthe Robert and Dominique Fernandez emerging as probably the most influential and certainly amongst the least abstruse.[6]

Within the context of this article to comment in any detail on more than a single text is impossible; and because of such constraints, even though some of the techniques of psychocriticism can be used to good effect, such an analysis, requiring according to Mauron's criteria the entire body of an author's work, is out of the question. Given these limits therefore a modified form of psychobiography seems, for present purposes at least, more appropriate.

The dangers inherent in the use of psychoanalysis for the study of literature are obvious. Not only does the critic risk having his own subconscious preferences and desires shape his assessment unbeknown to him (though this is arguably the case in any form of criticism) he may also be too readily satisfied with a facile correlation, direct or hidden, between, say, literary symbol or character development and behaviour, and certain verifiable features of the author's background and private life. Certainly in such an approach this latter element must play some part though it is essential, as Starobinski reminds us, that we should not be drawn into a study of what he defines as the 'préhistoire des œuvres',[7] at the expense of those literary qualities to which such knowledge should guide us. Whether or not we accept Freud's view that art is an activity by which the artist, consciously or otherwise, attempts to compensate for something which in real life he either did not or could not have, is not so vital as to recognize that whatever form it takes, it is an integral part of and therefore inseparable from life. Starobinski would in fact go further than this and argue that not only may a work of art be seen as consequential upon past events and influences, it is already part of a premeditated future and, as it becomes part of the past a formative factor in subsequent development.[8] While psychobiography may ultimately be open to the same kind of complex extension, it is in its basic form at least rather more restricted. Although its proponents[9] rightly acknowledge that the *formal* characteristics of a work should be considered as well as the more normal features of image and symbol, the starting point, which is the establishment of the facts of childhood and early family life, does lead to a form of determinism which in a way might be said to deny the artist (and his work) almost all freedom. Indeed in this sense psychobiographical criticism takes us close to Freud's view expressed in the *Psychopathology of everyday life* that an author's choice of words and forms of expression can be seen when analysed to reveal a meaning of which he was often unaware but which can nonetheless be retrospectively explained. While therefore within the limits of this essay all that I can hope to achieve is to suggest that some form of psychoanalytical study of Mauriac's work could have fruitful interpretive possibilities, such an examination might also be seen as a way of approaching that vexing question of his relationship with and the autonomy of his characters.

Although Mauriac never tried to deny that as a novelist he was always interested in the exploration and unravelling of the psychological problems of his characters, he always firmly rejected the idea that Freud's theories influenced his early writing in any specific way.[10] Whether or not we choose to accept this, it is undoubtedly true that from Mauriac's journals or essays of the 1920s there is little evidence that he was anything but sceptical, if not dismissive, of Freud's theories and analyses. In this he was not unlike his fellow Catholics Bernanos and Maritain, and his attitude is adequately summarised in *Le Roman* (1928) where he writes: 'Il y a un secret des cœurs qui est fermé aux anges, ouvert seulement à la science sacerdotale du Christ. Un Freud aujourd'hui, par des ruses de psychologue, entreprend de la violer'.[11]

How then do we respond to a novel like *Genitrix*? Of Mauriac's early novels it is one of the least well documented. Not only is the manuscript missing, but Mauriac's only private writing from this period currently available — extracts from a diary published as the *Journal d'un homme de trente ans* — contains only two or three allusions to his progress in writing *Genitrix*, and there are certainly no references to Freud or hints of any interest in psychological abnormality. Yet it is difficult, given its subject matter, not to speculate that a psychological analysis of *Genitrix* would be rewarding, particularly so in the light of Mauriac's dedication of the book to his brother Pierre, a doctor at the Medical Faculty in Bordeaux: 'A mon frère [. . .] Je confie *ces malades* en témoignage de ma tendre admiration'.[12]

There are of course at least two distinct ways of approaching the novel in psychological terms. The first (which McNab has already partly explored) is to analyse the novel purely in terms of its own frame of reference: in this way the conflicts which Mauriac develops in it may be seen merely as various features of a particular case history which he wishes for whatever reason to describe. The second is rather more wide-ranging (some would say fanciful) and attempts to assess through an analysis of the book's themes, imagery and structure, the importance which Mauriac's own psychological development had in its conception and creation.

Mauriac's first references of any length to *Genitrix* are to be found late in his life in the *Nouveaux Mémoires intérieurs* (1965) where he discusses it in relation to his own childhood and to the kind of society in which he grew up. Even without such recollections, however, it would be impossible from an acquaintance with Mauriac's earlier imaginative writing not to be aware of the mother-son or older woman-young man relationship as a recurring and dominant one. What is particularly interesting in the case of *Genitrix*, however, is that this novel is the first in which Mauriac develops the mother figure to any degree; hitherto in the five novels already published the mother had remained either marginal or caricatured, and even in the manuscript versions of *Le Mal*, Thérèse Dézaymeries was only the embodiment of certain moral and religious values threatened by the influence of Fanny.

It is generally recognized that Mauriac's most thinly disguised portrait of his own mother, who died in June 1930, is to be found in Blanche Frontenac (*Le Mystère Frontenac* (1933)). The underlying tenderness of this depiction is unquestionable, though the descriptions of the young Yves Frontenac's love for his mother may seem (especially when taken out of context) at times unusual; for example '[Yves] frottait sa figure aux genoux de Blanche, s'attachait à elle comme si un instinct l'eût poussé à rentrer dans ce corps d'où il était sorti'.[13] The facts of Mauriac's early years on which much of *Le Mystère Frontenac* is based are well known. Having lost his father when he was only twenty months old, Mauriac was brought up as the youngest of five children by his mother and grandmother. His sense of insecurity directly recalled in the quotation above is apparent too in the essays in *Commencements d'une vie* and in particular in accounts of his school experiences; but of his emotional and psychological development during the pre-war years much no doubt remains to be discovered. The passing reference in the *Nouveaux Mémoires intérieurs* to 'une mésaventure sentimentale',[14] an episode in his life which is also projected into *L'Enfant chargé de chaînes*, *Le Mystère Frontenac* and *Un Adolescent d'autrefois*, may or may not have made the impact on him which these novels suggest it did. Neither are there as yet any details concerning Mauriac's early years of marriage (he married Jeanne Lafon in 1913) though there is no reason to suppose that they were anything but happy. Yet it is worth noting that in the only currently available published account of the first ten years of his marriage, the *Journal d'un homme de trente ans*, there are relatively very few references to his family life; instead what emerges with most force are an obsession with age and loneliness ('vieillissement signifie solitude')[15] and with a private, hidden self described in one place as 'notre visage secret, notre visage de nuit'.[16] In the absence of more extensive intimate writing from this period it would be unwise, whatever the temptation, to draw too many conclusions from the *Journal d'un homme de trente ans*; and in any case it is to the earliest childhood years and to their formative influence that psycho-biography demands we should turn.

Mauriac's most sustained factual account of his relationship with his mother and the protection he found in it is recorded in the *Nouveaux Mémoires intérieurs*: 'Tout m'était horrible de cette vie separée de ma mère et de la maison, tout m'était insupportable . . .'.[17] In these same recollections, Mauriac also underlines the role played in general by women in this *bordelais* society:

Autour de moi, quand j'étais enfant, les femmes régnaient. Le veuvage avait rendu ma grand-mère et ma mère maîtresse de tout, chacune dans sa Maison [. . .] Elles en étaient les maîtresses absolues [. . .] Je n'imaginais pas que ce pouvoir qu'elle détenait eût été moindre si leurs époux avaient été encore au monde.[18]

'Le matriarcat' Mauriac recalls 'était la loi de la tribu' and 'autour de moi, une genitrix douce et redoutable exerçait le pouvoir et tenait les rênes en main'.[19] Yet his recollections of this 'monde enchanté'[20] of his childhood with its 'noyau tendre et rayonnant'[21] around his mother are not, as the adjective 'redoutable' already suggests, without a more sinister dimension. Indeed this is further emphasised by his description of the aging bachelors of this society, the 'vieux garçon[s]', unable to escape the clutches of 'une genitrix toute-puissante',[22] and by that of the alternative role open to women: 'Dans ce royaume de mon enfance, les femmes régnaient ou servaient. Elles étaient impératrices ou esclaves'.[23]

Although as we have already noted *Genitrix* offers the first developed portrait of a mother figure in Mauriac's published work, there are in the first drafts of *Le Mal*, written during or shortly after the war as a first person narrative, signs of the influence such a figure was beginning to exert. The description Fabien gives of Thérèse, for example, is strikingly similar to one Mauriac might have given of his own mother, even though the reference to the time of M. Dézaymaries' death makes a more precise family parallel impossible:

Une sainte femme, de ses mains posées sur mes yeux, me cachait le monde.
[. . .]
Jamais elle ne nous parlait de notre père mort avant ma naissance que comme d'un être faible. Elle ne se doutait point que pour connaître cet inconnu dont j'étais né, il me suffisait de regarder en moi-même, d'écouter mon propre cœur, de prendre conscience de ma faiblesse et de ce goût qu'il avait du silence, du reploiement.[24]

Mauriac's general dissatisfaction with *Le Mal* may well have been the true reason for his delaying the book's publication until 1935,[25] but it is distinctly possible, given in particular the eventual change from a first to a third person narrative, that such a portrayal of Mme Dézaymeries was both potentially embarrassing and something which he realized he could not allow himself to make public. Shortly after writing the third draft of *Le Mal* Mauriac began work on the first version of *Le Baiser au lépreux* in which Félicité Cazenave makes a first appearance as the step mother of the narrator, Jean Péloueyre, the closeness of the relationship in *Le Mal* thereby being marginally relaxed. Here the descriptions of her are much more physical and, together with the accounts of her total control over her son, her habit of sleeping in an adjoining bedroom, of tasting his food for him and of threatening any potential wife ('Elle avait dit un jour: si Fernand se marie, je tuerai ma bru'.)[26] are all to be found in the published version of *Le Baiser au lépreux* and directly anticipate *Genitrix*. And again there is a significant change of narrative point of view, with the first person of the two opening chapters being changed to Mauriac's more customary 'style indirect libre' for the final printed text.

Félicité's threat reported in *Le Baiser au lépreux* provides the starting point for *Genitrix*, a novel which many of Mauriac's critics consider to be the bleakest of his works. In terms of its basic theme of conflict, of the links between human psychology and temperament and the natural world of the *landes*, and of its 'classical' structure, *Genitrix* has regularly been the subject of critical attention. As yet, however, no one has gone beyond the text or related it in any detailed way to the facts of Mauriac's own life and in so doing suggested the kind of psychological analysis to which the novel seems eminently suited. Even McNab, while acknowledging the possible influence of various biographical facts, is hesitant, preferring to ignore such speculation and deal with the novel and its characters in its own right. Perhaps the most interesting clue to encourage a rather different approach (and one which McNab does record[27]) concerns the death of Fernand's father Numa Cazenave which he (Fernand) recalls having occurred 37 years prior to that of Mathilde; Mauriac wrote *Genitrix* during his 38th year, 37 years after the death of his own father. Furthermore the period in which the novel is set seems from the inscription on the railway tracks (Hommes 38-40 (p. 623)) to be just before the outbreak of the First World War. We should remember that in 1913 Mauriac met and married Jeanne Lafon . . .

In view of Félicité's remarks about a prospective daughter-in-law Mauriac's use of war as a referent in accounts of their relationship is appropriate. Each designates the other (or is described by the narrator) as *l'ennemie* and *l'adversaire*; Mathilde is *l'intruse*, her room '(un) territoire ennemi' or 'le pavillon de l'ennemie' and so on. This general context is also extended to include various aspects of the relationship between Fernand and his mother whose life together is described as '(un) combat quotidien' as Fernand attempts to escape from 'cette toile gluante que sa mère, *pour le protéger*, avait dévidée autout de lui pendant un demi-siècle' (618, my italics). Whatever conclusions we may ultimately come to about this relationship it is interesting to note that from an early point in the novel we learn that Fernand's desire to hurt his mother had existed even in childhood: 'Ce besoin de la faire souffrir qu'il eut toujours (enfant, il donnait des coups de genou dans le fauteuil de sa mère jusqu'à ce qu'elle criât grâce)' (605). In spite of Mathilde's temporary success when after her death she still 'l'[Fernand] occupait comme une forteresse' (605), Félicité does, ostensibly at least, emerge victorious, justifying the early descriptions and suggestions of her strength. Until her death in Chapter XIV there are numerous references to her as some kind of epic, earth mother ('une fondatrice de race' (508); 'la mère Cazenave' (597); 'vieille reine dépossédée' (606)) who, until temporarily denied her 'privilèges sacrés' by Mathilde's influence 'avait coutume de se tenir le buste droit, dans une attitude majestueuse, puissante' (611). And after her death as her influence reasserts itself she is recalled as 'la déesse redoutable' and 'la "genitrix" toute-puissante' (638). Throughout attention is focused on her stomach, a standard symbol of fertility, and on her head, in Freudian terms a substitute phallus signifying her dominance and masculine qualities — a suggestion reinforced by the references to the number of 'phallic' objects which she frequently handles (knitting needles (585, 606), scissors (585, 587, 588), a candle (597, 604, 611), a sun-shade (605)) and by Mauriac's use of verbs of erection and growth (*se dresser* (584); *être sur pied* (588) for example) in descriptions of some of her actions.

In marked contrast Fernand whose age is kept from us until Chapter III ('ce quinquagénaire timide' (590) — and we should not forget Mauriac's obsession with increasing age in *Le Journal d'un homme de trente ans*) is, especially until Félicité's death, referred to as a child: 'un collégien (593); 'ce même petit enfant' (506); 'ce vieil enfant pourri' (618). As we might expect, objects and verbs suggesting, in Freudian terms, sexual situations or events have an important role to play again: at the height of his adoration for the dead Mathilde his (phallic) candle is held most firmly and is lit (619); when he fails to confront Marie de Lados' relations it remains unlit (639). Likewise his cigarette is smoked and the melon eaten as signs of guilty defiance (593), and so much do his hands tremble that he has to put down the tongs which he holds shortly before his final dismissal of the de Lados clan. And, unless prompted directly by Félicité, his attempts at self-assertion are all ultimately stifled (586; 639). Indeed it is in this intimate relationship between mother and son that the real issue of the novel is to be found. As Mauriac clearly and importantly indicates as early as Chapter III, Mathilde remains very much a third party, exploited and helpless in a struggle which has far greater dimensions than her own with Félicité: 'Mathilde [. . .] avait dû comprendre [. . .] qu'elle n'était rien [. . .] qu'une arme dans le combat quotidien où jusqu'alors le fils avait toujours été jugulé par la mère' (590). It is of course in *jugulé* with its etymological meaning of 'strangle' that we have a clue both to the true nature of the relationship between mother and son and also to Mauriac's subconscious reasons for writing the novel. Everywhere evidence of Félicité's strangulating control over her son is apparent: her refusal to allow him a role in local politics (594); the platforms built onto the house from which she can spy on his every movement in the gardens (584); the 'deux chambres contiguës' (583) to which Fernand returns after his marriage ('Il n'avait pas fallu deux mois pour que le fils bien-aimé revînt dormir dans son petit lit de collégien tout contre la chambre maternelle' (587)) or the lavatory door 'où était déssiné un cœur' and through which they talk as they wait for one another. Furthermore, as McNab has rightly suggested, all such individual instances are subsumed within the role attributed to the property as a whole which, like many of the houses and estates described in Mauriac's novels, is ambiguously at once a place of protection and 'enforced claustration': 'Fernand is an embryonic being, literally outside his mother's womb, but figuratively contained in its symbolic equivalent, his mother's house and garden'.[28] Yet we can go further. Fernand is more than an 'embryonic being', and in her desire for possession Félicité has brought him up in ignorance and indeed fear of other women: 'La tendresse jalouse de la mère avait rendu le fils *impuissant* à nourrir en lui ce feu inconnu. Pour ne pas le perdre, elle l'avait voulu *infirme*, elle ne l'avait tenu que parce qu'elle l'avait *démuni*', (616, my italics).[29] The suggestion here of sexual impotence and of castration (with *démuni* echoing the earlier *jugulé*) indicates quite clearly that the struggle involves rather more than what McNab terms a 'mother fixation'.

That this is so is most firmly supported in Chapter VII. Here Félicité discovers the photograph from which Fernand has cut, in order to preserve it, the image of Mathilde, having at the same time significantly mutilated her head ('son propre sourire, son nez' (609)) and her stomach. What is more, to do this he has, ironically, used the 'ciseaux maternels'. By this the castration is reversed, Fernand having attempted to assert his own sexual potency by the symbolic destruction of the overpowering, masculine characteristics of his keeper. For a while he has some success: when, for example, he emerges from having spent a night in the dead Mathilde's room, the description contains strong hints of sexual possession and fatigue: 'Dans quel état le lui rendait la morte! Lèvres plus blanches que s'il s'était abreuvé de vinaigre — et les yeux pleins de sang . . . Elle était présente, non dans la chambre mais en lui, toute mêlée à sa chair' (614-15). Although shortly before she dies Félicité 'n'avait senti le bien-aimé à ce point détaché d'elle' (630), Fernand's escape from her through Mathilde is, like his pre-marriage visits to the Bordeaux prostitute, short-lived. As Mauriac observes in another 'epic' image in the closing lines of Chapter XV, the effect of Félicité's influence and control is far reaching — 'le soleil maternel à peine éteint, le fils tournait dans le vide, terre désorbitée' (634) — and the reassertion of her presence in him at the end of Chapter XVII (an ironic echo of course of Raymond's inability to remember the 'résurrection de la chair' section of the creed (629)) is to be expected. From this kind of physical manifestation it is tempting to infer that Fernand, having been inspired by Félicité to commit his one positive action, has been regained by her and has only to await death. Such a conclusion might be supported too, as Petit reminds us,[30] by Freud's theory that a loved one can be so absorbed by us that their influence can manifest itself in such a physical way after their death. Yet to conclude like this would be to undervalue the impression created by those elements which we have already noticed, and to pay insufficient attention to the dominant imagery and movement of certain key passages involving Fernand and his mother, and the manner in which in turn such passages also relate to the novel's overall structural pattern.

As we have seen, the descriptions of Fernand's cult of Mathilde have sexual overtones to them: the same is true, only more markedly so, of those involving Félicité, three in particular deserving some brief comment. The first occurs directly after Fernand accuses his mother of having killed Mathilde. He threatens to strike her — '[ses mains] frémissantes et levées' (621) — but fails to do so. Now while this failure is due ostensibly to his sudden realization that she is his mother, the description of the ensuing situation and of their mutual response to it could equally suggest frustrated satisfaction as they both recognize, if only within themselves, that an illicit sexual union has only narrowly been avoided:

Dégrisé, il regardait cette vieille femme haletante qu'il avait été au moment de frapper et dont il était né. Il regardait ce pauvre corps essoufflé, rendu — et enfin, brisant une dure écorce, l'obscure tendresse de l'enfance jaillissait dans un cri misérable:
'Maman !'
Comme elle s'était affaissée sur le canapé, il appuya sa tête contre l'épaule offerte. [. . .] Et elle, sans force, écrasée, goûtait, les paupières closes, ce bonheur d'un instant [. . .] [Fernand] se relève, il essuie du revers de sa main son front trempé de sueur . . . (621-22)

The last two episodes occur towards the end of the novel and are closely linked. Irritated by the presence of Marie de Lados' relations, Fernand makes a first attempt to dismiss them, inspired to do so by the influence or presence within him of his mother: 'Fernand avait redressé sa haute taille. Sa mère le poussait en avant; elle était en lui; elle le possédait' (639). Just as he had been unable to strike his mother in the earlier scene, however, so too does he fail here: 'ses jambes se dérobaient [. . .] Il se laissa choir [. . .] couché enfin, et sa bougie éteinte [. . .] Un apaisement lui venait' (639). His second attempt only hours later is successful. Again the same pattern emerges but possession and growth are on this occasion unchecked: 'Fernand Cazenave sentait naître, s'enfler en lui la vague furieuse; il laissait avec délices sa mère le pénétrer, l'envahir, le posséder' (641). And the chapter closes with lines which suggest a reincarnation of Félicité's spirit: 'il rejetait sa tête, le cou gonflé comme une Junon; — et l'on eût dit sa mère vivante' (642).

The unambiguous sexual allusions in both the imagery and the rhythmic patterns of these passages invite further attention. In view of the references throughout the novel to Fernand as a child held in check by his mother and in particular to his having been kept in sexual ignorance, what is being symbolically expressed in this last example is the final, complete manifestation of pubescence; hesitant but suppressed phallic growth already implied from early on in the novel by words like *dresser, lever* or *pousser* reaches its climax in the (surely penial?) *cou gonflé* of the closing sentence of Chapter XVII. But whereas prior to this, unfulfilled sexual climax is followed by relaxation or collapse, there is now a change and the final chapter of the novel assumes a rather different interpretation from that usually given to it, according to which the reappearance of Marie de Lados (the 'vierge noire') heralds death and/or the comfort afforded by faith. Fernand has achieved sexual maturity by virtue of his mother, the love-hate struggle which they endured in life being resolved in sexual terms but only after Félicité's death — the subconscious censor preventing any more explicit statement of the nature of the relationship. Mathilde is forgotten completely and the mother figure now in the form of Marie arrives to comfort or even forgive Fernand in his post-climactic (post-coital?) *apaisement.*

To maintain on the strength of such a tentative interpretation of this one small work that we can even begin to draw certain conclusions about Mauriac's early relationship with his mother or about his subconscious response to sexual development is clearly dangerous. (Unfortunately in the case of Mauriac there is no supportive material of the kind which Green and Vailland have published and in which they claim to have been threatened with castration as young children.[31]) Yet in the light of what Mauriac has said about his early relationship with his mother, of his reluctance to depict a mother figure in his published work before this date, his continuing fascination with the theme of incest in, for example, essays like *Blaise Pascal et sa sœur Jacqueline* or *Maurice de Guérin* and in novels like *Ce qui était perdu* or *Les Anges noirs*,[32] or by his description of Yves' feelings for his mother in *Le Mystère Frontenac*, it does not seem entirely unreasonable to suggest that we do have in *Genitrix* a subconscious expression of Mauriac's love for his mother which was at once both pure and, as is the case with many children, deeply sexual, if only subconsciously so. While this in no way invalidates or calls into question Mauriac's own marriage, it could go some way to providing an explanation for the morbid view of human love expressed in so much of his work. So too, for example, might it invite a psycho-structural reinterpretation of the seasonal pattern of so many novels — anticipation and preparation, climax, relaxation — or of the masculine characteristics of numerous female characters. Whatever new interpretations such an analysis may bring out, it does seem that *Genitrix* is the first full published expression of a relationship which developed in Mauriac's earliest years and from whose influence he would never fully escape. In spite of his declared suspicion of the work of Freud and of psycho-analysis in general the time does seem ripe for Mauriac's work to be submitted to a rigorous analysis of the psychobiographical or psycho-critical kind. As Dominique Fernandez has so pertinently observed: 'il est à noter . . . que les écrivains les plus hostiles à la psychanalyse sont ceux à qui on pourrait l'appliquer avec les résultats les plus fructueux'.[33] Mauriac is no exception.[34]

EXETER   J. E. FLOWER

---

[1] *Mauriac. OEuvres romanesques et théâtrales complètes*, I. Edition établie, présentée et annotée par Jacques Petit. (Bibliothèque de la Pléiade, no. 271). Paris, Gallimard, 1978. p. 1170. Hereafter referred to as P.I.

[2] ibid., p. 561.

[3] The first draft of *Le Mal* entitled *L'Homme qui craignait Dieu ou L'Evasion* dates almost certainly from late 1917. There are four manuscripts for the novel. This first one, the publication of which Mauriac has forbidden, was followed probably in late 1917 as well or early 1918 by a revised edition entitled *L'Emmuré* and by two subsequent ones both entitled *Le Mal*.

[4] Paris, Editions universitaires, 1970.

[5] *Hartford Studies in Literature*, Vol. 2, 1970, pp. 207-213.

[6] Important studies in these fields are Charles Mauron, *Des métaphores obsédantes au mythe personnel*, Paris, Corti, 1963; Dominique Fernandez, *L'Arbre jusqu'aux racines, psychanalyse et création*, Paris, Grasset, 1972; Marthe Robert, *Roman des origines et origines du roman*, Paris, Grasset, 1972. Mention should also be made of Janine Chasseguet-Smirgel, *Pour une psychanalyse de l'art et de la créativité*, Paris, Payot, 1977.

[7] 'Psychanalyse et critique littéraire', *Preuves*, No. 181, mars 1966, p. 27.

[8] ibid., p. 31.

[9] In particular Chasseguet-Smirgel.

[10] See for example *Le Dernier Bloc-notes*, Paris, Flammarion, 1971, p. 247.

[11] *Le Roman, Œuvres Complètes* (hereafter *OC*), Paris, Fayard, 1950-56 Vol. VIII, p. 269.

[12] All references are to the text printed in the Pléiade edition and will hereafter be given in the body of the article.

[13] *OC*, Vol. IV, p. 4.

[14] op. cit., Paris, Flammarion, 1965, p. 237. This in fact was an engagement which lasted for a few days only in 1911 and seems to have been prompted by Mauriac's future father-in-law's initial resistance to his daughter's proposed marriage. See Claude Mauriac, *Les Espaces imaginaires*, Paris, Grasset, 1975, pp. 208-9. A confirmation of this was given by Mme Mauriac to Mr Antony Wilcox in a letter of March 1977.

[15] *OC.*, Vol. IV, p. 261.

[16] ibid., p. 223.

[17] op. cit., p. 50.

[18] ibid., p. 130.

[19] ibid., pp. 133 and 131.

[20] ibid., p. 64.

[21] *Mémoires intérieurs*, Paris, Flammarion, 1959, p. 8.

[22] *Nouveaux Mémoires intérieurs*, p. 133.

[23] ibid., p. 134.

[24] Quoted in P.I. p. 1248. This description is not in the first draft of *Le Mal*. See note 3.

[25] *Le Mal* was published in the review *Demain* on 1 April 1924. Grasset was to have issued it in book form but Mauriac withdrew it at the last moment: 'Je fus si mécontent de ce récit bâclé que je renonçai au dernier moment à sa publication en librairie'. *OC*; Vol. IV, p. 1.

[26] Quoted P.I., p. 1139. In the final version of *Le Baiser au lépreux* this becomes: 'Si Fernand se marie, ma bru mourra'. P.I., p. 456. Much of the depiction of a mother-dominated son in the novel is directly based on Mauriac's in-laws. The platforms from which Félicité spies on Fernand's movements and the photograph (see below) are referred to by Claude Mauriac in *Le Temps immobile*, Paris, Grasset, 1974, p. 48.

[27] McNab, p. 207.

[28] ibid., pp. 210-212.

[29] In the first version of *Le Baiser au lépreux* Félicité spreads the rumour that Jean Péloueyre is impotent. See P.I., p. 1151.

[30] P.I., p. 1221.

[31] There is one fact which might be thought comparable. During his childhood Mauriac's bath water was coloured by some form of red dye: 'le rouge [. . .] troublait l'eau de mon bain pour que je ne 'me' voie pas'. (Letter to Jacques-Emile Blanche, 7 August 1926). The association with blood and the subconscious link that would be made between it and the sexual organs is obvious. I am indebted to Mr. Antony Wilcox for drawing my attention to this point.

[32] It is worth recalling Mauriac's rather interesting reaction to the theme of incest which he admits is to be found in his work. 'Comme il n'est aucune passion qui m'ait été plus étrangère que celle-là il serait curieux de chercher la clef de ce mystère. Mais c'est l'affaire des psychanalystes et non la mienne'. *OC*, Vol. V, p. ii.

[33] 'Introduction à la Psychobiographie', *Nouvelle Revue de Psychanalyse*, No. 1, Spring 1970, p. 35.

[34] I should like to express my thanks to my colleague Dr. Mark Waddicor for having had the patience to read this essay in a number of earlier versions and for having made various suggestions for ways in which it could be improved.

J. REED

THE PRESENTATION OF DIRECT SPEECH IN
THÉRÈSE DESQUEYROUX

Dialogue would seem to be an indispensable element in the traditional novel, particularly in third person narratives: it constitutes an essential device in the creation and structuring of a novelistic world, whatever the aims and aesthetic of the writer.[1] By 'dialogue' we mean not only conversation with two or more participants, but also soliloquy, the various ways of presenting the thoughts of a character including internal monologue, and even the device of authorial analysis which makes use of the negative, e.g. *elle ne dit pas . . ., elle ne songea pas . . .*, or of the potential, e.g. *elle allait dire . . ., si elle disait . . .* etc. One should also perhaps consider verbs such as *écrire* and *lire* as verbs introducing 'dialogue' in its widest sense. And most authors will at some time exploit the possibility of zero dialogue, e.g. *elle ne dit rien, elle se tut, il ne songe pas à protester*, etc. in which the power of silence, the inability or unwillingness to speak possess their own eloquence. Writers not only create the world of the word through the word, they express the different attitudes of the speaker to the faculty of speech including suspicion, distrust and ultimately, abstention.[2]

Dialogue permits the fictional world to model itself on, and represent the real world of human experience, both felt and expressed; through dialogue characters exist, achieve their own humanity and become recognizable and identifiable to the reader; dialogue recreates in the novel the temporal dimension (language being essentially linear), and contributes to the dynamic constructed by the writer and experienced by the reader; in many cases, dialogue *is* action in so far as it advances the individual in his quest for self-affirmation, and establishes, fosters and modifies relationships with others.

Mauriac, a successful playwright as well as master novelist, was fully aware of the manifold properties of dialogue and, as early as 1933, discussed them in his essay *Le Romancier et ses personnages*:

(. . .) le roman qui serre la réalité du plus près possible est déjà tout de même menteur par cela seulement que les héros s'expliquent et se racontent. Car, dans les vies les plus tourmentées, les paroles comptent peu. Le drame d'un être vivant se poursuit presque toujours et se dénoue dans le silence. L'essentiel, dans la vie, n'est jamais exprimé. (. . .) Le monde des héros de roman vit, si j'ose dire, dans une autre étoile, — l'étoile où les êtres humains s'expliquent, se confient, s'analysent la plume à la main, recherchent les scènes au lieu de les éviter, cernent leurs sentiments confus et indistincts d'un trait appuyé, les isolent de l'immense contexte vivant et les observent au microscope. (Livre de poche, pp. 116-7)

Dialogue in the novel marks essentially an impoverishment of the spoken word: the unique articulation of a concept which we take so much for granted in speaking cannot be reproduced by means of the written word. But the fictional universe does not require the exact transcription of the spoken word, rather it offers a range of possibilities, shared by author and reader, for the aesthetic exploitation of spoken language and the filtering out of irrelevant elements. In this, dialogue does not differ from a text of description or narrative as compared with reality: no description, no matter how detailed, *is* the object described, no narration *is* an event, it is a selection made by the author within the resources offered by a language of those elements which correspond to his vision and aesthetic intentions, and which will effectively communicate these to a discerning reader.

At the same time, an author is obliged by his privileged position to give a formal linguistic clarity to the conscious and unconscious world of the human spirit: the vague images and impressions, the various emotions to which a character is subject are inevitably formalized once they are presented in words and linguistic structures, as the internal workings of an individual mind, e.g. *il se dit . . ., il songe . . .* etc. This ultra-precision, although again in a sense an impoverishment of the complexity of the inner world of the psyche, privileges a character with an eloquence and an apparent clarity which are the hallmarks of the literary creation. Even modern novelists struggling with problems of 'communication' tend to accept the servitude of organized speech for without it there is surely no novel.

Traditionally, there are three principal modes of presenting dialogue: a) direct speech (DS) in which the spoken words or thoughts are presented as they are articulated by a character. This mode is normally marked by inverted commas or an equivalent. A verb of saying (VS) is not obligatory (autonomous DS), but is frequently used and in this case the dialogue can be considered as a direct object. There exists in addition a wide range of presentation formulae (PF) which do not include a VS.[3] b) indirect speech (IS) in which the dialogue is subordinated to a VS and suffers a number of transpositions due to grammatical servitudes, e.g. person, tense, mood, adverbs, indirect question forms, etc. In addition, the reader is left uncertain as to the degree of stylistic transposition since the text is now that of the narrator not the speaker. In the following extract does Queneau give any indication of what was actually said? 'Saturnin balayait devant la porte. Etienne le reconnut et lui demanda si sa santé était bonne.' (*Le Chiendent*, Gallimard, p. 100). c) free indirect speech (FIS) or *discours indirect libre* in which the VS is normally absent, but a number of transpositions of tense and person still take place. The question however remains in question form, exclamations remain and this contributes to maintaining something of the tone of DS. Stylistic transposition again takes place so that FIS is particularly powerful in creating ambiguity as to whether the text is to be attributed directly to the narrator or to the character through the transposition of the narrator, and, if it is attributed to the character, whether it is spoken or merely a formal articulation in the conscious or even unconscious mind.

These three modes[4] can be developed in a large number of ways and combined to achieve different effects, particularly in encouraging the reader to 'overhear' an authentic conversation in the case of DS and allowing him to draw his own conclusions; whereas in IS the reader is 'guided', he is presented with a ready-made, pre-digested form of dialogue which he is obliged to accept on trust; in the case of FIS, the reader has often the task of interpreting or deciphering to decide on the status of the text. Moreover in spite of Sartre's demand, 'Dans un roman il faut se taire ou tout dire, surtout ne rien omettre, ne rien "sauter"',[5] an author clearly has the right to omit and summarize dialogue, to interrupt it by description, narrative or comment, to vary the modes of presentation and thus provide a rich literary texture by means of which the reader can be flattered and manipulated into exploring the manifold dimensions of the work.

It is noteworthy that comparatively little has been written on the problem of the presentation of DS, whereas FIS, under its various labels, has been the subject of considerable analysis and explanations both by linguists and stylisticians, beginning with Charles Bally's seminal study 'Le style indirect libre' in 1912. A valid methodology for the study of DS has still to be elaborated although Gougenheim and Almenberg have opened up the field.

The present short article is an attempt to study the presentation of DS in Mauriac's *Thérèse Desqueyroux*; we hope to advance the elaboration of a general method as well as examining Mauriac's individual technique. General conclusions will be avoided since it is clear that there is considerable evolution and maturing in his writing, and in the case of DS the early works such as *Le Baiser au lépreux*[6] differ completely from the mature works.

Thérèse Desqueyroux, perhaps Mauriac's best known work, reveals an author in full command of an arsenal of literary devices, at the peak of his art. Although, at first sight, it might seem that dialogue would play an insignificant role in this book since the major part is an exercise in introspection, the preparation of a 'confession' by the heroine, constituting an original 'flash-back' technique, it is noticeable from the very beginning that Mauriac places considerable stress on dialogue and advances the novel by a series of scenes in which DS is a significant component. We make no distinction between those parts of the text narrated in the third person and those in which effectively the author allows the heroine herself to take over the role of narrator and so transposes to a first person narration (especially in Chapters VI and VII). As has already been noted, *Thérèse* offers a major contrast with *Le Baiser au lépreux* in novelistic technique and specifically in the control the author exercises over dialogue: the reader is accorded direct contact both with Thérèse herself and with the other characters through their utterances.

A number of features can be indicated briefly: DS is not in fact uncommon in *Thérèse*, and the author gives weight to dialogue (whereas in *Thérèse*, the proportion of UD (cf. note 3) of two or more sentences compared with a single sentence is 2 : 3, in the *Baiser* it is 1 : 4). The main VS is *dire* — Mauriac does not use *faire* in this meaning — together with *demander, interroger, répéter, répondre* and *songer*. Autonomous DS is about twice as frequent as 'introduced' DS.

The normal pattern in *Thérèse* is then either autonomous DS or dialogue introduced by a single VS. Two thirds of the verbs are prefixed; in a small number of cases, the VS, usually *dire*, follows the DS or is intercalated, e.g.

Prefix: Thérèse dit : 'Lisez ! lisez !' (p. 157)[7]

Suffix: 'Force-toi un peu . . . on se force', répétait Mme de la Trave. (p. 70)

Infix: 'Je ne désirais rien alors, songe Thérèse, j'allais, une heure, sur la route (. . .)' (p. 82)[8]

Against this framework of normality, Mauriac develops a wide, sophisticated and effective range of devices and structures, and it is these we now propose to analyse.

There are two examples of *encadrement* (i.e. the DS is framed by the PF) which seems to subordinate effectively the dialogue to the narrative which surrounds it, e.g.

Et depuis le drame : 'Toutes des hystériques quand elles ne sont pas des idiotes !' répétait-il à l'avocat. (p. 79)

Anne, trébuchant, répète : 'Je partirai (. . .) je le trouverai dans Paris . . .' mais du ton d'une enfant à bout de résistance et qui déjà s'abandonne. (p. 100)

It is rare to find Mauriac including two UD within one sentence, and when this happens it is inevitably two speeches by the same speaker. He may be addressing different people as when the lawyer cries 'Non-lieu' to the father before speaking to Thérèse (p. 7), it may be two stages in a development or two facets of an experience, e.g.

Thérèse, songeant à la nuit qui vint ensuite, murmure : 'Ce fut horrible . . .' puis se reprend : 'Mais non . . . pas si horrible . . .' (p. 45)

Mauriac may use a first verb for DS, a second for FIS, e.g.

Elle dit à voix basse : 'J'ai tant souffert . . . je suis rompue . . .' puis s'interrompit : à quoi bon parler? (p. 12)

The form here skilfully espouses the sense: the helplessness of Thérèse, her isolation, is mirrored in her ability to use the spoken word, her flight into reflection is symbolized by the use of FIS rather than DS.

The author is extremely sober in his choice of VS, he uses only a small number of standard verbs. In addition to those already mentioned we may note, *ajouter, avertir, insister, jeter, rabâcher, risquer, soupirer* — they all have in common that the subject of the verb is inevitably the speaker, but it is perhaps legitimate to include in this category a 'passive' alternative in which the grammatical subject is the recipient of the dialogue — verbs such as *écouter, entendre,* even *lire,* e.g.

Il la voit sourire; s'exaspère, hausse le ton, elle est obligée d'écouter : 'Moi, je vous tiens (. . .)' (p. 125)

It is possible to interpret such a sentence as an ellipsis of *dire,* but this type of construction is widely used (although rare in *Thérèse*) and has its own justification — verbs of hearing can take as their complements not only the person speaking, but also the text spoken. Compare the following example from *Le Mystère Frontenac*:

Le téléphone appela (. . .) Il entendit beaucoup de 'friture' puis : 'On vous parle de Bordeaux'. (p. 180)

This example is not unambiguous when placed against the forms used by Mauriac: is the DS a coordinated direct object of *entendre,* or is there an ellipsis after *puis*? We would add another clear example from Balzac's *Le Père Goriot*:

Trompé sans doute par les larmes, Goriot usa ses dernières forces pour étendre les mains (. . .) et l'on entendit faiblement : 'Ah! mes anges !' (Folio, p. 355)

DS is frequently placed in apposition to various nominals, usually containing the meaning of saying, e.g. *mots, phrase, réponse, aveu, exclamations, souvenirs* and sometimes used with a VS, e.g.

Et la dame rappelait des souvenirs de grossesse : 'Je me souviens (. . .)' (p. 70)

Elle entendait confusément leurs propos : 'Je recevrai demain (. . .)' (p. 7)

Thérèse, sur le conseil de Bernard, marchait beaucoup : 'L'exercice est le meilleur apértif'. (p. 168)

In the second example the verb brings in the person hearing or overhearing and introduces several UD shared between the two speakers; in the third the apposition is not with a direct object, and does not even follow directly the nominal, *conseil*. Finally, an elliptical construction:

Sans aucune autre réponse que : 'C'était couru!' (p. 121)

In some cases, the construction is extended to include nominals indicating the manner of speaking:

(. . .) impossible de ne pas entendre le fausset de son père : 'Je le lui ai assez dit (. . .)' (p. 10)

Ah! rappelle-toi sa stupéfaction non jouée, ce juvénile éclat de rire : 'Alors, vous croyez que je vais l'épouser? (. . .)' (p. 85)

(. . .) mais bientôt mon esprit s'accoutuma à cette volubilité : 'Me croire capable, moi, de souhaiter un tel mariage (. . .)' (p. 86)

and the concept of apposition is stretched to breaking point.

The verb *dire* (in most writers the most frequent and most neutral VS) is almost redundant in the PF — it is little more than a syntactic link between the subject i.e. speaker and the direct object i.e. the text of DS: an elliptical style will permit its omission, while retaining those elements deemed essential for the presentation of the dialogue, e.g. identity of speaker, manner of speaking, circumstances, etc. Mauriac uses this technique but with discretion, e.g.

Et Hector de la Trave : 'Elle nous reprocherait plus tard (. . .)' (p. 65)

Il murmura : 'Peur? Non : horreur'. Puis : 'Faisons vite (. . .)' (p. 126)

A double example occurs in the conversation between Thérèse and her husband in the last chapter: the speaker is inferred from the first part of the sentence, but there is no VS and the dialogue is effectively introduced by adverbs of manner:

Il observait le profil de Thérèse, ses prunelles qui parfois s'attachaient dans la foule à une figure, la suivaient jusqu'à ce qu'elle ait disparu; et soudain :
'Thérèse . . . je voulais vous demander . . .'
Il détourna les yeux, n'ayant jamais pu soutenir le regard de cette femme, puis très vite :
'Je voudrais savoir (. . .)' (p. 173)

The ellipses, the discontinuity in the syntax of the presentation is echoed in the staccato of the DS, itself a translation of Bernard's unease, uncertainty, doubts, characteristics which are new to him and which in their own way mark the conclusion of the novel, and the resolving of the relationship between the two characters.

Verbs other than VS are used to introduce DS in *Thérèse*, but Mauriac does not resort excessively to this economical device:

Il prit le bras de Thérèse: 'Monte vite; il est temps'. (p. 13)

Oui, sa confession finie, Bernard la relèverait: 'Va en paix, Thérèse (. . .)' (p. 25)

In such examples the PF will precede the DS and contain the identity of the speaker and the circumstances of the DS, so that one could add *et dit* or *en disant*. But the speaker may be indicated by other means:

Des millions de mouches s'élevaient des hautes brandes: 'Remets ton manteau pour entrer au salon; c'est une glacière . . .' (p. 33)

Here we are so absorbed into the consciousness of Thérèse as narrator that the dialogue breaks into the sensuous world evoked by the heroine, as it does into ours, as if disembodied and the voice is identified retrospectively as hers, rather than that of her companion.

We may also draw attention to the example:

Anne criait à la sourde d'inutiles paroles de bienvenue: 'Ne t'égosille pas chérie, elle comprend tout au mouvement des lèvres . . .' (p. 34)

Here the DS is not, as might be expected, in apposition to the noun phrase *d'inutiles paroles*. The context makes clear that the speaker is in fact neither Anne nor the deaf tante Clara but Thérèse who is not mentioned in the PF although present throughout the scene. The economy is extreme but suggests the dual conversation between the aunt and the two girls in which the dialogue is artificialized by the needs for a clear articulation, and the private, informal and natural communication between the two girls from which the aunt is excluded by her deafness.

Two further examples deserve comment:

Et comme Thérèse l'interrogeait du regard: 'Crois-tu qu'elle s'est amourachée du fils Azévédo? (. . .)' (p. 49)

We note here a subordinate clause preceding the dialogue, without an accompanying main clause; the speaker, as the context makes clear, is not Thérèse, subject of the verb, but Bernard = *le*, the direct object. The syntax is more startling here, but the identity of the speaker is not in doubt, and the omission of *il dit* can be seen as a device for reducing the role and impact of Bernard and focusing attention on the speech as Thérèse hears it.

Des métayers entrent, s'agenouillent, sortent, non sans avoir longuement dévisagé Thérèse debout au pied du lit: ('Et qui sait si ce n'est pas elle encore qui a fait le coup?') (p. 141)

The text of the DS would seem already to make clear who is speaking but Mauriac offers here exceptionally a typographical marker: the brackets seem to signify the special status of the dialogue, firstly as far as the identity of the speakers is concerned, but also as to the circumstances and mode of speaking, i.e. one is surely meant to suppose that such a remark could not be uttered in the presence or hearing of Thérèse, although it could be thought, and the author leaves ambiguous whether this represents a question posed aloud or a reflection of the *métayers*, whether it corresponds to an individual suspicion or whether the author has translated a group reaction, whether even Thérèse may be imagining what the *métayers* are thinking. This ambiguity, due to concision, does not seem in any sense a fault in the narrative technique: whichever interpretation the reader selects, the text maintains its integrity.

As has already been stated most UD are presented as autonomous or by a simple sentence containing a VS, but of course, compound and complex sentences are also used. We find the VS coordinated with another verb, both of which are placed before the DS, the VS preceding immediately the DS, e.g.

Elle jeta son chapeau sur un fauteuil; demanda: 'Où est-il?' (p. 98)

Il s'était rapproché de Thérèse; il criait: 'Celle-là est trop forte! (. . .)' (p. 49)

In addition, the coordinated VS may be intercalated into the DS or follow it, e.g.

Ici, Thérèse hésite; s'efforce de détourner sa pensée (. . .): 'Non, non, songe-t-elle, cela n'a rien à voir (. . .)' (p. 97)

Bernard, sur le seuil, guettait le retour de Thérèse: 'Je n'ai rien! Je n'ai rien!' cria-t-il, dès qu'il aperçut sa robe dans l'ombre. (p. 91)

It is noticeable that the part of the sentence coordinated with the VS has several functions: it may be merely narrative or descriptive, it may consist of FIS, e.g.

C'était impossible, à l'entendre, que je pusse supporter ce climat étouffant: 'Regardez, me disait-il, cette immense et uniforme surface de gel (. . .)' (p. 93)

Il ne fallait pas lui demander de travailler à la layette: 'Ce n'était pas sa partie', répétait Mme de la Trave. (p. 103)

Occasionally the coordinated verbs both follow, e.g.

'C'est nerveux', répétait-on à Bernard; mais lui sentait bien cette paille à même le métal — cette fêlure. (p. 75)

and in one case the VS does not precede directly the DS:

Prise de panique, Thérèse balbutie, tournée vers l'avocat (mais c'est au vieux qu'elle s'adresse): 'Je compte demeurer quelques jours auprès de M. Desqueyroux. (. . .)' (p. 15)

Again we may note the use of brackets which Mauriac finds a useful adjunct to his normal devices. Although the bracketed verb is itself a VS, ue dialogue must be seen as dependent on *balbutie*: the brackets themselves seem to symbolize the double orientation of Thérèse's remarks — the apparent and real recipients.

In the complex sentence, it is perhaps significant that the VS is more frequently found in a subordinate clause than in a main clause, e.g.

Si Bernard lui avait dit: 'Je te pardonne; viens . . .' elle se serait levée, l'aurait suivi. (p. 181)[9]

When the main clause contains the VS, it almost invariably follows the subordinate, e.g.

Comme à table, elle parlait enfin de sa rencontre, Bernard lui cria: 'Tu ne me le disais pas? (. . .)' (p. 92)

but we may draw attention to two exceptions:

Elle expliquait de sa voix monotone d'enfant qui récite une leçon (cette leçon qu'elle repassait durant ses nuits sans sommeil): 'J'ai rencontré sur la route un homme (. . .)' (p. 117)

It is surely logical to consider the DS as completing the verb *expliquer*, although it could also be seen as being in apposition to *leçon*. Again Mauriac uses the device of brackets.

Mme de la Trave répond à une réflexion de Bernard que Thérèse n'a pas entendue : 'Tout de même, sois prudent (. . .)' (p. 167)

The structure of the sentence can once again be interpreted as allowing the reader not only to understand Thérèse's position but in a symbolical sense almost to share it: the VS is not followed immediately by the dialogue which the reader might expect, he too is distanced from it, as is the heroine.

There are eight examples in this novel of written texts — twice the formula, the other six cases being letters. The prescription is first presented as an apposition to 'la formule inscrite sur l'enveloppe', (p. 20); on the second occasion there is a simple reproduction of the formula after the phrase 'le paquet cacheté de cire' (p. 137) with an ellipsis of the type 'qui porte l'inscription'.

The extracts from the letters which play an important part in the novel are presented in different ways: again by apposition (to 'ce cantique des cantiques, cette longue plainte heureuse' (p. 50), 'quelques mots' (p. 52), 'ce que déchiffrait Balionte' (p. 157)), by a verb of action with the ellipsis of 'elle lut' (pp. 51 and 60), and finally the DS of the letter continues on from a sentence of IS, 'Bernard annonçait qu'il rentrerait (. . .)' (p. 157). Written texts are thus presented in a similar way to authentic dialogue, although Mauriac does not enclose them in inverted commas.

So far we have seen in fact a close correlation between the use of inverted commas (and *tiret*) and the formal presentation of DS. It is time to examine this in more detail. In some cases inverted commas are used with a word or phrase, setting it apart, because of its colloquial or technical nature, e.g. 'sans le sou' (p. 31), 'd'arrache-pied' (p. 32), 'postes restantes' (p. 48), 'par retour du courrier' (p. 42), 'à la voie' (p. 89), un 'ciré' (p. 148) (this usage dates from 1906 according to the *Trésor de la langue française*), le 'collier de force' (p. 159), etc. These occur sometimes in dialogue, more usually in narrative. In some cases, the expressions are clearly meant to indicate the speech style of a particular character: 'qui s'en allait de la poitrine', (p. 41) is inserted into a passage of FIS.

But there are several other ways in which Mauriac uses this typographical device. In some cases, indirect speech is enclosed in inverted commas, e.g.

On se demandait, par exemple, 'pourquoi il avait traversé quatre fois la place dans la journée (. . .)' (p. 105)

Elle balbutia que 'ça ne l'ennuyait pas du tout d'y aller'. (p. 147)

Le fils Deguilhem, qui avait promis à sa famille 'de ne pas garder les yeux dans sa poche', se disait 'que c'était à tout le moins un manque d'empressement et qui donnait à penser'. (p. 160)

This use is rare, although not without precedents, and not easy to explain in Mauriac. It would seem however that he uses it to create an intermediary style between DS reproducing the spoken word and IS transposing the word of the speaker to the word of the narrator: it is as if the narrator through the use of inverted commas is not prepared to take full responsibility for the dialogue because the transposition is incomplete; at the same time it implies a greater degree of authenticity and accuracy because it retains something of the speaker's style. It allows the author to characterize and satirize his creations.

In a similar way Mauriac places FIS within inverted commas on occasion:

Elle avait demandé à Thérèse de lui décrire 'par retour du courrier' les robes des autres demoiselles d'honneur : 'Ne pourrait-elle en avoir des échantillons? (. . .)' (p. 42)

'Le tout était de le revoir; si elle le revoyait, il serait reconquis; il fallait le revoir'. (p. 98)

A further example, quoted already in another context, reveals a certain idiosyncrasy in Mauriac's technique:

Il ne fallait pas lui demander de travailler à la layette : 'Ce n'était pas sa partie', répétait Mme de la Trave. (p. 103)

It seems necessary to interpret both parts of the sentence as FIS, with Mme de la Trave indicated as the speaker of both, but the second half is formally marked, because it represents a typical expression of the speaker.

In other cases Mauriac inserts into IS or FIS a section enclosed in inverted commas corresponding to the speaker's original words, e.g.

(. . .) les gens ne s'entretinrent jamais de ces noces de Gamache (. . .) sans rappeler que l'épouse, 'qui sans doute n'est pas régulièrement jolie mais qui est le charme même', parut à tous, ce jour-là, laide (. . .) (p. 44)

The inverted commas allow and compensate for the rupture in the sequence of tenses as well as the spoken cadence within a very literary sentence (note the reference to *Don Quixote*). Once again, Mauriac creates an intermediary mode of dialogue.

We might consider one other use of inverted commas: in some cases, they seem to correspond not so much to the reproduction of a speaker's words or thoughts, as to an emphasising of the main point and thus to a summary of his views or attitude, e.g.

Quand son père proclamait 'un dévouement indéfectible à la démocratie', elle l'interrompait (. . .) (p. 81)

Il me décrivit : 'la grande aventure des mystiques', se plaignit de son tempérament (. . .) (p. 88)

Elle comptait suivre des cours, des conférences, des concerts, 'reprendre son éducation par la base'. (p. 171)

It is perhaps dangerous to overclassify and interpret such examples: in some cases more than one interpretation seems possible, in some an element of irony or doubt or ambiguity may well be the intention of the author in a text in which the search for truth, for understanding, for clarity is a basic theme.

A common feature of Mauriac's presentation of DS is to introduce it in the second part of a sentence, after a colon, usually without a VS. In some examples, this personal technique marks a variation in the mode of presentation of dialogue since the first part of the sentence is either IS or FIS, and it is as if Mauriac chooses, at a certain point, to enliven the dialogue, to give greater freedom to character and reader, by allowing a direct contact between them. After indirect speech:

(. . .) il m'assura que ce livre l'avait bouleversé: 'Vivre dangereusement, au sens profond, ajouta-t-il, ce n'est peut-être pas tant de chercher Dieu (. . .)' (p. 88)

Mais Mme de la Trave assurait qu'elle aimait sa fille à sa manière: 'Bien sûr, il ne faut pas lui demander de surveiller son bain (. . .)' (p. 108)

Le fils Deguilhem disait que l'hiver à la campagne, n'est pas si terrible pour une femme qui aime son intérieur: 'Il y a toujours tant de choses à faire dans une maison'. (p. 164)

Usually we find that the text in DS is longer than that in IS introducing it: in many cases the IS seems almost to state a theme which is then amplified, expanded, exemplified by the DS; sometimes the DS comes almost as a conclusion or climax to the UD, the most significant part of which appears in IS.

A similar pattern occurs with FIS followed after a colon by DS, without a VS, e.g.

Enfin l'essentiel était qu'elle ramenât la petite à la raison: 'Mes parents comptent sur toi (. . .)' (p. 49)

Le résultat cherché était acquis: 'Et puisque la messe, pour vous, ne signifie rien...' (p. 147)

Elle n'avait pas envie de lire; elle n'avait envie de rien; elle errait de nouveau: 'Ne t'éloigne pas: on va servir.' (p. 37)

With this construction clarity depends on a single speaker and on the interpretation of the first part as FIS and not authorial comment. However, Mauriac daringly does include two subjects:

Entre les mille sources secrètes de son acte, cet imbécile n'a donc su en découvrir aucune; et il invente la cause la plus basse: 'Naturellement: à cause des pins (. . .)' (p. 127)

The first part of the sentence represents the thoughts of Thérèse and could be prefixed by *elle se dit*, whereas the DS is articulated by Bernard. In fact, there is no ambiguity since essentially the DS is in apposition to the preceding noun and the subject of the clause is the speaker.

There are in addition a number of occasions where the part of the sentence preceding the DS is, or can be interpreted as, narrative. Frequently, there is an element of doubt but in the last chapter we have the following example:

Un agent à cheval approchait un sifflet de ses lèvres, ouvrait d'invisibles écluses, une armée de piétons se hâtait de traverser la chaussée noire avant que l'ait recouverte la vague des taxis: 'J'aurais dû partir (. . .)' (p. 180)

The text is narrated by the omniscient narrator who then reproduces Thérèse's words or thoughts (without a VS or indication of speaker). By the simple economic device of using a colon here instead of a full stop, the author is able to suggest not only that the scene is experienced by Thérèse, but that she is integrated into it: her inner voice is stimulated by her vision. Separate sentences would have allowed us to interpret the scene as mere background against which we should 'see' Thérèse.

More often the text is somewhat ambiguous: it can be seen as authorial comment, or possibly as the thoughts of the character concerned, perhaps existing in a pre-articulated form, e.g.

Mais sa solitude lui est attachée plus étroitement qu'au lépreux son ulcère: 'Nul ne peut rien pour moi (. . .)' (p. 121)

The form of the first half of the sentence with the powerful comparison suggests the narrator, but in the context it is quite possible to see this as an indication of Thérèse's introspection. A more trivial example:

Bernard n'avait jamais bu de vin du Rhin: 'Pristi, ils ne le donnent pas.' (p. 55)

can again be interpreted as authorial comment — of a rather gratuitous type —, but viewed in terms of Mauriacian practice, we can consider the first part as FIS (*Bernard dit* or *Bernard se dit*). This interpretation is surely more coherent since there is no other satisfactory way of linking semantically and grammatically the two parts of the sentence. Moreover the following sentence reads, 'Mais ça n'était pas tous les jours fête.' The *ça* is a marker of FIS.

A further example of concision shows the variety of Mauriac's technique: he almost imperceptibly switches from an authorial point of view to that of a character — or perhaps brings us to question the status of narrator in certain parts of the story. Has the narrator allowed a character to replace him? Has the narrator *become* a character?

Anne de la Trave avait un manteau de petit-gris, un chapeau de feutre sans ruban ni cocarde ('mais, disait Mme de la Trave, il coûte plus cher, sans la moindre fourniture, que nos chapeaux d'autrefois (. . .)'). (p. 160)

The description seems to begin objectively, the inverted commas and brackets mark a change of status for the second part, and the verb of saying and present tense indicate the passage to DS. It may be that we should see the bracketed section not only as a personalized comment, i.e. a comment by Mme de la Trave, but an indirect authorial comment on Mme de la Trave.

One last extract of DS is worth quoting:

M. de la Trave soupirait à mi-voix: 'Oh! un voyage avec nous . . . Rien! rien!' répondait-il à sa femme qui, un peu sourde, l'interrogeait: 'Qu'est-ce que tu as dit?' (p. 66)

It is extremely rare to find three UD with three VS in the same sentence, particularly in Mauriac, but it is also strange to see the chronological sequence of the speeches changed: in reality, the sequence is M. de la Trave's barely audible remark, followed by his wife's question and finally his reply 'Rien! rien!' Mauriac has blocked the two speeches by M. de la Trave, making the second incomprehensible until we reach the end of the sentence. One must admire the originality of the technique and wonder why it is not used more in literature to interrupt strict chronology and causality, although it inevitably places greater strain on the reader.

We hope we have been able to show something of the variety and subtlety of Mauriac's approach to the problem of presenting (or in some cases, suggesting — by the use of inverted commas) direct speech in this novel. There is here within an aesthetic founded on concision a real virtuosity of technique which, as we have demonstrated, is never gratuitous. We would claim that Mauriac has rarely been given credit for his technical sophistication; indeed, he has, as in the famous Sartre article already quoted, been attacked unfairly for creating a particular dense literary 'code', the deciphering of which demands the reader's full attention. Not only does Mauriac constantly vary his presentation of dialogue, he explores the space between the standard modes or styles of dialogue, and in our view disposes of a much richer palette than many novelists. Moreover, in the case of *Thérèse Desqueyroux*, the multiple significance of the articulated word, both spoken and thought, the clarity of which Thérèse seeks and Bernard (and the reader) demands, is successfully mirrored in the extreme diversity of the literary form which Mauriac creates and exploits.[10]

BIRMINGHAM   J. REED

---

[1] '(. . .) c'est seulement en donnant la parole à leurs personnages (je songe ici à ces longues tirades de Charlus ou de Vautrin, ou des héros de Dostoïevski) que le romancier parvient à nous donner le sentiment que leur langage est, si j'ose dire, en prise directe sur leurs pulsions profondes (. . .)' Michel Raimond in *Cahiers François Mauriac*, 2 (1975), p. 194.
[2] For a literary and biographical exploration of this theme in Mauriac, see the article by M. Parry, quoted in note 10.
[3] The following abbreviations will be used:
    DS = direct speech
    IS = indirect speech
    FIS = free indirect speech
    VS = verb of saying
    PF = presentation formula
    UD = unit of discourse, i.e. a 'speech', a continuous sequence of dialogue.
[4] For further discussion of this topic, see the article by A. Kalik-Teljatnicova listed in note 10.

[5] *Situations I*, p. 53.

[6] '(. . .) il n'y a pas un seul dialogue proprement dit dans *Le Baiser au lépreux*', P. Croc in *Cahiers François Mauriac*, 2, p. 31.

[7] Page references are to the Livre de Poche edition (1970). We should note that there is some variation in the use of inverted commas from edition to edition: we have for example observed some differences in the Calmann Lévy edition of 1927 and *Les Chefs-d'œuvre de François Mauriac*, t. 3, Grasset, n.d.

[8] We have been obliged to abridge some examples. Normally the abridging, indicated by (. . .), is limited to the dialogue as it is not the subject of this study.

[9] The Livre de Poche edition prints 'Elle' (i.e. with capital letter).

[10] The following works have been consulted:

Dagmar Almenberg, 'La présentation des répliques chez quatre romanciers contemporains', *Studia Neophilologica*, XXX (1958), 200-213.

Cahiers François Mauriac, 2, Paris, Grasset, 1975.

Marcel Galliot, 'Le "Présentatif du discours"', *Défense de la Langue française*, janvier 1963 (17), 9-13.

Keith Goesch, *François Mauriac: Essai de bibliographie chronologique 1908-1960*, Paris, Nizet, 1965.

Georges Gougenheim, 'La présentation du discours direct dans *La Princesse de Clèves* et dans *Dominique*', *Le Français Moderne*, 6 (1938), 305-320.

A. Kalik-Teljatnicova, 'De l'origine du prétendu "style indirect libre"', *Le Français Moderne*, 33 (1965), 284-294 & 34 (1966), 123-136.

Anne Gertrude Landry, *Represented Discourse in the Novels of François Mauriac*. Washington D.C., Catholic University of America Press, 1953. (Studies in Romance Languages and Literatures, XLIV).

Marguerite Lips, *Le style indirect libre*. Paris, Payot, 1926.

Maurice Maucuer, *Thérèse Desqueyroux: Analyse critique*. Paris, Hatier, 1970. (Profil d'une Œuvre, 9)

François Mauriac, *Œuvres romanesques et théâtrales complètes I*. Edition établie, présentée et annotée par Jacques Petit. Paris, Gallimard, 1978. (Bibliothèque de la Pléiade, 271) *II*, 1979 (Bibliothèque de la Pléiade, 279).

Georges Mounin, 'Structure, fonction, pertinence: A propos de *Thérèse Desqueyroux*', *La Linguistique*, 10, 1 (1974), 21-32.

M. Parry, 'The Theme of Silence in the Writings of François Mauriac', *Modern Language Review*, 71 (1976), 788-800.

Jean-Paul Sartre, 'M. François Mauriac et la liberté' in *Situations I: Essais critiques*. Paris, Gallimard, 1947. (Dates from 1939).

Jan Adriaan Verschoor, *Etude de grammaire historique et de style sur le style direct et les styles indirects en français*. Groningen, 1959.

C. R. P. MAY

SAINT-DENYS GARNEAU:
A CANADIAN CATHOLIC READER OF MAURIAC
IN THE 1930s

The Catholic Church was the institution most influential in the creation of New France. If the professed aim of the sixteenth-century explorers — the evangelisation of the Indians — has been treated with much scepticism, the missionary zeal of their successors in the seventeenth century has never been in doubt. The first settlements — Sainte-Croix and Port Royal in the Bay of Fundy — were founded by the Jesuits. The work of the Society in Canada has been vividly recorded in their annual *Relations* published for forty years from 1632. These reports, popular in Paris for their excitement and strangeness, led directly to the establishment in Quebec in 1639 of the Ursulines, a teaching and nursing order which began a long tradition of Catholic healing and education. Montreal was no simple trading post. It was founded by a group of French Catholics who dedicated their venture to the Virgin and named their settlement Ville-Marie. The accounts of early martyrdoms only served to increase the enthusiasm in France for the mission to the savages. The *Relations* recount the massacre of the Jesuit Mission to the Hurons in 1649 and the deaths of Jean de Brébeuf and others subsequently canonized. By the middle of the century, men and women in religious orders accounted for a sizeable proportion of the population — 150 out of 500 in the town of Quebec in 1663.

The outstanding personalities in the colony in its early days were men like the first Bishop, François de Montmorency Laval, who created by his benign but firm paternalism the Catholic spirit and ecclesiastical structures of New France, conservative, puritan and ultramontane, and women like Mère Marie de l'Incarnation, Superior of the Ursulines, whom Bossuet called the 'Thérèse of New France'.

From 1627, Richelieu decreed that neither Jews nor Huguenots should come to the colony and though the morals of some of the immigrants have been the subject of controversy, it seems safe to assert that the Manon Lescauts of France went to the easier societies of the Caribbean and Louisiana whilst the kind of material needed to face the perils of forest and climate was directed to the Valley of the St. Lawrence. Lahontan, a needy aristocrat who visited the colony in the 1670s, left in a hurry, appalled by the interference of the clergy in the private lives of their parishioners.

It was this parish clergy which was the saving of Quebec in the years following the Treaty of Paris which in 1763 gave the province to the British. Forsaken by army and administration who were repatriated, bereft of the merchant class who were rapidly bankrupted, the rural folk society had only its priests to turn to. These became the mentors of their flock in every sense and were largely content to persuade obedience to the authorities. When revolutionary France apostasised, Quebec assumed her role as elder daughter of the church. A movement for parliamentary reform produced a flash of armed revolt in 1837-38 and this and the Voltairean 'Institut canadien' with its anticlerical 'rougisme' provided the pretext for a full-scale crusade imposing an orthodoxy as rigid as anything promoted by Pius IX in Europe.

Twentieth-century French Canada inherited this rather monolithic, obscurantist clericalism with the church massively present in the University, secondary education, primary education, hospital and social welfare services, in the unions, publishing, pioneering in remote areas and in foreign mission fields. Indirectly, the clergy were influential in politics and by dictating the pattern of parish life and by a powerful censorship they determined the culture of the community in every sphere.

Commentators on the Church in Quebec foresaw the vulnerability of such a clerical structure in the event of a wave of liberalisation and but for the shrewd leadership of Cardinal Léger in the nineteen-fifties and sixties, discreetly, drastically contracting the scale and scope of the Church's activities, pulling it out of education and the unions and disestablishing it, the impact of the 'Quiet Revolution' after 1960 on Quebec Catholicism would have been even more devastating than it, in fact, was.

The brief, dramatic spiritual itinerary of Hector de Saint-Denys Garneau in the 1930s illustrates perfectly the plight of a sensitive and educated Quebec Catholic wishing to live his faith responsively in such a society. The Quebec of the thirties provided only one model of piety — the religious observance, unthinking and simplistic, of a homogeneous society intolerant of heterodoxy, in which religion was a social reflex, superficial, non-internalised. Such a cultural background becomes unbearable to middle-class adolescent boys, racked by scruples, over-earnest, incapable of healthy compromise with principles, too expert at suppressing the pleasure principle in exchange for the tawdry nobility of suffering.

Saint-Denys Garneau inherited a double set of impossible standards. His mother, a Juchereau-Duchesnay, descended from the seigneurial gentry abolished in 1854, was preternaturally pious, unwilling to attend for confession in a church which was not completely empty. Through his father, he was descended from the poet Alfred Garneau and the historian François-Xavier Garneau. From both, Saint-Denys Garneau received an excruciating perfectionism. However, his early years brought him happiness and success. He won literary competitions, enjoyed sports and was surrounded by a friendly group of young people of his own age. The education he received at the private Collège Saint-Jean de Brébeuf and at the Beaux-Arts in Montreal was the best available and developed his propensities as an artist and writer. However, ill-health — the discovery of heart lesions in his early twenties — made him increasingly paranoiac and he withdrew progressively into himself until his death at 31 in 1943. Whether the silence of his last four years was the silence of a deep mystical experience or a sympton of catatonic withdrawal is likely to remain an open question.

His only published work was a short volume of free verse, *Regards et jeux dans l'espace*, of 1937, and a few articles which appeared in the journal *La Relève* which Garneau produced from 1934 with a group of friends. His poetry, dwelling on the fleeting beauty of the objective world, the inadequacy of language to express the poet's vision, the tenuous grasp he has on the true self and the precarious nature of art in a materialist, philistine cultural milieu, resembles that of fellow-American Jules Supervielle, though Supervielle is inclined to be more content with his lot, less solemn, less word-bound. Garneau's *Journal* and his correspondence which contain impressive pages of self-analysis as well as sensitive art, music and literary criticism have been published posthumously.

In his *Journal*, the bulk of which was contained in school exercise-books for the years 1935 to 1939, he recorded personal confidences, transcribed poems and letters, stuck magazine cuttings, noted the music he listened to and the books he read and even his petty cash accounts — the parallel with Baudelaire's *Journaux intimes* cannot be missed. Like his numerous letters to friends, the *Journal* is the work of a solitary and of a perfectionist, compensating in writing for the frustration he feels at his failure to communicate meaningfully with others.

The culture shock of the French Catholic writers, obviously, could not but be profound. Garneau and his friends read, discussed, commented on the writings of Mounier, Mauriac, Maritain, Jouhandeau, Bernanos, du Bos, Claudel, Chateaubriant and, as filtered through the Catholic critics (Stanislas Fumet, for example), the tragic ontology of Dostoievsky and Baudelaire. Through Maritain, who visited Quebec and whose lectures Garneau attended, the group of *La Relève* were in touch with the review *Esprit* whose idealistic spirituality they shared.

Garneau's reading of European authors has been carefully studied by Roland Bourneuf, thematically rather than by individual author. The same writer has looked at Garneau's reading of Baudelaire in an article in *Études Littéraires*. Bourneuf devotes a dozen pages to François Mauriac in his thesis and this section has been discussed, expanded and criticised in an article in *Liberté* by Léon Debien which draws on his own unpublished thesis of 1966. Bourneuf's thematic approach means that his analysis of Garneau's relations with individual authors is necessarily cursory. Debien finds that the judgement of Bourneuf and Gilles Marcotte on Garneau's attitude to Mauriac (Garneau's willingness to revise his view, his integrity as a critic) is inaccurate. Debien's own careful and thoughtful study of Garneau's reading of Mauriac permits him to see that Garneau, commenting on Mauriac at two points in the year 1935, does so at two times of deep personal crisis. The affinity between the Canadian and the Frenchman is a factor in each of these crises, a decisive one even. Garneau found in Mauriac a kindred sensibility. The foregoing will have made the resemblance apparent: slow or arrested moral development, obsession with morbid introspection, fixation in the moral problems generated by a middle-class, puritanical, family-centred milieu, the alienation and solitude of the sensitive, artistic temperament, ill-served by the prevalent Catholic ethos which is unquestioning and crudely mechanistic, finally, the resulting crisis of inter-personal communication. The parallel need not be laboured. Garneau uses Mauriac as a spring-board for his own intense feelings. Time and again, we observe him responding to his reading in a way that is almost entirely symptomatic of his mood at the time, though this does not prevent him from making perceptive comments or from profiting tremendously from the authors he frequents.

Léon Debien very rightly points to the importance of putting Garneau's reflexions on Mauriac in the *Journal* back into the context of his other entries at the time. Mauriac is first mentioned in February 1935 at the beginning of Garneau's serious diaries. The beginning of the year was a difficult time for the young poet. Christmas and New Year were spent in the peace and seclusion of the family country home at Sainte-Catherine-de-Portneuf, though the New Year imposed on him a number of social calls which he found irksome. This was nothing to his reluctance to return to Montreal, to the big city and his studies. The *Journal* reflects all this in passages which are often quoted:

Grande fatigue, abattement, exaspération comme sur la fine marge de ma possibilité d'exister . . . Besoin pour ma guérison de sortir de moi-même, et défaut de force pour y réussir; la musique seule me permettait une contemplation désintéressée où je me reposais . . . Retour du thé chez les Vaillancourt. De plus en plus je me sens dépaysé parmi cette société, même composée d'êtres aimables et qui, chacun, ont du bon . . . J'ai connu la semaine dernière une expérience intérieure de délaissement, d'humiliation, de solitude . . . Dieu m'a certes visité de sa grâce durant cette période de désarroi . . . j'ai été éclairé étrangement sur la nécessité de la sainteté . . . Que le bonheur est dangereux, et toute puissance, et toute ivresse! . . . Apprends à jeter ta joie même humaine sur Dieu et dépense tout cela à t'en rapprocher.[1]

Amongst these reflexions, Garneau pastes a cutting from *Le Canada*, a review Mauriac wrote of a Toscanini concert, first published in *Le Figaro*.[2] Garneau responds in the margin to the article which dwells mainly on Beethoven's ninth, the fourth movement of which is a setting of Schiller's *Ode to Joy*. Whereas Debussy's *Iberia* creates a picture which our subjectivity is powerless to modify, the Beethoven leaves us completely free to colour our listening with the exact shades of our own personal drama. Mauriac confesses to a need to use the works of the masters to give a face to the world of unexpressed passion we carry in us. He takes issue with Beethoven, feeling that though the theme of the ninth is 'joy through suffering', nevertheless joy should be more involuntary. He argues that Beethoven calls on Schiller and the human voice to stifle the cries of despair of the music and to cover his suffering with 'une immense nappe de fausse joie'. Beethoven could not trust his instrumentalists — an interesting explanation of the unprecedented introduction of a choir and a text into a symphony.

Garneau reacts querulously to Mauriac's suggestion that Beethoven is incapable of expressing joy. He accuses Mauriac of being so subjective that his judgment is distorted (Mauriac readily admits his partiality) and of excessive pessimism amounting to heretical Jansenism. These comments are heavy with barely conscious irony. Many entries in this same *Cahier* of the *Journal* find Garneau using music to explore his own psyche and to sort out his own moral imperatives and he must have put more than a hint of self-mockery into his reference to Mauriac as 'ce remâcheur de lui-même'. Our quotations from the *Journal* above show the young writer tortured by his own powerlessness to transcend the self, finding some relief through music but defeated by his mistrust of simple happiness in the name of some unattainable joy. The affinity between the two writers amply explains Garneau's tetchiness.

Review and marginal notes are followed by a short article comparing Mauriac's attitude to evil with that of Bernanos and Claudel. The latter writers' realistic recognition of evil is favourably contrasted with what Garneau sees as Mauriac's poetic nostalgia for sin. Again, Garneau feels that Mauriac's characters have their objectivity clouded by a long heredity of evil, an atavism which the light of grace seems powerless totally to dispel. This view of evil which is finely observed by Garneau though the expression is awkward at times, makes of Mauriac a 'retardataire', wilfully ignoring the advances in self-analysis in the modern world, 'un fruit corrompu de la civilisation en désarroi dont nous voulons nous détacher'.

This last sentence offers a firm clue to the source of Garneau's attitude. He reacts to Mauriac in the terms of the movement for spiritual renewal associated with Jacques Maritain. He had read *Art et scolastique*. French Canadian Catholicism was based on orthodox Thomism and Garneau admires Maritain's asceticism and his aesthetics.[3] In another undated article on Mauriac which reads like a gloss on the one of February 1935, the link between Garneau's criticisms and Maritain's programme for moral renewal is even clearer. Mauriac's subjective art is seen as dangerous in an age 'où se fait sentir la nécéssité d'un ascétisme impitoyable pour toute complaisance à soi-même'. Excusing his severity towards the works of Mauriac which he cannot but admire, Garneau describes him as powerless to transcend himself at a time when an attitude of detached objectivity is essential to 'la reconstruction impérieuse de la personnalité humaine dissolue par tant de siècles d'analyse . . .' (p. 674). The names of Mauriac and Maritain are linked again in similar terms in an entry on 17 May 1935 (p. 355).

Garneau's attitude to the writing of Mauriac emerges then as one of more than grudging respect for a master of French prose and fiction. He is clearly very strongly drawn to the French writer, as can be seen from the first reference to Mauriac in a letter of 19 February 1931 where *Le Jeune homme* is described as a 'volume admirable'. In 1935, he acknowledges the 'grandeur du *Baiser au lépreux*' and '"la sérénité transparente" qu'on attribue justement au *Nœud de vipères*' and he seems, too, to except *Le Mystère Frontenac* from his strictures (p. 355). In the Spring of 1937, he appears afraid to accept that Mauriac could be right when he states in *Le Nœud de vipères* (is he confusing it with *Thérèse Desqueyroux*?) that there are no monsters in the sight of God, so appalled is he by his own monstrosity in which he feels compelled to believe (p. 493). In the undated text (identical in many respects to that of February 1935) he again excepts from his attacks 'le plus haut de l'œuvre de Mauriac, *Le Nœud de vipères, Le Jeudi saint, Souffrance et bonheur du chrétien*'.

A terse comment of May 1935 reveals Garneau's anxieties:

Drame de la multiplicité de la personnalité dans l'artiste, dont se plaint François Mauriac et dont Maritain montre le danger dans sa *Lettre à Cocteau* et le tiraillement intérieur. (p. 355)

At this juncture in his personal development, the parallel with Mauriac is too close for comfort. The resemblance with Yves Frontenac is striking:

Plus sa poésie rallierait de cœurs, et plus il se sentirait appauvri; des êtres boiraient de cette eau dont il devait être seul à voir la source se tarir. Ce serait la raison le cette méfiance de soi, de cette dérobade à l'appel de Paris (. . .) et enfin de son hésitation à réunir ses poèmes en volume.[4]

Everything fits, an easy success based on a misunderstanding, the loneliness created by an ambivalent attitude to mother and family, a failure to be truly at ease either in the capital or at home in the provinces, finally and most tellingly, his fear of publication which he sees as a betrayal. How could he not greet with mixed joy and pain Mauriac's confessions in *Souffrances du pécheur*:

Tel garçon de vingt-cinq ans possède toutes les grâces, mais toutes ses amours sont malheureuses. Si d'abord il est aimé, cela ne dure guère et il n'a de cesse qu'il n'ait repris son rôle de victime: c'est toujours lui qui finit par être torturé.[5]

The occasional indiscretion in the *Journal* and the poems indicates that Garneau knew the torments of love which as a mystical craving was doomed to fail. Like Jean Péloueyre in *Le Baiser au lépreux*, he seeks the anonymity of the metropolis or the solitude and silence of the country to avoid being crushed by the bitter disappointment his relations with others always lead to.

Garneau needs not someone to mirror his own *angst* about the Catholic writer's dilemma but a firm lead to help him make clear moral choices. He rejects Mauriac's marvellous complicity with his characters on moral grounds, unaware, perhaps, of the qualms of conscience the Catholic novelist suffered on this score and the trouble it gave him with his readers. It is regrettable that Garneau's comments on Mauriac come at moments of spiritual crisis when a fair evaluation is denied him. His need for an ascetic, his commitment to moral reconstruction, makes him turn against a writer whom he had read with obvious pleasure and whose insights he clearly valued. Those who have caught themselves reacting to Mauriac in just these ways will no doubt treat his young Canadian reader with sympathy and respect.

BIRMINGHAM   C. R. P. MAY

---

[1] Hector de Saint-Denys Garneau: *Œuvres*. Édition critique établie par Jacques Brault et Benoît Lacroix, Presses de l'Université de Montréal, 1971, pp. 331, 333, 340, 341, 342. (Page references to the *Journal* given in the text are to this edition.)

[2] Ibid., p. 335-8. This review is also published in Mauriac's *Journal, 1932-1939*, La Table Ronde, 1947, pp. 175-179, 'Note d'après le concert'.

[3] The following brief quotation from Maritain's *Art et scolastique*, in *Œuvre philosophique*, *La Revue thomiste*, s.d., pp. 126-7, gives some idea of the identity of views of Garneau and his French mentor, striking at once to any reader of Garneau:

La beauté appartient à l'ordre transcendental et métaphysique. C'est pourquoi elle tend d'elle-même à porter l'âme au-delà du créé . . . Les règles certaines dont parlaient les scolastiques ne sont pas des impératifs de convention imposés du dehors à l'art, elles sont les voies d'opération de l'art lui-même, de la raison ouvrière, voies hautes et cachées. Et tout artiste sait bien que sans cette forme intellectuelle dominatrice de la matière, son art ne serait qu'un gâchis sensuel.

[4] François Mauriac, *Le Mystère Frontenac*, Grasset, 1933, p. 152.

[5] Idem, *Souffrances et bonheur du chrétien*, Grasset, 1937, p. 69.

S. B. JOHN

THE MIRROR OF THE STAGE:
VICHY FRANCE AND FOREIGN DRAMA

In so far as literature is not life itself but, in varying degrees, an abstraction from life, it might be said that its characteristic tendency is always metaphoric, though we may value prose-fiction, for example, because its particularity and concreteness, its local effects offer themselves as a guarantee of authentic experience. In a comparable way, the metonymic character of naturalistic plays is constantly eroded or challenged by the conventions and artifices of stage performance and so moves toward the metaphoric even when the rendering of real-life experience forms the substance of the play.[1] In all the plays I propose to deal with elements of realism are insistently present, whether in the furniture of the settings, the references to local geography and actual historical episodes, the care in relating dramatic time to chronological time, or the general concern with realistic motivation in the characters. But it is also true that in a number of these plays we meet a deliberate and self-conscious striving to redeem the naturalistic mode and to raise the historical vicissitudes of individuals to the level of a metaphor about the human condition.

This sense of the play as metaphor is the necessary complication which faces any critical reader or spectator when he attempts to define with any precision the way in which the life of the drama can be said to relate to society and historical experience, or to have significance for our understanding of a period as burdened with violence and conflicts of value and loyalty as the German occupation of France between 1940 and 1944. I accept that the metaphor of the 'mirror' of the stage, used here as a kind of convenient shorthand, is profoundly unsatisfactory unless one conceives of the play not as the passive reflection of a real historical world 'out there', but as a medium for interpreting reality. The ambiguities and contradictions of a play dealing imaginatively with historical conflicts are valuable precisely because they restore an adequate sense of the complexity of the relations between public and private acts, and express what is above and beyond ideology in historical experience.[2] Although the plays I propose to study vary considerably in the degree to which they achieve formal control, verbal tact and imaginative insight, each, in embodying a given dramatist's vision of the world, creates the *analogy* of a lost world of feeling and belief which enables us to enter more fully into it specific values and assumptions. At their most finely realized moments, these plays offer insights into human activity that are not as immediately or vividly available in document or testimony. At their best, they recreate, in Richard Hoggart's eloquent phrase, 'the experiential wholeness of life — the life of the emotions, the life of the mind, the individual life and the social life, the object-laden world'.[3]

It is, of course, true that all attempts to reorder imaginatively the historical realities of occupation and resistance in France necessarily involve the writer, whether he is poet, novelist or dramatist, in inventing forms that both capture and distance the living experience. So it could be argued that the aesthetic success and moral significance of plays inspired by the ordeals of France under the Vichy régime do not depend on whether the plays are imagined by Frenchmen under the shadow of the events and experiences they transpose, or by foreigners in countries remote from these ordeals, or by Frenchmen or foreigners writing years after the war is over. But this is not incompatible with arguing, as I shall, that distance in time or space does necessarily affect the tonality of these foreign plays and colour the perspectives in which events, struggles and aspirations are viewed. There is something else, an aesthetic problem put succinctly by a distinguished art-historian: 'In fact great artists seldom take any interest in the events of the outside world. They are occupied in realising their own images and achieving formal necessities. As is well-known, the images that are the basis of Guernica occur in drawings that antedate by over a year the bombing of the Basque town'.[4] The point being made here seems to me greatly exaggerated when applied to literature, but I do see that the qualification, 'great artist', is important. I would not want to claim that any of the playwrights I have chosen to study is 'great', even if the best exhibit high technical skill and marked imaginative power, so they would not need to conform to the rule embodied in Clark's first sentence. However, what is spelled out in his second clearly applies to them, as to all creative writers. Their plays are certainly written out of an intense awareness of the tragic possibilities inherent in a great public theme, that of the social, political and moral fate of a conquered nation, but are not to be understood uniquely by reference to the events and dilemmas that inspire them. They have also to be related to the sensibility of the individual playwright as it is expressed in the characteristic settings, preoccupations and images which mark his literary production in general, and which make up that distinctive and essentially mythopeic world that each artist creates from the disparate materials of his actual and imagined experience.

Of the plays I wish to discuss, two were actually written during the Second World War and both in the United States. John Steinbeck's *The Moon is Down: a play in two parts* (1942) is a dramatic transposition of his novel in eight chapters, dating from the same year. Bertolt Brecht's *Die Gesichte der Simone Machard* (*The Visions of Simone Machard*) was written in collaboration with Lion Feuchtwanger in California, largely between December 1941 and February 1943, though it had to wait until 1957 for its first stage production, at the Städtische Bühnen in Frankfurt. So both plays must be thought of as directly inspired by the pressure of events and both as seeking to express a gesture of solidarity with European nations occupied by the German armies. In Brecht's case there is a special charge of personal feeling. He himself was a political exile; his friend, the critic Walter Benjamin, had committed suicide in 1940 on the French frontier with Spain rather than risk being handed over to the Gestapo, while his collaborator, Feuchtwanger, interned outside Aix-en-Provence in 1940, had managed to escape and cross the Pyrenees at the point where Benjamin had been turned back. As for Steinbeck, *The Moon is Down* appears to have grown out of a 'serious discussion' with William J. Donovan of the Office of Strategic Services on techniques for aiding resistance movements in German-occupied territories in Europe.[5] As a consequence, both plays tend to present heroic images of resistance and to indulge a tone that is sometimes disconcertingly hortatory.

Steinbeck's occupied town has been overrun swiftly and methodically with the aid of a local quisling, Corell. It is both a fishing-port and a mining community; the names and climate are Nordic rather than French, and there is small sense of the attitudes and forms of social life characteristic of France. The untidy, brave and unassuming local mayor, Orden, and his shrewd and philosophic friend, Dr Winter, are conceived very much in the spirit of the folksy, unsung heroes of Thornton Wilder's *Our Town* (1938). Essentially, the dramatic action, episodic like that of the novel, is articulated about the attempts of the occupying forces to win the cooperation of the locals, and, when that is not volunteered, to compel it by terror. The struggle is epitomized in the conflicts of interest and clashes of will played out in the Town Hall between Mayor and Medical Officer, on the one hand, and officers of the invading army, on the other. The struggle for survival in the microcosm of the Town Hall is echoed in the growing resistance activities of the larger community outside. All we get of these are 'noises off', so to speak, involving sabotage in the mines and on the railways and reports of young men escaping by fishing-boat to England. But the play also focuses on two individual cases which break through the anonymity of the resistance: the killing of the officer Bentick by the miner Alexander Morden and, in a contrived and melodramatic episode, the stabbing to death by Morden's pretty wife, Molly, of Lieutenant Tonder whose nerve has failed under the strain of isolation and covert public hatred. The shot that wounds Lieutenant Prackle comes out of the anonymous crowd at the very moment when Morden is executed in the public square, and coincides with the coming of the winter snows, a metaphor for the pitiless struggle that lies ahead. After the first 'drop' of explosives by parachute, engineered by the allies to aid the local resistance movement, Orden refuses to appeal to the community to collaborate with the occupying authorities by handing in the explosives. The weary professional, Colonel Lanser, quite without illusion about what the future holds, orders Orden to be led away as a hostage and executed in the event of further resistance activity. As the mayor goes, explosions can be heard from the direction of the mines and then from nearer the Town Hall. Resistance will clearly continue with or without the mayor.

It is difficult not to see in this play an over-schematic picture in which conventional images of patriotic unity and sacrifice quite efface the physical suffering, psychological bewilderment, and moral and political divisions normally experienced by an occupied people. Collaboration is identified with a single quisling whose motives are never explored, local status never explained, and self-styled patriotism never examined. Orden believes that free men will always triumph over 'herd-men', but, given the appalling realities of Nazi methods, there is something too unthinkingly optimistic about this view of the certain victory of spirit over brute force. Nor, indeed, can it be said that the officers of the occupying army are *shown* to be 'herd-men'. In fact, with the exception of the rigid and ambitious Captain Loft, they all exhibit varying degrees of frailty, humanity and idiosyncrasy.

The general sense of abstraction and contrivance created by the play is powerfully reinforced by the exchanges between Orden and Winter which virtually close it. To Orden's echo of the death of Socrates in Plato's *Phaedo* ('Crito, I owe a cock to Asclepius; will you remember to pay the debt?'), Winter responds with dramatic irony: 'The debt shall be paid'. Here, as violence explodes outside, the studied appeal to the glories of European philosophical thought seems intended to transcend and cancel out the surrounding barbarism. The effect is too facile to be persuasive. Such sheer theatricality is at variance with the drab naturalism of the rest of the play, and the self-conscious cultural allusions inconsistent with the plain man Steinbeck has created for us in Orden. However, it is easy to understand why French readers who encountered this fable in its original form as a novel, when it circulated clandestinely in February 1944 under the title *Nuits noires*, reacted enthusiastically to it. Its exalted tone, unblemished heroism, confidence, and large appeals to liberty had the impact and immediacy of a propagandist tract. The translator's note admirably crystallizes this aspect of the work: '*Nuits noires* n'est pas une œuvre réaliste, les générations futures pourront la trouver utopique comme elles pourront juger chimérique *Le Silence de la mer*'.[6]

In spite of its good will and admirable sentiments, the sense which Steinbeck's play provokes of being remote from the events it embodies, is generally absent from Brecht's *The Visions of Simone Machard*, chiefly because of the care he takes to place his characters in their social setting and in the framework of concretely rendered economic and ideological interests. The drama critic, who reported on the first French production of Brecht's play at the Théâtre de la Commune d'Aubervilliers in the winter of 1967, confirms this when he expresses astonishment that Brecht in California 'ait senti, deviné, les réactions "de classe" que l'occupation allait provoquer'.[7] There is something almost paradoxical about this comment when one reflects that Brecht's play is structured about a sequence of nine scenes in which realistic representations of war, civil confusion and social discord in the little French country town of Saint-Martin in June 1940 alternate with dream-interludes in which the young hotel skivvy, Simone Machard, imagines herself to be Joan of Arc called to rescue France from the German invader. In the real-life episodes Simone, prompted by the intimations supplied by her dream-interludes, stops her profiteering employer from taking all the hotel's food and transport with him on his flight to the south; distributes food to hungry refugees; sets fire to the town's petrol reserves so as to prevent the enemy using them; and is eventually handed over to the nuns running the local mental institution, though not before the refugees have followed her example and set fire to the village hall. In the four dream-interludes the real personages in Simone's life are transformed into the historical figures of the Joan of Arc story, while her own brother who is away serving in the French army, appears as an angel.

This 'doubling' of the characters is an ingenious and economical device for connecting past and present, establishing a sense of national community and, above all, for throwing into bold relief the very Brechtian notion of the supremacy of economic and class interests. In this perspective the paradox I have alluded to is more apparent than real since the dream-interludes are not used in *The Visions of Simone Machard* in order to point to a spiritual realm. They simply assemble the properties of the familiar historical legend, not so as to suggest that France is under some kind of divine protection, but so as to provide a vivid device for reinforcing Simone's sense of her patriotic duty in the face of the invasion. Such a device rests a little uncertainly in the hands of a dramatist as thoroughly secular and political as Brecht, since he has necessarily to invoke a legend profoundly coloured by Christian faith while at the same time neutralizing its religious significance. This he does by surrounding the story of the Maid of Orleans with ironic and satirical touches that imply a radical social and political critique of the French propertied classes, seen unsparingly as preferring their own survival as the beneficiaries of capitalism to the survival of France as an independent nation. So the anachronisms of the dream-interludes, in which the vacillating mayor figures as Charles VII; Henri Soupeau, proprietor of the hostelry, as the Connétable; his mother, Marie, as Queen Isabeau; Fétain, the wealthy vineyard owner, as the Duke of Burgundy; and the French colonel who has deserted his troops as the Bishop of Beauvais, graphically clinch for us Brecht's conviction that the central historical reality is that of the class-war. In this play the poor are quite simply sacrificed to the rich, and in the dream-interludes the gorgeous apparel of the notables present at Joan's rigged trial conveniently epitomizes this.

No doubt there is something too simplistic here, and too sentimental in the treatment of Simone as a humble and selfless worker embodying all courage and virtue. In fact, in making Simone little more than a child, Brecht risks destroying her interest as a character and her plausibility as a leader of resistance. Yet it cannot be said that the other workers are spared his criticism. On the contrary, Simone's obsequious and time-serving parents and the shifty and opportunistic employees of the hostelry are shown in a bad light, seeming much closer to the *attentistes* of the Pétain years than to the dedicated minority of resistance fighters. So the temptation to simplify and idealize, to persuade rather than to show, enters into Brecht's portrait of resistance, but is offset by a much more satisfying and concrete picture of motive, loyalty and social differences than we get in Steinbeck. In addition, Brecht's exploitation of the theatrical medium is altogether more assured, vivacious and inventive, more successfully adapted to conveying a large and significant action than Steinbeck's sequence of static tableaux. Brecht has brought a characteristic political resonance to an act of instinctive resistance, but Simone's essentially childish perception of the world and her lack of self-awareness make it impossible for us to view her as a tragic agent in history, so that *The Visions of Simone Machard* does not achieve that 'recovery of history as a dimension for tragedy' which Raymond Williams detects in Brecht's mature work.[8]

Brecht, I have argued, secularizes Simone/Joan's visions and conscripts them to the task of political satire. Carl Zuckmayer, on the contrary, strains to invent a dramatic form that will redeem the naturalism of historical events and connect the transient and the eternal, the profane and the sacred, the human and the elemental. In *Der Gesang im Feuerofen* (*The Song in the Fiery Furnace*), first produced at the Deutsches Theater, Göttingen in November 1950, the plot, based on an actual war-time incident, is simple but the treatment complex and episodic, constantly eluding the naturalistic mode. In December 1943 a group of the Maquis are celebrating Christmas in a deserted château in the Savoy Alps; they are betrayed to the Germans who set fire to the building and burn to death all those inside. Just as *The Moon is Down* reflects something of Steinbeck's trust in the folklore of American democracy, and *The Visions of Simone Machard* something of Brecht's reliance on Marxist ideas, so *Der Gesang im Feuerofen* repeats and orchestrates themes and insights that recur in Zuckmayer's work.

For example, Zuckmayer's characteristic admiration for feminine loyalty and devotion finds lyrical expression in the scene where the wife of a sick and exhausted Jewish husband, on the run from the authorities, refuses to abandon him and find safety for herself. The overtones of racial persecution not only echo moments in other plays but have a particular resonance for Vichy France where racial laws had been adopted as early as October 1940 and savagely reinforced by the legislation and deportations of 1942. In much the same way, the theme of bastardy which recurs in Zuckmayer's plays is here reflected in the figure of the treacherous Creveaux and his relationship with the sinister and drunken La Soularde. But two particular themes which persist in Zuckmayer's theatre are central to the meaning of *Der Gesang im Feuerofen*. The first is his concern with personal and spiritual freedom, which he here connects with a process of spiritual purification that transforms suffering into a higher order of love and enables the victims of the fire to attain inner peace and harmony.[9] The second is his fascination with the dilemmas of patriotism, obedience and moral integrity, perhaps most vividly illustrated in his play of 1946, *Des Teufels General* (*The Devil's General*), and related in the present play to resistance and collaboration in France. Though *Der Gesang im Feuerofen* is rooted in a dense network of local and private bonds and allegiances, it moves constantly beyond them, showing how the acts of individuals are caught up in the highest ethical and spiritual imperatives. In unquestionly obeying orders the French policeman, Albert, and the German commander, Mühlstein, are alike in using the concept of duty as a means of legitimizing their moral abdication. Sylvaine, having persistently taunted and humiliated the collaborator, Creveaux, who will betray his countrymen to the Germans, experiences a profound emotional and spiritual awakening when she falls in love with the German radio-operator, Sylvester Imwald. Similarly, Sylvester's decision to warn the Maquis of Creveaux's treachery is an act of betrayal that nevertheless answers to a higher moral law than patriotism. Marcel Neyroud, who epitomizes the fervent patriot's duty to hate the enemy, is won over by the priest Francis Leroy to accepting that love transcends mere patriotism and is moved, in the blazing chapel of Act III, to forgive Sylvester at the moment of death. On the other hand, Marcel's father, a loyal supporter of the legally constituted government of Vichy, acts as a servant of the state against his private conscience and ironically brings about the death of his own son.

But all these acts, set within the web of family, friendship and army, and against the landscape of Haute-Savoie, are in some sense transfigured by a series of devices which tend deliberately to produce a symbolic and metaphysical dimension over and above the world of social and political fact. Through these devices we are led to judge actions from a standpoint outside history, from a kind of eternal realm where angels and the personified elements meet and where the nature of human responsibility, guilt and atonement can be seen more clearly. Some of these devices are limited in their effects. The fleeing Askenasi family are simply referred to as 'Mother', 'Father', 'Son', etc., and this lack of individuation lends them a kind of archetypal status as persecuted Jewry. Elsewhere, the haunting ballad about an unmarried mother sung by La Soularde, as she cradles a bottle in her arms like a child, similarly lifts the play out of the particular into the world of folktale. But by far the most ambitious use of the devices which blur or cancel out historical time is that of introducing two angels (doubling for the characters Michelle and Francis) and three figures personifying the elements of Wind, Frost and Mist. Significantly, these figures, suggesting a dimension beyond human time, actually frame the entire action of the play. Act I opens with two angels speaking the heightened language of verse, while Wind, Frost and Mist open Act II and close Act III, also in poetic vein. Particularly suggestive is this final appearance in which the elements, prefiguring the coming of Spring and the return of new life to the earth, intone the solemn line: 'Gross ist die Macht der Toten' ('Great is the power of the dead'), and so recall for us the scene of the Maquis in the burning chapel, a scene itself raised above naturalism by the illuminated presence of cross and altar and by the triumphant excerpts from the liturgy declaimed by Francis: 'Te Deum laudamus! Te Dominum confitemur!' In this perspective it is not difficult to see why one critic thinks of the play as reflecting 'the need for God and His help'.[10]

Whatever *Der Gesang im Feuerofen*'s uncertainties of tone, lapses into banality or ultimate failure to achieve a coherent dramatic design, Zuckmayer's large ambition to fuse such different levels of experience and to carry history beyond chronicle and polemic compels admiration. The imaginative energy at work here, and the reverence for life which underlies Zuckmayer's awareness of the baffling variety and contradictions of human behaviour, often raise this play above its formal and technical imperfections and lend to the cruel dilemmas and sacrifices of resistance and counter-resistance in France in 1943 a significance which transcends time and place.

This vein of anguished reflection on ends and means, and on the limits of obedience, is central to Charles Morgan's *The River Line*, first staged at the Lyric Theatre, Hammersmith in September 1952. It is a play written at sufficient remove from the events it describes to be able to reorder the experience rather than use it as a means of encouraging certain attitudes, which is what tends to happen with Steinbeck and Brecht. In the scenes it specifically devotes to clandestine resistance in France it conveys a strong sense of the tenseness, risks and uncertainty which attach to such activity. It also shares with *Der Gesang im Feuerofen* the desire to find a structure, tone and language that are appropriate for dealing with the powerful issues of conscience involved. Far more restricted than Zuckmayer in the range of effects he deploys, Morgan exhibits more unity and restraint, but also less breadth of vision and human sympathy.

This three-act play centres on an incident which occurs in July 1943, not far from Toulouse, in a disused granary belonging to Pierre Chassaigne and his daughter, Marie. The building is being used as a staging-post in an escape line operated by the French resistance so as to enable Allied servicemen to make their way into Spain from where they may rejoin their units in Britain. The incident itself, shockingly abrupt and unexpected, involves the murder of one of the escapers, Heron, suspected of being 'un faux Anglais', a German agent who has infiltrated the line in order to inform German intelligence of its members and organisation. In two ways Morgan attempts to rescue this episode from becoming simply another sensational accident in a long and bloody modern war. The first is through the dislocation of normal chronology. The murder takes place in Act II, scene 3, framed between the first and third acts which are set in July 1947 in the pastoral charm and serenity of an eighteenth-century dower house in Gloucestershire where three of the original participants in the murder are gathered. The second way is through the use of a heightened formal prose, not breaking entirely with normal speech, as in the case with the choric interventions of angels and personified elements in Zuckmayer's play, but perfectly distinct from everyday usage and from the cadences of ordinary speech. In Act I, scene 1 Marie Chassaigne, now married to Julian Wyburton, the naval commander who killed Heron in the granary at her order, says 'And when one whom we have loved, however silently, is dead, all account of him from those who were with him when we were not is precious, seeming . . . seeming to extend his life in our memory which cannot now be extended in our experience'.[11] This stilted language is excused on the grounds of her being French, but in scene 2, Mrs Muriven, one of the guests at dinner, expresses herself in a way that is hardly different: 'Why, then, in the direction of responsibility. Which doesn't mean counting appetites and calling them progress or counting voices and calling them the voice of God. It means responsibility *within your destiny*. Like a pilot's responsibility for his ship, moving on a tide' (p. 39). The same is true of Valerie Barton's language in Act III, scene 2: '. . . You see, there was no question of his forgiving or not forgiving them. They bore their responsibility in the predicament of the world. Blame and forgiveness he was leaving behind. All our debts and credits were emptied out . . .' (p. 162).

The broken chronology means that the act of taking life is surrounded, before and after, by a kind of envelope of ethical intimations and can thus, or so Morgan seems to imply, be raised to a level of generality it could with difficulty attain if just presented in a straight narrative of adventure. Certainly the rearrangement of the chronology means that Act I can be used to stimulate our curiosity so that we become anxious to learn more about the strange wartime encounter spoken of at dinner by the American, Philip Sturgess. Following on this, Act II affords a vivid picture of the old granary with its masked lamps, 'huge ominous shadows' and clutter of discarded furniture, as it does of the extreme isolation and vulnerability of the men on the run, and of the heroic courage of their helpers in the resistance. In enables us to grasp more fully the sense of the hints, silences and hesitations we note in Act I, and prepares us for the rather contrived rush of revelations that comes in Act III after a series of tense interventions by each of the principal characters ('The secret is almost out', says the terse stage direction). Only then do we learn the whole truth: that Heron/Lang was killed in error; that Julian and Marie have known it for four years but concealed it from each other; that Valerie Barton, whom Philip loves and wants to marry, is Heron's half-sister. By the end of the play Valerie recognizes that Julian, Marie and Philip were all implicated in her half-brother's death and forgives them.

One flinches a little at the melodramatic coincidences here while accepting that the dramatic structure as a whole articulates and sustains suspense, just as the murder of Heron in Act II, scene 3 graphically embodies the play's central concern with violence, guilt and atonement. Yet it seems to me that Morgan's decision to frame this moment between the elaborate moral reflexions voiced by the principal characters in Act I and III is ultimately mistaken. No doubt, the image of the country house in peacetime is deliberately juxtaposed to that of the gaunt granary in order to contrast the contemplative with the active, and order with contingency: an entirely legitimate effect in the theatre. But the images of poise and civilised ease do tend to suggest that reflexion on moral dilemmas is peculiarly the business of a privileged élite, and the rarefied language of the exchanges between characters creates the impression of high seriousness only at the cost of extinguishing any real sense of life. What is more, the self-conscious refinement of the language so aestheticizes actual experience that the appeal seems directed not to humanity at large, but to a coterie. It is clear that Morgan intends this language to be evidence of an exceptional moral sensibility on the part of those who use it (and all do, in a quite undifferentiated way), but it emerges less as an instrument perfectly attuned to probing moral and spiritual complexities than as a form of preciosity which denatures experience.

Yet it is easy to sympathise with Morgan's underlying ambition to find a dramatic form that will use a shocking episode in the French resistance as a means of asking how we are to exercise moral responsibility in a world of violence that has lost its traditional, and specifically Christian, values.[12] Certainly the moral centre of the play is located in the dramatic reversal of rôles which brings Philip Sturgess in Act III, scene 2 to discard the democratic optimism, which has previously characterized him, in favour of a philosophy of tragic suffering, guilt and expiation, movingly summed up in his question: 'Do you really believe that only the sins we commit knowingly are to be expiated and forgiven?' (p. 150). This truth is vitally important to Morgan, as his letter of 27 July 1949 to T. Warner Allen makes clear: 'If there is no sin without the will to sin, then there is no Grace without our deserving it; and it is the root of Christianity that Grace, like poetry and like love, comes not by our own deserving'.[13] I do not personally find that the language, characterisation and plotting of *The River Line* persuasively embody this truth, and I think the argument about violence, guilt and expiation is flawed by Morgan's unconvincing attempt, in the character of Commander Wyburton, to grant an exceptional ethical value to the code of military obedience, to what he calls the 'very ordinariness of discipline'.

In this play, Charles Morgan's intense concern with moral scruple is linked, though not always successfully, with Christian belief in sin, expiation and grace. In the last play I propose to deal with, Arthur Miller's *Incident at Vichy* (1964), the same moral intensity prevails but is articulated with greater directness and humanity than in *The River Line*. Where Morgan ultimately appeals to the divine, Miller wrestles painfully and uncertainly with guilt and evil and tries to find an answer in fallible man, deprived of any transcendent truth. Alone among the plays I have chosen, *Incident at Vichy* explores the moral climate of Vichy France and the consequences for French citizens of racialist legislation passed by a French government supported, or at least accepted, by the great majority of Frenchmen in 1942, the period in which the play is set. Though references to forged papers, the Unoccupied Zone, extermination camps and lists of proscribed books reinforce the sense of historical authenticity, the play is not primarily concerned to examine the working of anti-semitic laws in France but to probe the more general human experience of evil, guilt, responsibility and atonement.

The situation is stark: six men and a boy, suspected of being Jews or members of other 'inferior' races, are seated on a long bench in a 'place of detention', a bare, grimy building that might be a warehouse or armoury. The stage directions specify that they are caught 'in attitudes expressive of their personalities and functions, frozen there like members of a small orchestra at the moment before they begin to play'.[14] Subsequently they are joined by three others. The action is continuous, without formal division into acts or scenes, emphasizing the ineluctable passage of time within a closed space. Characters are carefully 'placed' in terms of trades or professions or social status: Lebeau, an artist; Marchand, a business-man; Bayard, an electrician; Monceau, an actor; Leduc, a psychiatrist; von Berg, a prince; Hoffman, a German scientist working for the Gestapo; a German army major; a waiter; a boy; a gypsy; an old Jew; Ferrand, a café proprietor. And this rather self-conscious placing, tending to give characters the status of types rather than individuals, is Miller's way of modifying the intrinsic naturalism of the play so as to lend the action a more general, perhaps even universal, resonance.

The suspects are interrogated in turn in an atmosphere of growing tension, especially after Ferrand learns from the callous French police investigators in the inner office that Jews are to be deported and burned to death in furnaces. In the agonized interplay between the suspects, each attempting to come to grips with the imminence of deportation and death, the whole range of human feeling is explored: appalled unbelief, self-deception and rationalizing of the situation, despair, resignation, even revolt (when Leduc and the boy are on the verge of making a break for it). Miller uses this crisis in the lives of the characters to strip away illusions and to confront us as spectators with the 'banality of evil', to borrow Hannah Arendt's phrase. Essentially, *Incident at Vichy* is Arthur Miller's attempt to reverse the imaginative failure he detected in the stage version of *The Diary of Anne Frank*: 'There is something dramatically wrong, for instance, when an audience can see a play about the Nazi treatment of a group of Jews hiding in an attic, and come away feeling the kind of — I can only call it gratification — which the audience felt after seeing *The Diary of Anne Frank*'. What was necessary 'to break the hold of reassurance upon the audience, and to make it match the truth of life, was that we should see the bestiality in our own hearts, so that we should know how we are brothers not only to these victims but to the Nazis . . .'[15]

This process of peeling away all human pretence and facile self-justification constitutes the central argument of the drama. With the exception of the silent old Jew, an archetypal figure of persecution, the other Jews are not sustained by any vital religious faith. Indeed, they are either indifferent, or positively hostile, to their Jewishness. Effectively each man is alienated from the next, each failing to see the degree he is like the others. Lebeau eventually settles for submission, feeling the guilt for being a Jew that anti-semites do so much to foster: 'Maybe it's that they keep saying such terrible things about us, and you can't answer' (p. 66). The communist Bayard draws comfort from a simplistic picture of the world, abdicating personal responsibility to the Party and the 'inevitable' progress of history that will make the working class 'master of the world' (p. 46), though he cannot explain why one should repose such trust in the workers, given that they are such staunch supporters of the Nazi régime. The actor, Monceau, utterly dependent on others, and especially spectators, for a sense of his own identity, will only act for the effect he produces. Hoffman and the major look respectively to a false racial anthropology and the fraudulent sanctity of a military oath to legitimate their complicity in mass murder. Only Leduc and von Berg strive strenuously to know themselves and to understand the nature of evil in a secular world. In his progress toward self-knowledge, von Berg, Aryan, aristocrat and lover of the arts, has to pass beyond Kierkegaard's aesthetic stage, beyond the false aestheticism which can only see the Nazis as 'vulgar'. When Leduc convinces him that through association with his anti-semitic cousin, Baron Kessler, he has been an accomplice to the evils of the Nazi régime, von Berg decides to atone by a freely chosen act of self-sacrifice, giving up his own 'white pass' so that Leduc can go free and rejoin his wife. In doing so, von Berg accepts Leduc's argument that nothing can come out of this suffering unless those who are not victims recognize their own complicity in what has happened, and the potential hatred and murder in themselves: 'Each man has his Jew; it is the other. And the Jews have their Jews' (p. 85). Here it is possible to see von Berg's act as establishing a 'moral norm',[16] in the sense that he becomes the only authentic moral agent in the play, inventing his values, in a very Sartrean fashion, in the absence of objective or transcendent criteria to which he might appeal. But Leduc, released into life by the sacrifice of his 'Jew', finds himself in the most fragile moral position.

He has yet to merit the sacrifice by any act of his own or to manifest his solidarity with the victims he is now able to leave behind. It is easy to see why a critic like Philip Rahv, reared on the radicalism of the old *Partisan Review*, criticizes the surprise ending for going contrary to the 'dialectic of guilt' embodied in the play, and rejects so general a notion of moral responsibility: 'Responsibility cannot be other than specific: if all are responsible, none are (*sic*) responsible'.[17] Such a view clearly recognizes the degree to which Miller is pronouncing an elegy over radical optimism. The experience of French Jewry in 1942 is used to illuminate a larger dilemma: that no social or political system will be likely to end man's exploitation of man, but that guilt can be exchanged for responsibility if man accepts his own complicity in evil.[18] There is a kind of difficult and moving idealism at work here, too often couched in a language that is banal or sententious, too often lodged in characters who are merely vehicles for ideas, but, at least, reaching out beyond Vichy France to the age of violence in which we live.

SUSSEX   S. B. JOHN

[1] As David Lodge has argued in *The Modes of Modern Writing* (London: Edward Arnold, 1979), pp. 82-83.

[2] Pierre Macherey, *Pour une théorie de la production littéraire* (Paris: Maspero, 1966), p. 155.

[3] *Speaking to Each Other, Volume Two: About Literature* (Harmondsworth: Penguin Books, 1973), p. 20.

[4] Kenneth Clark, *The Other Half: a Self-Portrait* (London: John Murray, 1977), p. 72.

[5] Lewis Gannett, 'John Steinbeck: the Novelist at Work', reprinted in: John Steinbeck, *Two-in-One* (London: The Reprint Society, 1947), p. 17.

[6] *Nuits noires* (Paris: Editions de Minuit, 1944), p. 7.

[7] 'Les Visions de Simone Machard de Bertolt Brecht', *Le Figaro littéraire* (4-10 December, 1967).

[8] 'A rejection of tragedy: Brecht', in *Modern Tragedy* (London, Chatto & Windus, 1966), p. 202.

[9] Ausma Balinkin, *The Central Women Figures in Carl Zuckmayer's Dramas* (Bern/ Frankfurt: Peter Lang, 1978), pp. 52-54.

[10] Murray B. Peppard, 'Moment of Moral Decision: Carl Zuckmayer's Latest Plays', *Monatshefte* 44 (7), (November 1952), p. 356.

[11] *The River Line: a Play* (London: Macmillan, 1952), pp. 17-18.

[12] As Morgan argues in his introduction to the play: 'On Transcending the Age of Violence', in *The River Line: a Play*, p. xvi.

[13] Eiluned Lewis (ed), *Selected Letters of Charles Morgan* (London: Macmillan, 1967), pp. 192-93.

[14] *Incident at Vichy* (London: Secker and Warburg, 1966), p. 11.

[15] 'The Shadows of the Gods', reprinted in Robert A. Martin (ed), *The Theater Essays of Arthur Miller* (New York: The Viking Press, 1978), pp. 186-187.

[16] Lawrence D. Lowenthal, 'Arthur Miller's *Incident at Vichy*: a Sartrean interpretation', *Modern Drama*, xviii, i (1975), p. 38.

[17] Philip Rahv, 'Arthur Miller and the fallacy of profundity', in *The Myth and The Powerhouse* (New York: Farrar, Straus and Giroux, 1965), p. 227 and p. 231.

[18] Lowenthal, *loc. cit.*, p. 39.

BACKTRACKING BECKETT[1]

Commentators have had a good deal to say about the 'naturalism', 'realism', *particularité*, or 'local colour' they find in Beckett's first radio play, *All That Fall*. 'On a été surpris par le réalisme, le pittoresque, la couleur locale d'une composition aussi récente que *All That Fall*', writes V. Ballardini.[2] *Fin de partie*, according to J.-J. Mayoux,[3] 'se déroule entre des personnages et dans un décor de type expressionniste, je veux dire non localisé, et reste apparenté à l'ensemble des fictions de Beckett. La particularité est beaucoup plus poussée dans *All That Fall*. Ici en effet, à ce qu'on pourrait appeler la particularité intérieure se joignent des références identifiables au monde extérieur'. The authors of *A Student's Guide to the Plays of Samuel Beckett*[4] speak of the processing of sounds to rid them of excessive naturalism and create 'the enclosed subjective realism' of the play. For the most part, they opine, 'Beckett's text reinforces the unreal realism'. Yet the radio play seems to start in the same place as *En attendant Godot*, on a *'route à la campagne'*, as the printed text of the stage play indicates. On the stage, however, the road is nowhere in particular and leads nowhere in particular[5] and the action has no topographical or temporal flavour, whereas in *All That Fall* the road goes to a real place (with a fictitious name) and the dialogue bears the stamp of a definite period.

Beckett's acceptance of the invitation from the B.B.C. in 1956 to submit the script of a play for broadcasting seems to have led to two violent reversals in his practice. Firstly, the suppression of the visual component eliminated the direct representation of movement in general and, in particular, of individual gesture, which was such a feature of the stage plays, *Godot*, *Fin de partie* (recently completed) and, if blurred recollections of what happened nearly fifty years ago can be trusted, *Le Kid*.[6] Those who heard Mr Beckett lecture on Molière in the early thirties will recall his insistence on this element in the comic theatre, his references to 'muscular dialogue generated by gesture' and his repeated allusions to Charlie Chaplin. Deprived of this resource, unable to concentrate (visual) attention upon the stage puppets, he perhaps felt obliged, in his first venture, to abandon that strict observance of the unity of place[7] that characterized *Godot* and *Fin de partie* and to create an (aural) illusion of movement on the part of his main character, Maddy Rooney, and those 'going in the same direction', by the sounds of shuffling steps, cartwheels, bicycle bell and brakes, rattling van and private car.[8] Betty Rojtman has shown how Maddy's return with her husband is illustrated by the recurrence in the dialogue of themes first occurring on her way out.[9]

Secondly, the B.B.C. offer forced Beckett to produce, for the first time in over ten years, a work in the English language forsaken by him since *Watt*. The return to the mother tongue was accompanied by the clearest and most sustained evocation of the mother land or, at least, of that strictly circumscribed part of it that had once been part of his daily life. Whatever efforts have been made to generalize the unseen landscape, resistant memories fix the dialogue-action in a place and period. Both Vivian Mercier[10] and Deirdre Bair[11] offer descriptions of the locality and Cooldrinagh, the Beckett home, but even in the nineteen-twenties and early thirties Foxrock, the 'Boghill' of the play, was little more than a place-name, a fashionable residential suburb developing in a rural setting. Its only real centre was the railway station and, in its immediate vicinity, one high-class grocery shop and a post-office. This station provided the link with the city and the outside world for the new population, since bus services developed late in Ireland. Torquay Road runs alongside the now disused railway line south to the station and continues in the same direction under the name of Brighton Road, passing Cooldrinagh about half a mile further on. This is the path trodden daily in real life by Beckett during the earlier part of his undergraduate career and, in the play, by Mrs Rooney on her way to meet the train, the 'hellish road' that Dan longs to trudge for the last time (p. 27). At the station it is intersected by Westminster Road which, by a level crossing, led to Leopardstown race-course immediately alongside the up platform.

In the play the station provides a fixed point to which the unseen action can be related, not unlike the pine or olive trees of the *chanson de geste*[12] or their descendent, the single tree beside which Estragon and Vladimir wait in vain, a kind of *lieu vague*. Nevertheless, 'the best kept of the entire network', as Maddy with historical accuracy reminds Mr Barrell (p. 23), 'the pretty little wayside station' beside the 'race-course with its miles and miles of white rails and three red stands' (p. 22), it has kept its identity. Mr Rooney grumbles at the short flight of stone steps leading to the down platform:

I have been up and down these steps five thousand times and still I do not know how many there are. When I think there are six there are four or five or seven or eight and when I remember there are five there are three or four or six or seven and when finally I realize there are seven there are five or six or eight or nine. Sometimes I wonder if they do not change them in the night. (p. 26).

But if Dan does not know or, playing the Beckett numbers game, chooses not to remember how many steps there are, his creator not only retains the visual memory of the place, but also recalls with obsessive accuracy the timing of trains on this somewhat ramshackle and underused system, the Dublin and South-Eastern Railway, or Dirty, Slow and Easy, as its users still called it even after its absorption in 1926 into the ambitiously styled Great Southern Railway. The great moments of the day on this stretch of line were when the 'up mail' and the 'down mail' passed through without stopping, linking Dublin with Rosslare Harbour and the G.W.R. Fishguard steamer. The up mail that Mrs Rooney is so worried about at the beginning of the play would probably have left Rosslare at 8.25 a.m. and Bray at 12.32, arriving at Harcourt Street, Dublin, at 1.05 after passing through Foxrock (Boghill) at about 12.48, fifteen minutes after the arrival time of the slow train from Dublin.[13] But on that Saturday the local train, delayed by the child's fall,[14] is a quarter of an hour late, entering the station as the boat train passes through (p. 46).

Alec Reid says that Beckett's method in all his plays is to reduce the specific to a minimum,[15] but in this play we find not only a specific, identifiable, railway station, trains running at specific, identifiable times, but also a specific station-master. Unruly, disrespectful commuting schoolboys in the nineteen-twenties delighted in exciting the wrath of the irascible and brightly complexioned little ruler of Foxrock station who kept his domain so trim. Not even on the D.S.E.R. was the post of station-master hereditary, but Beckett, not content with a lively presentation in word and action of this admirable functionary, resorts to the device of placing in Mrs Rooney's mouth a description she obviously cannot give of the Barrell she is addressing and therefore invents a Barrell *père*. 'You stepped into your father's shoes, I believe, when he took them off', she says, 'I remember him clearly. A small ferrety purple-faced widower, deaf as a doornail, very testy and snappy' (p. 17). My own father was a railway official and when, some time after the first broadcast of *All That Fall*, I asked him if he could remember the name of the rather cantankerous Foxrock station-master of my schooldays, he immediately replied 'Mr Farrell'.

The text of *All That Fall* provides indications of a fairly specific period, other than train times and local characters. Mrs Rooney, offered a lift by Mr Slocum, says 'But would I ever get in, you look very high off the ground today, these new balloon tyres, I presume'. (p. 13). The excellent *Student's Guide*, already quoted, notes 'Inflatable as opposed to solid tyres'. (p. 78). This interpretation would push the action into the remote past indeed! The first reference to these tyres given by the *Supplement to the Oxford English Dictionary* reads '*Motor* 27 May 1924 "The low-pressure or balloon tyre manufacturers in the United States have adopted the straight-sided type of rim exclusively."'[16] They could still be new in Ireland in the mid-twenties. As Mrs Rooney and Miss Fitt toil up the station steps they are greeted by 'cackling laughter' and Maddy says 'Now we are the laughing-stock of the twenty-six counties. Or is it the thirty-six?' (p. 21). The partition of Ireland had become effective in 1922 and divided the twenty-six counties of the Irish Free State from the six counties of Northern Ireland but took some years to sink into the habit of thought of the ordinary citizen and Mrs Rooney hates counting (p. 26). Again, after the establishment of the Free State in 1922 Irish Gaelic became the official, if widely unknown, language of the state and all public notices. For some time this provided the material for trivial comment. So Mr. Rooney, explaining the lateness of his arrival, says 'I got down and Jerry led me to the men's or Fir as they call it now' (p. 33).

Mr Rooney's rail journey is of course identical with that described in *Watt* some ten years or more before Dan's creation. The blind man must have tapped his way up the winding stairs to the platform after first mounting the steps to the colonnaded frontage of Harcourt Street station (enough perhaps to confuse him about the other station steps that faced him), just as the newsagent in the novel made the wearisome ascent weighed down by his heavy bicycle each morning only to carry it down again each evening at closing time.[17] This character, Mr Evans, described in comic detail,[18] and the porter, with his stage-Irish imprecation 'the devil raise a hump on you',[19] and his milk-churn business[20] create the same Abbey Theatre unreal reality here as do Mr Barrell and Tommy at Boghill. Incidentally, the *real* up mail was also the milk train. Watt like Dan Rooney, although not blind, mistakenly thinks that he is alone on the hard wooden seat of the D.S.E.R. third-class compartment.[21] The train moved 'across a land for ever still' until 'the race-course now appearing, with its beautiful white railing, in the fleeing lights, warned Watt that he was drawing near, and that when the train stopped next, then he must leave it. He could not see the stands, the grand, the members', the people's . . . with their white and red, for they were too far off'.[22]

It is by night too that Watt sets out on his return journey, arriving at the country station in the small hours to find it shut.[23] Mounting Mr Rooney's 'cursed steps' to the wicket gate he admires the permanent way, stretching on either hand, in the moonlight, and the starlight, as far as the eye could reach, as far as Watt's eye could have reached, if it had been inside the station.'[24] 'He contemplated with wonder also the ample recession of the plain, its flow so free and simple to the mountains'.[25] Climbing the locked wicket, he turns

to gaze [through it] the way back he had come, so recently. Of the many touching prospects thus offered to his inspection, none touched him more than the highway, now whiter somehow than by day, and of a fairer onrush, between its hedges, and its ditches. This highway, after an unbroken course of considerable length, dipped suddenly, and was lost to view, in a deplorable confusion of vertical vegetation.

The chimneys of Mr Knott's house were not visible, in spite of the excellent visibility. On fine days they could be discerned from the station. But on fine nights apparently not.[26]

What Watt sees, turning southwards, is Brighton Road, the Beckett road, the Rooney road, dropping away beyond Cooldrinagh with its high-perched chimneys which on a fine day would be visible from the raised station platform.[27] In the station Watt finds only the signalman still on duty 'an elderly man of the name of Case',[28] here described with the same care as Mr Evans at the beginning of the book, and who will still be in his cabin in *All That Fall* (p. 22) though neither heard nor described.

Although the radio play, Beckett's first English work for over ten years, is thus linked with *Watt* and Beckett land by rail (and road), the tracks and wheels still run on in the intervening years. In *Textes pour rien*, dating according to the publishers from 1950, here is the narrator

dans la salle d'attente de troisième classe de la gare du Sud-Est, je n'osais jamais me déclasser en attendant le départ, si j'y attendais toujours le départ, pour le sud-est, le sud plutôt, à l'est c'était la mer, tout le long des rails, en me demandant où mais où descendre, ou l'esprit loin, ailleurs. Le dernier départ était à vingt-trois heures trente,[29] ensuite on fermait la gare pour la nuit. Que de souvenirs, ça c'est pour me faire croire que je suis mort, je l'ai dit cent mille fois. Mais les mêmes reviennent, tels les rais d'une roue qui tourne, toujours les mêmes, et se ressemblant tous, comme des rais . . . Mais zut me revoilà loin du terminus, au joli péristyle classique.[30]

On 1 January, 1959, Harcourt Street terminus was closed, not for the night but for ever, and the line abandoned. Foxrock (Boghill) station has fallen into decay and only three of Mr Rooney's unknown sum of steps remain. But *All That Fall* soon became *Tous ceux qui tombent* and in January 1963 O.R.T.F. put out a televised version of the play. For this purpose Boghill station was recreated, apparently by the simple device of displaying the appropriate name-plates on the platform and station buildings at Romilly-sur-Andelle in the *arrondissement* of Les Andelys in the Eure.[31] This production was enthusiastically received by the public and the critics, especially Mauriac, first in *Le Figaro* and then in *Le Figaro littéraire*. Jacques Siclier declared in *Le Monde* (26 January 1963) that 'avant tout un texte de Beckett est fait pour l'oreille. Celui-là mis en images n'a pourtant rien perdu de son pouvoir'. Mitrani's production was awarded the Albert Olivier prize and is praised by Pierre Mélèse[32] for maintaining 'un équilibre entre le réel et le singulier', although he adds: 'Mais cette expérience suffit à l'auteur, qui par la suite refusa à Roger Blin l'autorisation de porter *Cendres* au petit écran'.[33]

W. H. LYONS

Did Beckett perhaps, having created a work that richly compensated for the absence of direct visual impact, find the re-introduction of this element destroyed a carefully contrived balance? Or did Romilly-sur-Andelle, despite a vague similarity in its station building, clash too painfully with a transmuted memory of Boghill?

SHEFFIELD   W. H. LYONS

---

[1] Some apology seems appropriate for the intrusion into this field of one whose academic interests have lain elsewhere. Vivian Mercier, whose contributions to Beckett studies are numerous, nevertheless starts his recent book (*Beckett/Beckett*, Oxford, 1977) with a prologue recounting a 'long-distance relationship with Beckett'. Unlike Professor Mercier I did not follow Beckett to his boarding-school, but commuted on the Harcourt Street line to a Dublin day-school and, like the latter, for some time to university. I entered Trinity College to read French and English in 1930 when Mr Beckett joined the staff and so I had the good fortune to enjoy the stimulus of his teaching during the four terms he gave to Trinity. The late Dr Luce acted as College tutor to all three of us in turn and, I learn from Deirdre Bair (*Samuel Beckett*, London, 1978), used in speaking of Beckett a phrase he once addressed to me (and doubtless many others) about 'being one of the just who have little need of a tutor'. In 1934, four years after Beckett's departure from the Ecole Normale Supérieure, I in my turn went there as *lecteur*, only to return at the end of my stay, to teach in the preparatory school he had attended. Though I did not live in Foxrock I was a frequent visitor to a house beside Cooldrinagh.
[2] 'Beckett — écrivain irlandais?', *Langues modernes*, 61 (1967), pp. 90-96.
[3] 'Le Théâtre de Samuel Beckett', *Etudes anglaises*, 10 (1957), p. 35.
[4] Beryl S. Fletcher, John Fletcher, Barry Smith and Walter Bachem, *A Student's Guide to the Plays of Samuel Beckett*, London, 1978, p. 73.

⁵ Unless it is *'au marché de Saint-Sauveur'* to which Pozzo is leading Lucky (*En attendant Godot*, Paris, 1952, p. 51), a passage omitted from the English translation. Presumably *'Saint-Sauveur, ch.-l. de c. (Yonne)* . . . *Marché (chevaux).'* (*Nouveau petit Larousse illustré, 1954*).

⁶ Performed at the Peacock Theatre, Dublin, in 1931, by the Dublin University Modern Language Society, but unpublished.

⁷ Vivian Mercier, after recalling the prominence given to Racine in the T.C.D. course, observes 'Not only is the unity of place rigorously observed in all Beckett's stage plays, but, true to the rules of Racinian tragedy, the scene is always a *lieu vague* neither here nor there'.

⁸ *All That Fall*, London, Faber and Faber, 1957, pp. 1, 9, 10, 12.

⁹ 'Un retour à l'origine: étude structurale de *Tous ceux qui tombent'*, *Romance Notes*, 18 (1957), pp. 11-17.

¹⁰ *Beckett/Beckett*, Oxford, 1977, pp. 20ff.

¹¹ *Samuel Beckett*, London, 1978, pp. 9ff.

¹² See, for example, *La Chanson de Roland*, Paris, Bibl. Bordas, 1969, 11. 114, 168, 366, 406-7, etc.

¹³ See, for example, *Bradshaw's Monthly Railway Guide*, June-July, 1925, p. 961.

¹⁴ It is curious that the unspecific 'little child' (*'un petit enfant'* in the French translation) has become for J.-J. Mayoux *'une petite fille'* (loc. cit. p. 352) and that Hugh Kenner says 'it seems meaningless to ask whether he pushed her there'. (*A Reader's Guide to Samuel Beckett*, London, 1973, p. 160)

¹⁵ *All I Can Manage, More than I Could*, Dublin, 1968, p. 32.

¹⁶ Oxford, 1972, Vol. 1, p. 193.

¹⁷ *Watt*, London, 1963, p. 24.

¹⁸ Ibid., pp. 23-24.

¹⁹ Ibid., p. 22

²¹ Ibid., p. 24.

²¹ Ibid., p. 25. But Dan, of course, in real life, almost certainly would not have found an uncrowded compartment on races day!

²² Ibid., p. 27. Compare Mrs Rooney's description quoted above.

²³ Ibid., p. 223.

²⁴ Ibid. The tracks ran in a straight line from near Stillorgan almost to Carrickmines.

²⁵ Ibid. Compare Mrs Rooney 'The entire scene, the hills, the plain . . .'.

²⁶ Ibid., p. 224.

²⁷ A photograph of the house appears in Deirdre Bair (op. cit. after p. 115).

²⁸ *Watt*, p. 227.

²⁹ The last train to Bray always left at 11.30.

³⁰ Samuel Beckett, *Nouvelles et Textes pour rien*, Paris, 1965, pp. 177-78.

³¹ The production was not, of course, visible in this country, nor have I been able to trace a videotape. Thanks, however, to the kindness of Monsieur de Lacroix of French television technical service and the courtesy of the *Société française de productions et de créations audiovisuelles*, I have obtained some photographs of the actors and the setting.

³² *Samuel Beckett*, Paris, 1966, pp. 99-100.

³³ See also *A Student's Guide to the Plays*, already quoted, p. 72, 'But Beckett . . . has not been happy with either this production or with a German stage presentation'.

NARRATIVE STRUCTURE IN *LES MANDARINS*

The question of narrative technique in the novel is one in which Simone de Beauvoir has shown a longstanding interest. In the late thirties she and Sartre admired the American writers Dos Passos and Faulkner who were experimenting in the field, and in her second published novel *Le Sang des autres*, begun in 1941, she introduced a complex technique permitting the hero to recount events in both first and third person narrative. Her interest is still manifest in her more recent fictional work: *La Femme rompue*, published in 1967, presents three short stories each exemplifying a different use of monologue.

It is by no means fortuitous therefore that the author's fourth novel, *Les Mandarins* (1954), evinces considerable attention to narrative problems, and not surprising that these problems are approached in a somewhat unusual way. Unlike most novels which quickly establish a dominant narrator, albeit supplemented by a second one (such as the opening 'nous' in *Madame Bovary*), *Les Mandarins* has two narrators of broadly equal weight in terms of the length of their narratives, and who alternate throughout the novel. One is Anne Dubreuilh: she speaks in the first person and is one of the figures in the novel ('homodiegetic' narrator). The second is an unspecified narrator who speaks in the third person and who remains outside the fictional structure ('heterodiegetic' narrator).[1] This second narrator cannot be assumed to be simply identical with the author; we shall designate him/her simply as the external narrator. The present study proposes to characterise in detail the two narrative situations present in the novel, before going on to consider what the author has to say about her choice of a double narrative and the question of what this technique might be said to achieve.

The opening section of the novel is narrated by the external narrator, and in order to discover what kind of relationship he has with the events and figures he is presenting it is useful to examine the first few sentences of his narrative:

Henri jeta un dernier regard sur le ciel: un cristal noir. Mille avions saccageant ce silence, c'était difficile à imaginer; pourtant les mots se carambolaient dans sa tête avec un bruit joyeux: offensive stoppée, débâcle allemande, je vais pouvoir partir. Il tourna le coin du quai.[2]

These few lines already suggest that we are not dealing with an overt omniscient narrator likely to provide us with a blueprint of Henri's previous history, physical appearance and moral qualities and defects. The reader will be required to piece together for himself as the novel proceeds that Henri Perron is a writer and journalist whose relations with Anne's husband Robert Dubreuilh form a major theme of the novel. Henri is simply presented without any explanation of who he is, a technique — deixis — which involves an effacement of the narrator and implies that the character evoked possesses an individual specificity. Further evidence of effacement by the narrator may also be elicited from the opening sentences cited above. The narrator's authority, for instance, can be seen to be limited to the character's knowledge of the situation: the information we are given about the air-battle has Henri as its source since (as we shortly learn) he had heard this news on the radio earlier in the evening. Equally, the narrator's visual powers are restricted since only what is within the character's own visual field is described — as Henri looks at the sky so do we. This restriction must of necessity though, be only a partial one. Although it is generally true throughout the sections narrated by the external narrator that descriptions of the external world correspond to the visual field of the character, the narrator nevertheless 'fixes' the character in the scene. Thus in the opening lines of the novel quoted above, Henri cannot see himself looking at the sky or turning the corner, and the narrator's presence is therefore indicated.

It remains to decide whether any of the other elements of the opening sentences may be attributed directly to the narrator. The remarks towards the end of the section ('offensive stoppée, débâcle allemande, je vais pouvoir partir') can easily be characterised as unmediated presentations of Henri's thoughts. The early statements ('un cristal noir. Mille avions saccageant ce silence, c'était difficile à imaginer') might be accepted as indirect presentation of Henri's thoughts, if we allow that the images 'cristal' and 'saccageant' are sufficiently banal to occur spontaneously to a character who is after all an artist. The remaining phrase, however, ('pourtant les mots se carambolaient dans sa tête avec un bruit joyeux') is more difficult to ascribe to Henri; here we may well conclude that the narrator is describing from the outside Henri's state of mind.

The pattern which we have noted in the opening sentences in the novel of adoption of the character's perspective, coupled with occasional discreet interpolations by the external narrator, remains constant as the first section proceeds and the majority of the characters assemble for a Christmas Eve party. Much of the narrative consists of direct and indirect presentation of Henri's thoughts and large portions of dialogue between Henri and newly introduced characters are reported in direct speech. In the case of dialogue reported in this way, the narrator's presence is evident only in speech-tags, as in the following example: 'Paule sourit mystérieuse-ment: "J'avais pris mes précautions. (. . .)"' (p. 9). Even in instances such as these however, where 'mystérieusement' is an interpretative interpolation, the comment remains well within Henri's perception and competence, even if it is not attributed to him. It does not draw attention to an interpreting external narrator. The same is not true of course of speech-tags attached to Henri's own statements. Although these are kept brief and relatively infrequent, the suggestion by the external narrator that Henri has spoken 'gaiement' or 'avec décision' inevitably contributes to the reader's image of Henri.[3]

One of the functions of the party scene is to present the majority of the characters (in fact Henri, Paule, Anne and Robert Dubreuilh, Nadine, Lambert, Lenoir, Julien, Sézénac, Chancel, Claudie, Preston, Scriassine and Luc all appear and receive some sort of identification however perfunctory), and this is a function which one might well expect to reveal the overt presence of the external narrator. In fact the major characters — Paule, Anne, Robert, Nadine — are like Henri introduced deictically, and any early impressions of them are presented in such a way as to be acceptable as an indirect report of Henri's reflections. As the minor characters arrive, however, the narrator reverts to labelling them rather summarily or inserting passages of biographical material. An example is furnished by the presentation of Lenoir and Julien:

Ils [Henri and Nadine] s'approchèrent du buffet; Lenoir et Julien étaient en train de se disputer: c'était chronique. Chacun reprochait à l'autre d'avoir trahi sa jeunesse de la manière qui n'était pas la bonne. Autrefois, trouvant l'extravagance du surréalisme trop mesurée, ils avaient fondé ensemble le mouvement 'para-humain'. Lenoir était devenu professeur de sanscrit et il écrivait des poèmes hermétiques; Julien était bibliothécaire et il avait cessé d'écrire, peut-être parce qu'après de précoces succès il avait redouté une mûre médiocrité (. . .). (pp. 20-21)

The motivation for this mass of detail is provided by the fact that Henri has just approached the two characters, and goes on to speak to them immediately afterwards. Yet is it really possible to suppose that the sight of his friends leads Henri to mentally summarize their previous history? Both the implausibility of this supposition and the expository tone of the passage indicate the presence of the external narrator. The ambiguity which arises in this kind of example is also often present when direct or indirect report of Henri's thoughts introduces information about his past. The following example introduces a passage of explanation of the history of Henri's relations with Paule:

Il [Henri] se dit avec décision: 'En revenant du Portugal, j'irai m'installer à l'hôtel'. C'est tellement agréable de rentrer le soir dans une chambre où personne ne vous attend! Même au temps où il était amoureux de Paule, il avait toujours tenu à avoir ses quatre murs à lui. (p. 11)

The first sentence is direct report of Henri's thoughts; the second sentence in free indirect speech acts as a bridge for the third and following sentences which present explanatory biographical material, and where the narrator's intervention is more overt. We have seen then that the distinction between the external narrator's voice and Henri's view of events can be a difficult one to make. This is for two main reasons: firstly, the information supplied by the external narrator is usually within Henri's competence to supply and is only presented by the external narrator in the interests of narrative economy (it would be an elaborate process to mirror every piece of information in Henri's consciousness); secondly, the information which the external narrator supplies is presented largely in a colloquial spoken form virtually indistinguishable from the register in which Henri habitually thinks and speaks. There is no formal narrative voice breaking in on Henri's thoughts and creating an awareness of a rupture in the narrative mode. This is an important point, since strong criticism has been levelled at Simone de Beauvoir for the informality of the narrative voice employed (Cottrell, for example, has called it 'graceless' and 'vulgar').[4] It has perhaps not been sufficiently appreciated that one reason for the use of this colloquial (and we would argue lively) register, is the attempt to retain maximum flexibility in moving from the characters' perspective to that of the external narrator, and to keep the latter's voice as covert as possible.

We cannot fail, however, to be particularly interested by those moments where the external narrator's voice is audible, because they may provide a different perspective on events from those offered by the characters themselves. This is a relatively rare case in *Les Mandarins*, but at least one such example may be cited. It occurs at a point in the novel where a temporary 'wrong' turning in Henri's development is discreetly underlined. This could not of course be achieved simply by reference to Henri's consciousness. Henri is in a state between wake and sleep in a mountain-hut on a cycling holiday. He has recently decided to make his paper the organ of Dubreuilh's political movement, the S.R.L. He is thus at the end of a long debate with himself and he feels a certain self-satisfaction at the outcome:

Pas de regrets, pas de questions: cette insomnie était aussi sereine qu'un sommeil sans rêve. Il avait renoncé à beaucoup de choses, il n'écrivait plus, il ne s'amusait pas tous les jours, mais ce qu'il avait gagné en échange, c'est qu'il avait sa conscience pour lui, et ça c'était énorme. Loin de la terre et de ses problèmes, loin du froid, du vent, de son corps fatigué, il flottait dans un bain d'innocence: ça peut être aussi capiteux que la volupté, l'innocence. (p. 217)

The choice of image in 'bain d'innocence', the emphasis on the fact that Henri is 'loin' from anything resembling reality, here underline the illusory nature of Henri's reflections. Only a few days later he is shocked into writing again, and by the end of the novel he learns that innocence and a clear conscience are luxuries that he cannot afford.

The narrative mode in the sections of *Les Mandarins* where the external narrator is present may thus be summarized as follows: a form of third person narrative in which the heterodiegetic narrator has severely limited powers and adopts wherever possible the perspective of a central figure in the novel — Henri Perron. With a few exceptions (such as the case of speech tags relating to Henri and interpretative comment of the type exemplified above), the narrator does not offer opinions or information outside the character's knowledge or competence, and where he does speak in his own voice instead of reporting through the medium of Henri's consciousness, rupture of the narrative situation is avoided by employing the same register for both Henri's and the narrator's voice. This kind of narrative situation in which the narrator largely 'disappears' behind a central figure of the novel has been variously labelled 'covert narration' (Chatman), 'focalisation interne' (Genette) and perhaps most clearly 'figural narration' (Stanzel).[5] It is generally considered to be a flexible narrative mode, since it allows momentary shifts to the authorial narrative mode (where the narrator's voice is audible) without noticeable disruption, and to be particularly suitable for following fluctuations in the mental processes of a central figure. Most of the 'action' of *Les Mandarins* in which Henri is involved in fact consists of moral crises and the making of choices — should Henri keep his paper independent or would it be more effective as the organ of a political movement? Should he publish details of the Russian labour camps? Should he perjure himself and save an ex-collaborator from justice in order to protect his mistress? Should he, finally, retire to Italy and write books or stay in France and participate in a political action which may well be ineffectual? The figural narrative mode which the external narrator largely adopts has obvious advantages for the recounting of those 'aventures de la pensée' which Simone de Beauvoir argues are as real as any other kind of adventure.[6] The advantages and disadvantages of the use made by the external narrator of the figural mode cannot however be discussed in isolation, since they are materially affected by the existence in the novel of the second narrator — Anne Dubreuilh.

The narrative mode in what may be termed for convenience 'Anne's sections' seems at first sight to present no difficulty of definition. Her narrative opens in the second part of the first chapter; she is lying in bed in the early hours of the morning reflecting on death and the meaning it has for her, and intermittently thinking over the party which she has attended earlier in the evening and which has already been recounted by the external narrator in the first part of the chapter. The narrative time (point in time at which the narrating process takes place) is clearly pinpointed as 4 a.m. and this is reinforced by several references to 'tout à l'heure' and 'demain'; furthermore the use of the present tense for reflections of a general nature, future tense for references to the following day, and perfect tense for evocation of events at the party or memories dating further back to her childhood seems quite consistent with the monologue form. Other features, however, are less easy to account for: the lengthy explanations of the past, and biographical summaries such as the account of Nadine's former lover Diégo, now dead; the often prolonged stretches of dialogue reported in direct speech; the use of the past historic tense which in some quite extensive passages replaces the perfect tense. However this first section of Anne's narrative ends as it begins in the present tense, and so the reader's sense of being in the presence of unmediated monologue is largely retained. It is when we come to the succeeding stretches of narrative where the past historic becomes the dominant tense and the present tense is used only occasionally, and where we are no longer given any indications of narrative time, that we see that unmediated monologue has largely given way to narrative of events in the past. In other words the two selves which make up the first person narrator, the experiencing self and the narrating self, have now become visibly disassociated. The difference between those parts of the narrative in which narrating and experiencing selves come together in monologue, and those parts in which the narrating self recounts events in the past, can be seen by comparing the opening of Anne's first stretch of narrative in chapter one and the opening of her fourth stretch of narrative in chapter six. Her narrative in chapter one begins:

Non, ce n'est pas aujourd'hui que je connaîtrai ma mort; ni aujourd'hui, ni aucun jour. Je serai morte pour les autres sans jamais m'être vue mourir. (p. 26)

Chapter six opens as follows:

J'étais égarée de joie et de curiosité le soir où j'atterris à La Guardia; je passai la semaine qui suivit à ronger mon frein. (p. 302)

In the first extract we have direct access to the experiencing character's thoughts, as she thinks them, at a fairly specific moment of time. In the second extract the narrating character is more overtly addressing the reader and organizing the narrative, as can be seen for instance from the time-summary in the second part of the sentence. We do not know at which point in time events are being narrated, except that it postdates those events. Yet despite the loss of unmediated access to the experiencing character's consciousness which occurs in passages like the second one above, attention remains focused on the experiencing self, largely because the narrating self shows no evidence of increased maturity or change of perspective (as for instance the narrator does in *Adolphe*). Indeed the present tense reflections which the narrating self occasionally reverts to are identical in tone to those which are attributed to the earlier experiencing self. Further, the reflections of the narrator never postdate the events of the novel as a whole (this is achieved by ending the novel in the present tense), and if narrative time must be presumed, it can only be presumed to be a series of different moments which all remain within the bounds of the moments at which the events recounted in the novel begin and end.[7]

The narrative of Anne's sections can thus be seen to be a mixture of unmediated monologue (in which experiencing and narrating self coincide) and first person narrative of past events (in which the disassociation of narrating from experiencing self can more easily be inferred). The author herself distinguishes two narrative modes in Anne's sections when she comments in *La Force des choses*: 'le récit d'Anne est sous-tendu par un monologue qui se déroule au présent, ce qui m'a permis de le ['récit'] briser, de le raccourcir, de le commenter librement'.[8] The author, then, clearly considers the major narrative mode to be the 'récit', the narrative of past events, with the monologue serving the important but subsidiary role of interrupting and interpreting the account. We have already argued that the monologue and the narrative of past events in fact do not so much offer different interpretations of events as simply reflect on them in a very similar way; there can be little doubt however, that the monologue does serve the function of providing some variety in what would otherwise be a long and perhaps rather limiting first person account.

The dominating role which monologue plays in the first section of Anne's narrative can now be seen to be rather untypical. Of the seven sections of Anne's narrative only the last contains anything approaching the same quantity of monologue as the first; the other five stretches of her narrative are characterised chiefly by narrative of past events, interspersed only infrequently with elements of monologue. The rather privileged place which monologue holds in Anne's discourse is not therefore the result of a dominance in terms of the number of pages on which it occurs, but rather the result firstly of the inherent advantage of its form — the impression of direct communication between the character's consciousness and the reader which it creates — and secondly of the simple fact that Anne's narrative opens in chapter one with monologue and closes the novel at the end of chapter twelve with monologue. Anne's 'récit' thus finds itself enclosed within passages of monologue, and when in the last line of the novel Anne asks 'Qui sait? Peut-être un jour serai-je de nouveau heureuse. Qui sait?' (p. 579), the reader is left with the impression of dealing directly with the experiencing self. The narrator is not placed

227

at a superior vantage point in time to the reader, and the answer to this final question is thus left open for both reader and narrator.

We have now identified four major narrative modes in the novel: figural narration with elements of authorial narration on the one hand, alternating with first person narrative of past events and monologue on the other hand. The figural narration and the monologue correspond to each other in so far as both purport to present processes of consciousness without interference or distortion. The authorial narration and first person narrative of past events are also similar in some respects, since both permit a greater flexibility in organizing and summarising narration of events, but the interpretative heterodiegetical function of the authorial mode is not assumed by Anne's narrating self. The two pairs of narrative modes can thus be seen to perform broadly similar functions: both try to give direct access to a central figure's consciousness, both employ a more distanced narrative mode to supplement the experiencing character's point of view, both maintain a single register when switching from one narrative mode to another. The distance between experiencing character and distanced narrator is of course much greater in the case of the external narrator and Henri than it is in the case of Anne's experiencing and narrating self, and it is this greater distance which permits the external narrator to comment and interpret more freely than Anne's narrating self.

Given the broad similarity of function of the two pairs of narrative modes in the novel, we must ask why it is useful to employ two sets of modes at all. Let us first examine the author's explanation of her choice. Simone de Beauvoir has argued that her novel is not a 'roman à thèse' and that it does not propose solutions to the characters' dilemmas. The role of literature, she suggests, is rather to 'manifester des vérités ambiguës, séparées, contradictoires'.[9] The advantage of establishing two distinct narratives might thus be seen to be that Anne and Henri can each represent a different set of 'vérités' which can be experienced by the reader as equally valid, since each set is communicated more or less directly to him. The contradictions and ambiguities of each set of 'vérités' can emerge all the more clearly since the dual narrative permits the same events to be viewed from different perspectives.

What differing interpretations of events do the two narratives then offer? A significant difference between the perspectives of Henri and Anne arises from Anne's preoccupation with death, with old age and with the passing of time. When Henri and Robert spend anguished hours debating the question of whether to publish the evidence of the existence of labour camps in Russia, Anne's own monologue on the subject opens up new perspectives which reduce the issue to meaninglessness:

Tout passe, tout casse, tout lasse, tout se dépasse; les camps seront dépassés et aussi ma propre existence; c'est dérisoire, cette petite vie éphémère qui s'angoisse à propos de ces camps que l'avenir a déjà abolis. (p. 336)

This provides a very different view from that of Henri, for whom the question of the existence of the camps is a pressing personal and political problem. Yet does Anne's view provide a real alternative to Henri's? The above reflections do not prevent Anne herself discussing the question at length with Robert, and precisely on the personal and political level. Anne makes it clear that she agrees with Henri that the evidence of the camps should be published. Anne's 'goût de la mort' does not really undermine Henri's view of events, it simply provides an additional and usually subsidiary subject for reflection. Where Anne's particular perspective does substantially inform our overall view of events is of course in those chapters which narrate her three visits to America and her relationship with Lewis Brogan. The external narrator does not narrate these events — it would not be consistent to do so since Henri has no knowledge of them — so that Anne's ideas about the meaning of individual existence, her fears of death and the ageing process are major themes in this part of the narrative.

Yet these events and the ideas which are expressed about them, never really seem relevant to the problems and concerns of Henri and Dubreuilh. They remain a set of moral and emotional problems which concern a particular individual — Anne — and we are not led to question Henri and Dubreuilh's actions in the light of Anne's experience in America. The major part of the novel concerns events and people in France, and the viewpoints offered by Anne and Henri on these events and people tend to be either similar or indeed identical. Let us take for example the figure of Paule. Henri's view of her is presented early in the first chapter:

[. . .] Henri se glaça. Leur vie commune avait été tellement morne pendant cette dernière année que Paule elle-même avait paru s'en dégoûter; mais elle avait brusquement changé au début de septembre; à present, dans toutes ses paroles, ses baisers, ses regards, il y avait un frémissement passionné. (pp. 11-12)

We may at this point suppose Henri's analysis to be rather subjective, in view of his relationship with Paule. But we are forced to accept it as objective when Anne, in the second section of the same chapter, confirms Henri's view with a remarkably similar explanation:

Elle [Paule] avait compris pendant ces quatre ans qu'Henri ne lui accordait plus qu'une affection ennuyée; mais depuis la Libération, je ne sais quel espoir fou s'était réveillé dans son cœur. (p. 32)

Both here and elsewhere in the novel Anne and Henri display some sympathy towards Paule, but both implacably view her as over-theatrical in dress, gesture and speech, the sad victim of illusions whose error is to have no activities except those relating to Henri. The two narratives do not provide a multi-dimensional view of Paule.

Much the same point may be made in relation to Dubreuilh. It is true that Anne has information about Dubreuilh's personal life to which Henri may not have access, but these details are scarce. As J.-R. Audet has pointed out,[10] Dubreuilh is something of a substitute Deity for both Anne and Henri, and when Henri breaks off relations with Dubreuilh, Anne echoes this on a minor level by doubting the rightness of Robert's decision for the first time ever. Politically, Anne and Henri both argue in favour of publishing the evidence of the Russian camps; artistically, Anne praises Henri's play enthusiastically and adds: 'Moi, j'aime tous les livres d'Henri, ils me touchent personnellement [. . .]' (p. 400).

Two episodes in particular suggest Anne and Henri's sympathy for each other, and hint that this sympathy borders on intimacy. At the Christmas party Henri dances several times with Anne and thinks that 'il lui aurait volontiers fait un doigt de cour' (p. 17). Anne makes a similar statement when the two are separated from their other friends on Victory night:

L'intimité, la confiance de cette heure, nous aurions pu la prolonger jusqu'à l'aube: par delà l'aube peut-être. Mais pour mille raisons il ne fallait pas essayer. Ne fallait-il pas? En tout cas, nous n'avons pas essayé. (pp. 192-3)

The two principal consciousnesses then to which we have direct access, are too close in opinion and sympathy to provide a significantly different account of events which they discuss in the light of often shared values and experiences, and indeed this fact is hardly surprising when we note that both characters are semi-autobiographical. Simone de Beauvoir goes so far as to detail in *La Force des choses* how she distributed auto-biographical elements between the two characters;[11] perhaps this explains in part Anne's conviction that an affair between herself and Henri is taboo.

Anne's narrative does sometimes provide an additional perspective on events, one tending to reduce all forms of action and choice to the absurd; but since she herself continues to make choices and in fact eventually rejects the notion of suicide, this perspective cannot really be said to undermine the dominating ethos of the novel, which is that of choice, responsibility and action. It is clear then, that whatever the author's intention, the choice of a dual narrative does not in fact ensure that the work will incorporate equally valid and different truths, each receiving the same weighting. The attempt to avoid the didacticism evident in some of her earlier work is not entirely successful.

Yet this is by no means to say that the narrative technique employed in *Les Mandarins* is ineffective. Some advantages of the use of first person and figural narration have already been alluded to, and it can be further argued that the alternate use of these two narrative modes has a number of important advantages. One major consequence of the dual account of events is the creation of consistency and verisimilitude. Anne's narrative constantly supports and elaborates on Henri's observations, creating a rounded and credible fictional world. A second important consequence is the way in which each narrator is lent concrete existence by the other's description of him or her, an effect difficult to achieve by the use of figural or first person narrative alone. This effect takes on a particular importance in the context of existentialism, since it permits the avoidance of the situation where one character's consciousness is always 'sujet' and every other character is 'objet de regard'. The relation between consciousnesses is of course a frequent theme in Simone de Beauvoir's fiction, and appears in *Les Mandarins* as one of Anne's preoccupations. She remarks for example: 'quand je devine au fond d'une conscience étrangère ma propre image, j'ai toujours un moment de panique' (p. 38), and on a later occasion when looking out of Paule's window in a vain attempt to see the world as Paule sees it, she concludes:

Non. Jamais le petit sapajou ne verrait avec des yeux d'homme. Jamais je ne me glisserais dans une autre peau. (p. 176)

The use of the dual narrative perspective can be said to be an effective means of capturing this 'otherness' of others, and of ensuring that the 'sujet' which perceives will also be perceived as 'objet'.

A more functional advantage of the use of two distinct narratives is the fact that the narrative is able to proceed in two locales simultaneously.[12] In the same way the technique allows an extension of the characters' knowledge of events which can be drawn on, since Anne and Henri have a greater competence between them than either one could have singly. On this level, the advantage of the use of two narratives can be seen to be that whilst each narrative retains the immediacy which derives from the use of narrative restricted to a single consciousness, the two narratives when taken together create many of the advantages which traditionally derive from the use of the omniscient narrator. Finally, the dual narrative offers the reader the possibility of being both aware of the characters' perspective and at the same time superior to it, since he possesses a more complete view of events than either Anne or Henri and must make his own synthesis. This is perhaps the nearest the technique approaches to offering the choice of 'vérités' which the author intended.

An analysis of *Les Mandarins* shows how seriously the author considered problems of narrative technique. Simone de Beauvoir's fiction, which has largely been discussed in terms of its political and philosophical content, surely also deserves critical attention on the grounds of its more formal literary merits.

BIRMINGHAM   ELIZABETH FALLAIZE

[1] These terms, based on Gérard Genette's usage in *Figures III* (Seuil: 1972), have been widely adopted by narrative theorists. Genette defines the terms in the above work as follows: 'On distinguera donc ici deux types de récits: l'un à narrateur absent de l'histoire qu'il raconte (exemple: Homère dans l'*Iliade*, ou Flaubert dans *L'Education sentimentale*), l'autre à narrateur présent comme personnage dans l'histoire qu'il raconte (exemple: *Gil Blas* ou *Wuthering Heights*). Je nomme le premier type, pour des raisons évidentes, *hétérodiégétique*, et le second *homodiégétique*'. (*Figures III*, p. 252)

[2] Simone de Beauvoir, *Les Mandarins* (Gallimard: 1954), p. 9. All subsequent page references are to this edition.

[3] See *Les Mandarins*, p. 9 and p. 11, for examples of this.

[4] Robert Cottrell, *Simone de Beauvoir* (Ungar: 1976), p. 120.

[5] Seymour Chatman, *Story and Discourse* (Cornell University Press: 1972); Gérard Genette, (op. cit.); Franz Stanzel, *Narrative Situations in the Novel* tr. James Pusack (Indiana University Press: 1971). Other critics, notably Tzvetan Todorov in 'Les catégories du récit littéraire', *Communications*, 8 (1966), 125-147, use a form of classification based on J. Pouillon's work, and they classify this kind of narration as 'la vision "avec"'.

[6] Cited by Maurice Nadeau in '*Les Mandarins*', *Les Lettres Nouvelles*, 22 (1954), p. 883.

[7] Narrative time in chp. 1 is made clear. In chp. 2 there is some suggestion that narrative time corresponds to a period of reflection whilst Anne is gazing into a mirror in her room. In chps 4, 6, 8 and 10 there is no real evidence of narrative time and in most cases even surmise is difficult.

[8] Simone de Beauvoir, *La Force des choses* (Gallimard; 1963), p. 291. All subsequent page references are to this edition.

[9] *La Force des choses*, p. 282 and p. 289.

[10] J-R. Audet, *Simone de Beauvoir face à la mort* (Editions L'Age d'homme: 1979), p. 52.

[11] *La Force des choses*, p. 287-8.

[12] A problem of the dual narrative which is related to its ubiquity is the problem of chronology and transition between narrators. An analysis of the chronology of events in the novel shows that whilst there is no significant period of time between Christmas 1944 and Autumn 1948 (the years the novel spans) that is not narrated by one or other of the narrators, there are gaps varying from a few days to six months in the separate narratives. Anne's narrative has more continuity than Henri's, because whereas Anne is in a position to fill in details on elements of the plot concerning Henri, the latter is not in a position to relate events in America concerning Anne. Anne's narrative achieves the necessary extra time compression by time-summaries which on occasion draw attention to the narrating voice in a very marked way (see for example the opening to chp. 4 where two paragraphs summarize a period of a month).

NINETTE BAILEY

DISCOURS SOCIAL:
LECTURE SOCIO-CRITIQUE DU *VICE-CONSUL*[1]
DE MARGUERITE DURAS

Les textes durassiens accueillent tous, à divers degrés, une lecture fondée sur les concepts du manque et de la jouissance. Il nous a semblé, cependant, que si le *Vice-Consul* relève lui aussi d'une économie libidinale, dans ce roman s'articule également un discours social, mise en signe de la Référence dont l'effet est de mettre à jour le discours que la société tient sur elle-même, exposant ainsi à la critique ses stéréotypes et ses contraintes. Discours de la société donc et discours sur la société: on se propose de montrer ici la mise en évidence du social aux multiples niveaux du *Vice-Consul* et le travail de subversion idéologique que le texte poursuit en contrepoint.

Discours articulé sur une thématique sociale, tout d'abord, résultant dans une obscuration du romanesque au niveau anecdotique. Le texte, en effet, semble proposer simultanément une histoire d'amour, le récit d'un acte criminel et celui du périple d'une jeune Cambodgienne, expulsée de sa famille pour être tombée enceinte. Trois anecdotes individuelles donc mais dont la représentation est brouillée par une problématique sociale: l'histoire de l'amour du personnage titulaire se dissout en cours de texte — le sentiment qui le pousse vers l'ambassadrice de France est en vérité un désir, excentré, intolérable, de lui dire l'inacceptable pauvreté des masses indigènes en Inde. Cette même révulsion devant leur souffrance est par ailleurs à l'origine de l'acte criminel qu'il a commis en tirant sur les lépreux de Lahore. Conduite qui est à lire, par conséquent, non pas comme le comportement d'un individu déséquilibré, dans la perspective singularisante du romanesque, mais comme un geste symbolique (anti-social) de protestation sociale. Quant au troisième centre d'intérêt romanesque, il s'inscrit aussi dans une problématique sociale. C'est un narrateur de relais, Peter Morgan, qui est chargé, dans un récit secondaire, de retracer les pérégrinations de la Cambodgienne, échouée à Calcutta, et vivant dans la mendicité. Or ce périple est totalement fictif: si Peter Morgan choisit de raconter — en l'inventant — l'histoire d'une jeune fille qui aurait transgressé les lois du groupe familial, c'est afin de pouvoir lui-même transgresser la frontière qui le tient, lui, homme, Blanc, privilégié, séparé de la masse des populations souffrantes que symbolise la mendiante de Calcutta. Peine infinie qu'il voudrait assumer: 'Peter Morgan est un jeune homme qui désire prendre la douleur de Calcutta, s'y jeter et que son ignorance cesse avec la douleur prise' (p. 29). Son entreprise narrative est donc un mouvement de participation affective avec une société. On n'oublie pas pour autant que le romanesque n'exclut pas le social. A condition cependant que la figuration d'un destin particulier, essentielle au roman, ne soit pas mise en cause. Or dans *Le Vice-Consul* cette figuration est insidieusement minée. Nommé, reconnaissable, pris, sinon certes dans une intrigue, du moins dans une activité identifiable, le personnage durassien ici semble 'réel'. Son existence cependant s'inscrit dans une tentative de mise en scène psychanalytique — qui reste en dehors de notre étude — et dans un effort de problématisation des coordonnées sociales. A son niveau anecdotique, le texte ne respecte donc pas la formule romanesque d'une histoire d'amour ou de scandale qu'il semble pourtant proposer.

C'est cependant sur toute l'étendue du texte que se fait la mise en évidence du social dans *Le Vice-Consul*. En effet, non seulement les trois centres d'intérêt anecdotique (amour, folie, faute) sont déplacés par une commune préoccupation sociale, mais aussi le texte procède à un codage social de tous ses éléments dont l'effet est de mettre en relief les marques de la socialité aux dépens de la particularisation romanesque. Surcodage du social, par conséquent.

Récit surcodé socialement signifie d'abord que l'activité des divers protagonistes connote fortement le social. La mendiante mise à part, tous les actants du *Vice-Consul* actualisent ce qui dans le social le définit le mieux: activité du travail, communication langagière. L'activité laborieuse étant celle de la domesticité, au travail s'ajoute un autre indice social, la division hiérarchique de maître et serviteur. Hiérarchie visible aussi dans le secteur actanciel de la communication qui se fait ici au niveau mondain. On est, en effet, dans le milieu diplomatique de Calcutta. Officielle, la brillante réception que donne l'ambassadrice de France manifeste le signe doublement social de l'institution et du mondain, observance du rituel diplomatique et des conventions du savoir-vivre. Le surcodage social joue également au niveau individuel du personnage. Sa présentation est lacunaire, faite à partir des rumeurs de la voix publique, fondée, par là même, sur une information douteuse. Echappant totalement au doute, par contre, est son identité officielle, son état-civil. Inlassablement, sa fonction administrative est rappelée, proclamant 'quoi' il est, alors que savoir 'qui' reste, en somme, interdit. Innommable dans une perspective singularisante puisque son patronyme s'arrête à une initiale: Jean-Marc de H., le personnage titulaire se replie sur cette fonction, tantôt réduite à la mention de son rang, le vice-consul, souvent précisée par une indication d'origine et de localité: le vice-consul, de France, à Lahore. Le texte fait mention de lui sous cette forme plénière un nombre excessif de fois, excessif puisqu'au niveau de l'information le rappel n'ajoute rien au message. Insistance de valeur indicielle, par conséquent. Il en est de même pour les autres personnages: l'ambassadrice de France, Anne-Marie Stretter, sera désignée telle, en toutes lettres, sans égard au coût de cette information, tandis que par ailleurs, référence entière est faite au nom et prenom de Peter Morgan, Charles Rossett, Michael Richard, etc. Onomastique de distantiation: ainsi désignés, les personnages n'offrent que l'endroit social de leur envers romanesque, toute intimité interdite au lecteur.

Récit surcodé socialement signifie aussi que l'organisation des personnages se fait selon une structure de différentiation dont l'effet est de connoter les positions conflictuelles inséparables de la situation politique du roman, ici société de Blancs isolés dans l'immensité de l'Inde. Cette structure oppositionnelle est allusivement posée dès le seuil du texte, impliquée dans sa phrase inaugurale: 'Elle marche, écrit Peter Morgan'. Est proposée ici, en effet, une différence: celle des sexes séparant 'elle' — la jeune Cambodgienne — du protagoniste masculin, le vice-consul, instauré par le titre dans cette position privilégiée, la séparant aussi du narrateur masculin, Peter Morgan. Différence — de sexe — accentuée par la différence de race: placée (coincée) entre deux Blancs, 'elle', femme de couleur. En plus, relation de subordination. Soumise, en effet, à la merci d'un arbitraire, celui de son scripteur qui invente son histoire, elle n'est qu''objet' de narration.

Programmée dans l'incipit, cette opposition s'actualise pleinement à mesure que se construit le texte, s'étendant du niveau actanciel des personnages, à la topographie comme aux objets romanesques. La structure d'oppostion contrôle ainsi l'espace entier du texte. On propose cependant de l'étudier d'abord sur un de ses fragments. Situé vers la fin du roman, ce fragment présente l'avantage — au niveau actanciel — d'être le seul passage où sont mis en présence des Blancs avec des indigènes, tandis que par ailleurs il constitue une des rares séquences descriptives du roman. On pourra donc voir comment le texte, manipulant à divers niveaux ses éléments fictionnels, signifie la structure oppositionnelle qui le sous-tend.

Rare passage descriptif, en effet, dans un texte dominé par les échanges verbaux de ses personnages, ce passage décrit le voyage aux Iles d'Anne-Marie Stretter accompagnée de ses intimes. Tant par le choix des diverses composantes de cette page — p. 176 — que par son articulation discursive, est mis à jour un schéma de différentiation.

D'une part, le groupe des Blancs, très petit, Anne-Marie avec Michael Richard et Charles Rossett. Ils roulent en auto entre les rizières du Delta en route vers le luxe de l'hôtel 'Prince of Wales' et de la villa diplomatique. Autour d'eux, l'immensité du paysage se peuple de la foule des indigènes: 'mille sur les talus, ils transportent, posent, repartent les mains vides . . .' Prolifération effrayante: 'mille, dix mille, partout, cent mille, partout, en grains serrés sur les talus ils marchent, procession continue, sans fin'. (ibid.) Sont donc mis en présence pour la seule fois, le contact avec la domesticité indienne excepté, des Blancs, sortis de l'enceinte protectrice de la Résidence, d'une part, de l'autre, des indigènes. Dans le reste du roman les 'hordes dolentes de Calcutta' (p. 32) n'existent que dans le discours du texte, évoquées dans l'indistinction d'une voix commune, inarticulée: 'De nouveau crie doucement Calcutta' (p. 158) — 'De sourds braillements encore, le long du Gange' (p. 154). Ici, bien que toujours anonyme et muette, la foule est dénombrable, innombrable d'ailleurs face aux trois Blancs. Contraste numérique par conséquent dans le nombre des personnages, sans doute légitime dans une situation romanesque mais que le texte a pris soin de rendre ici extrême. Contraste aussi entre les Blancs en auto — portés — et les indigènes, à pied, — porteurs, de sacs, de bidons —; les Blancs, dans la détente de leur voyage d'agrément face aux masses travailleuses qui forment cette procession continue de labeur sans fin. La main des indigènes est mise en évidence: 'ces gens aux mains nues' (p. 175), en évidence aussi chez les Blancs grâce à la main d'Anne-Marie, posée sur celle de son compagnon. Main posée.. reposée, inactive. 'Il prend sa main et l'embrasse longuement' (ibid). Geste qui la définit comme objet non-fonctionnel alors qu'il est dit des indigènes: 'De chaque côté d'eux pendent leurs *outils* de chair nue' (ibid).

L'auto roule dans un pays fluviatile: 'Jonques noires qui avancent dans les voies d'eau, entre les rizières d'eau noire. De loin en loin il y a des semis, des espaces de verdure éclatante et moelleuse, de la soie peinte' (ibid). Contraste cette fois entre les éléments qui composent le paysage, le noir redoublé des jonques noires et de l'eau noire, connotant, comme il se doit, l'indigène, tandis que les rares taches de couleur, verdure connotant le pays d'origine des Blancs, sont irréalisées par la substance du tissu et le trompe-l'oeil de la peinture: 'de la *soie peinte*'. Opposition à lire ici: noire 'réalité' du contexte indigène, brillante irréalité des notations liées aux Blancs. Plus bas, contraste interne, c'est-à-dire différence au sein du même, opposition inacceptable donc et que le texte assume pourtant: 'On est dans un pays d'eau, à la frontière entre les eaux et les eaux, douces, salées, noires, qui dans les baies se mélangent déjà avec la glace verte de l'Océan' (ibid). Dans une même substance, l'eau, s'inscrit l'opposition doux/salé, noir/vert; paysage qui offre ainsi dans sa figuralité l'image des oppositions — inacceptables aussi — entre les êtres, Noirs/Blancs, inscrites pourtant dans une même matière humaine.

Au cours de ce fragment, essentiellement descriptif, une seule question, laissée sans réponse, 'Ça va?', énoncé désoriginé qu'aucun des actants ne prend en charge. Il ne serait pas difficile de l'attribuer à un des voyageurs, Michael Richard ou Charles Rossett qui l'aurait adressée à Anne-Marie

Stretter. Le texte la place en effet à la suite de ce court paragraphe: 'Elle vient de se réveiller. Elle a posé sa tête contre l'épaule de Charles Rossett. — Ça va?' Lecture réaliste, parfaitement valable. Elle n'exclut cependant pas une interprétation qui ferait de la question un énoncé-charnière amenant le paragraphe qui suit: 'Mille sur les talus, ils transportent . . .' consacré, on l'a vu, à décrire la marche des indigènes. Foule anonyme que le texte réifie: '*chapelets* de gens aux mains nues' (p. 175) qui marchent 'en *grains* serrés', dans une procession continue, dans un sens unique donc, et à qui, par conséquent l'expression toute faite: Ça va?, défaite en Ça = la foule chosifiée, va = marche, pourrait s'appliquer sans heurter la logique ni la syntaxe du texte. De la sorte, ce qui peut se laisser lire comme une formule de communication (question de politesse, ou même d'intérêt entre les voyageurs blancs) pourrait aussi constituer un moyen textuel de communication, la tacite mise en relation des deux groupes raciaux par un énoncé à double utilisation. Que le discours du texte vise à un tel effet de mise en rapport par quoi deux mondes distincts sont placés en présence l'un de l'autre, dans une confrontation silencieuse, est vérifié par un deuxième énoncé, semblable au précédent en ce qu'il est, lui aussi, typographiquement en évidence: un seul mot, 'fatigue', placé entre deux paragraphes. Enoncé constatif, que ne précède aucun signe de la déclaration, réduit à un substantif, ne demandant par conséquent aucune prise en charge par un locuteur. Enoncé flottant, totalement libéré. Ce qui n'en découvre que mieux la fonction d'articulation qu'il lui est demandé de remplir et qui est de relier le paragraphe sur les indigènes, dont on donne la dernière phrase, avec celui, qui à l'aide du pronom 'ils', se refère aux Blancs: 'De chaque côté d'eux pendent leurs outils de chair nue.

Fatigue.

Ils ne parlent pas pour ne pas la réveiller, ils n'ont rien à se dire d'ailleurs sur les jonques noires . . .' Enoncé disponible, valable pour l'un ou l'autre paragraphe, l'un ou l'autre groupe et qui ne lève pas son ambiguïté. A qui est attribuée cette fatigue que la syntaxe laisse ainsi en suspens? Fatigue de la foule, des files indiennes (doublement indiennes), fatigue d'Anne-Marie Stretter qui s'étant réveillée un moment vient de se rendormir, fatigue mille fois motivée dans un cas par le labeur et le mouvement, honteuse fatigue de l'oisiveté et de l'immobilité dans l'autre, structure oppositionnelle donc signifiée par le texte dans son discours, c'est-à-dire par le choix des termes et la disposition typographique.

Programmée dans l'incipit, réalisée dans ce fragment descriptif, la structure oppositionnelle, en fait, sous-tend le texte dans son entier.

Au niveau actanciel le contraste le plus scandaleux sépare les surnourris des affamés. Le récit de la mendiante par lequel s'ouvre le

roman est tout d'abord un récit de la faim. Faim proprement affolante
puisque la jeune fille, au début de son périple, ne trouvant rien à manger
'ramasse une poignée de poussière et la met dans sa bouche'. (p. 22) Le
récit principal lui aussi commence par poser la faim mais pour la faire
cesser par la surabondance des restes. La première fois qu'Anne-Marie
Stretter est actualisée dans le texte, c'est dans sa fonction de bienfaitrice,
assurant pour les pauvres une distribution de nourriture après une
réception à l'ambassade: elle 'va dans les dépendances, elle répète que les
restes doivent être donnés aux affamés de Calcutta' (p. 36). Disette d'un
côté, surplus de l'autre. La réception est le lieu de l'alimentation coûteuse,
surabondante: champagne, foie gras. Pendant que les invités s'empiffrent
ou se saoûlent (p. 160), les affamés de Calcutta, dans le noir des jardins
de la Résidence, attendent pour manger que se remplissent les poubelles
de l'ambassade. A deux reprises, le texte intercale cet épisode obscur dans
la scène illuminée des salons de la Résidence et insiste sur le contraste,
personnifié par la mendiante de Peter Morgan, 'elle, *maigreur* de Calcutta
pendant cette nuit *grasse*'. (p. 149) Contraste également scandaleux dans
les objets du roman: luxe coûteux d'une part, 'fougères fragiles venues de
France' (p. 93), objets de standing, les autos de l'ambassade et même la
bicyclette rouge d'Anne-Marie Stretter 'abandonnée, sans emploi' (p. 49),
connotant le gaspillage par cette sous-utilisation ainsi que, par ailleurs, est
connoté le souci, social par excellence, de ce qui en impose. Dans les trois
demeures des Blancs, en effet, le luxe de l'ameublement est invoqué mais à
fin seule de le provoquer à lever son masque, luxe trompeur des apparences:
'faux lustres, du creux, du faux or' dans la Résidence à Calcutta, lustres
aussi à l'hôtel 'Prince of Wales' qui sont du 'creux, du faux or' (p. 178),
comme dans le salon de la villa des Iles se trouvent de 'fausses consoles
encore, les faux lustres, le creux, le faux or' (p. 189). Par contraste les
indigènes sans abri, dormant dans les jardins, sous les buissons, au bord du
Gange, quand ils sont des lépreux ou des affamés, mais partout marqués
d'un indice de pauvreté: 'gens qui repartent les mains *vides*, gens autour de
l'eau *vide* des rizières' (p. 176).

Contraste également dans le colorisme, parcimonieux, réaliste aussi
quand il s'agit de la lumière crépusculaire des moussons, mais ailleurs axé
sur la structure d'opposition qui sépare Blancs des indigènes. Présent
déjà dans la figuralité du fragment descriptif étudié plus haut, le colorisme
est plus significatif vers la fin du roman qui couvre le séjour aux Iles.
L'hôtel 'Prince of Wales': 'immense bâtiment blanc' (p. 177), 'grandes salles
à manger blanches', personnel indien 'en gants blancs et pieds nus' (p. 178),
du blanc pour le contact par les mains gantées avec les Blancs, tandis que
par ces pieds nus le noir touche au sol natal. Dans la villa diplomatique
flotte une odeur de citronnelle, 'blanche odeur' qui est 'la meilleure façon

d'éloigner les moustiques' (p. 189), et sur laquelle le texte insiste: 'l'odeur de citronnelle revient à la surface, blanche odeur' (p. 190). Blanche odeur ou odeur pour les Blancs qui tient à distance ce qui est du pays, moustiques sans doute mais aussi — symboliquement — indigènes.

Tenir à distance, séparer: cette connotation se dégage plus nettement encore du découpage topographique du texte, espace clôturé sur toute son étendue. Tandis que Calcutta est délimitée par des enceintes concentriques (p. 165), celles des Blancs ne s'incluent pas l'une dans l'autre; marquées par l'obstacle visible et concret de la grille, elles tiennent séparés les deux mondes. L'ambassade a un nombre symptomatique de ces grilles, autour du parc, intérieurement autour des tennis, petite grille à l'entrée des domestiques, fins grillages aux fenêtres . . . Leur nombre augmente encore aux Iles où leur fonction séparatrice est évidente: ainsi, l'hôtel bâti sur une grande île, à *l'autre extrémité* de laquelle il y a un village, séparé donc de lui 'naturellement', requiert de plus une séparation artificielle: 'Entre ce village et l'hôtel un grand grillage s'élève et les sépare' (p. 177). La phrase continue: 'Partout, au bord de la mer, dans la mer, d'autres grillages contre les requins' (ibid). Troublante juxtaposition . . . A l'intérieur de l'île, un autre grillage encore, le plus effectif, approuvé par les Blancs: 'La palmeraie du Prince of Wales est célèbre, dit le directeur du Cercle européen, un grillage électrique la protège du côté nord. Bonne chose que ce grillage' (p. 84). Actualisation du sème de la clôture donc dans l'espace géographique du texte repris également dans son espace social: 'Les cercles fermés aux Indes, c'est le secret' (p. 103).

★ ★ ★

Le codage social des éléments fictionnels du *Vice-Consul* est ainsi un surcodage: insistance, aux dépens de la particulisation romanesque, sur ce qui relève d'une visée sociale, structure du texte homologue à la structure sociale, présence, ainsi, sinon présentation, du collectif. Or, le texte actualise la collectivité dans son discours même; il met en signe la Référence, le discours social envahissant l'espace textuel au point de subvertir la narration romanesque. Dans les limites de cette étude cependant, négligeant ici la perturbation du narratif, on voudrait montrer le caractère discursif du texte d'une part et de l'autre dégager les marques de la socialité dans ce discours.

Par discursivité du texte on entend que le récit se laisse recouvrir par son propre discours. En effet, les données romanesques ne sont pas seulement inscrites dans une problématique sociale, elles représentent d'autre part une quantité de matière diégétique fort petite: expulsion de la jeune Cambodgienne, acte criminel du vice-consul. De plus, cette matière diégétique est refoulée en dehors de la représentation romanesque: le crime du vice-consul a eu lieu avant l'ouverture du récit principal, le périple de la jeune fille n'est qu'une simple hypothèse. Pré-textuelle par son repère chronologique, déréalisée par son ancrage imaginaire, la narration est ainsi mise en cause. Mise en suspens également: il ne sera jamais dit à quel autre poste se fera la nouvelle affectation du vice-consul, principal sujet des conversations (et du texte) ni si la mendiante chauve de Calcutta est bien la jeune Cambodgienne qu'avait connue l'ambassadrice.

Que reste-t-il pour meubler un espace narratif si vide? A la place du récit des événements, une activité discursive incessante: *les* discours constituent *le* discours du texte. Visites au Cercle européen, réception à l'ambassade, réunions des intimes d'Anne-Marie Stretter, ainsi sont naturalisés ces discours, incessants commentaires qui font des actants de ce roman surtout des parlants. C'est aussi par la parole — des autres — qu'est donnée l'information sur les principaux personnages: exilée de son Indo-Chine natale, la mendiante est frappé de mutisme, un seul mot surnageant dans sa mémoire abolie. Son existence textuelle est tout entière dérivée des discours — écrits — que Peter Morgan tient sur elle et des conversations qui tournent autour d'elle. Par contre le vice-consul est à certains endroits du texte extrêmement volubile: on ne sait de lui cependant que ce qu'il décide de dire, dans un interminable échange avec le directeur du Cercle, afin que ses propos soient répétés: 'Directeur, parlez à qui veut l'entendre, racontez à qui veut l'entendre tout ce que je vous raconte' (p. 88). Propos colportés qui alimentent d'autres conversations à son sujet pendant la réception à l'ambassade, au cours des réunions intimes de l'ambassadrice. Quant à cette dernière, sa situation locutive est un compromis entre le mutisme de la mendiante et la loquacité du vice-consul. Mais comme eux, elle est surtout sujet de conversations, objet de la parole des autres. Et le tout-Calcutta diplomatique ne se fait pas faute de parler.

Ainsi le texte — récit obscuré par les discours — est presqu'entièrement fait de paroles, parole sociale en ce qu'elle est l'énonciation d'un groupe, discours social en ce que cette parole exhibe les marques de la socialité que l'on se propose maintenant de relever. 'Le discours social, dit Claude Duchet, est le "on" du texte et sa rumeur . . . le romancier peut céder plus ou moins sa parole à ce tout-dit multifocalisé, saturé et structuré par l'idéologie dominante dont il est la forme résiduelle, vécue comme le "parce que cela se fait", "parce que cela se dit" . . .' (*Poétique*, No 16, 1973, p. 453). Si l'étude d'un tel discours présente un intérêt à propos du *Vice-Consul*, c'est que la situation narrative qui lui est réservée le met particulièrement en évidence — l'histoire de la réception où il se manifeste surtout occupe un tiers de l'espace textuel — et que par ailleurs la discursivité du texte, que l'on vient d'établir, favorise son actualisation.

Si l'on parle, en effet, beaucoup dans le *Vice Consul*, c'est de plus 'on' qui parle dans le texte. Sur toute son étendue mais plus particulièrement dans le segment de la réception, le degré de fréquence du pronom indéfini est exceptionnellement élevé. A titre d'échantillon: quatorze occurrences sur deux pages (p. 98-99), huit dans une seule page (p. 137). A retenir surtout que cet emploi de 'on' relève très rarement du code gnomique: peu de réflexions de moraliste ici. Par contre la valeur déictique du terme est mise en relief: 'on' refère à des participants à la communication. Rappelons d'autre part que 'la quantité d'information apportée par le segment 'on' est la moins grande de tout le système' (Dubois, *Grammaire structurale du français: nom et pronom*, 1965, p. 114). Participation donc mais dans l'anonymat: ce sont de tels énoncés, imputables à des personnes présentes, absentes cependant dans leur présence même puisqu'elles demeurent anonymes, irrepérables, de tels énoncés qui forment la rumeur publique, ce qu'on dit et le qu'en dira-t-on. Précisément dans le texte durassien c'est le verbe dire qui remplit le plus fréquemment la fonction déclarative: on dit, on dit que, dit-on. Aucune tentative pour varier la formule: 'On dit: Regardez quelle audace. On dit: Non seulement elle danse avec le vice-consul mais elle va même lui parler. On dit: le dernier venu c'est . . .' (p. 121). Le souci d'esthétiser l'énonciation n'est pas plus apparent que celui d'effectuer une économie dans l'information: à côté l'un de l'autre sont juxtaposés le discours du texte et le discours social du 'on dit': 'Il ne peut pas ne pas l'inviter à danser. C'est la première fois. On dit: c'est la première fois, va-t-il lui plaire?' (p. 106) D'autre part, paroles citées dans le dialogue sans que les locuteurs soient nommés, redites, redondances. Le segment de la réception est principalement fait de ces énoncés désoriginés, disséminés, réitérés, incontrôlés: 'On parle, c'est ainsi on parle' (p. 121). *People will talk.*

Répétitive, confuse, anonyme, la parole de la société, d'une société de Blancs à l'étranger, s'inscrit dans *Le Vice-Consul* côte à côte avec ce qui est discours social dans une autre acception. Il s'agit alors du discours de l'Autorité marqué du double indice de l'officiel et du prescriptif.

Le texte, en effet, cède par endroits sa parole à une voix administrative. Sans doute la situation anecdotique légitime le procédé: ainsi le vice-consul ayant à expliquer à ses supérieurs son acte de Lahore fait une déposition écrite, rédigée nécessairement dans un langage officiel. Ce langage cependant s'étend, par contagion, à la suite du fragment et le passé du vice-consul dont il est question est alors, non pas raconté, mais établi (cf. p. 38). Dossier qui n'est pris en charge par aucun membre de l'ambassade, voix officielle libérée de toute attache locutive donc qui intervient dans la continuité narrative sans que le contexte immédiat puisse justifier cette intrusion. De même les renseignements donnés ailleurs dans le texte sur le personnage titulaire ont une forme schématique, et lui constituent une carte d'identité au lieu de s'ordonner en une présentation — classique — du personnage (cf. pp. 33-34). Quant au discours prescriptif, il est inscrit au fronton du livre, dès ses premières lignes, dans toute la première page: 'Elle marche, écrit Peter Morgan. Comment ne pas revenir? Il faut se perdre. Je ne sais pas. Tu apprendras . . '. Il faut être sans arrière-pensée . . . Il faut apprendre que . . .' Série d'impératifs que le récit principal va réactiver sous la forme adoucie du rituel mondain: 'Il faut inviter Anne-Marie Stretter à danser lorsqu'on est reçu à l'ambassade' (p. 97); ou des conseils d'hygiène : 'Pendant la chaleur . . . il ne faut boire que du thé vert brûlant' (p. 163). Discours de l'autorité bureaucratique, de l'autorité morale, et surtout des 'pesanteurs idéologiques' (Duchet), ce qui se dit mais aussi ce qui se pense ou doit se penser selon les stéréotypes en vigueur, conformité . . . ici aux valeurs dominantes d'un groupe de Blancs sortis de leurs pays. La thématique du *Vice-Consul* met en avant une telle conformité.

En effet, l'acte du personnage titulaire — anecdote centrale du roman — est somme toute un crime. Conduite (de protestation sociale) anti-sociale. Pourtant est déclenché non pas un procès juridique mais le processus de la parole d'une société qui cherche à expliquer un tel acte par un recours aux stéréotypes qui lui sont familiers. Symbolique destruction de la lèpre, elle-même symbolisant 'la douleur des Indes', le crime du vice-consul est récupéré par une motivation qui ne tient aucun compte de la situation qui l'a généré. 'Je préfère qu'on en reste aux conjonctures habituelles, qu'on cherche dans l'enfance', dit l'ambassadeur (p. 42). Se conformant — ironiquement — à l'usage, le vice-consul s'invente un passé d'orphelin, enfant négligé, élevé dans une pension disciplinaire, qu'il raconte complaisamment au Directeur du Cercle chargé d'enquêter sur lui et qui lui rappelle à quoi vise cette enquête: 'Ils insistent sur l'enfance, monsieur' (p. 87).

Stéréotype de l'enfance malheureuse ou encore de la conduite sexuelle: 'Il a dit qu'il était vierge au directeur du Cercle. Que croyez-vous? Alors, serait-ce cela? (p. 114). Autre explication toute faite: 'On dit: il s'ennuyait à Lahore, c'est peut-être ça' (p. 116). Ennui qui accompagne la condition du Blanc exilé: 'sentiment d'abandon colossal, à la mesure de l'Inde elle-même, ce pays donne le ton' (ibid).

Enfance, abstinence sexuelle, ennui, chacun de ces stéréotypes explique en excusant. Mais l'excuse qui réhabilite le plus complètement est celle de la race. Dans une situation symétriquement inverse de celle de Meursault dans *L'Etranger*, le vice-consul de France à Lahore, Blanc privilégié parmi les hommes de couleur, est blanchi de son crime. Il a tiré *dans le noir*, dans le tas noir des lépreux, la nuit. 'Il tirait la nuit sur les jardins de Shalimar où se réfugient le lépreux et les chiens. — Mais des lépreux ou des chiens, est-ce tuer que de tuer des lépreux ou des chiens?' (p. 94). Confusion . . . pardonnable, sur laquelle le texte ironise. Telle cette mauvaise foi du locuteur qui ayant entendu crier prétend ne pas pouvoir différencier les chiens des lépreux: 'Puisque vous le savez, pourquoi avez-vous dit des lépreux ou des chiens? — J'ai confondu de loin, comme ça, à travers la musique, les aboiements des chiens et ceux des lépreux qui rêvent. — Cela fait bien de le dire ainsi' (p. 95).

Discours des convenances terminologiques — ce qu'il convient de dire — et discours des convenances idéologiques — ce qu'il convient de penser, le texte du *Vice-Consul* propose donc bien un discours social saturé par une idéologie dominante, en l'occurrence celle des Blancs dans une situation coloniale.

En contrepoint cependant s'articule un tout autre discours dont la fonction est précisément de miner les positions stéréotypées que le discours social met en avant. Une première indication de cette dialectique discursive apparaît dans les pages d'ouverture. Dé-localisant sa situation géographique, le texte propose une lecture non réaliste qui met en cause l'extrême naturalisation de son discours et permet alors de repenser les stéréotypes qu'il charrie. L'anecdote, en effet, se donne un lieu réel, déréalisé: 'une ville au bord du Ganges qui sera ici capitale des Indes et nommée Calcutta' (p. 35), fixée à un moment immuable de son développement 'dont le chiffre des habitants reste toujours le même, cinq millions, ainsi que celui, inconnu, des morts de faim qui vient d'entrer aujourd'hui dans la lumière crépusculaire de la mousson d'été (ibid). Avec de telles références spatio-temporelles ce n'est pas tant le récit qui est discrédité que la notion même de Référence, ce soubassement idéologique sur lequel s'appuie toute écriture réaliste. En cours de texte un questionnement se poursuit, en effet, touchant aux notions les plus fondamentales, controversant l'incontrovertible. Concept de l'origine, raciale surtout, sans doute le concept le plus pertinent dans la situation coloniale du roman. Face au stéréotype qui explique par son enfance malheureuse la conduite criminelle du vice-consul, le texte propose un autre passé — une origine différente — pour Jean-Marc de H. Alors 'qu'on cherche avec lassitude qui était le vice-consul avant Lahore' (p. 115), il est dit que son origine est précisément Lahore: 'c'est de Lahore qu'il vient, je crois, oui' (p. 111). Parallèlement, Anne-Marie Stretter, née à Venise de père français, situe elle aussi son origine ailleurs que dans son pays natal: 'C'est un peu simple de croire que l'on vient de Venise seulement, on peut venir d'autres endroits qu'on a traversés en cours de route, il me semble' (ibid). Remise en question de ce qui ne saurait être questionné, geste de défi ou de protestation contre ce qui semble devoir catégoriser les êtres sans appel: lieu de naissance, appartenance raciale. A sa façon la mendiante, ce troisième centre anecdotique, fait, elle aussi, un semblable geste de protestation lorsqu'elle réussit à se débarrasser de son bébé, à le 'vendre' pour une piastre à une dame blanche au cours de son long périple. Cette vente du bébé racontée par l'ambassadrice à Peter Morgan — seul épisode qu'il n'ait pas inventé — symbolise bien la rupture avec l'origine puisque la jeune fille se coupe de son enfant comme sa mère qui l'avait chassée s'était coupée d'elle. Convergence des trois personnages principaux qui chacun à sa manière provoque un questionnement du concept de la provenance — raciale — comme par ailleurs est questionné celui de l'appartenance — sociale — posé par l'exil de la Cambodgienne et l'exclusion du vice-consul, isolé parmi les Blancs. Quant à Anne-Marie, elle figure dans le texte l'abolition de toutes les différences, la possibilité d'une parfaite indifférentiation: 'Certaines femmes rendent fou d'espoir . . . Celles qui ont l'air de dormir dans les eaux de la bonté sans discrimination . . . celles vers qui vont toutes les vagues de toutes les douleurs, ces femmes accueillantes' (p. 100). Articulé à chaque niveau par des structures d'opposition, le texte tient donc aussi un discours de l'indifférentiation, proposant que se fasse 'l'enchevêtrement . . . la confusion de toutes les douleurs' (p. 100).

Ainsi actualisant le discours social, le texte le mine sourdement, discours de la société qui assume les stéréotypes et accuse les différences mais que l'écriture durassienne, du seul fait de le mettre en évidence, retourne contre cette société même.

LONDON   NINETTE BAILEY

---

[1] Les références renvoient à l'édition Gallimard (Paris, 1966).

LIST OF SUBSCRIBERS

D.Adamson, Goldsmiths' College, London.

I.W.Alexander, 2 Menai Dale, Siliwen Road, Bangor, Gwynedd.

L.J.Austin, Department of French, Sidgwick Avenue, Cambridge.

R.Bales, Department of French, Queen's University, Belfast.

G.V.Banks, Department of French, University of Birmingham.

C.A.Burns, Department of French, University of Birmingham.

Mrs Paule Chicken, Department of French, University of Birmingham.

P.H.Collin, George Harrap & Co, 182, High Holborn, London W.C.1.

R.F.Cousins, Department of French, University of Birmingham.

C.Crossley, Department of French, University of Birmingham.

Ms Elizabeth Fallaize, Department of French, University of Birmingham.

J.F.Falvey, Department of French, University of Southampton.

D.J.Firth, Newman College of Education, Bartley Green, Birmingham.

F.W.A.George, Department of French, St. David's University College, Lampeter, Dyfed.

R.E.Hallmark, Department of French, University of Birmingham.

E.J.Hathaway, Department of French, University of Birmingham.

F.M.Higman. Department of French, University of Nottingham.

Miss Nicole Hodgson, Newman College of Education, Bartley Green, Birmingham.

The Lord Hunter of Newington, University of Birmingham.

J.S.Jones, 83 Woodholm Road, Sheffield.

B.Kite, Department of French, University of Birmingham.

F.W.Leakey, Department of French, Bedford College, Regent's Park, London, N.W.1.

W.H.Lyons and Margaret Lyons, 38 Hill Turrets Close, Sheffield.

C.R.P.May, Department of French, University of Birmingham.

Mrs E.Nasralla, 41, Godward Road, New Mills, Stockport.

R.Pickering, Downing College, Cambridge.

I.Pickup, Department of French, University of Birmingham.

J.Reed, Department of French, University of Birmingham.

Mrs J.M.Robinson, Goffs School, Goffs Lane, Cheshunt, Herts.

A.Rodocanachi, 11, Rue Barbet de Jouy, 75007 Paris.

Miss Marjorie Shaw, Department of French, University of Sheffield.

J.P.Short, Department of French, University of Sheffield.

C.N.Smith, School of Modern Languages, University of East Anglia, Norwich.

A.J.Steele, 17 Polwarth Grove, Edinburgh.

A.V.Subiotto, Department of German, University of Birmingham.

Miss Margaret Tillett, 20 St. John's Road, Cosham, Portsmouth.

D.M.Wood, Department of French, University of Birmingham.

A.S.Zielonka, Department of French, University of Birmingham.

LIBRARIES

Aberdeen, The University.
Amsterdam, Vrije Universiteit.
Berlin, Freie Universität.
Birmingham, The University.
Birmingham, The French Department, The University.
Birmingham, Newman College of Education.
Bolton, Institute of Technology.
Bonn, Das Romanische Seminar der Universität.
Bradford, The University.
Brighton, The University of Sussex.
Bristol, The University.
Buffalo, State University of New York.
Cambridge, Faculty of Modern and Medieval Languages.
Cambridge, Jesus College.
Cambridge, Sidney Sussex College.
Cambridge, Massachusetts, Harvard University.
Cape Town, The University.
Coventry, Lanchester Polytechnic.
Downsview, Ontario, York University.
Exeter, The University.
Giessen, Romanisches Seminar der Justus Liebig-Universität.
Gothenburg, Universitetsbibliotek.
Groningen, Rijksuniversiteit.
Lampeter, Saint David's University College.
Lausanne, Bibliothèque cantonale et universitaire.
Leeds, Brotherton Library, The University.
Leeds, The French Department, The University.
Leicester, The University.
London, Goldsmiths' College.
London, Westfield College.
London, Polytechnic of Central London.
London, St. Pancras Library.
Loughborough, The University.
Manchester, The Polytechnic.
Milan, Università Cattolica.
Montreal, McGill University.
Nedlands, University of Western Australia.
Newcastle-upon-Tyne, The University.
Norwich, The University of East Anglia.
Oxford, The Taylor Institution.

Pietermaritzburg, The University of Natal.
Poole, Dorset Institute of Higher Education.
Quebec, Université Laval.
Regensburg, Universitätsbibliothek.
Reims, Bibliothèque de l'Université.
Saarbrücken, Universitätsbibliothek.
St. Andrews, The University.
Stanford, The University.
Stirling, The University.
Toronto, Metropolitan Library.
Vancouver, University of British Columbia.
Wellington, The Victoria University.
Williamstown, Massachusetts, Williams College.

★　★　★

In addition to the subscriptions listed above, a number of orders have been placed with bookshops. These subscribers unfortunately remain anonymous, but thanks are due to them no less than to the individuals and libraries mentioned here.